Love Me,
Love Me Not

7

IO SAKISAKA

Contents

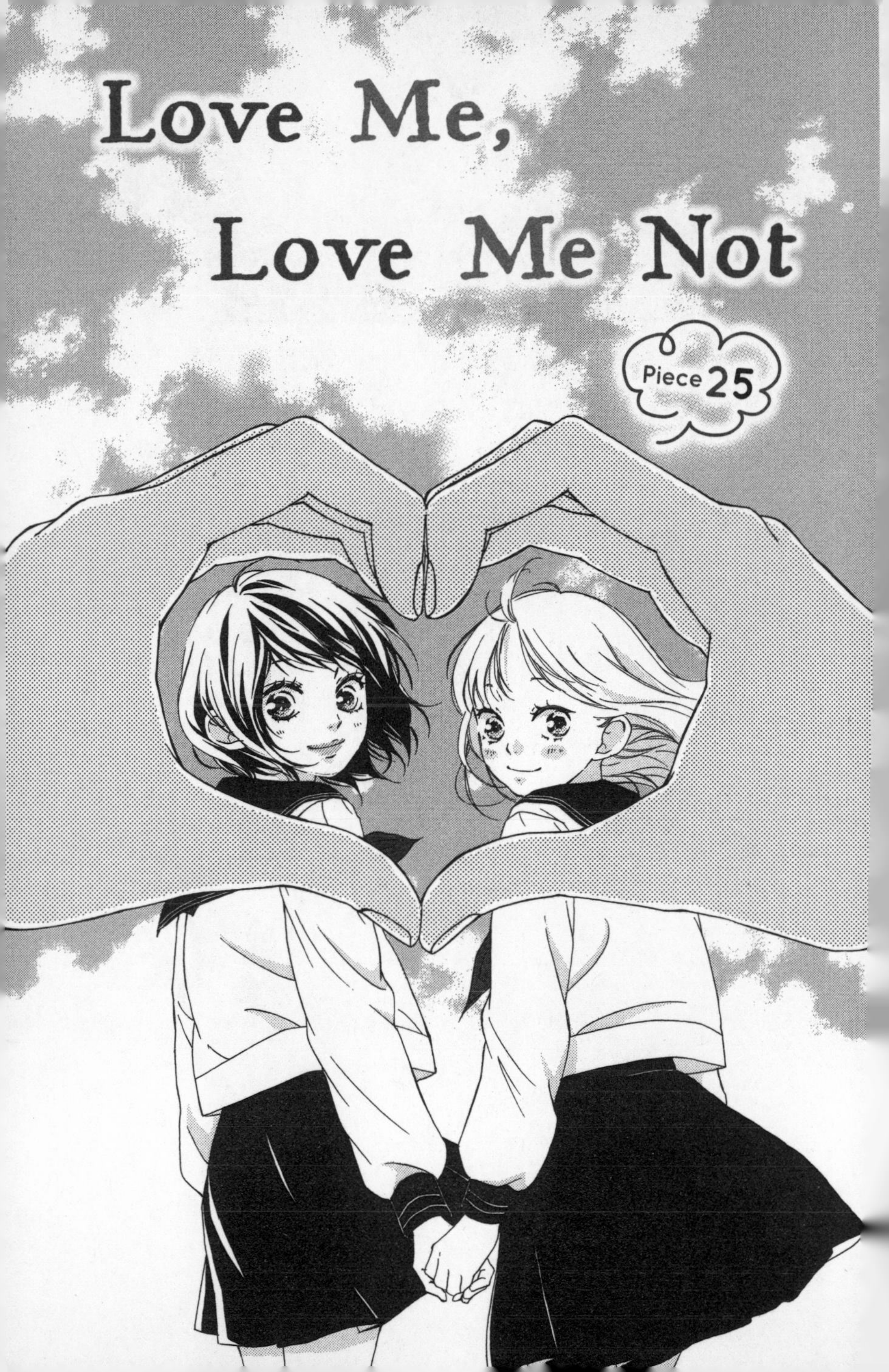
Love Me, Love Me Not
Piece 25

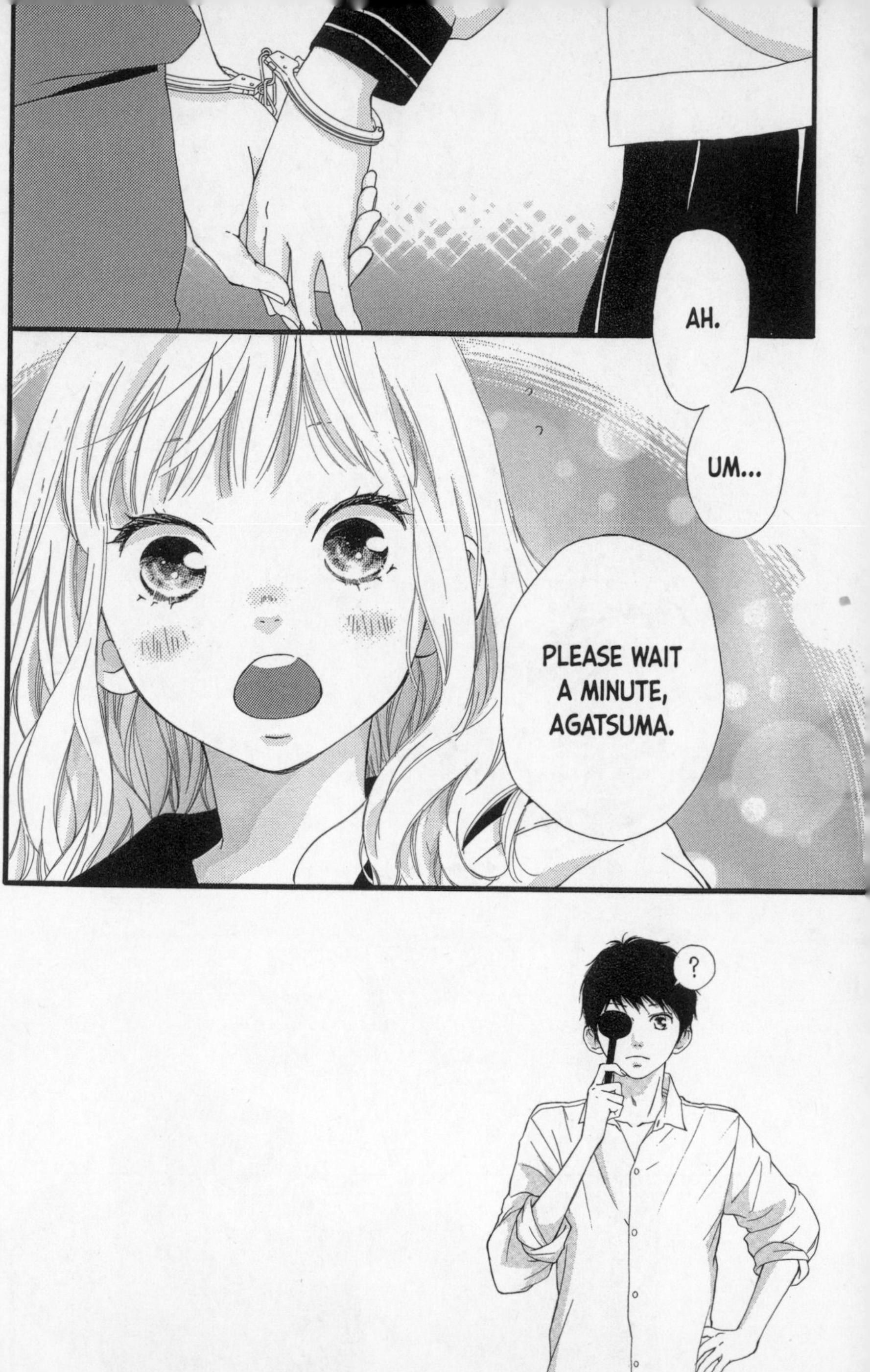
AH.
UM...
PLEASE WAIT A MINUTE, AGATSUMA.
?

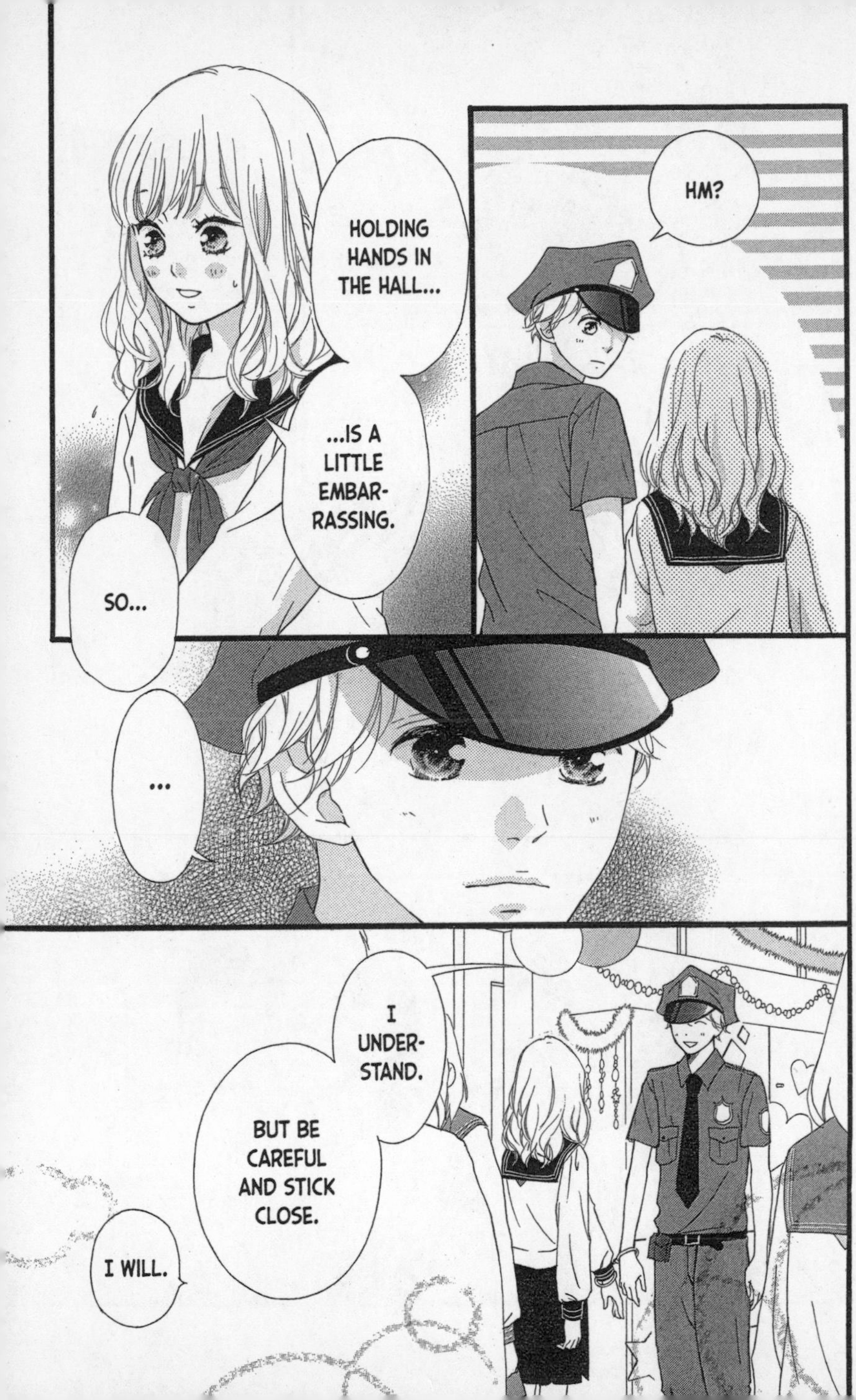
HM?
HOLDING HANDS IN THE HALL...
...IS A LITTLE EMBAR-RASSING.
SO...
...
I UNDER-STAND.
BUT BE CAREFUL AND STICK CLOSE.
I WILL.

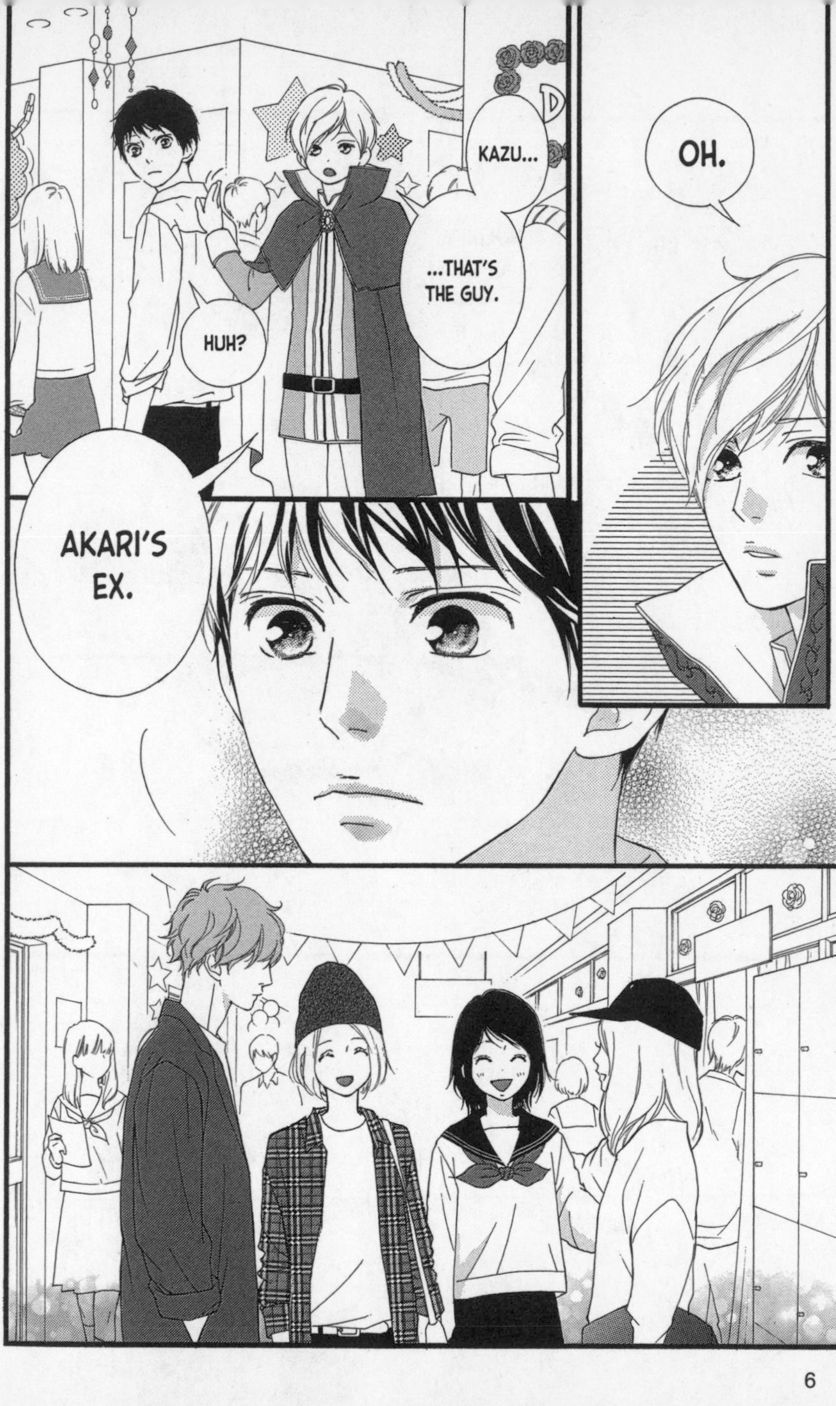
OH.
KAZU...
...THAT'S THE GUY.
HUH?
AKARI'S EX.

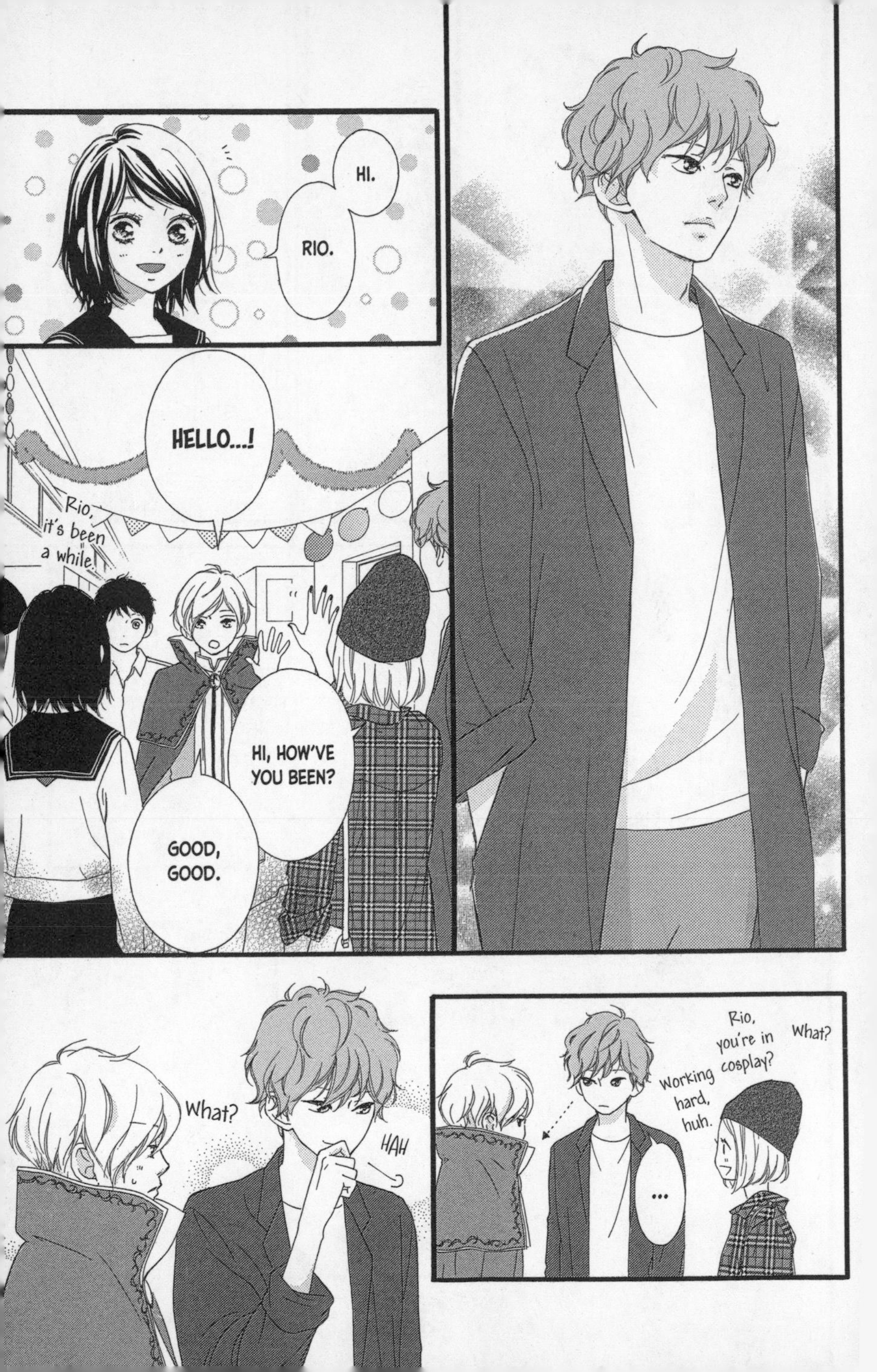
HI.
RIO.
HELLO...!
Rio, it's been a while.
HI, HOW'VE YOU BEEN?
GOOD, GOOD.
What?
Rio, you're in cosplay?
Working hard, huh.
...
HAH
What?

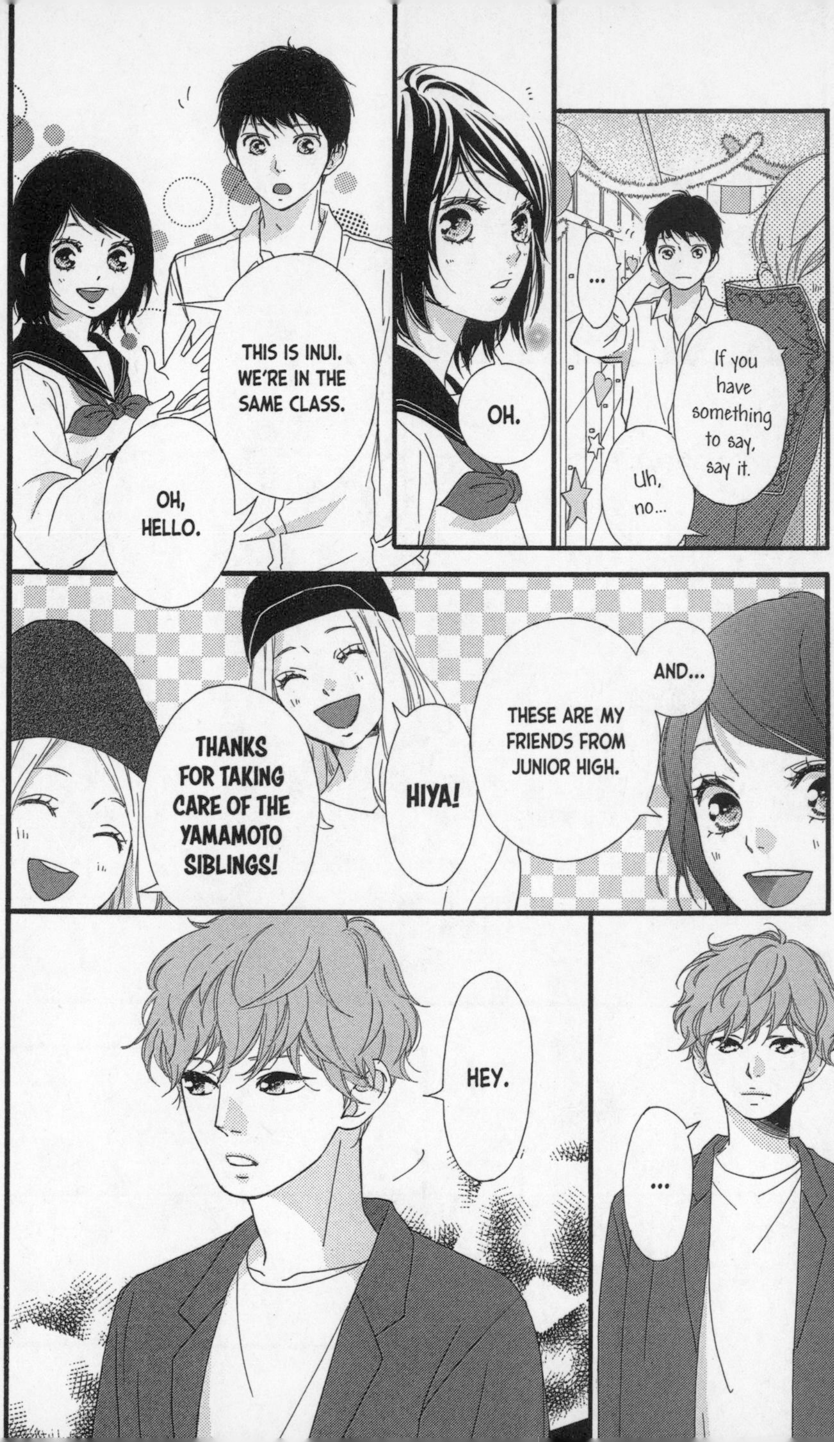
...
If you have something to say, say it.
Uh, no...
OH.
THIS IS INUI. WE'RE IN THE SAME CLASS.
OH, HELLO.
AND...
THESE ARE MY FRIENDS FROM JUNIOR HIGH.
HIYA!
THANKS FOR TAKING CARE OF THE YAMAMOTO SIBLINGS!
...
HEY.

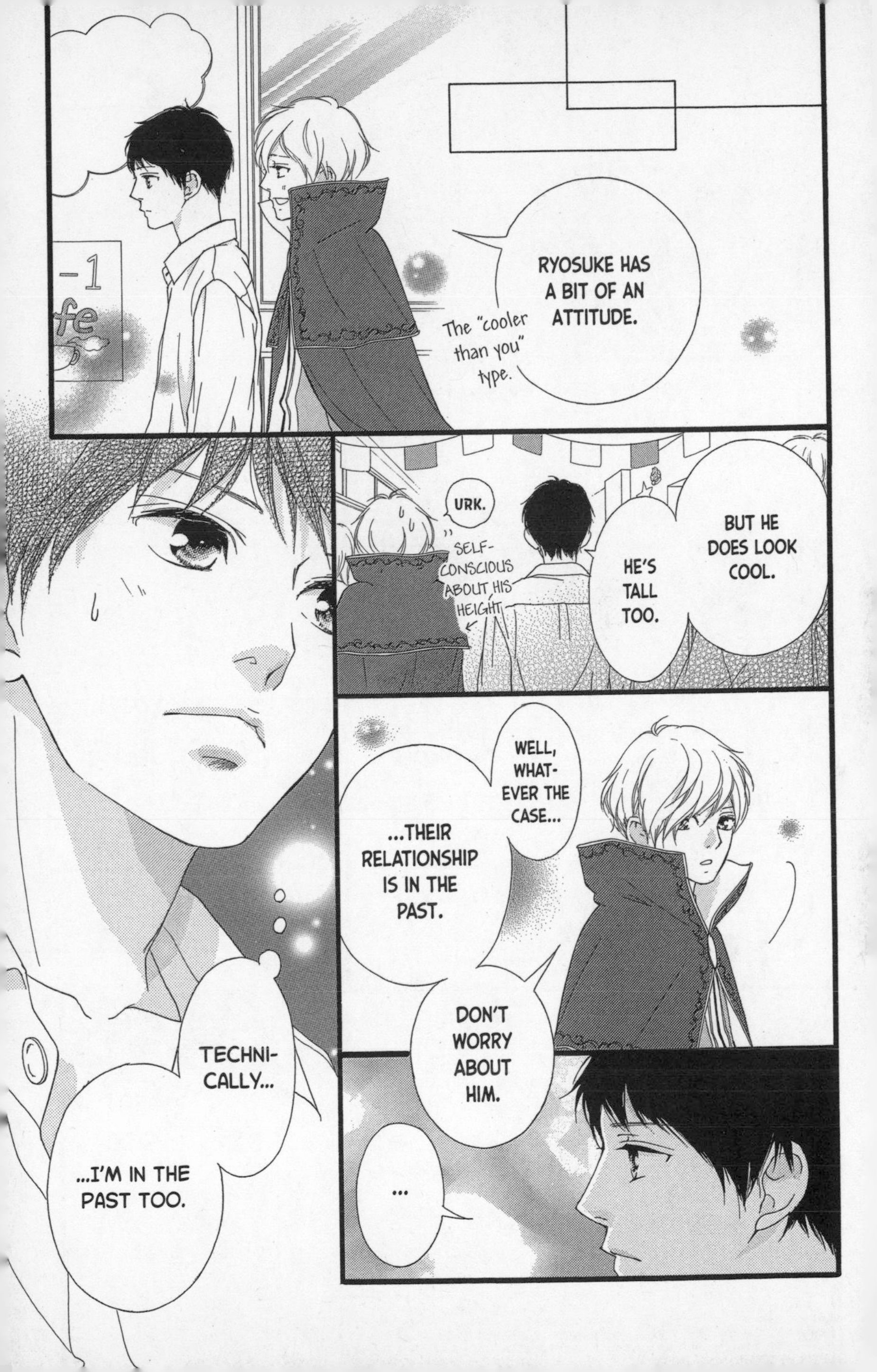
RYOSUKE HAS A BIT OF AN ATTITUDE.
The "cooler than you" type.
BUT HE DOES LOOK COOL.
HE'S TALL TOO.
URK.
SELF-CONSCIOUS ABOUT HIS HEIGHT
WELL, WHAT-EVER THE CASE...
...THEIR RELATIONSHIP IS IN THE PAST.
DON'T WORRY ABOUT HIM.
...
TECHNI-CALLY...
...I'M IN THE PAST TOO.

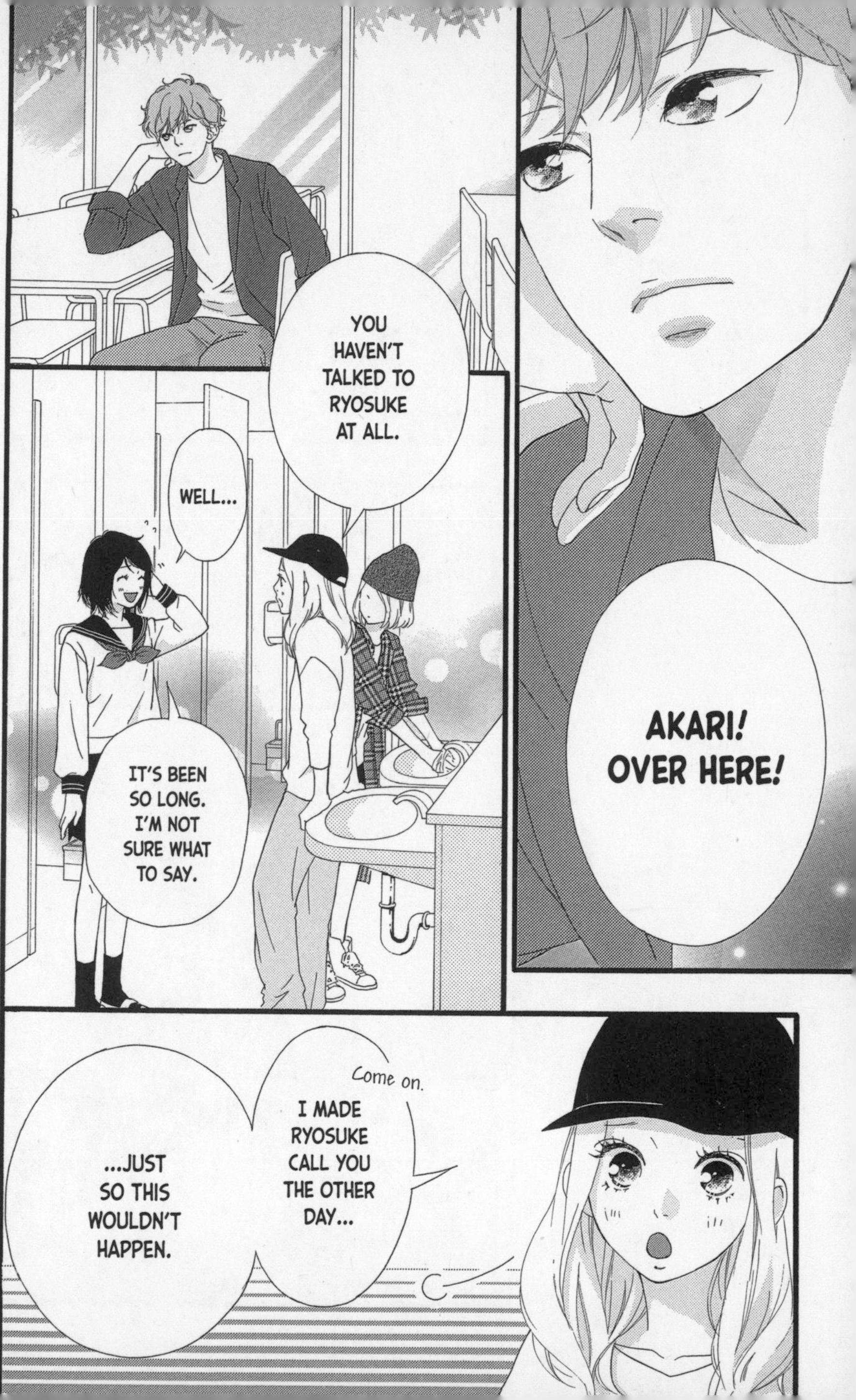
AKARI! OVER HERE!
YOU HAVEN'T TALKED TO RYOSUKE AT ALL.
WELL...
IT'S BEEN SO LONG. I'M NOT SURE WHAT TO SAY.
Come on.
I MADE RYOSUKE CALL YOU THE OTHER DAY...
...JUST SO THIS WOULDN'T HAPPEN.

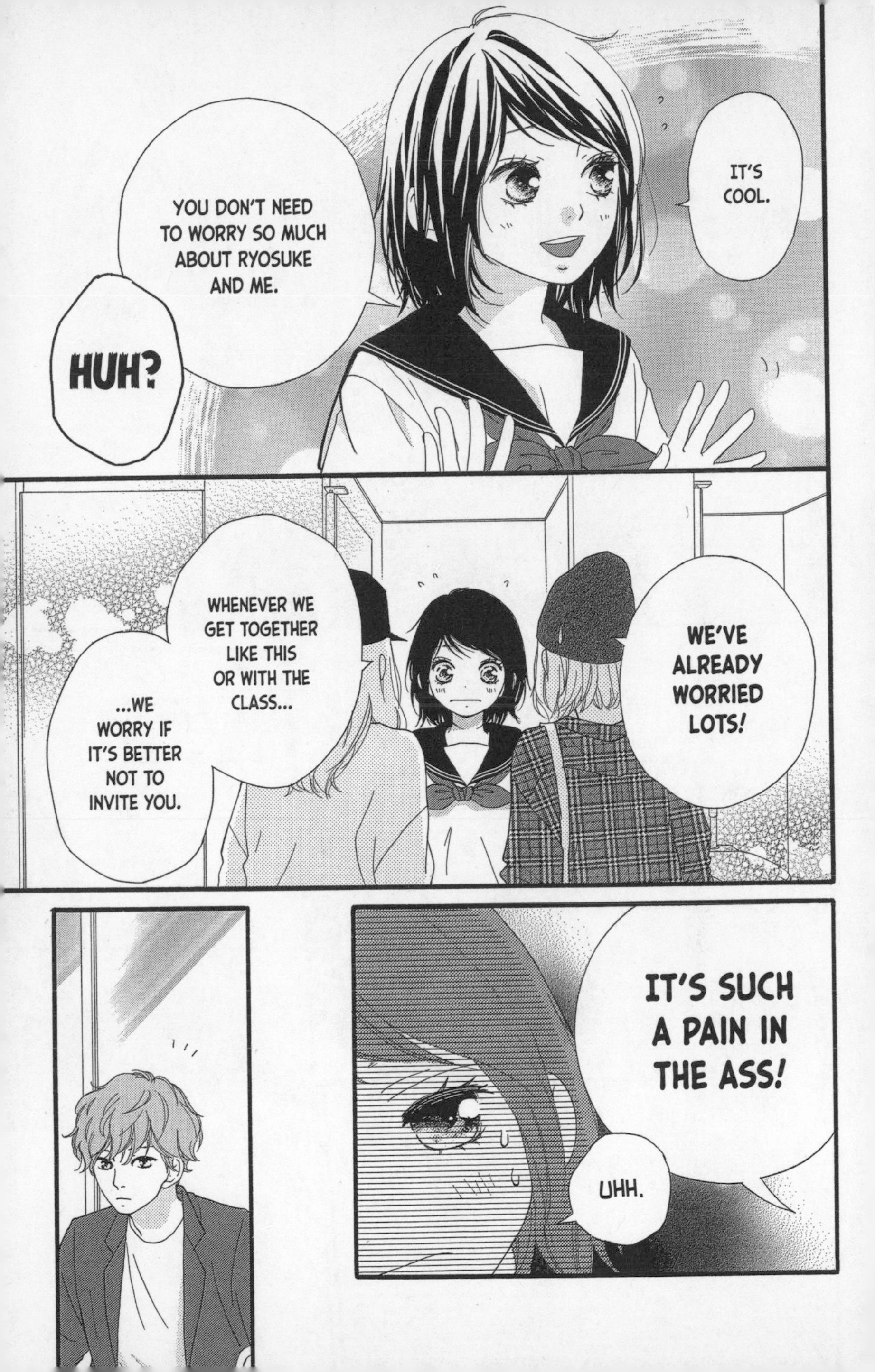
IT'S COOL.
YOU DON'T NEED TO WORRY SO MUCH ABOUT RYOSUKE AND ME.
HUH?
WE'VE ALREADY WORRIED LOTS!
WHENEVER WE GET TOGETHER LIKE THIS OR WITH THE CLASS...
...WE WORRY IF IT'S BETTER NOT TO INVITE YOU.
IT'S SUCH A PAIN IN THE ASS!
UHH.

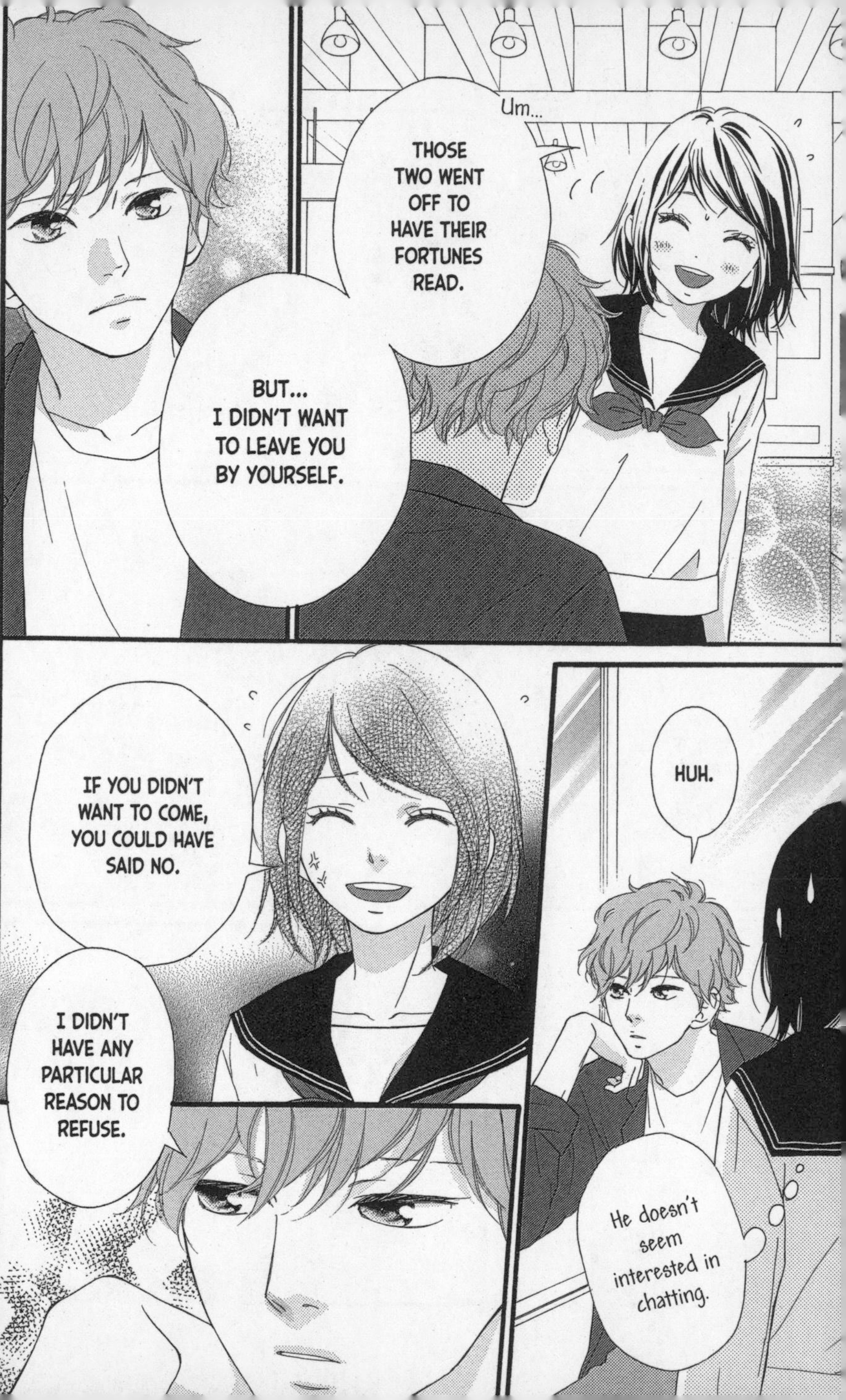
Um...
THOSE TWO WENT OFF TO HAVE THEIR FORTUNES READ.
BUT... I DIDN'T WANT TO LEAVE YOU BY YOURSELF.
HUH.
He doesn't seem interested in chatting.
IF YOU DIDN'T WANT TO COME, YOU COULD HAVE SAID NO.
I DIDN'T HAVE ANY PARTICULAR REASON TO REFUSE.

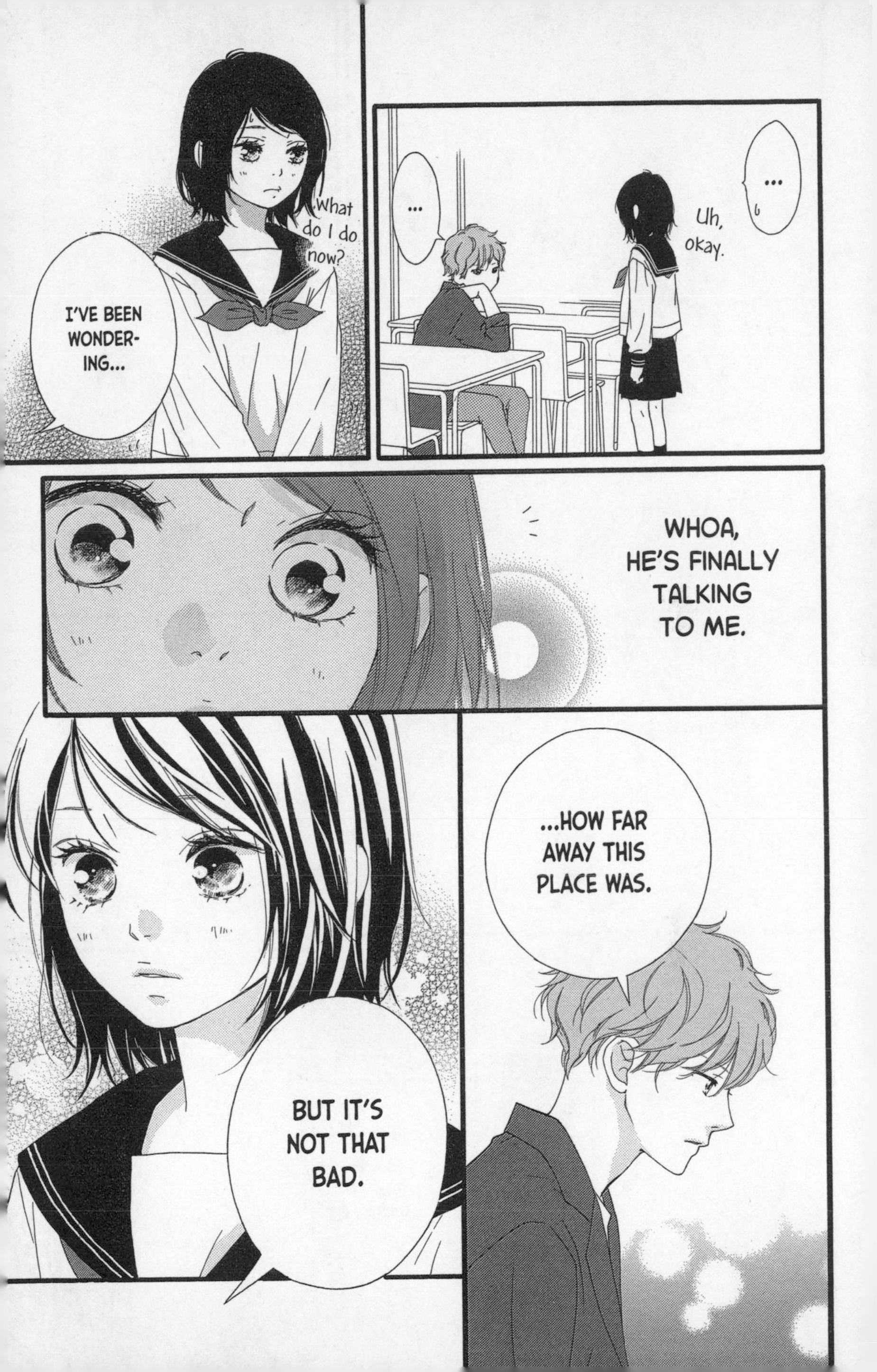
...
Uh, okay.
...
What do I do now?
I'VE BEEN WONDERING...
WHOA, HE'S FINALLY TALKING TO ME.
...HOW FAR AWAY THIS PLACE WAS.
BUT IT'S NOT THAT BAD.

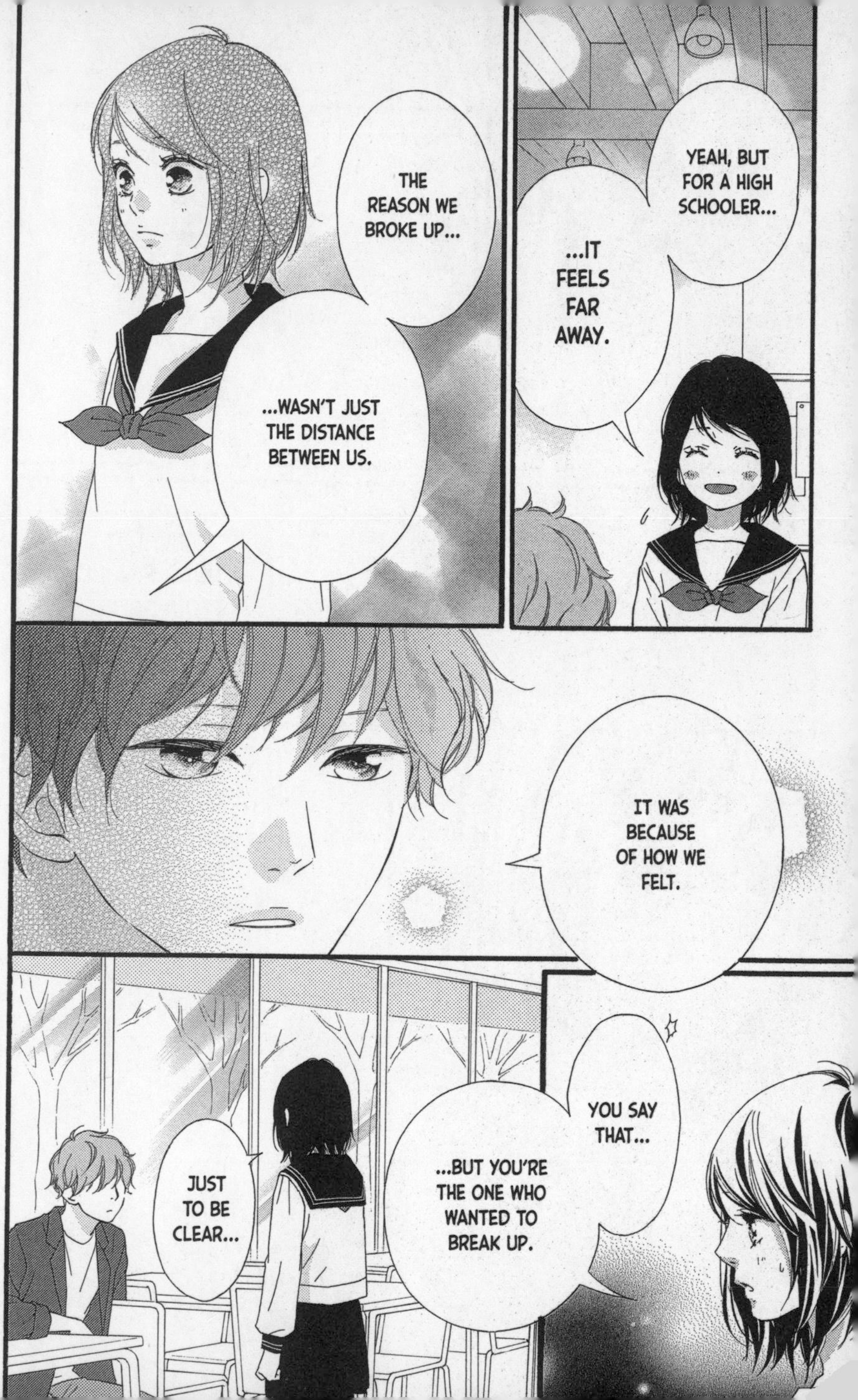
YEAH, BUT FOR A HIGH SCHOOLER...
...IT FEELS FAR AWAY.
THE REASON WE BROKE UP...
...WASN'T JUST THE DISTANCE BETWEEN US.
IT WAS BECAUSE OF HOW WE FELT.
YOU SAY THAT...
...BUT YOU'RE THE ONE WHO WANTED TO BREAK UP.
JUST TO BE CLEAR...

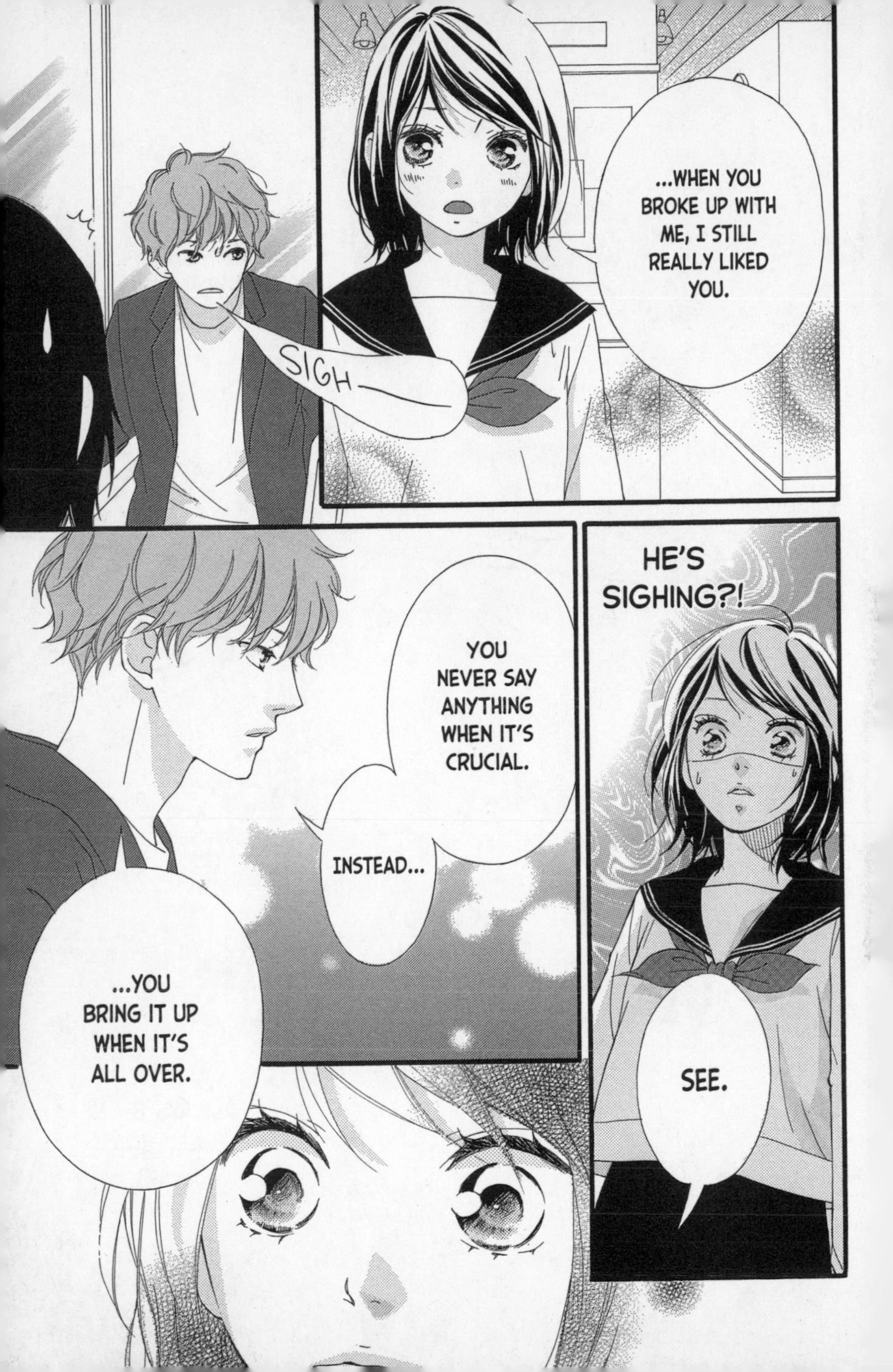
...WHEN YOU BROKE UP WITH ME, I STILL REALLY LIKED YOU.
SIGH
HE'S SIGHING?!
SEE.
YOU NEVER SAY ANYTHING WHEN IT'S CRUCIAL.
INSTEAD...
...YOU BRING IT UP WHEN IT'S ALL OVER.

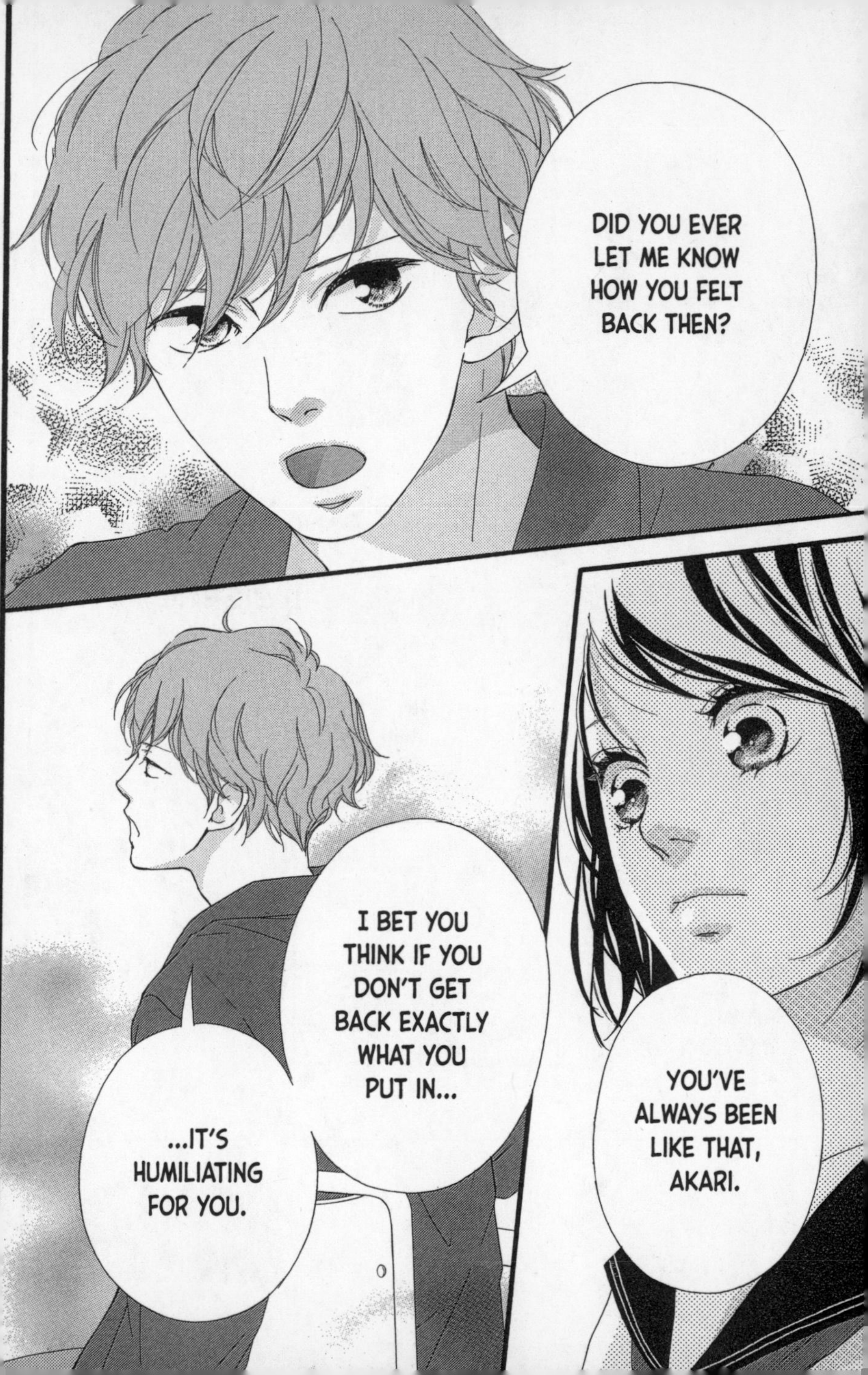
DID YOU EVER LET ME KNOW HOW YOU FELT BACK THEN?
YOU'VE ALWAYS BEEN LIKE THAT, AKARI.
I BET YOU THINK IF YOU DON'T GET BACK EXACTLY WHAT YOU PUT IN...
...IT'S HUMILIATING FOR YOU.

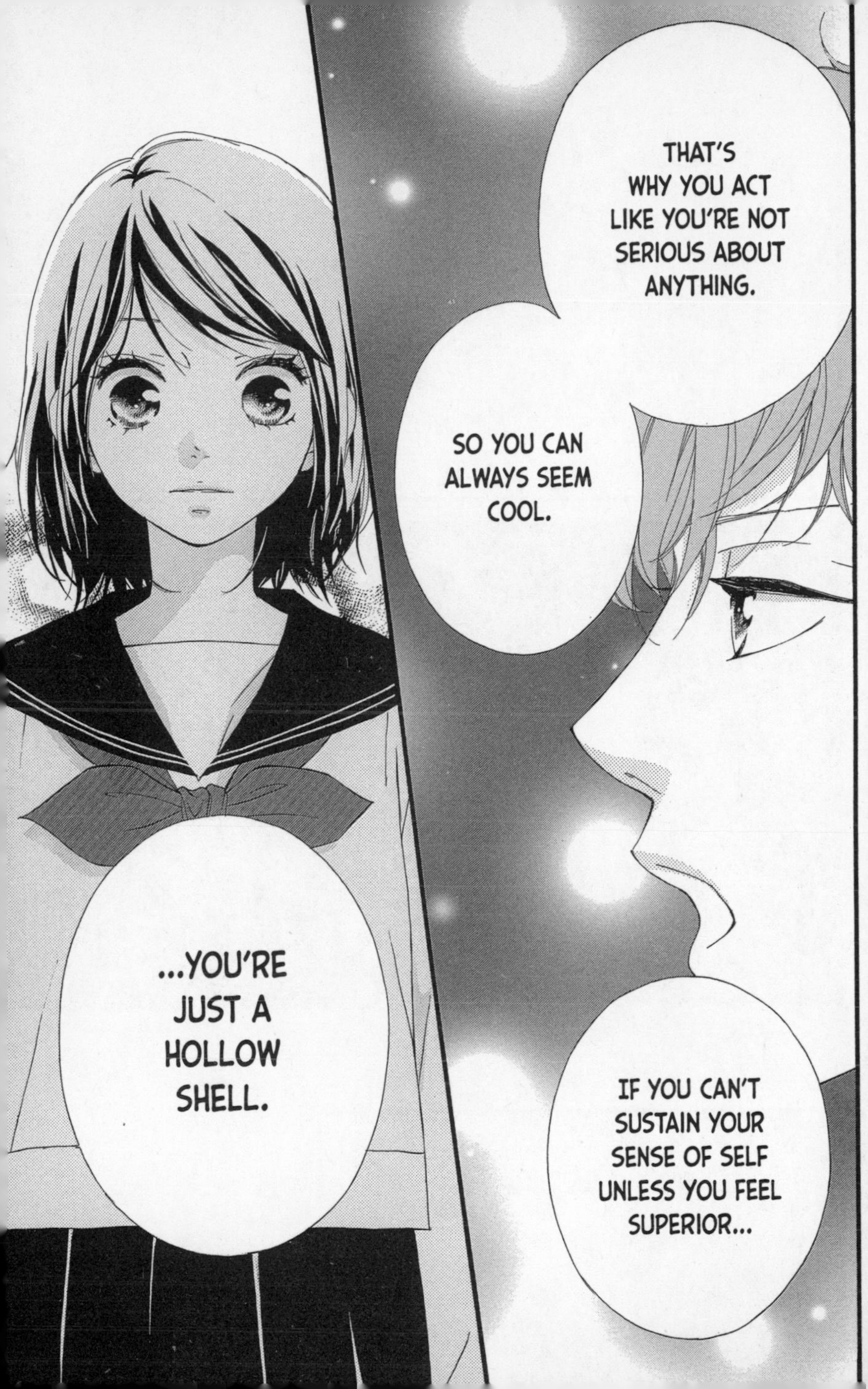
THAT'S WHY YOU ACT LIKE YOU'RE NOT SERIOUS ABOUT ANYTHING.
SO YOU CAN ALWAYS SEEM COOL.
IF YOU CAN'T SUSTAIN YOUR SENSE OF SELF UNLESS YOU FEEL SUPERIOR...
...YOU'RE JUST A HOLLOW SHELL.

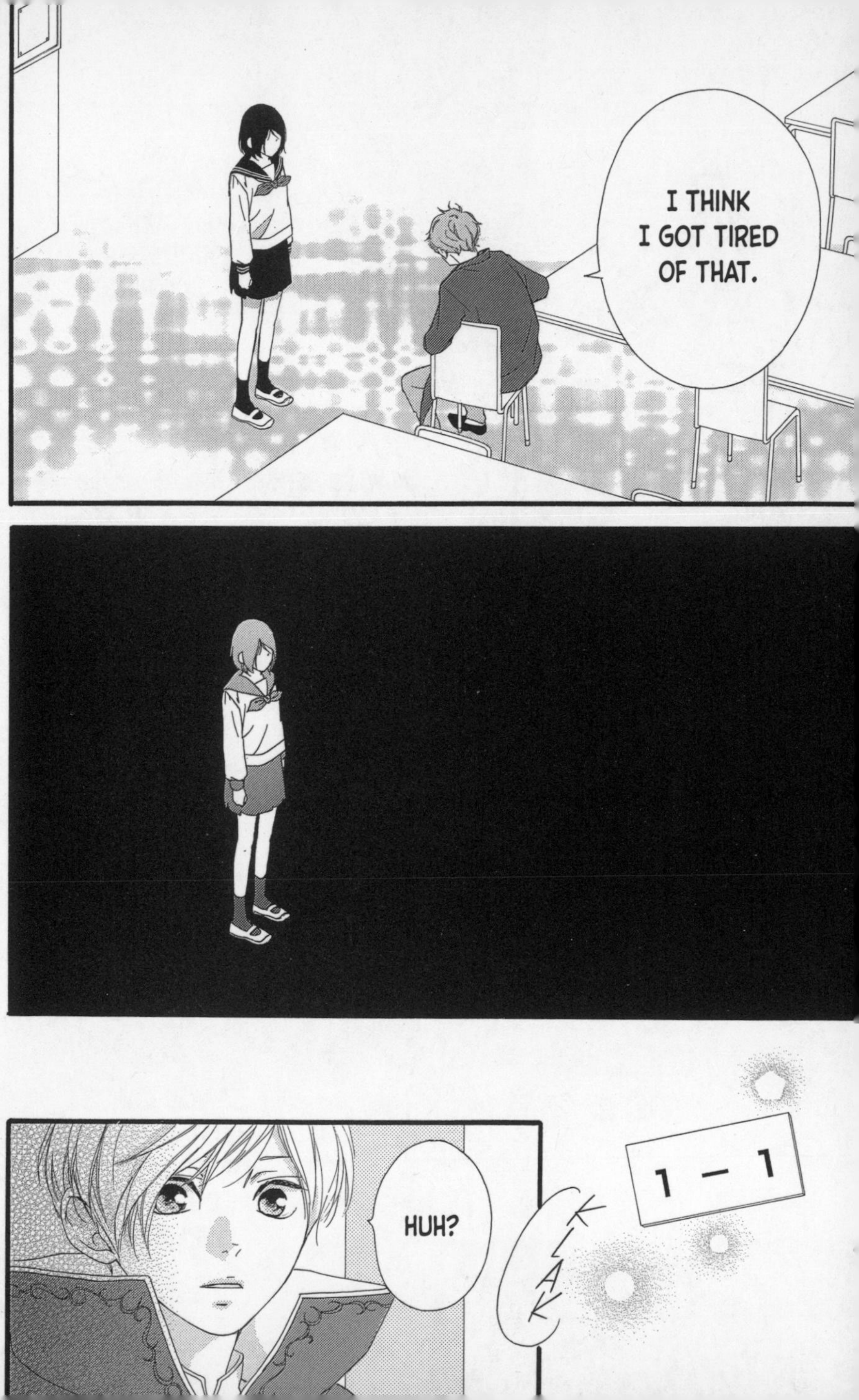
I THINK I GOT TIRED OF THAT.
1 — 1
KLAK
HUH?

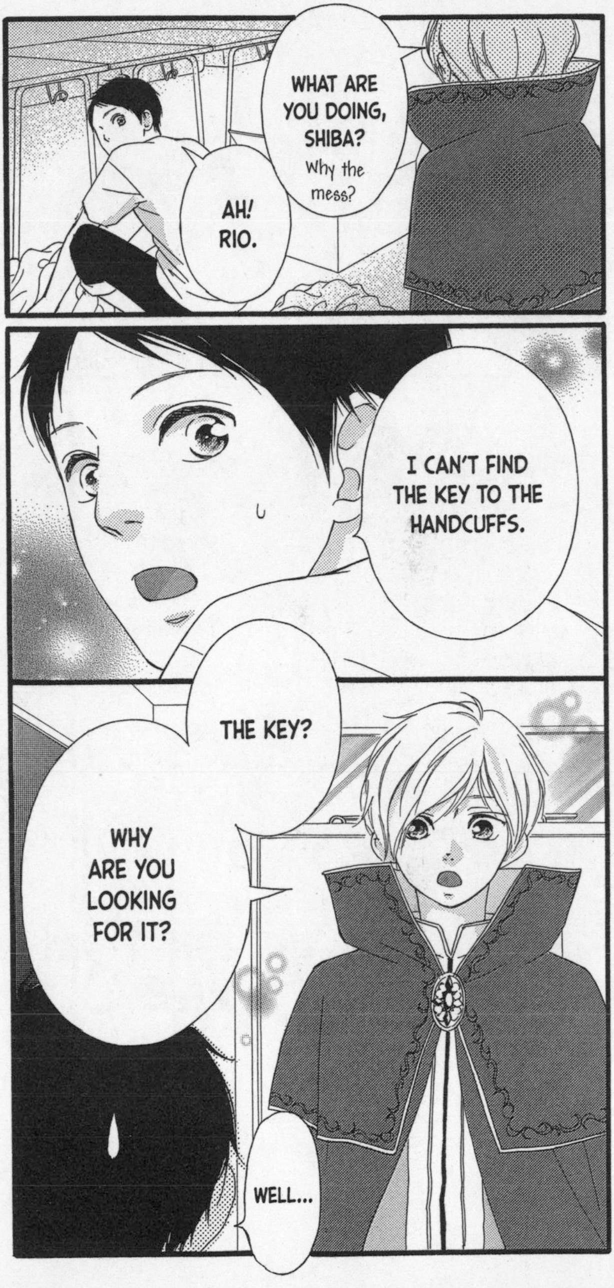
WHAT ARE YOU DOING, SHIBA? Why the mess?
AH! RIO.
I CAN'T FIND THE KEY TO THE HANDCUFFS.
THE KEY?
WHY ARE YOU LOOKING FOR IT?
WELL...

The other day I went to Disney Sea for the second time in my life. It all started when the assistants were chatting about the underlings of villains. I was the only one who asked what that was, and they filled me in. The villains have made their underlings human and sent them to our world. What an amazing concept! Seeing how blown away I was by that, they said, "Let's go." So off we went. During the underlings' show, I failed at securing a good viewing spot, so it was a little hard to see, but everyone who was watching was so happy that it made me happy too. I really saw how feeling happy spreads to those around you. By the way, Jack Hart is my favorite. We all had different favorites, so that made it fun too. Next time I want to have a better view.

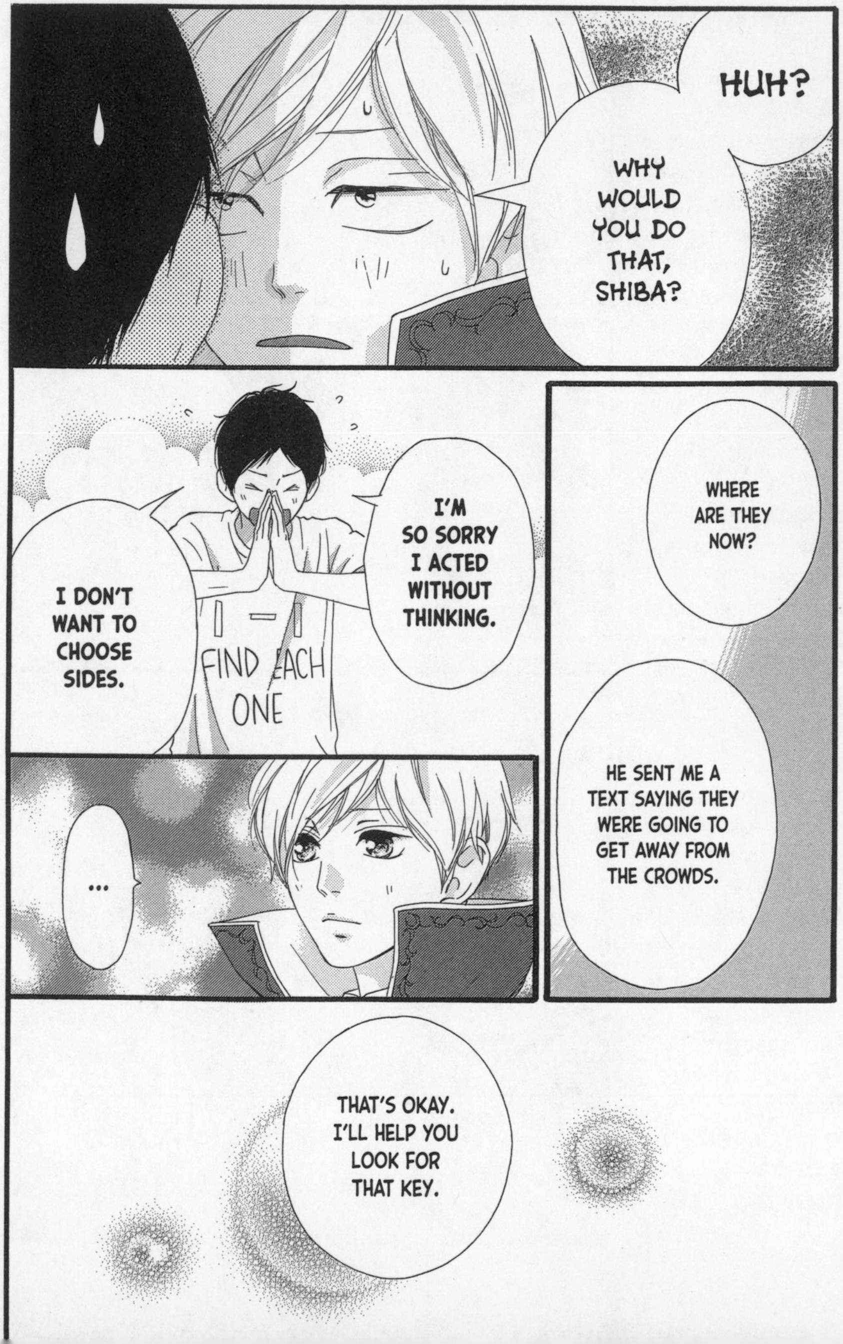
HUH?
WHY WOULD YOU DO THAT, SHIBA?
WHERE ARE THEY NOW?
HE SENT ME A TEXT SAYING THEY WERE GOING TO GET AWAY FROM THE CROWDS.
I'M SO SORRY I ACTED WITHOUT THINKING.
I DON'T WANT TO CHOOSE SIDES.
FIND EACH ONE
...
THAT'S OKAY. I'LL HELP YOU LOOK FOR THAT KEY.

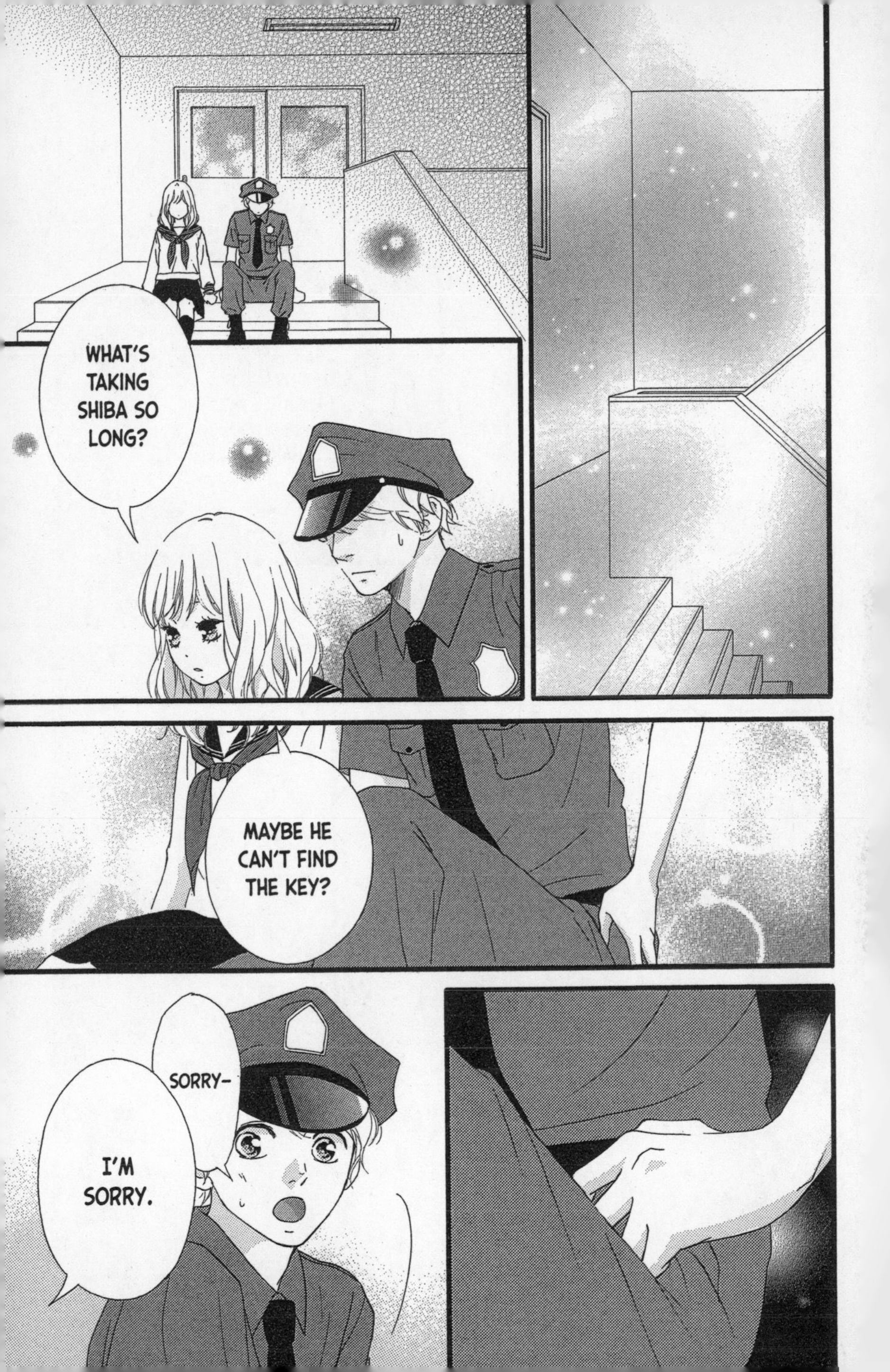
WHAT'S TAKING SHIBA SO LONG?
MAYBE HE CAN'T FIND THE KEY?
SORRY–
I'M SORRY.

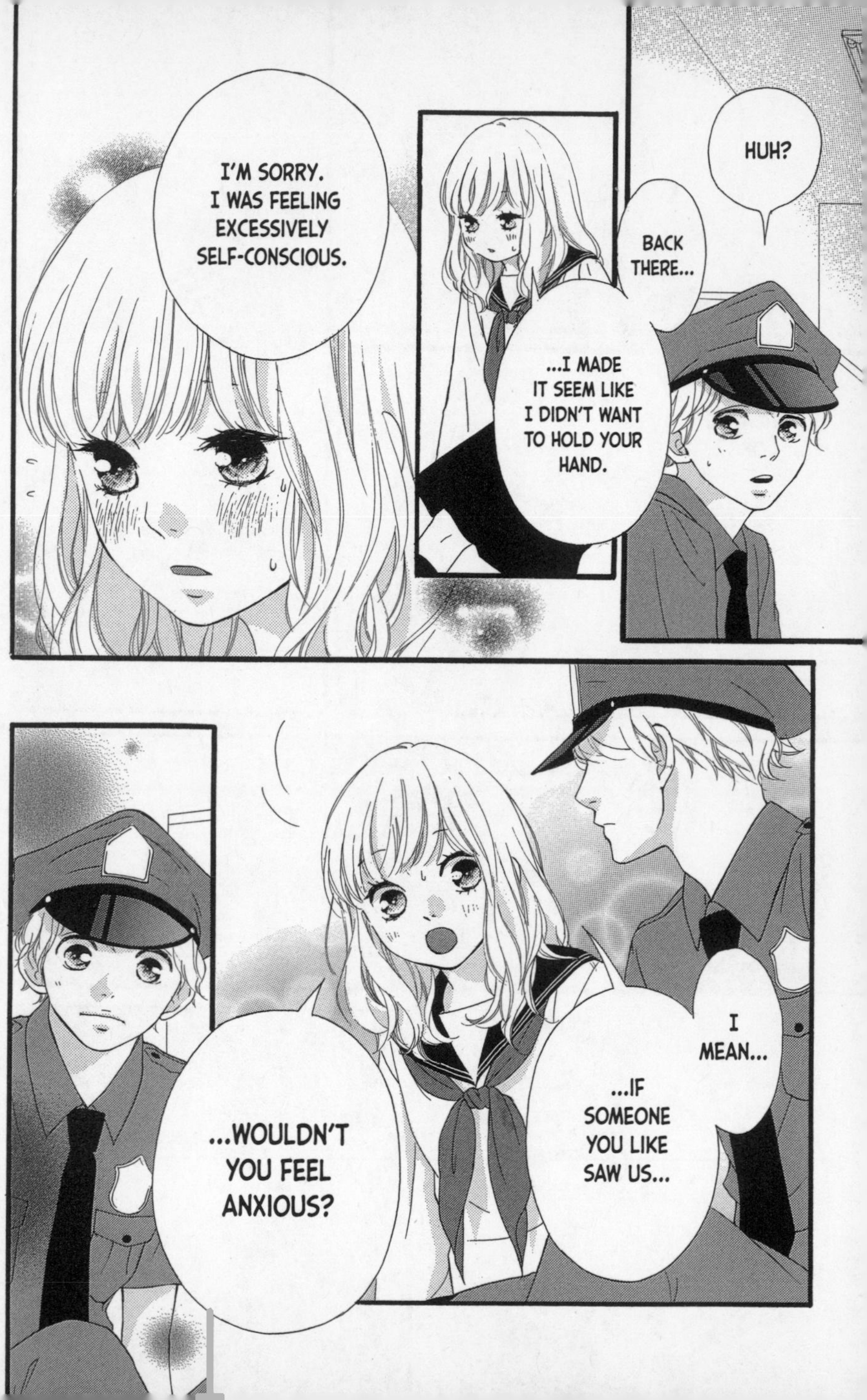
HUH?
BACK THERE...
...I MADE IT SEEM LIKE I DIDN'T WANT TO HOLD YOUR HAND.
I'M SORRY. I WAS FEELING EXCESSIVELY SELF-CONSCIOUS.
I MEAN...
...IF SOMEONE YOU LIKE SAW US...
...WOULDN'T YOU FEEL ANXIOUS?

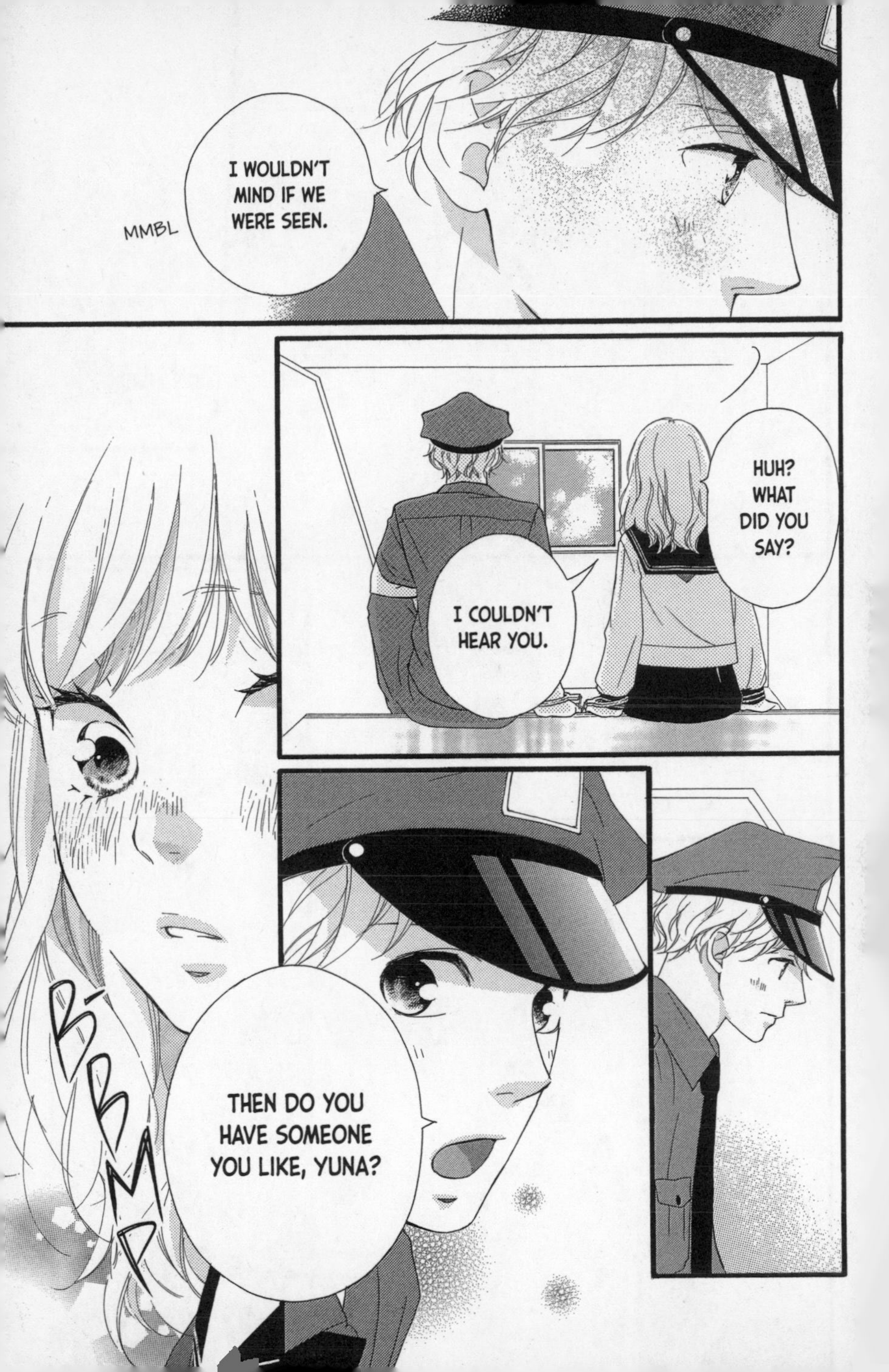
I WOULDN'T MIND IF WE WERE SEEN.
MMBL
HUH? WHAT DID YOU SAY?
I COULDN'T HEAR YOU.
THEN DO YOU HAVE SOMEONE YOU LIKE, YUNA?
B-BMP

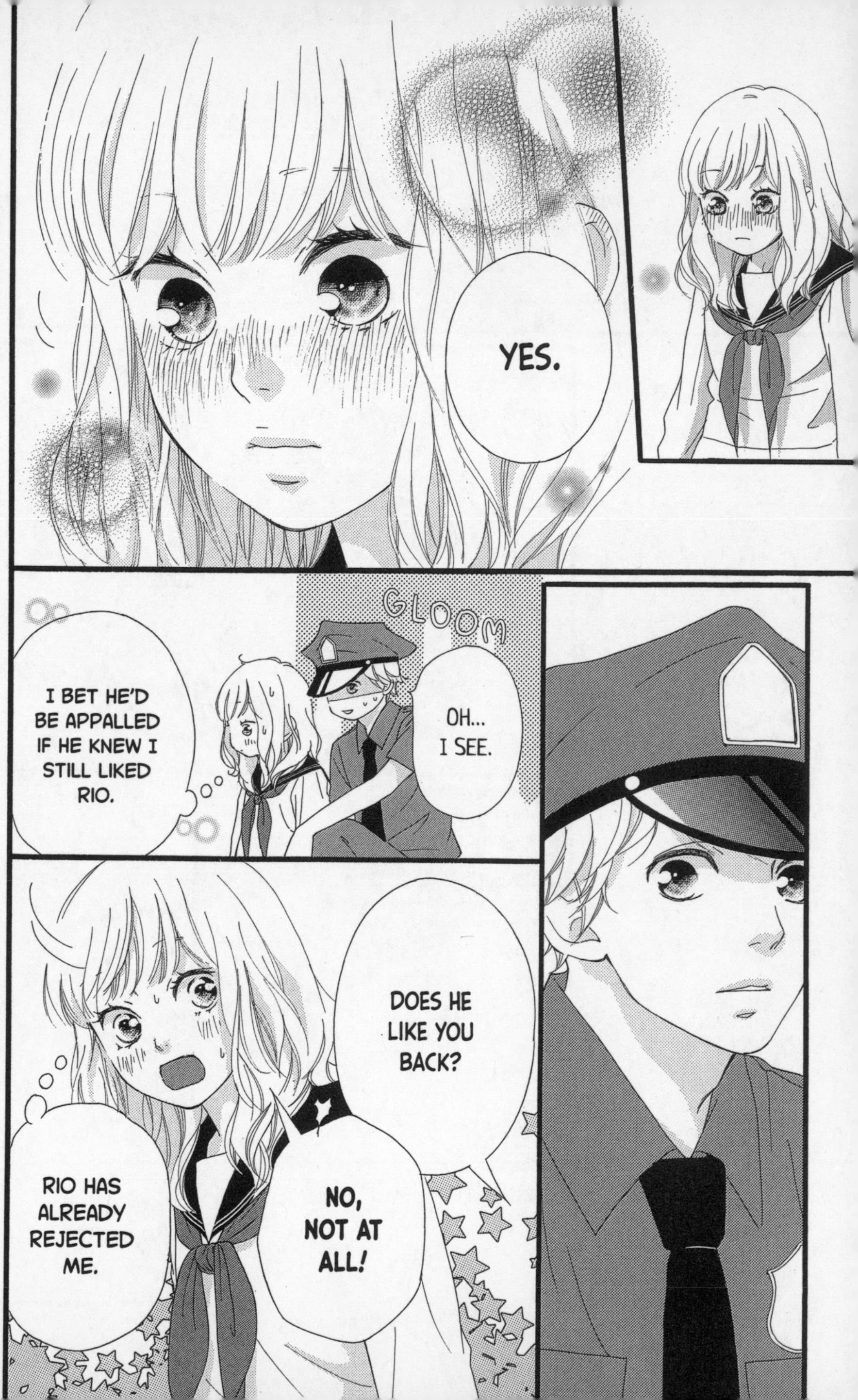
YES.
GLOOM
OH... I SEE.
I BET HE'D BE APPALLED IF HE KNEW I STILL LIKED RIO.
DOES HE LIKE YOU BACK?
NO, NOT AT ALL!
RIO HAS ALREADY REJECTED ME.

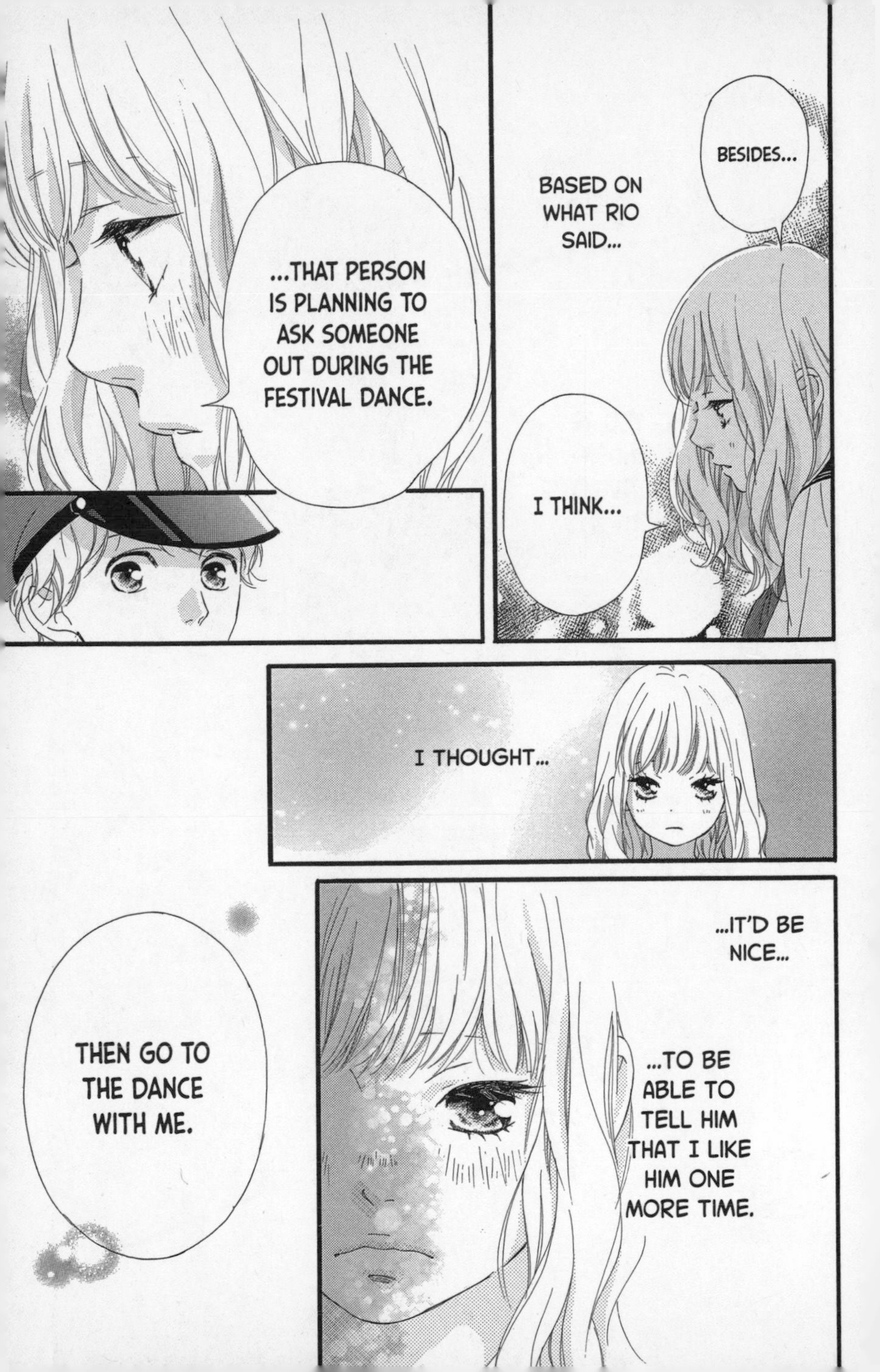
BESIDES...
BASED ON WHAT RIO SAID...
I THINK...
...THAT PERSON IS PLANNING TO ASK SOMEONE OUT DURING THE FESTIVAL DANCE.
I THOUGHT...
...IT'D BE NICE...
...TO BE ABLE TO TELL HIM THAT I LIKE HIM ONE MORE TIME.
THEN GO TO THE DANCE WITH ME.

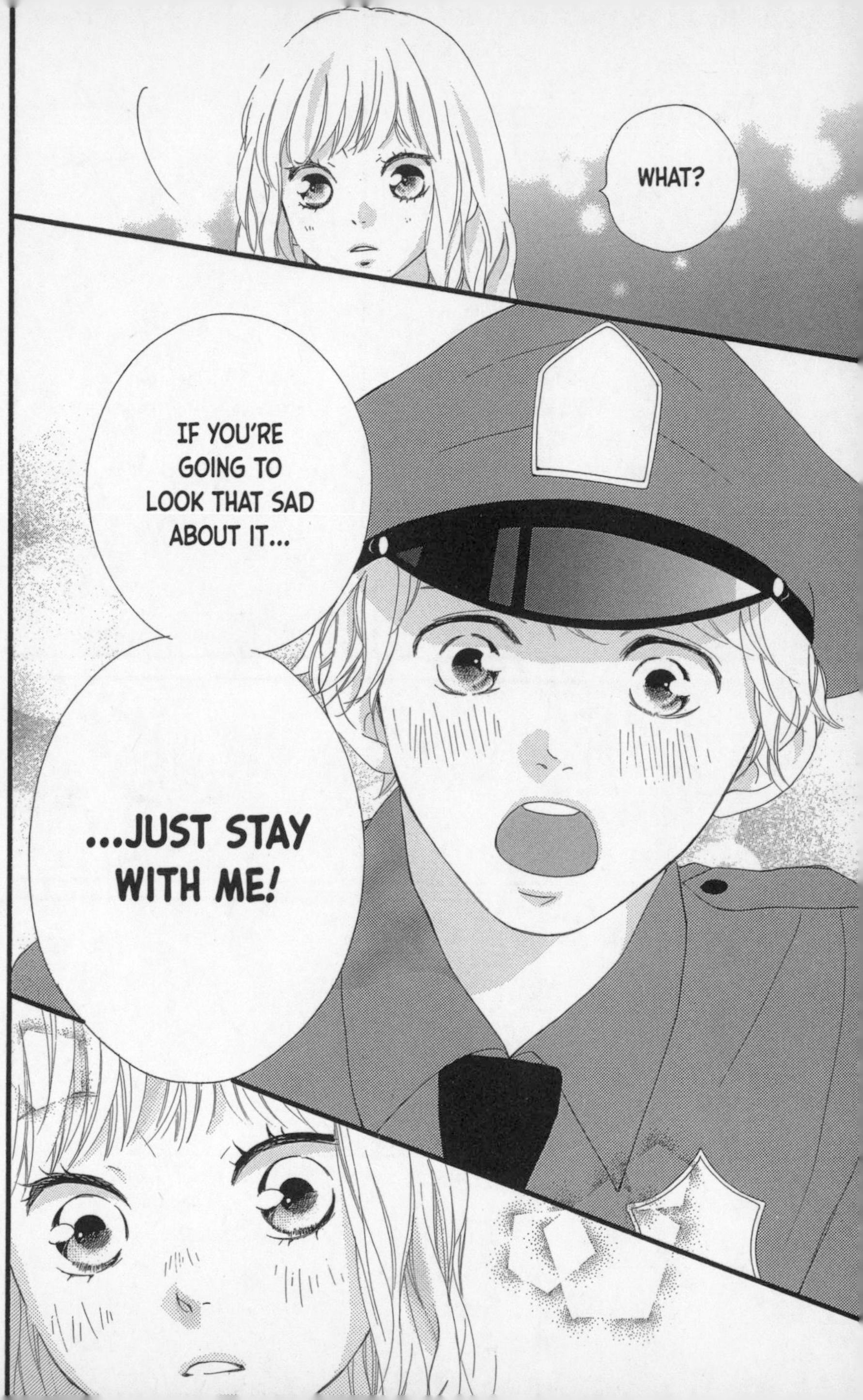
WHAT?
IF YOU'RE GOING TO LOOK THAT SAD ABOUT IT...
...JUST STAY WITH ME!

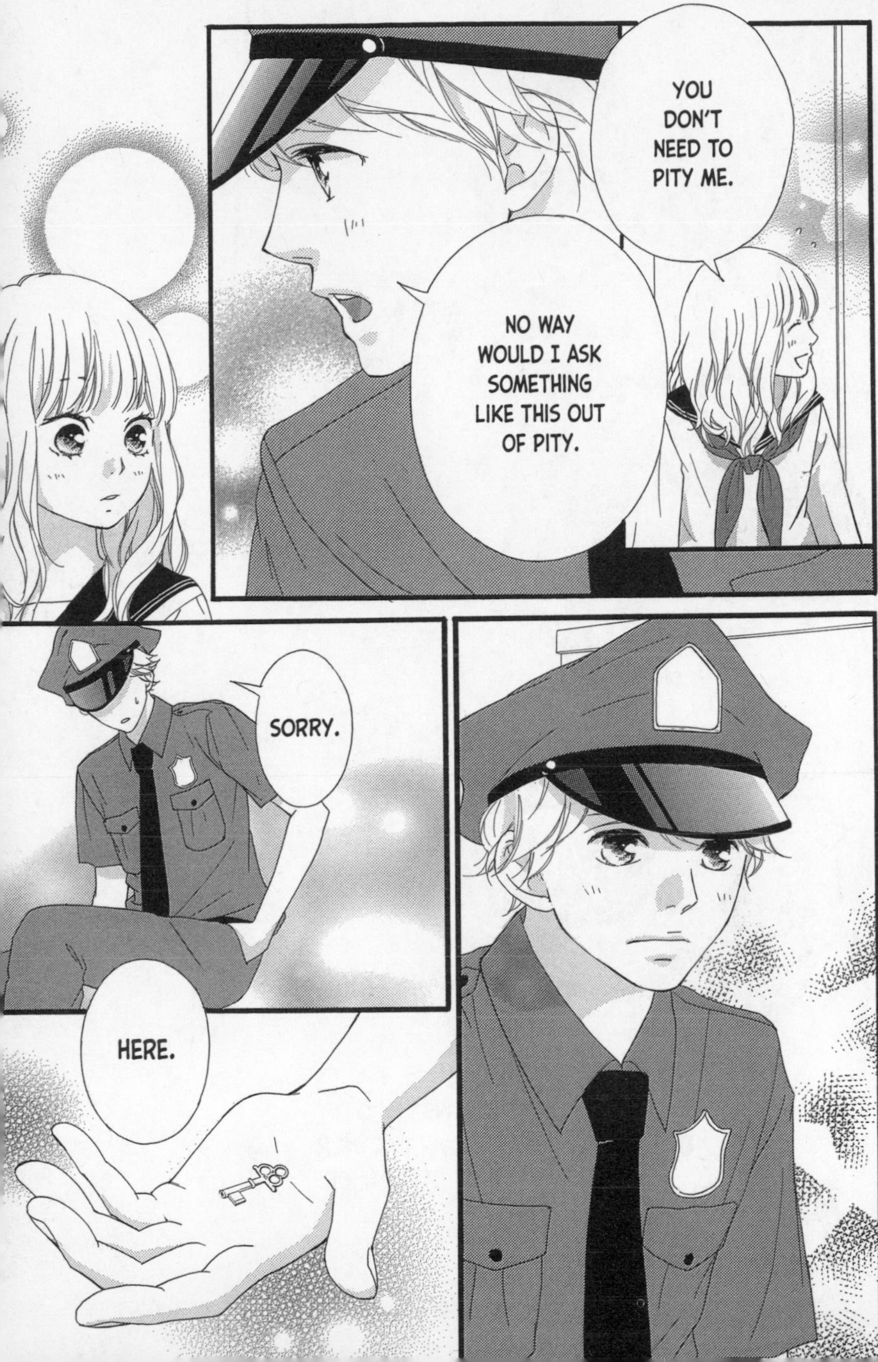
YOU DON'T NEED TO PITY ME.
NO WAY WOULD I ASK SOMETHING LIKE THIS OUT OF PITY.
SORRY.
HERE.

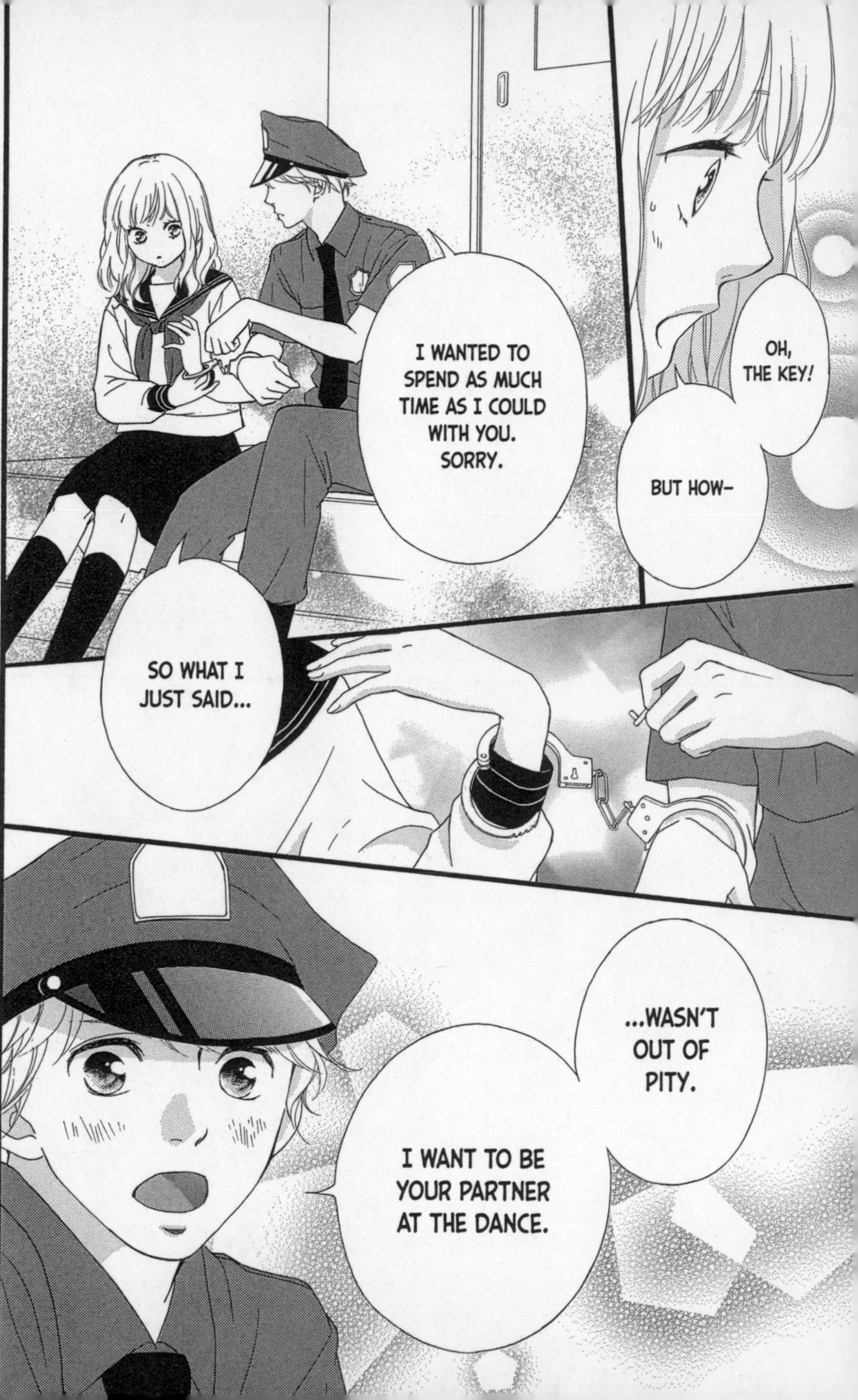
OH, THE KEY!
BUT HOW–
I WANTED TO SPEND AS MUCH TIME AS I COULD WITH YOU. SORRY.
SO WHAT I JUST SAID...
...WASN'T OUT OF PITY.
I WANT TO BE YOUR PARTNER AT THE DANCE.

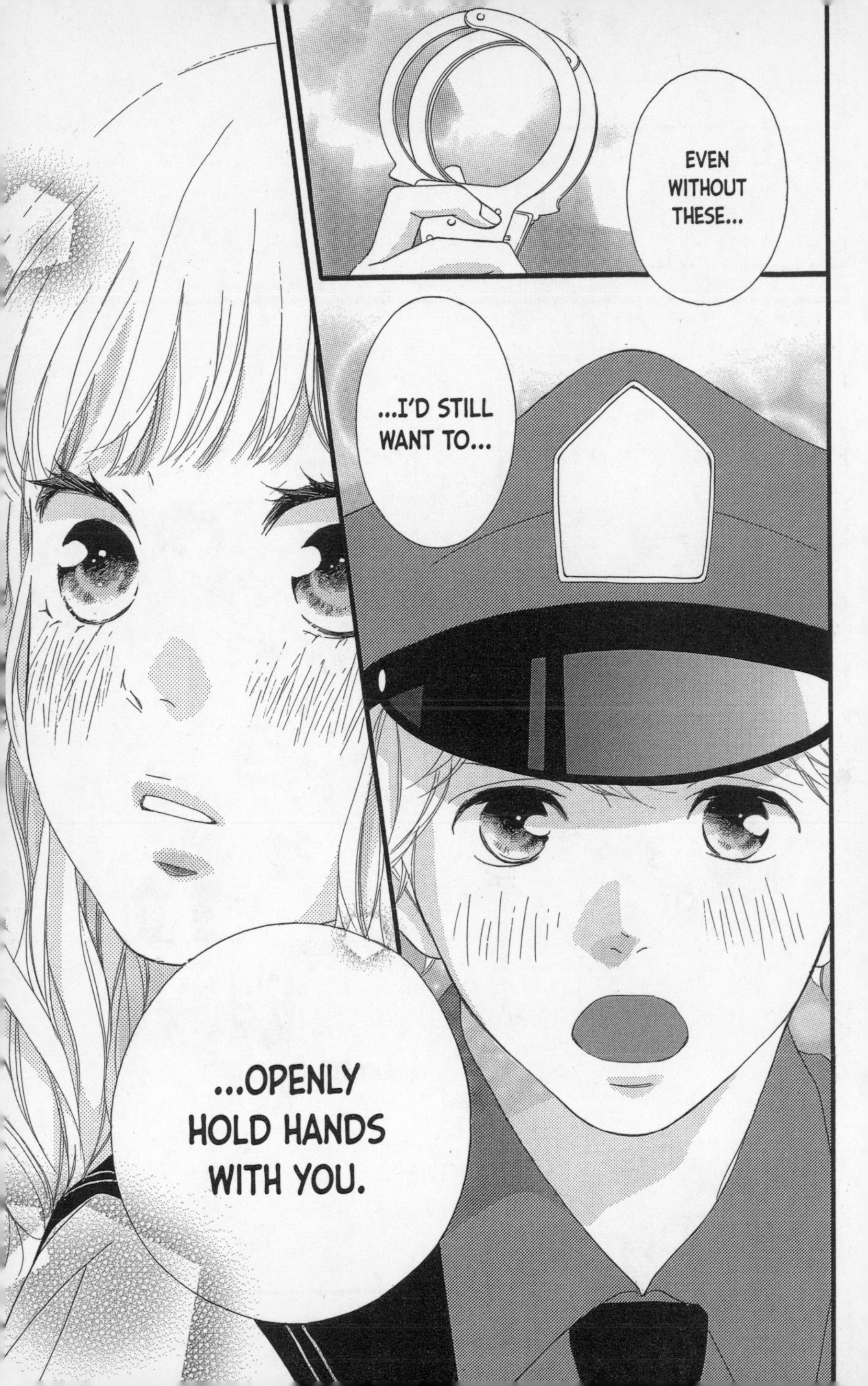
EVEN WITHOUT THESE...
...I'D STILL WANT TO...
...OPENLY HOLD HANDS WITH YOU.

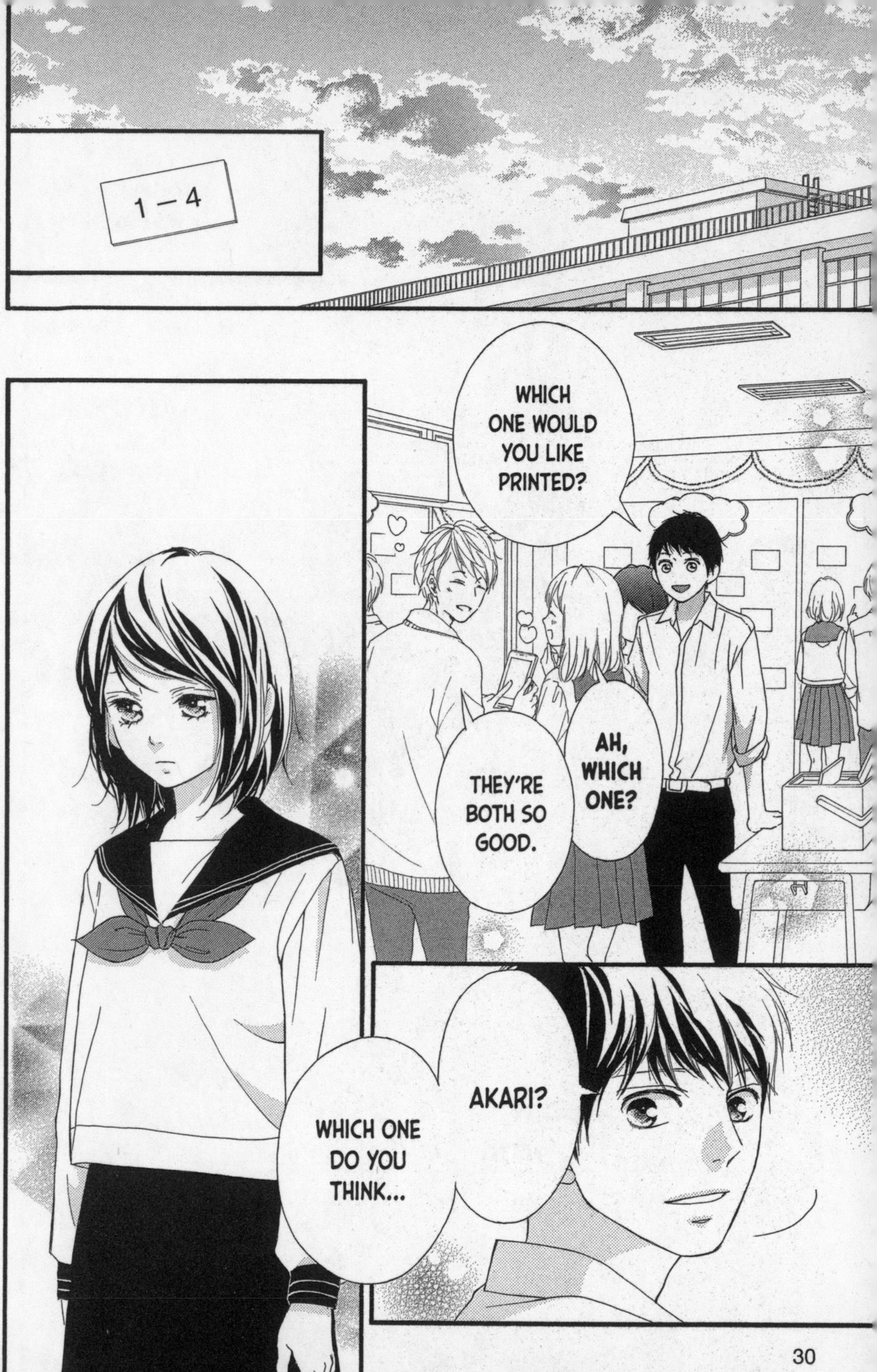
1-4
WHICH ONE WOULD YOU LIKE PRINTED?
AH, WHICH ONE?
THEY'RE BOTH SO GOOD.
AKARI?
WHICH ONE DO YOU THINK...

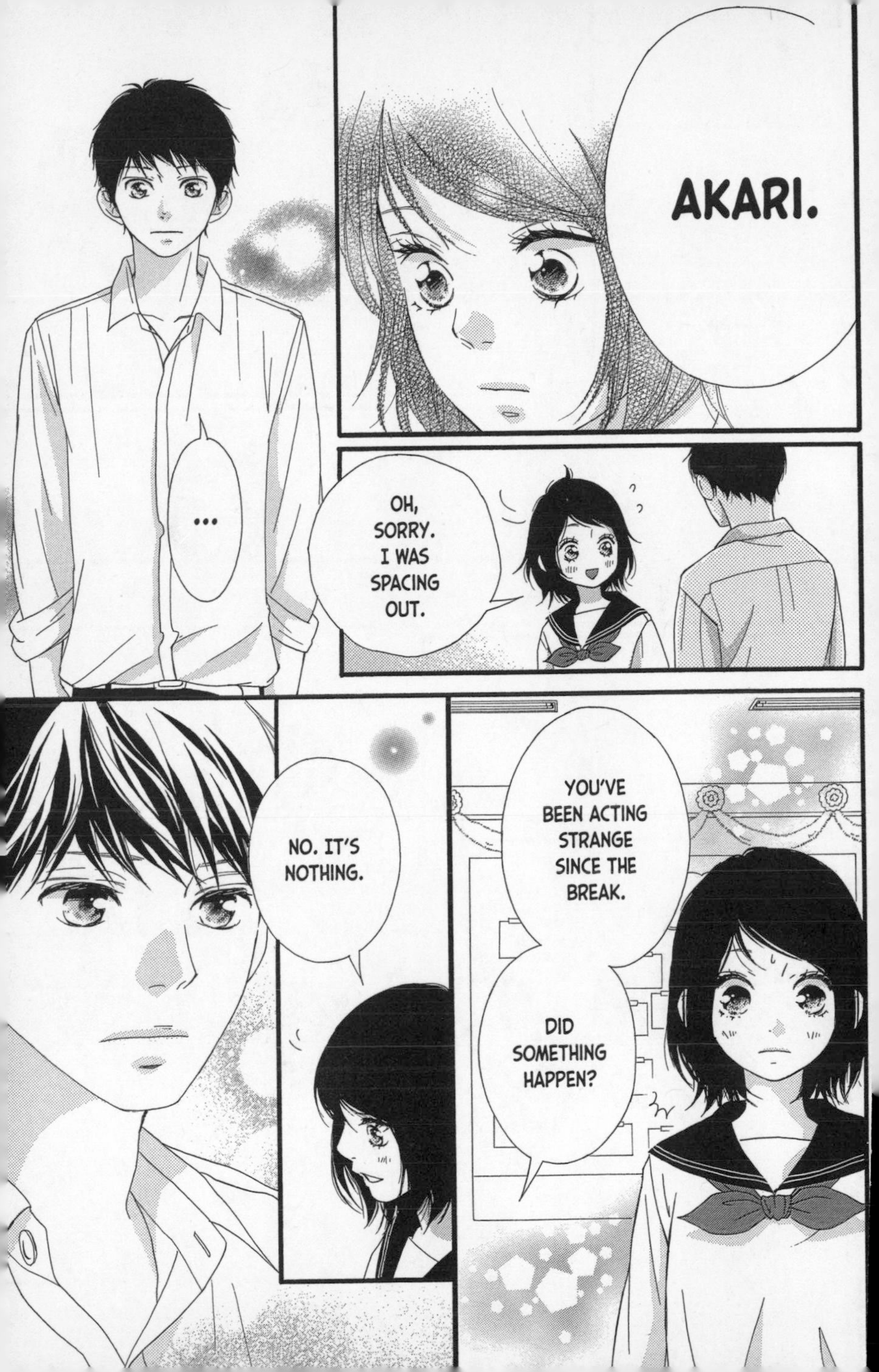
AKARI.
OH, SORRY. I WAS SPACING OUT.
...
YOU'VE BEEN ACTING STRANGE SINCE THE BREAK.
DID SOMETHING HAPPEN?
NO. IT'S NOTHING.

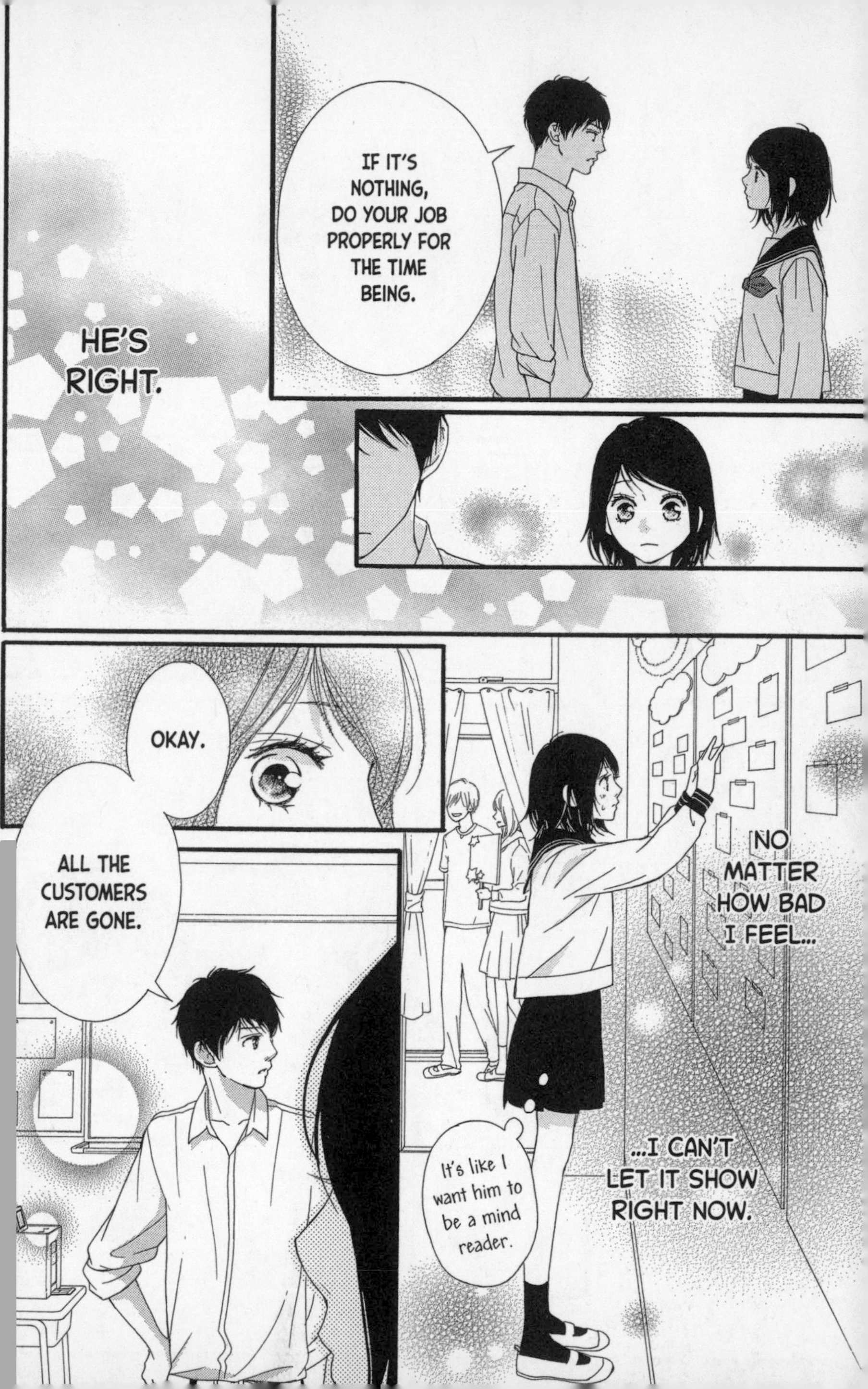
IF IT'S NOTHING, DO YOUR JOB PROPERLY FOR THE TIME BEING.
HE'S RIGHT.
NO MATTER HOW BAD I FEEL...
...I CAN'T LET IT SHOW RIGHT NOW.
It's like I want him to be a mind reader.
OKAY.
ALL THE CUSTOMERS ARE GONE.

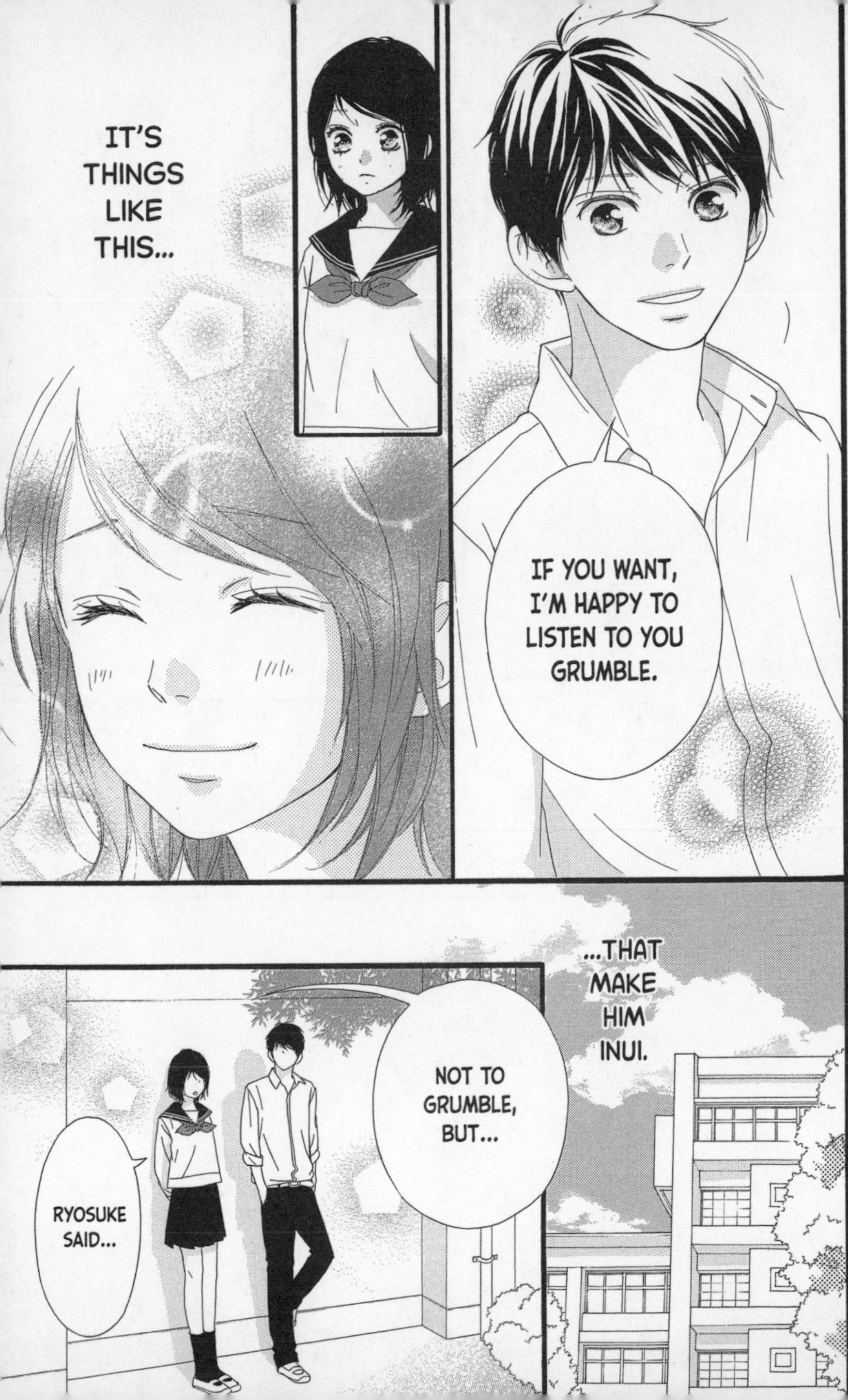
IF YOU WANT, I'M HAPPY TO LISTEN TO YOU GRUMBLE.
IT'S THINGS LIKE THIS...
...THAT MAKE HIM INUI.
NOT TO GRUMBLE, BUT...
RYOSUKE SAID...

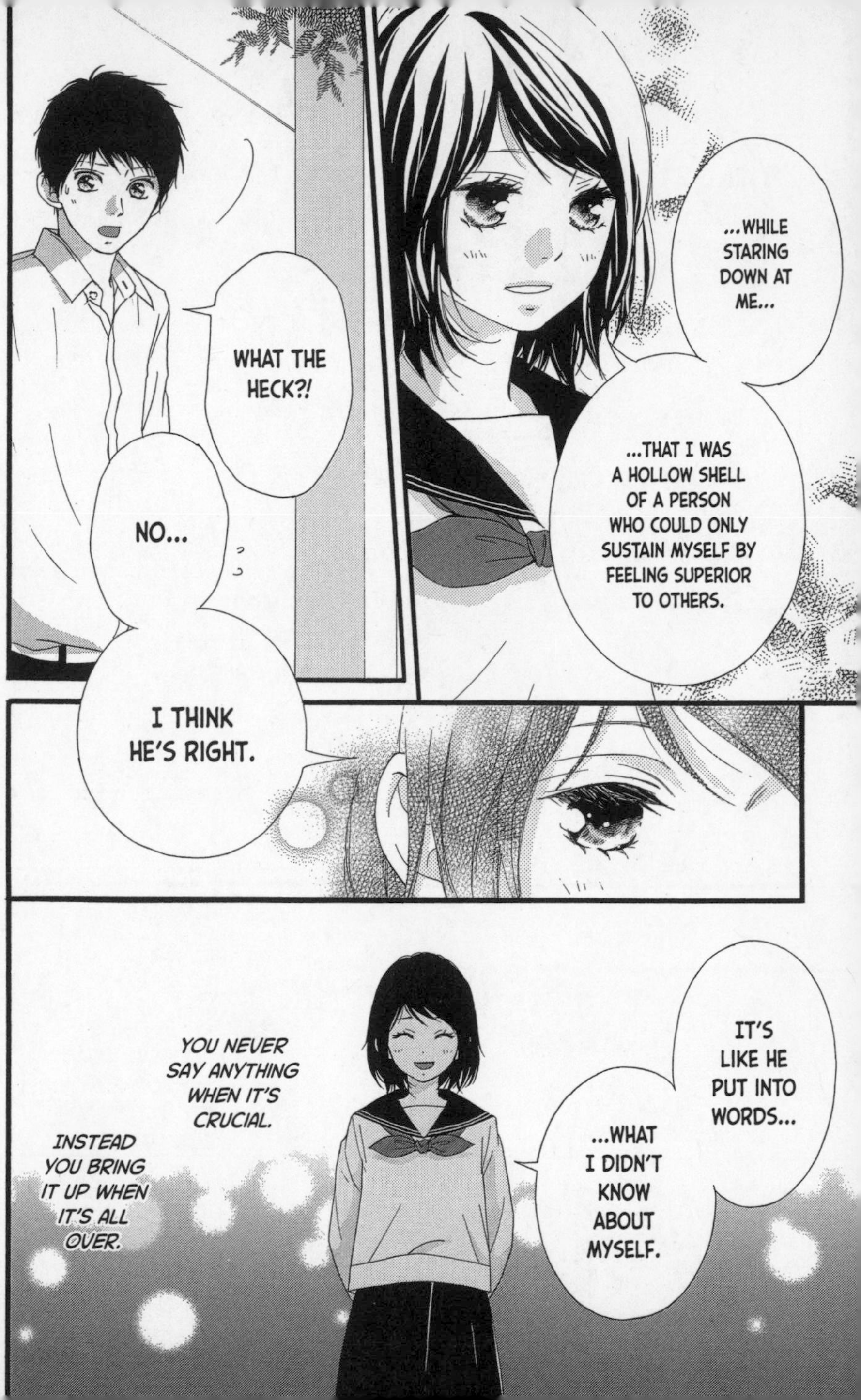
...WHILE STARING DOWN AT ME...
...THAT I WAS A HOLLOW SHELL OF A PERSON WHO COULD ONLY SUSTAIN MYSELF BY FEELING SUPERIOR TO OTHERS.
WHAT THE HECK?!
NO...
I THINK HE'S RIGHT.
IT'S LIKE HE PUT INTO WORDS...
...WHAT I DIDN'T KNOW ABOUT MYSELF.
YOU NEVER SAY ANYTHING WHEN IT'S CRUCIAL.
INSTEAD YOU BRING IT UP WHEN IT'S ALL OVER.

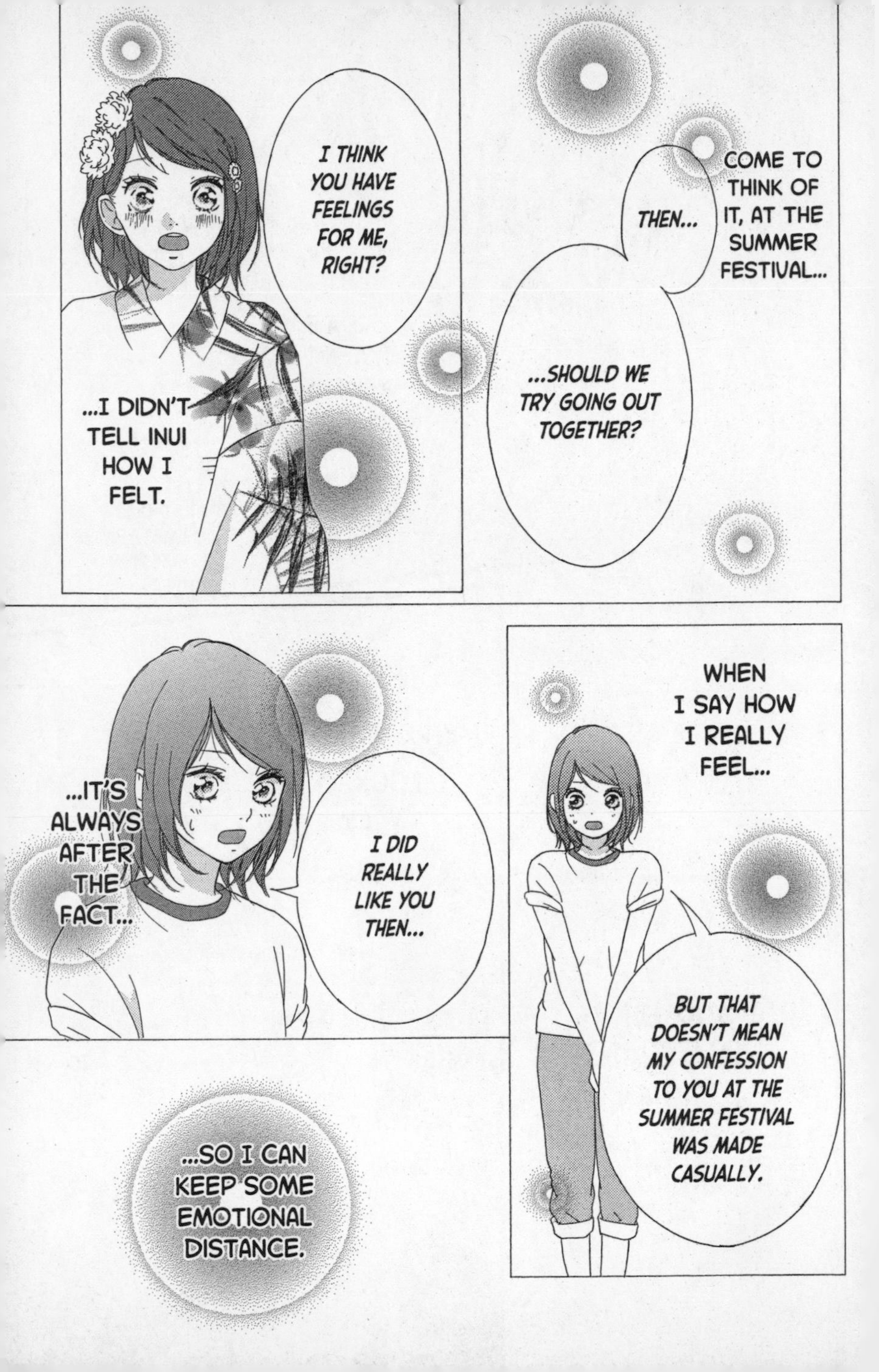
COME TO THINK OF IT, AT THE SUMMER FESTIVAL...
THEN...
...SHOULD WE TRY GOING OUT TOGETHER?
I THINK YOU HAVE FEELINGS FOR ME, RIGHT?
...I DIDN'T TELL INUI HOW I FELT.
WHEN I SAY HOW I REALLY FEEL...
BUT THAT DOESN'T MEAN MY CONFESSION TO YOU AT THE SUMMER FESTIVAL WAS MADE CASUALLY.
I DID REALLY LIKE YOU THEN...
...IT'S ALWAYS AFTER THE FACT...
...SO I CAN KEEP SOME EMOTIONAL DISTANCE.

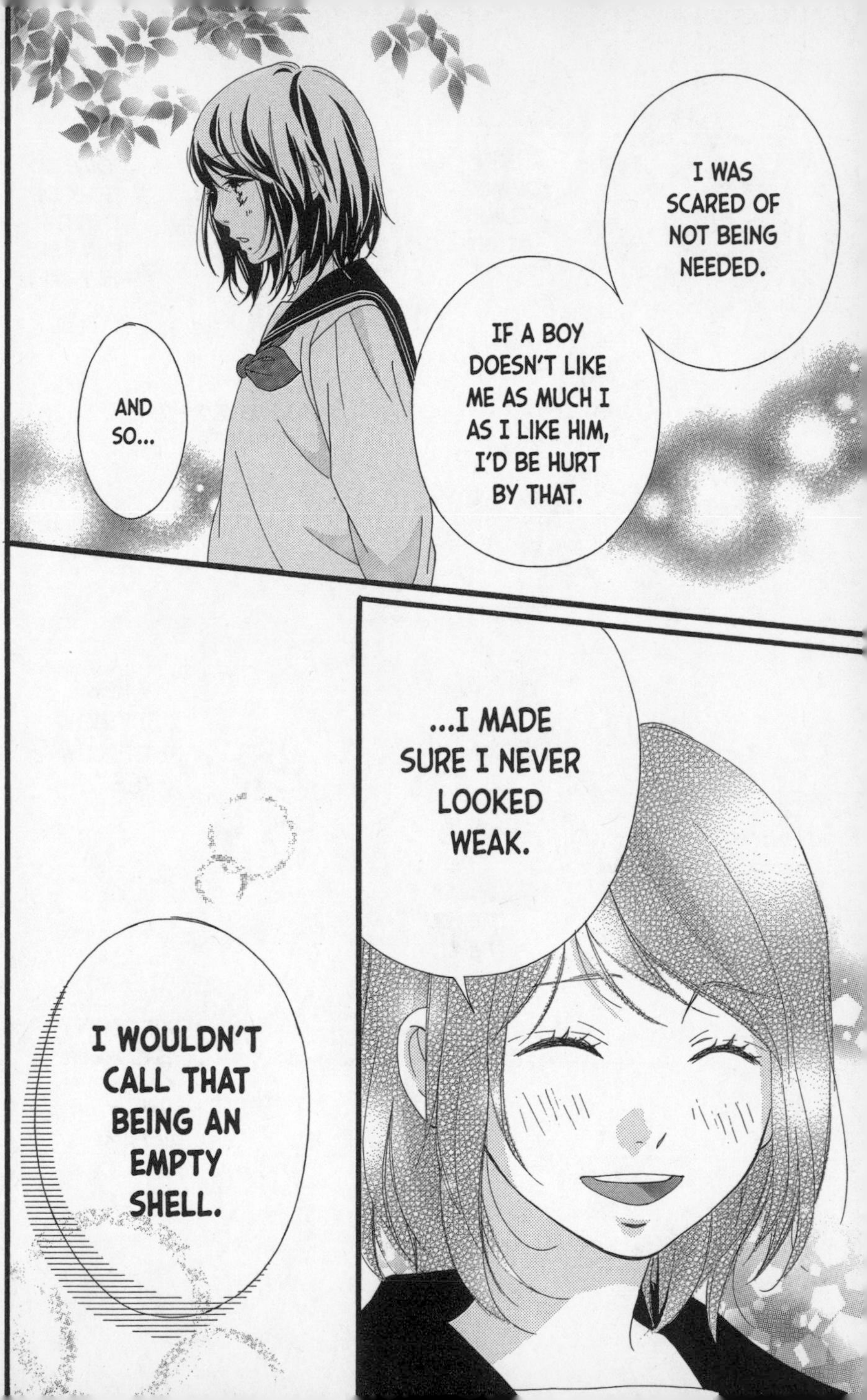
I WAS SCARED OF NOT BEING NEEDED.
IF A BOY DOESN'T LIKE ME AS MUCH I AS I LIKE HIM, I'D BE HURT BY THAT.
AND SO...
...I MADE SURE I NEVER LOOKED WEAK.
I WOULDN'T CALL THAT BEING AN EMPTY SHELL.

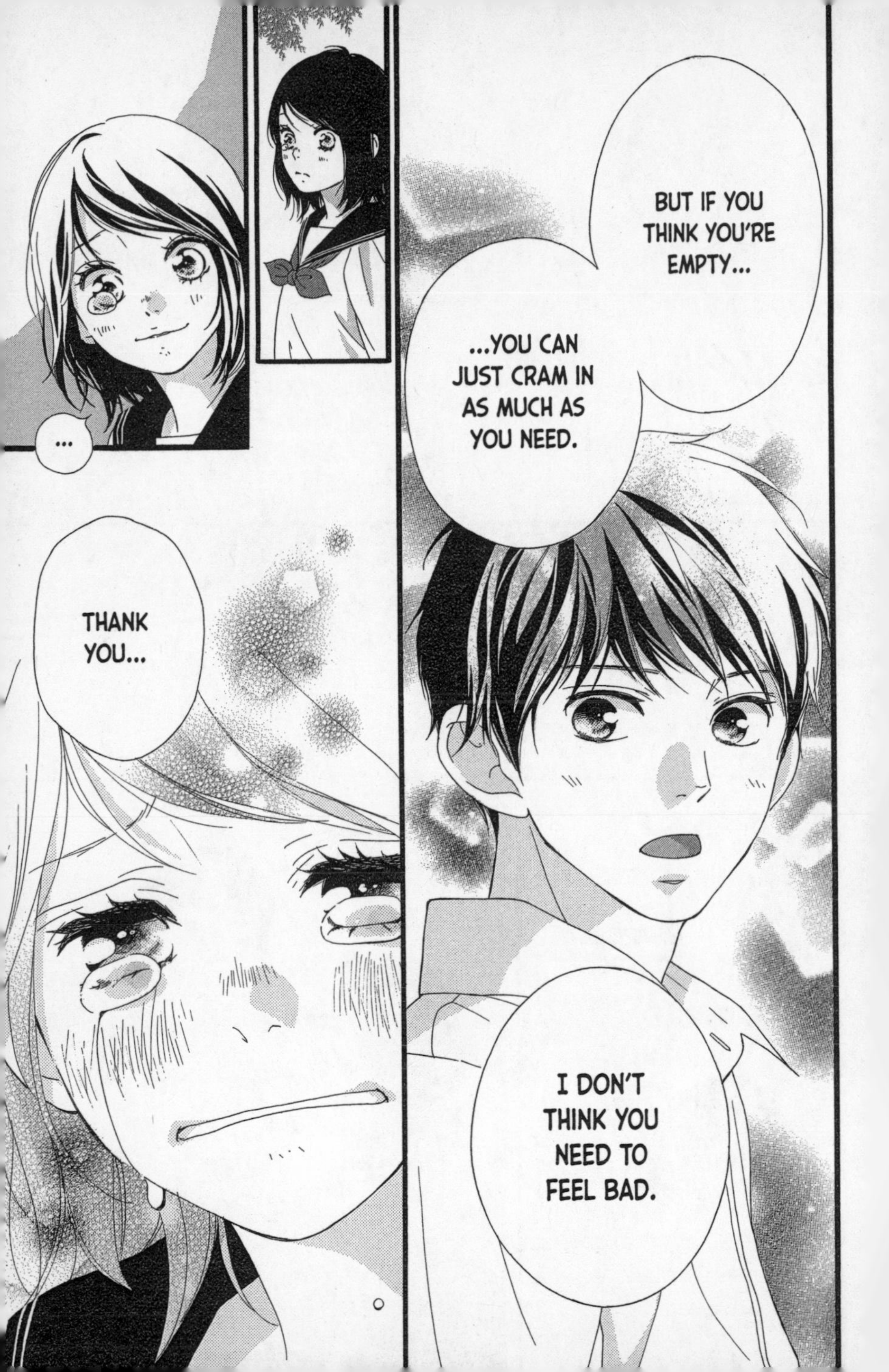
BUT IF YOU THINK YOU'RE EMPTY...
...YOU CAN JUST CRAM IN AS MUCH AS YOU NEED.
I DON'T THINK YOU NEED TO FEEL BAD.
...
THANK YOU...

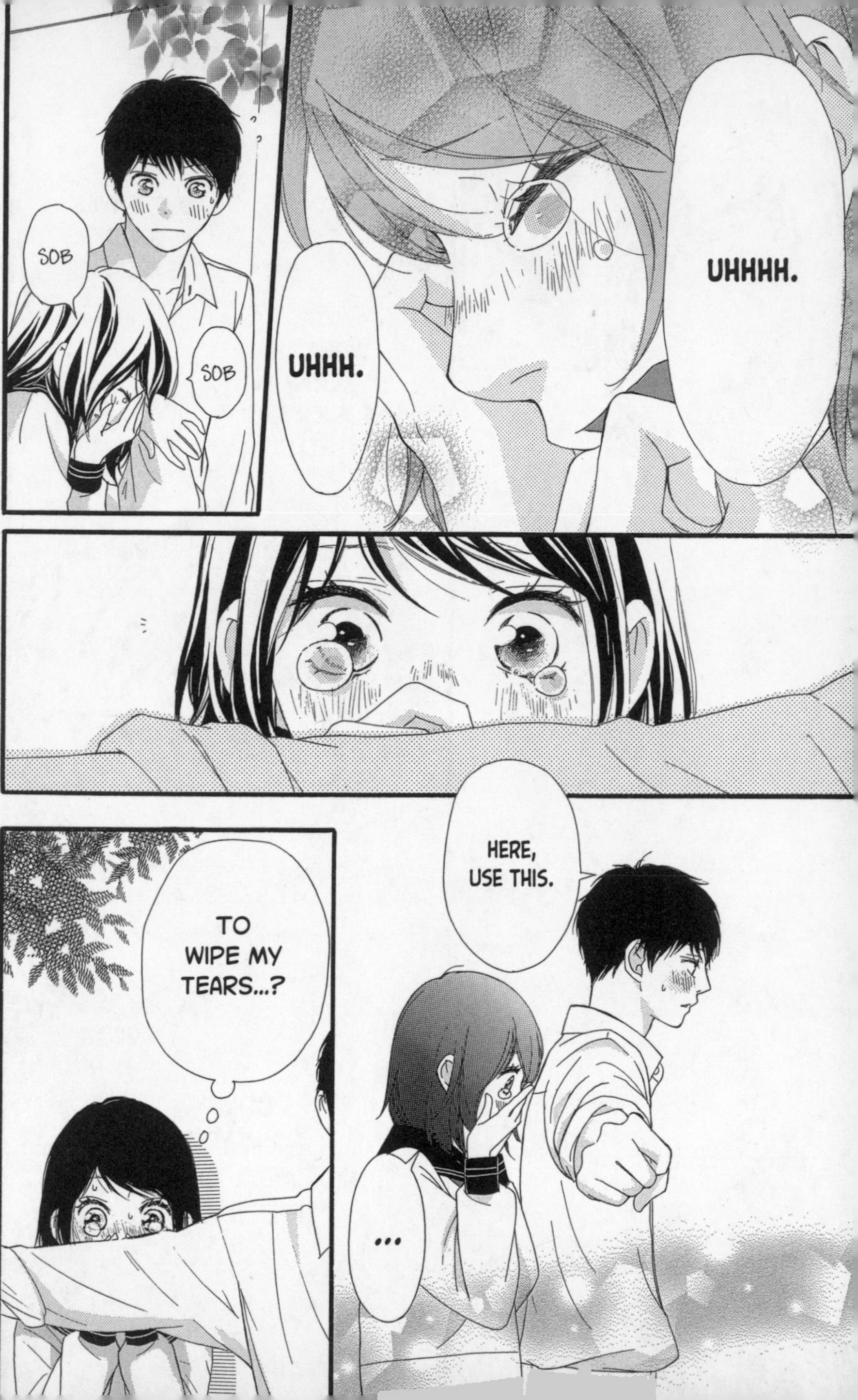
UHHHH.
UHHH.
SOB
SOB
HERE, USE THIS.
...
TO WIPE MY TEARS...?

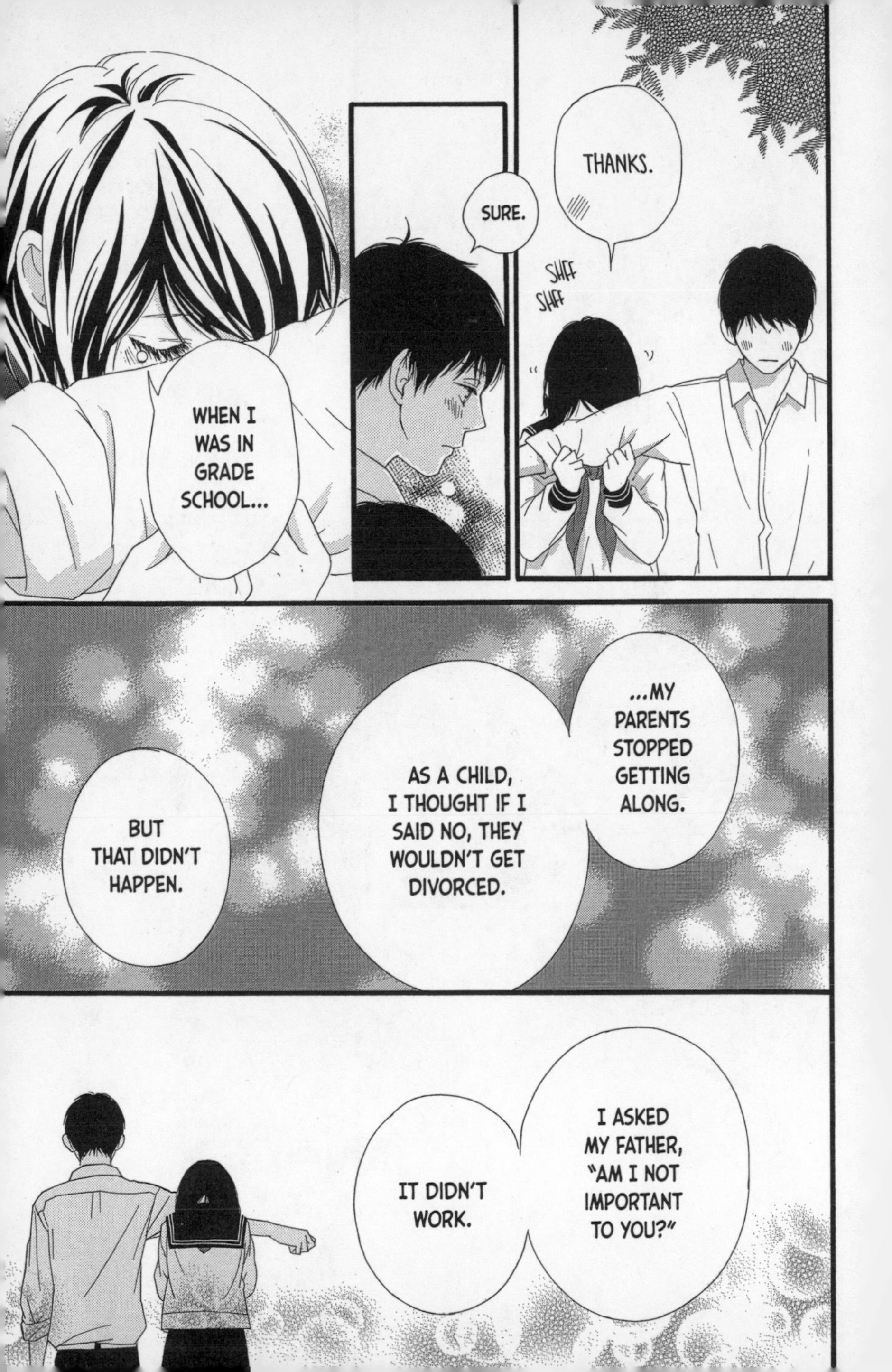
THANKS.
SHFF SHFF
SURE.
WHEN I WAS IN GRADE SCHOOL...
...MY PARENTS STOPPED GETTING ALONG.
AS A CHILD, I THOUGHT IF I SAID NO, THEY WOULDN'T GET DIVORCED.
BUT THAT DIDN'T HAPPEN.
I ASKED MY FATHER, "AM I NOT IMPORTANT TO YOU?"
IT DIDN'T WORK.

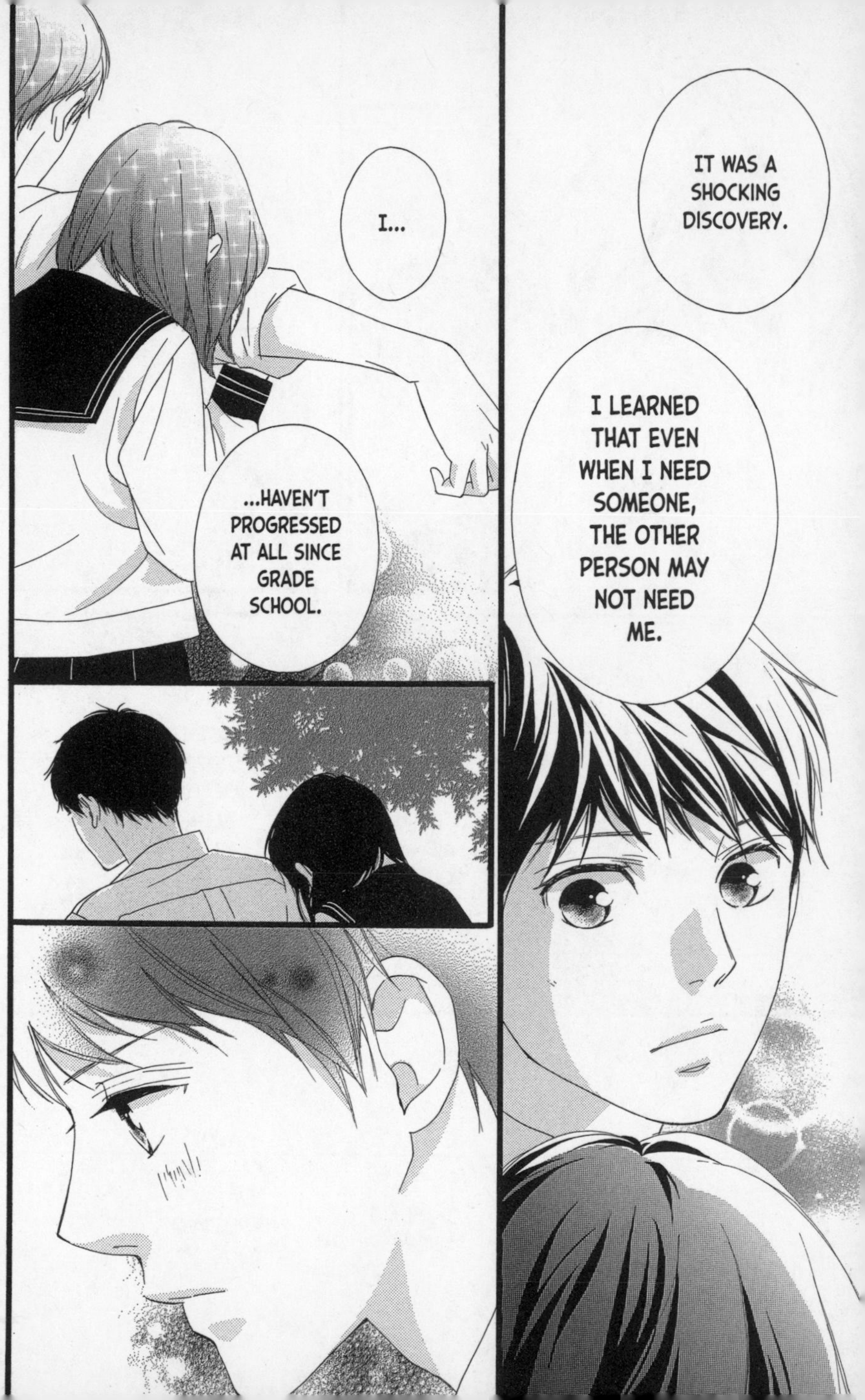
IT WAS A SHOCKING DISCOVERY.
I LEARNED THAT EVEN WHEN I NEED SOMEONE, THE OTHER PERSON MAY NOT NEED ME.
I...
...HAVEN'T PROGRESSED AT ALL SINCE GRADE SCHOOL.

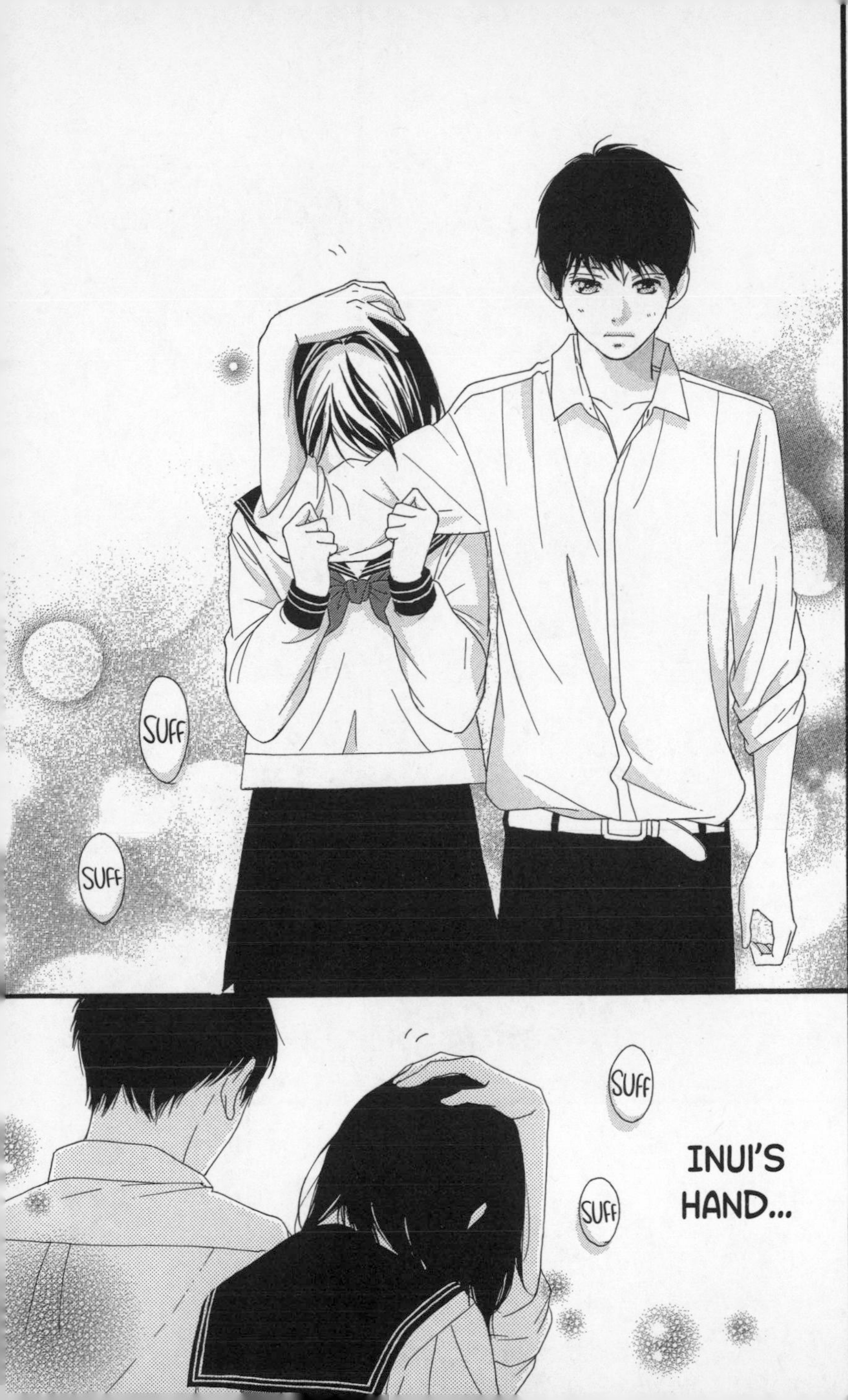
SUFF
SUFF
INUI'S HAND...
SUFF
SUFF

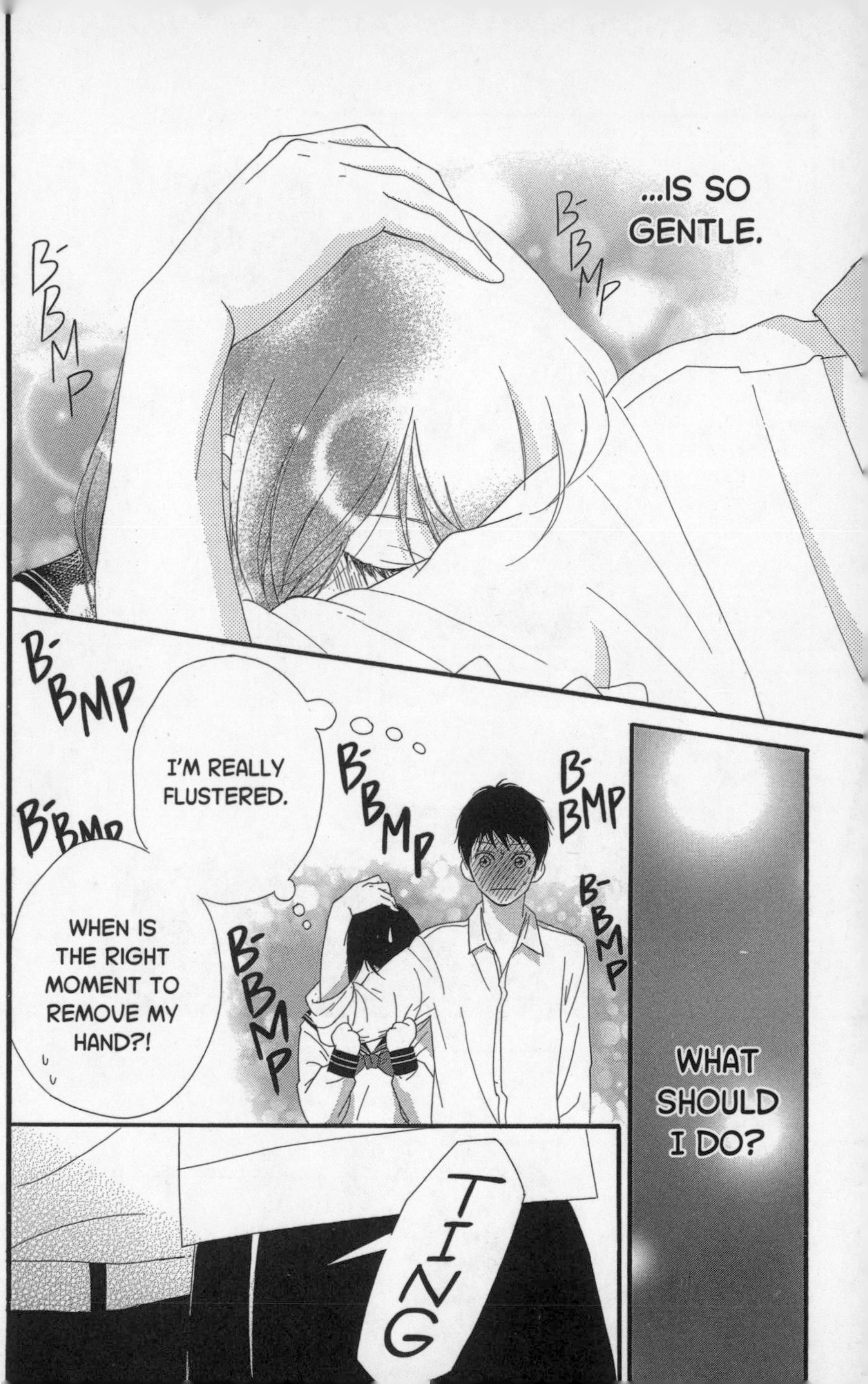
...IS SO GENTLE.
B-BMP
B-BMP
WHAT SHOULD I DO?
B-BMP
B-BMP
B-BMP
I'M REALLY FLUSTERED.
B-BMP
WHEN IS THE RIGHT MOMENT TO REMOVE MY HAND?!
B-BMP
B-BMP
TING

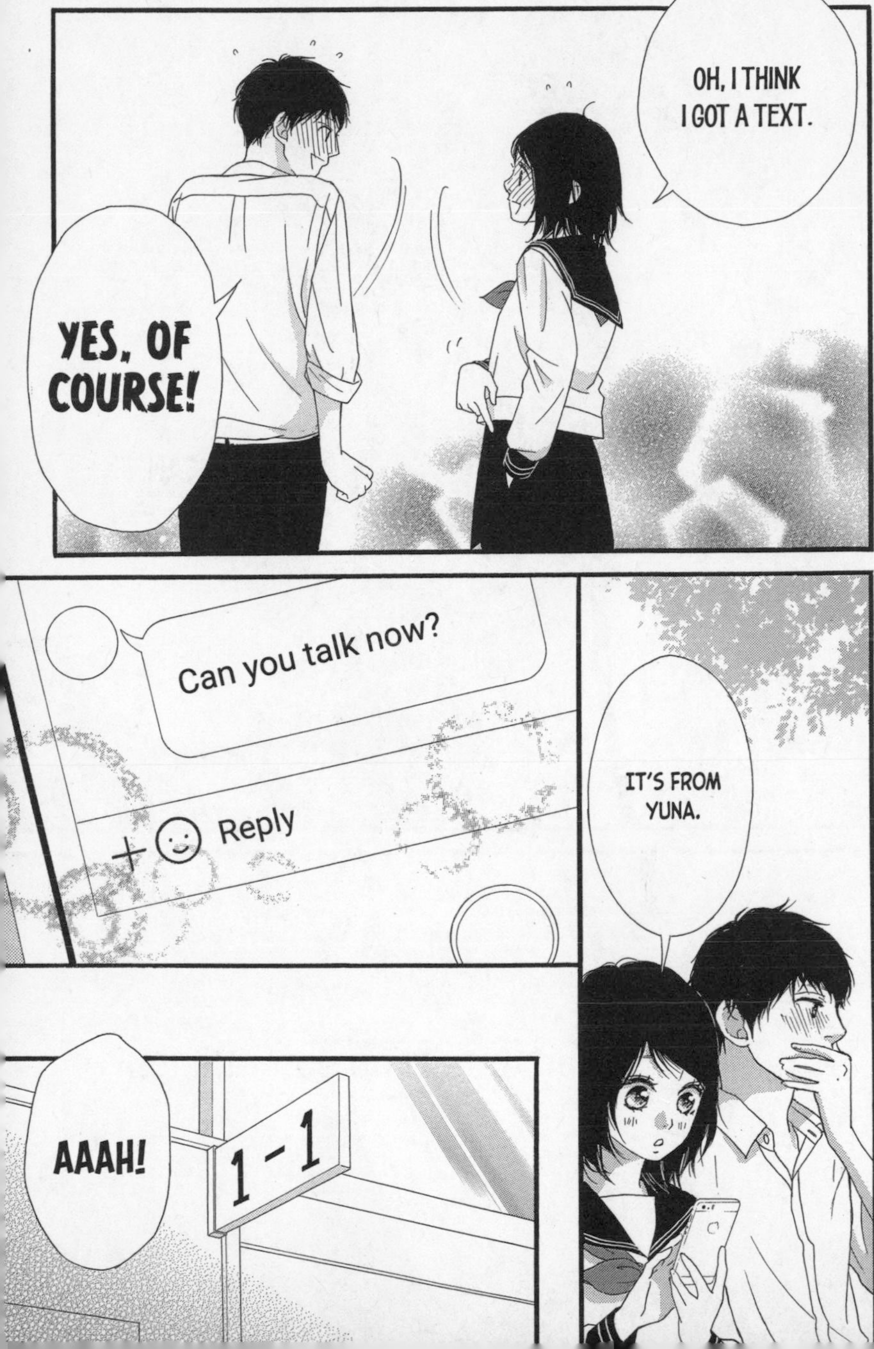
OH, I THINK I GOT A TEXT.
YES, OF COURSE!
IT'S FROM YUNA.
Can you talk now?
Reply
AAAH!
1-1

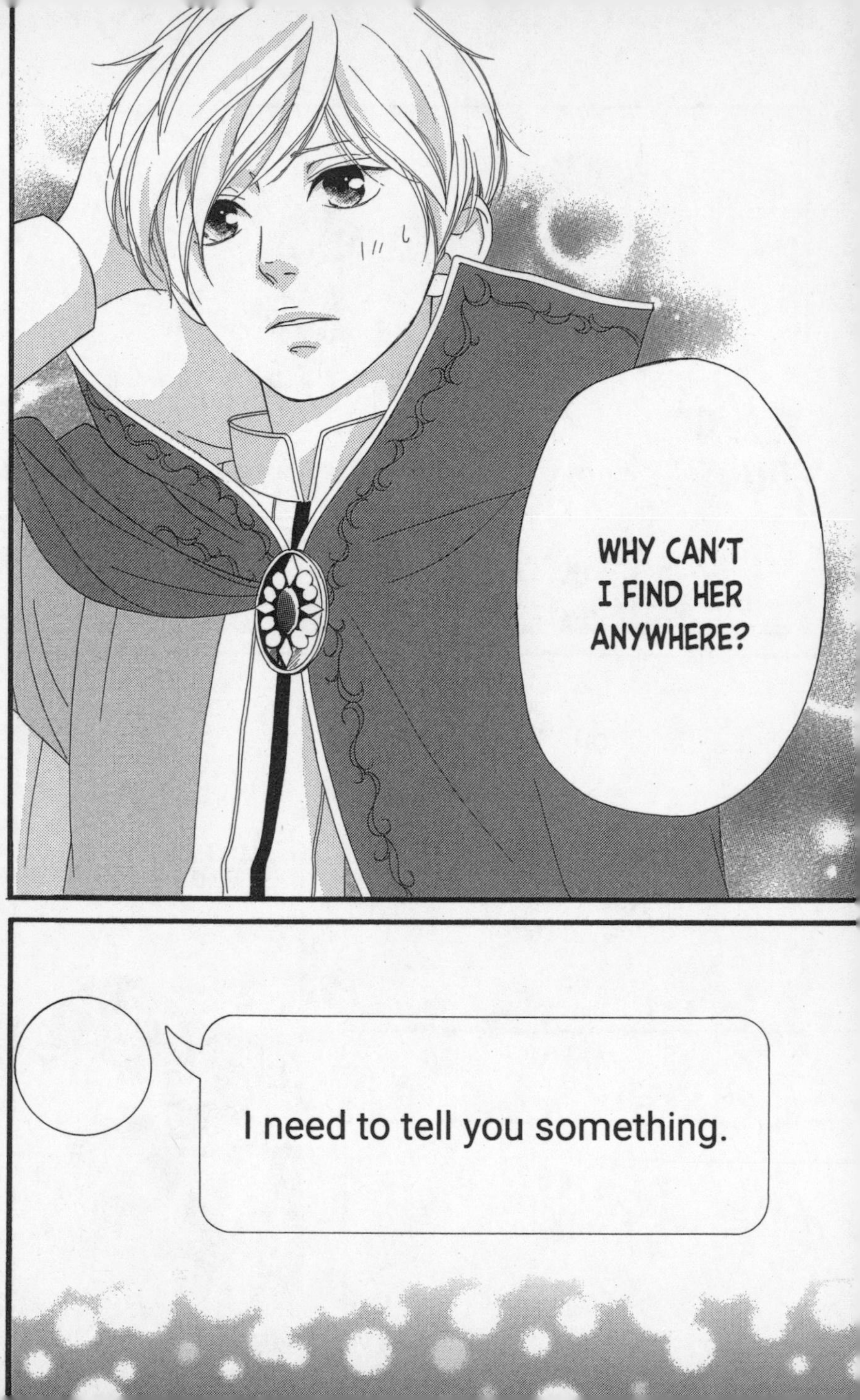
WHY CAN'T I FIND HER ANYWHERE?
I need to tell you something.

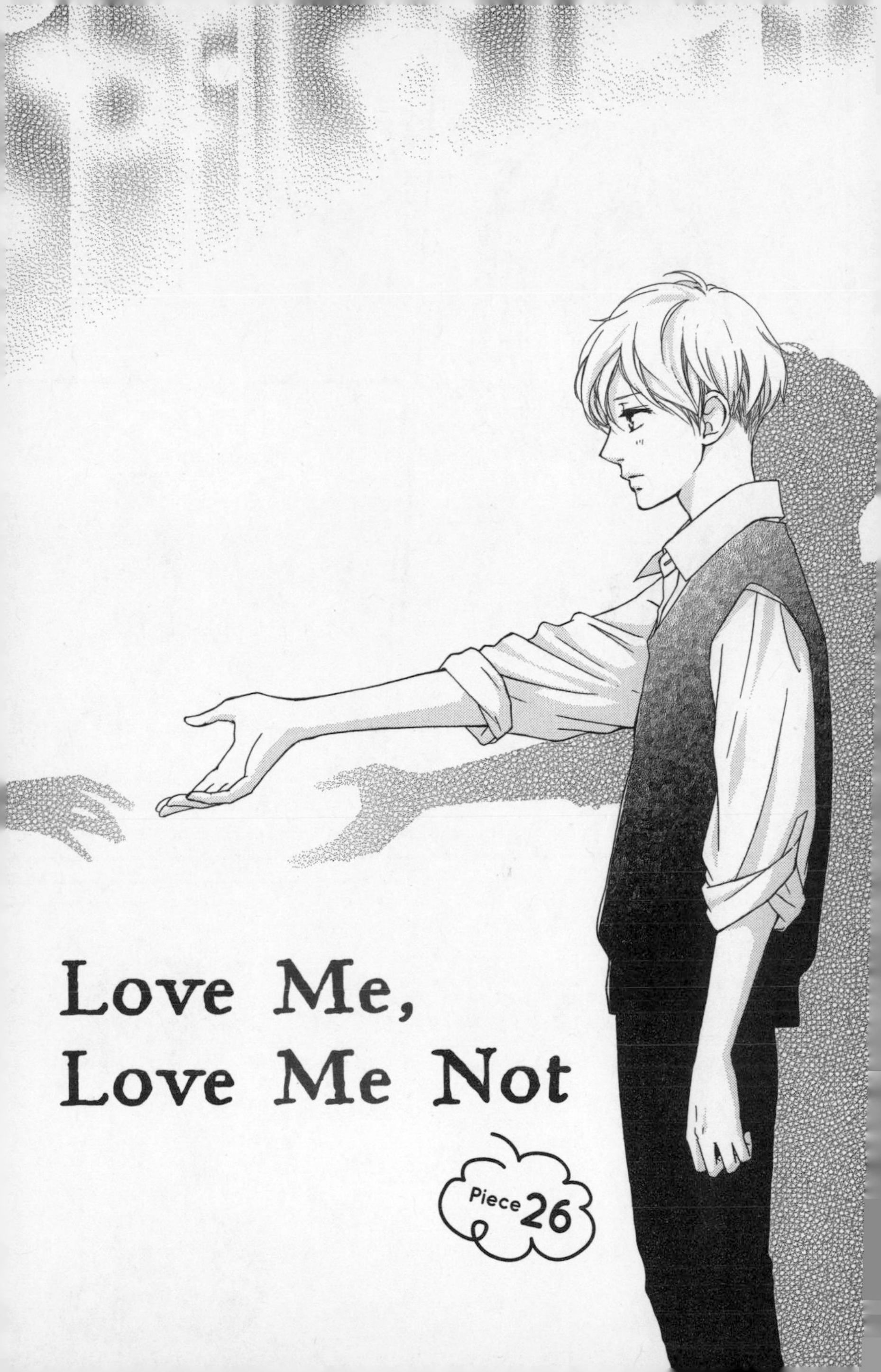
Love Me,
Love Me Not
Piece 26

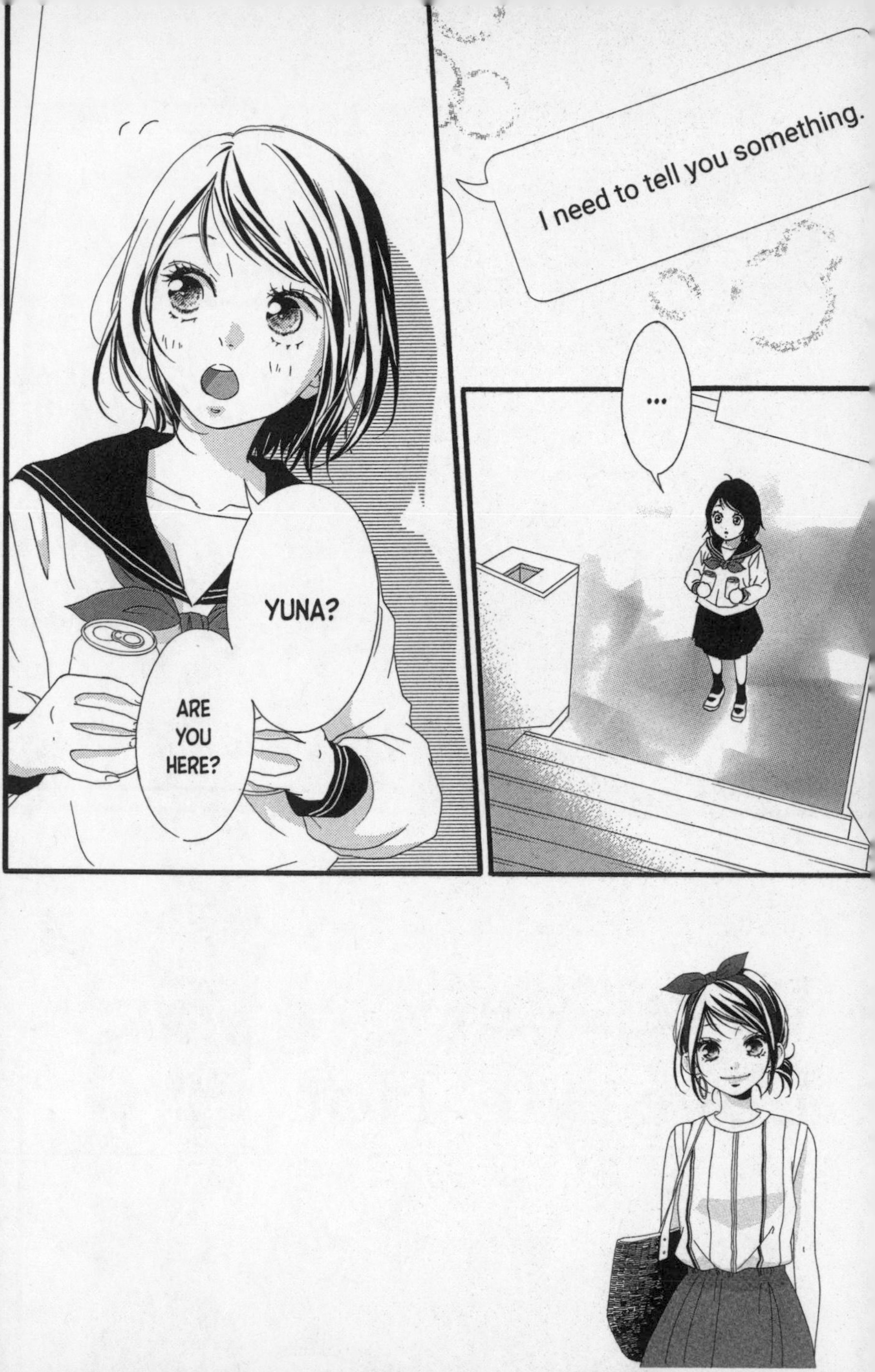
I need to tell you something.
...
YUNA?
ARE YOU HERE?

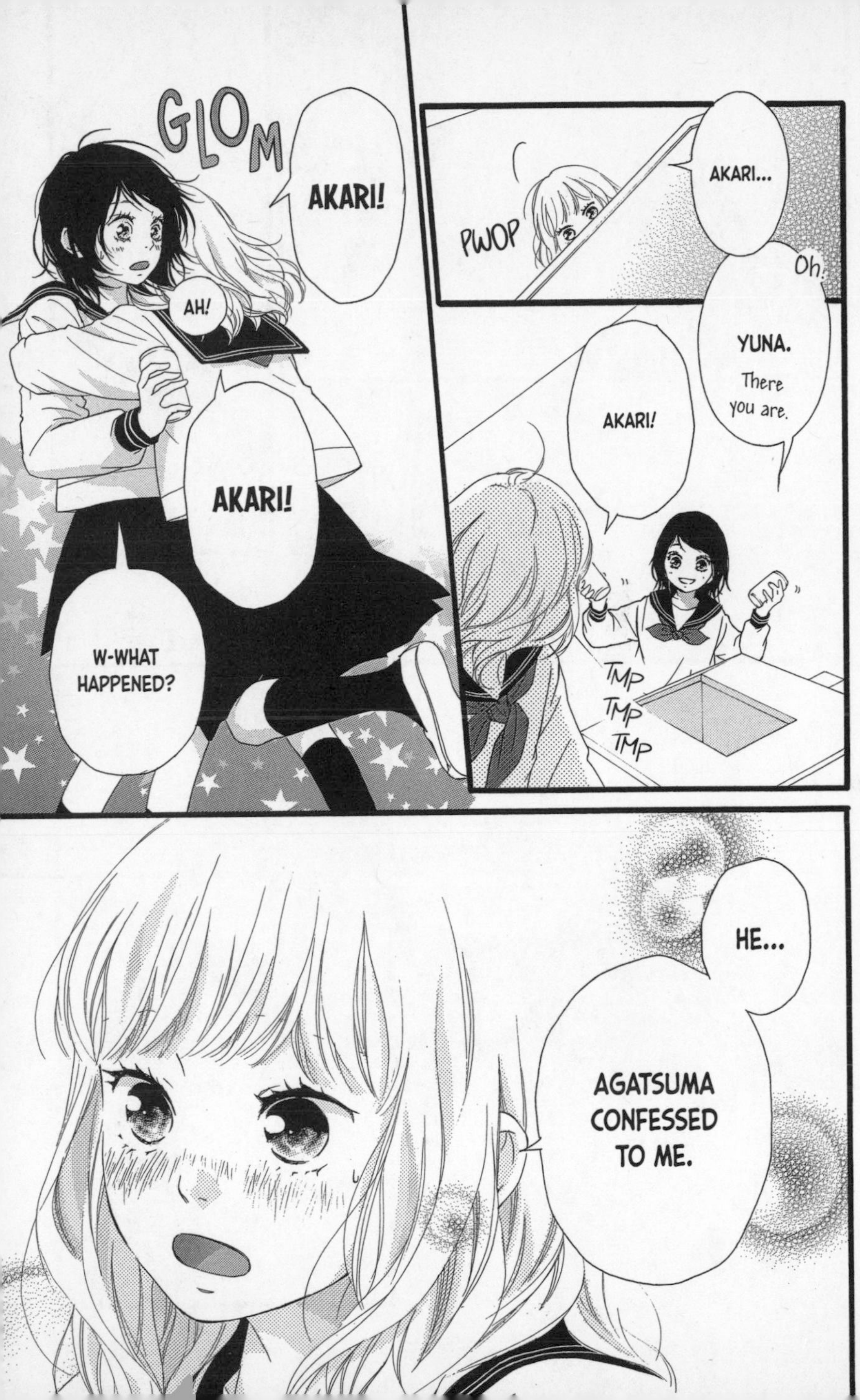
AKARI...
PWOP
Oh! YUNA. There you are.
AKARI!
TMP TMP TMP
GLOM
AKARI!
AH!
AKARI!
W-WHAT HAPPENED?
HE...
AGATSUMA CONFESSED TO ME.

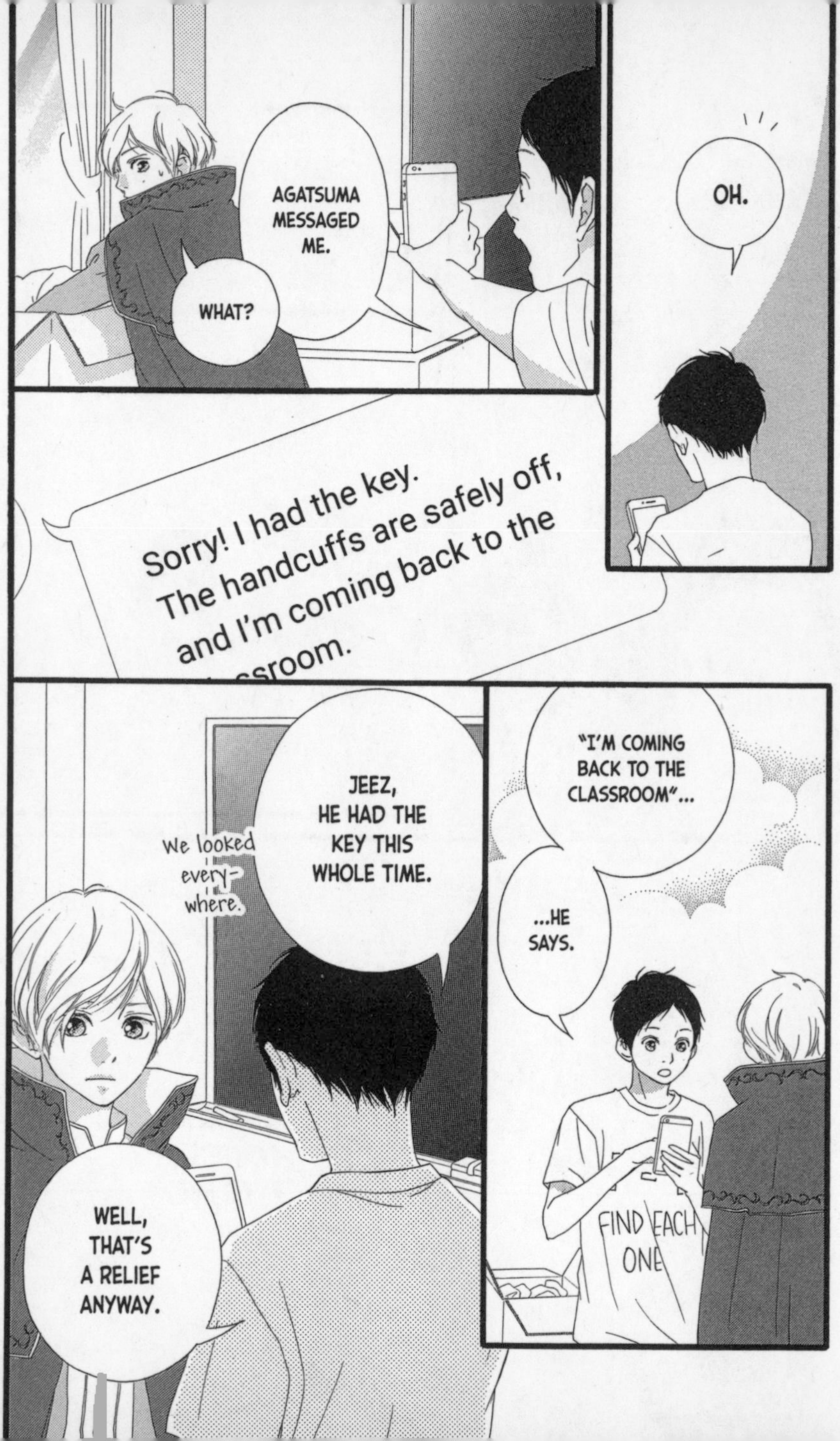
OH.
AGATSUMA MESSAGED ME.
WHAT?
Sorry! I had the key. The handcuffs are safely off, and I'm coming back to the
ssroom.
"I'M COMING BACK TO THE CLASSROOM"...
...HE SAYS.
FIND EACH
ONE
JEEZ, HE HAD THE KEY THIS WHOLE TIME.
We looked every-where.
WELL, THAT'S A RELIEF ANYWAY.

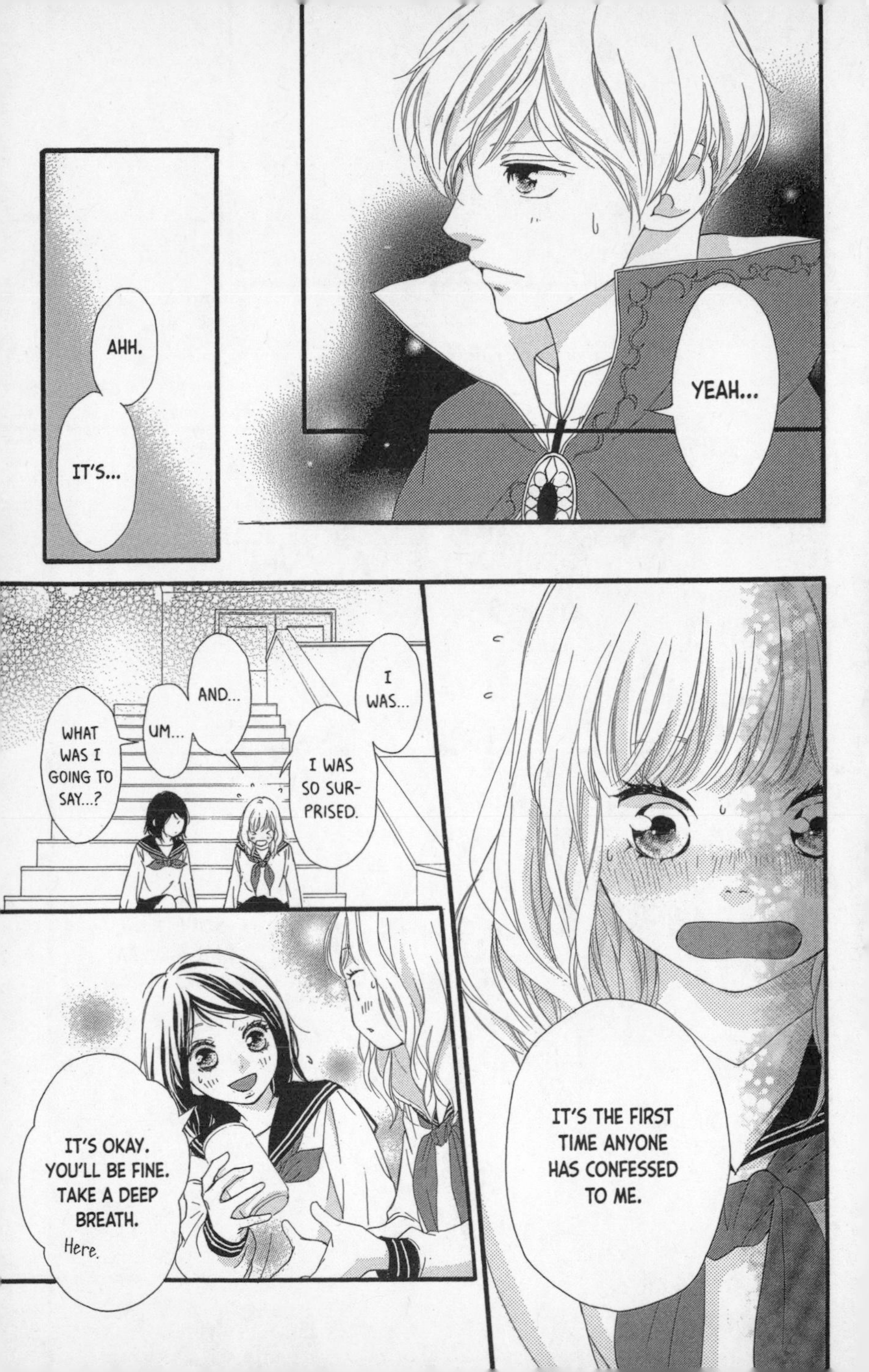
YEAH...
AHH.
IT'S...
IT'S THE FIRST TIME ANYONE HAS CONFESSED TO ME.
I WAS...
I WAS SO SURPRISED.
AND...
UM...
WHAT WAS I GOING TO SAY...?
IT'S OKAY. YOU'LL BE FINE. TAKE A DEEP BREATH.
Here.

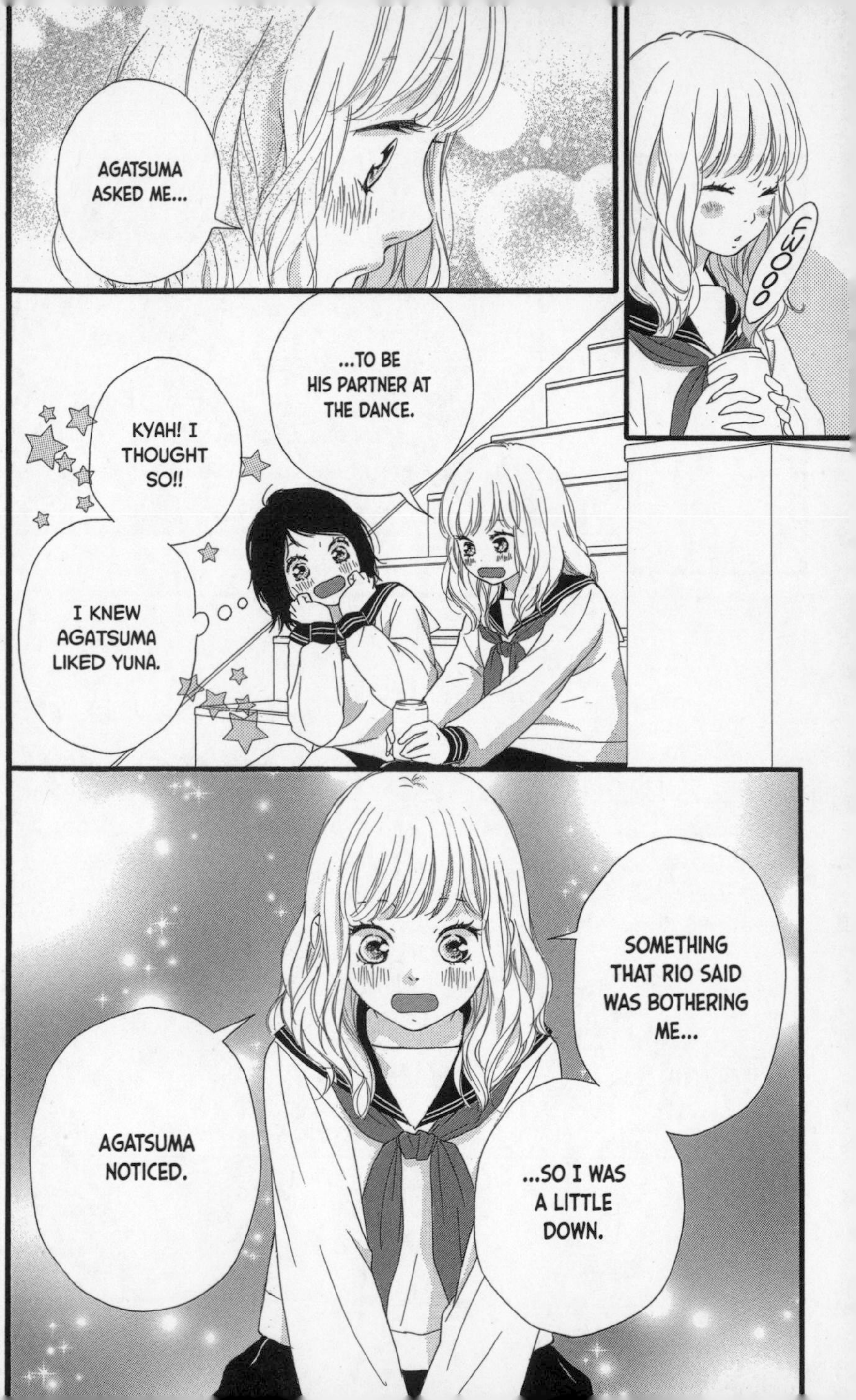
FWOOO
AGATSUMA ASKED ME...
...TO BE HIS PARTNER AT THE DANCE.
KYAH! I THOUGHT SO!!
I KNEW AGATSUMA LIKED YUNA.
SOMETHING THAT RIO SAID WAS BOTHERING ME...
...SO I WAS A LITTLE DOWN.
AGATSUMA NOTICED.

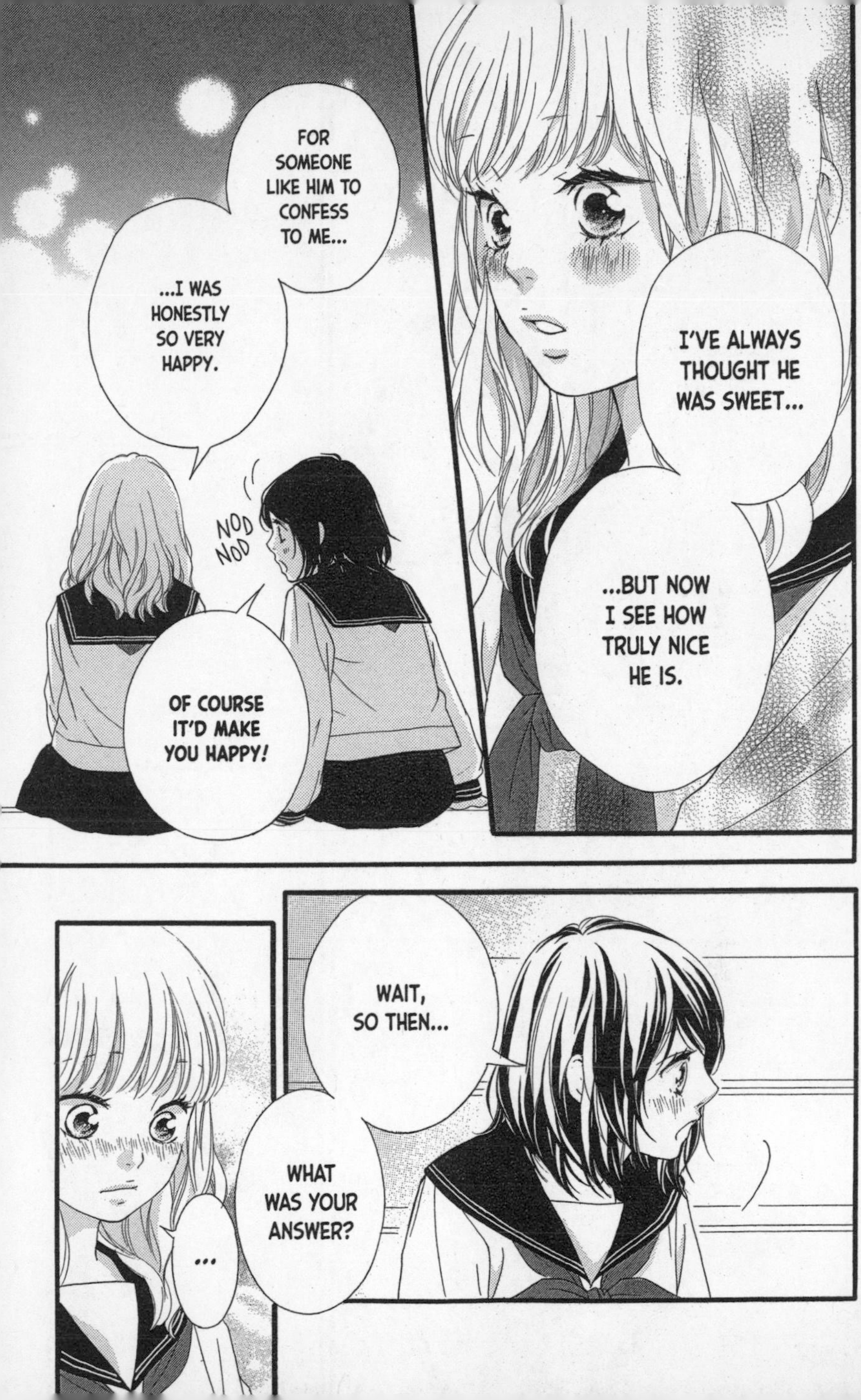
I'VE ALWAYS THOUGHT HE WAS SWEET...
...BUT NOW I SEE HOW TRULY NICE HE IS.
FOR SOMEONE LIKE HIM TO CONFESS TO ME...
...I WAS HONESTLY SO VERY HAPPY.
NOD NOD
OF COURSE IT'D MAKE YOU HAPPY!
WAIT, SO THEN...
WHAT WAS YOUR ANSWER?
...

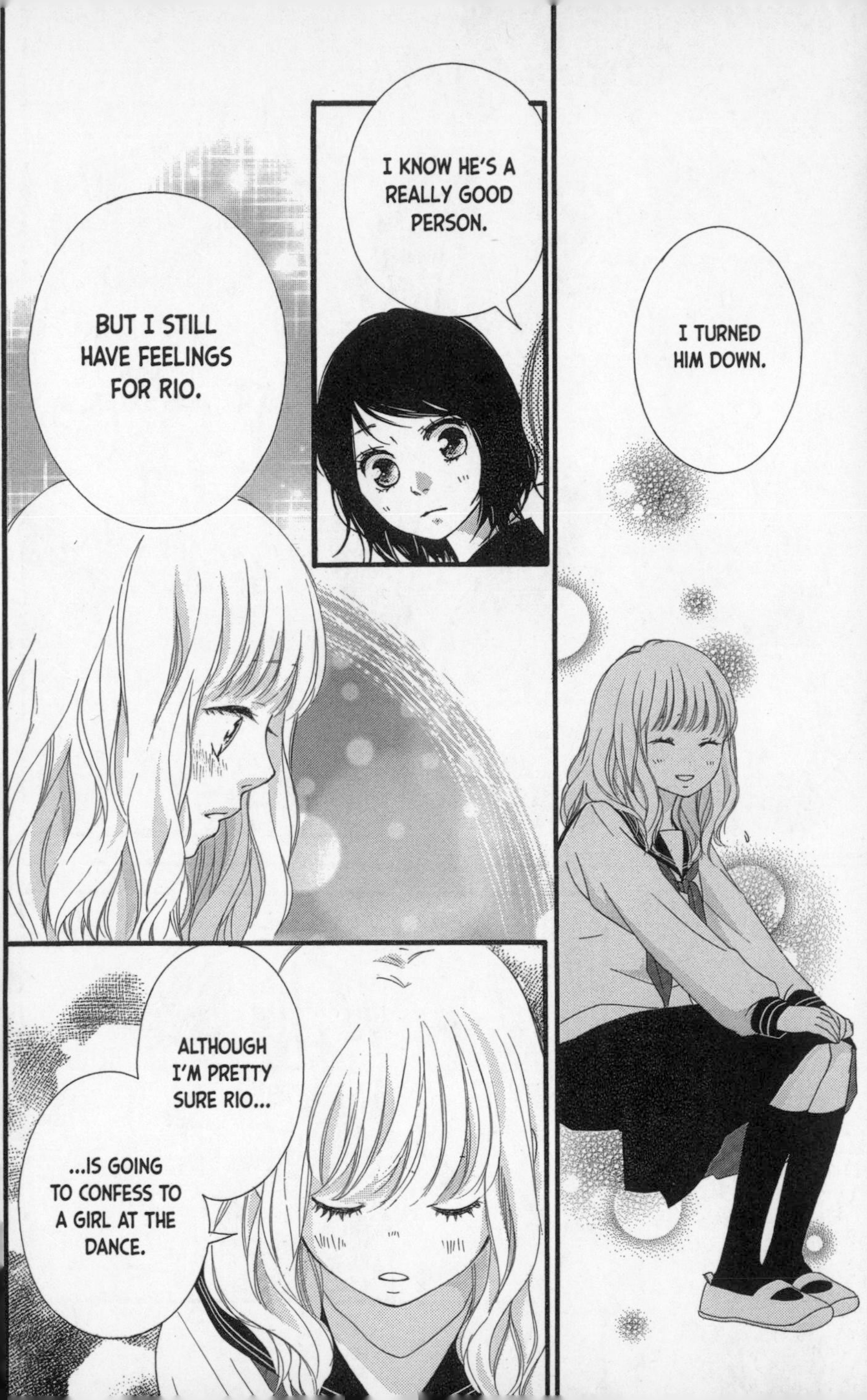
I TURNED HIM DOWN.
I KNOW HE'S A REALLY GOOD PERSON.
BUT I STILL HAVE FEELINGS FOR RIO.
ALTHOUGH I'M PRETTY SURE RIO...
...IS GOING TO CONFESS TO A GIRL AT THE DANCE.

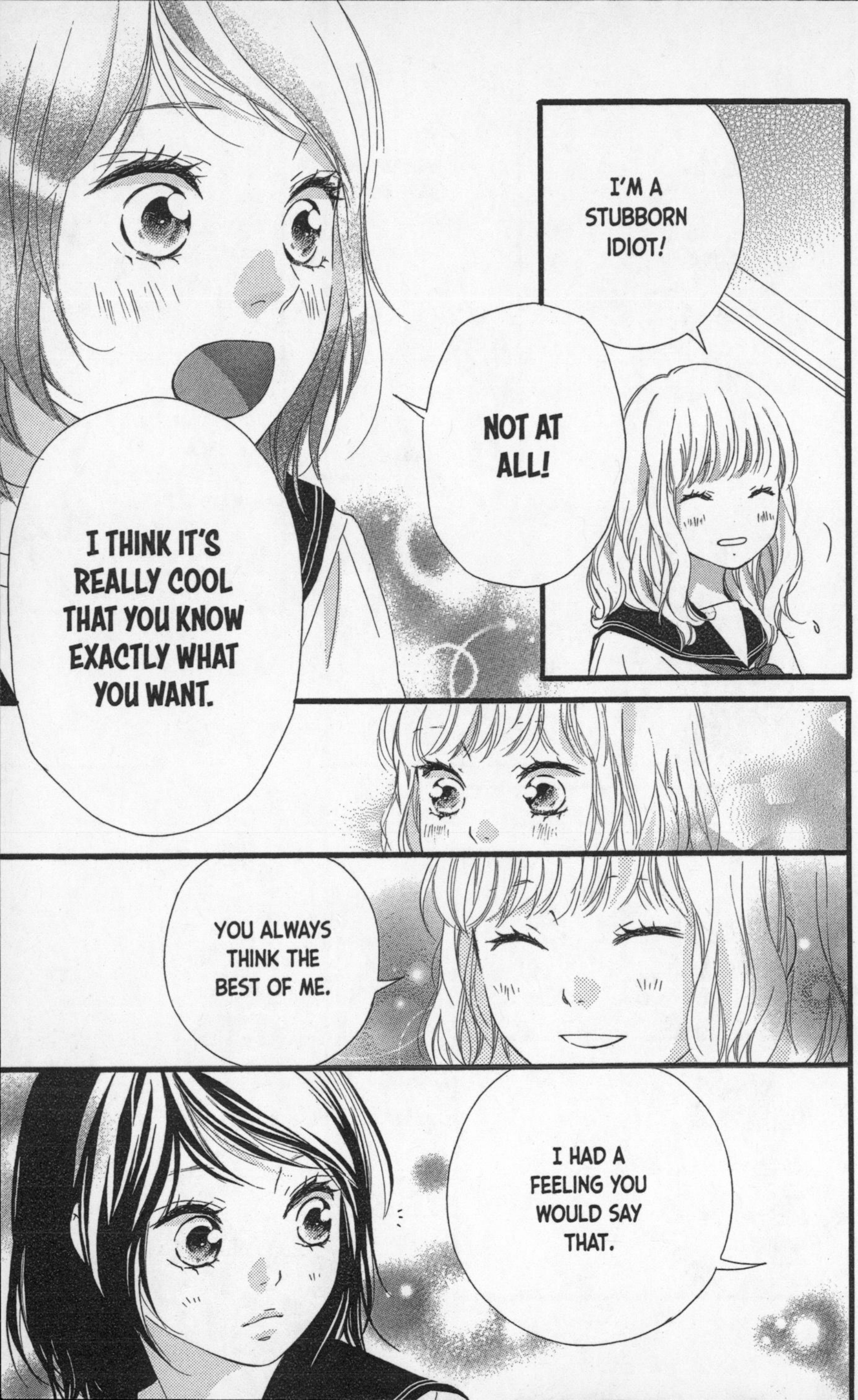
I'M A STUBBORN IDIOT!
NOT AT ALL!
I THINK IT'S REALLY COOL THAT YOU KNOW EXACTLY WHAT YOU WANT.
YOU ALWAYS THINK THE BEST OF ME.
I HAD A FEELING YOU WOULD SAY THAT.

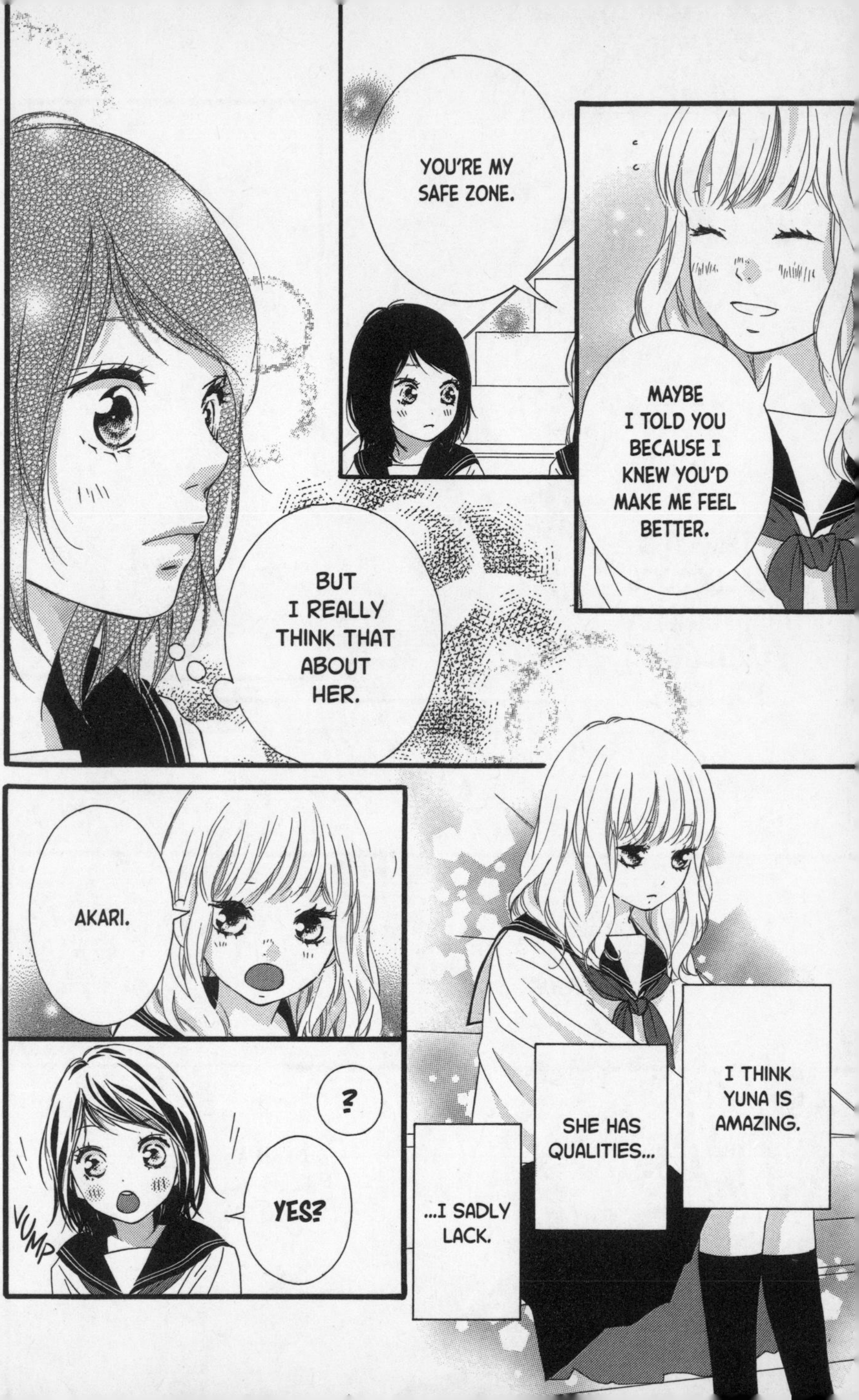
MAYBE I TOLD YOU BECAUSE I KNEW YOU'D MAKE ME FEEL BETTER.
YOU'RE MY SAFE ZONE.
BUT I REALLY THINK THAT ABOUT HER.
I THINK YUNA IS AMAZING.
SHE HAS QUALITIES...
...I SADLY LACK.
AKARI.
?
YES?
VUMP

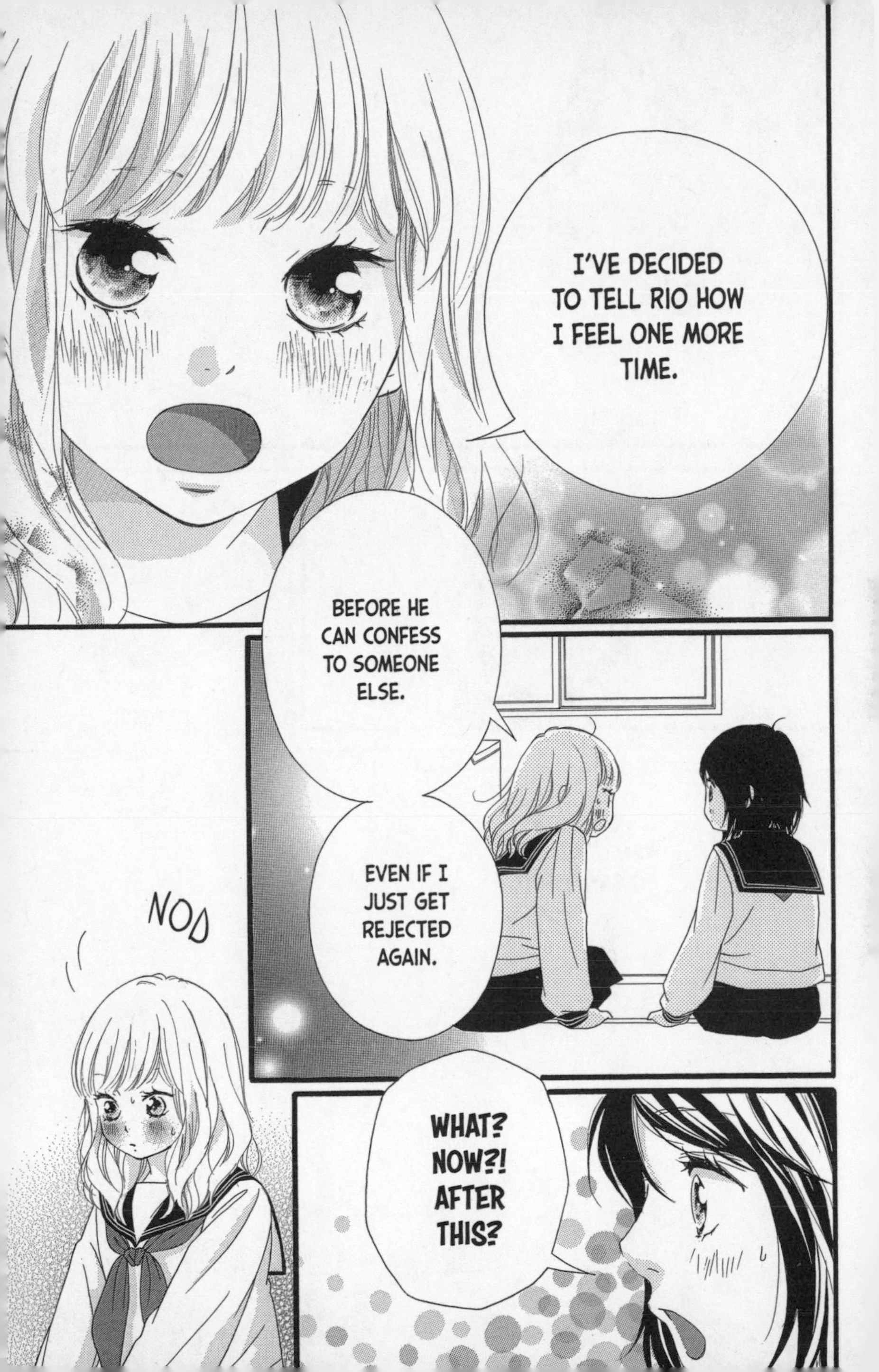
I'VE DECIDED TO TELL RIO HOW I FEEL ONE MORE TIME.
BEFORE HE CAN CONFESS TO SOMEONE ELSE.
EVEN IF I JUST GET REJECTED AGAIN.
WHAT? NOW?! AFTER THIS?
NOD

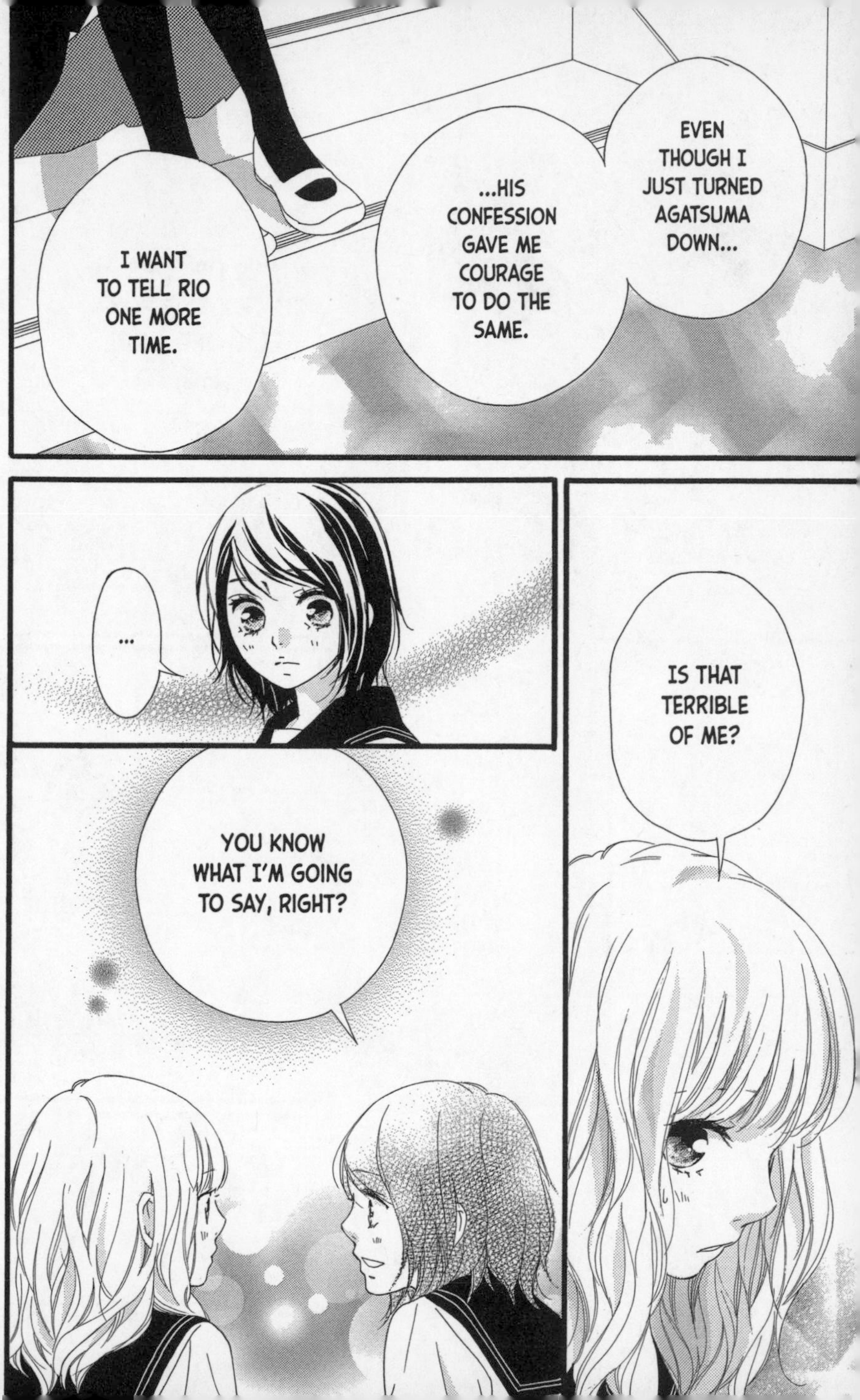
EVEN THOUGH I JUST TURNED AGATSUMA DOWN...
...HIS CONFESSION GAVE ME COURAGE TO DO THE SAME.
I WANT TO TELL RIO ONE MORE TIME.
IS THAT TERRIBLE OF ME?
...
YOU KNOW WHAT I'M GOING TO SAY, RIGHT?

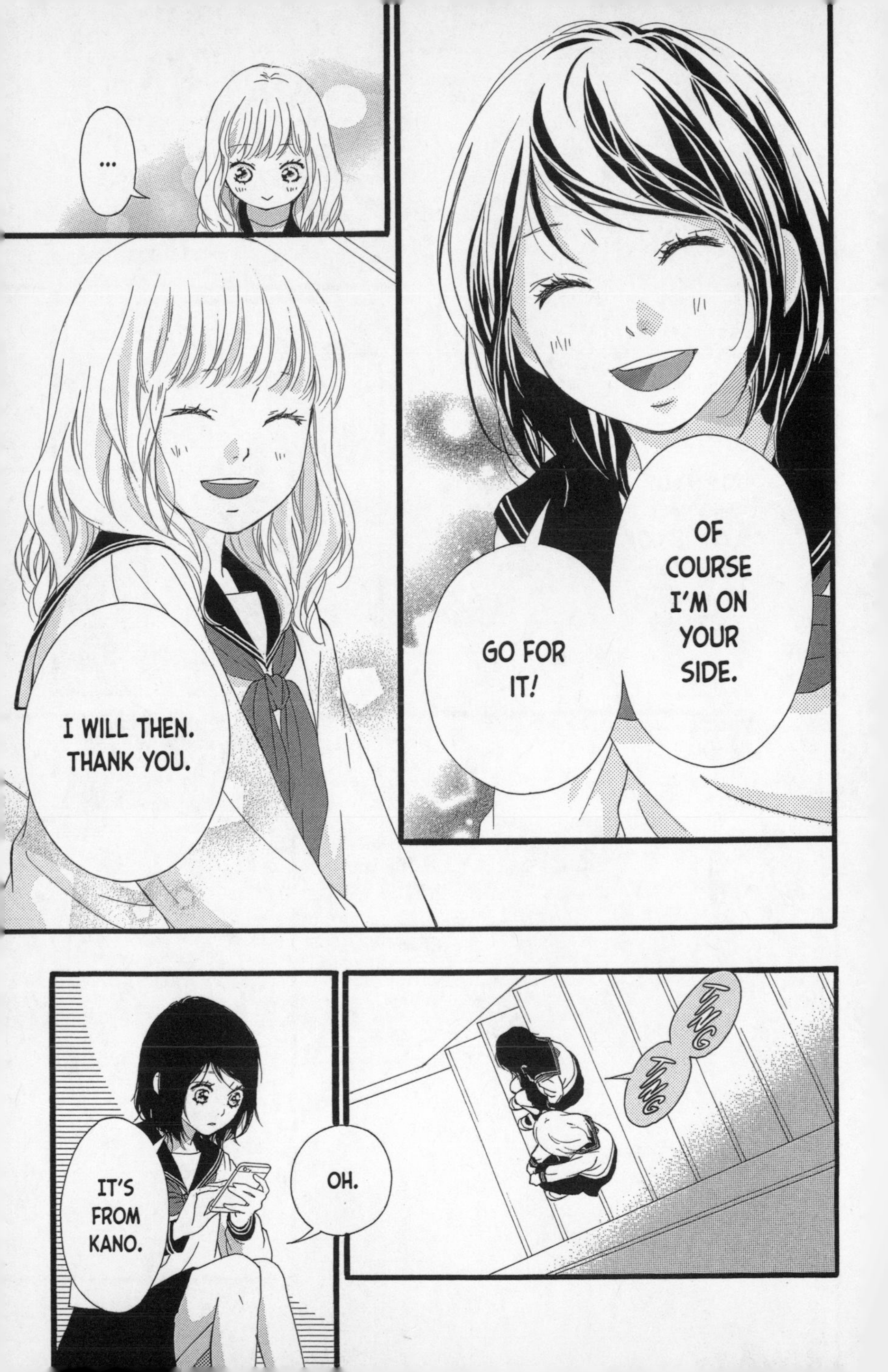
OF COURSE I'M ON YOUR SIDE.
GO FOR IT!
...
I WILL THEN. THANK YOU.
TING TING
OH.
IT'S FROM KANO.

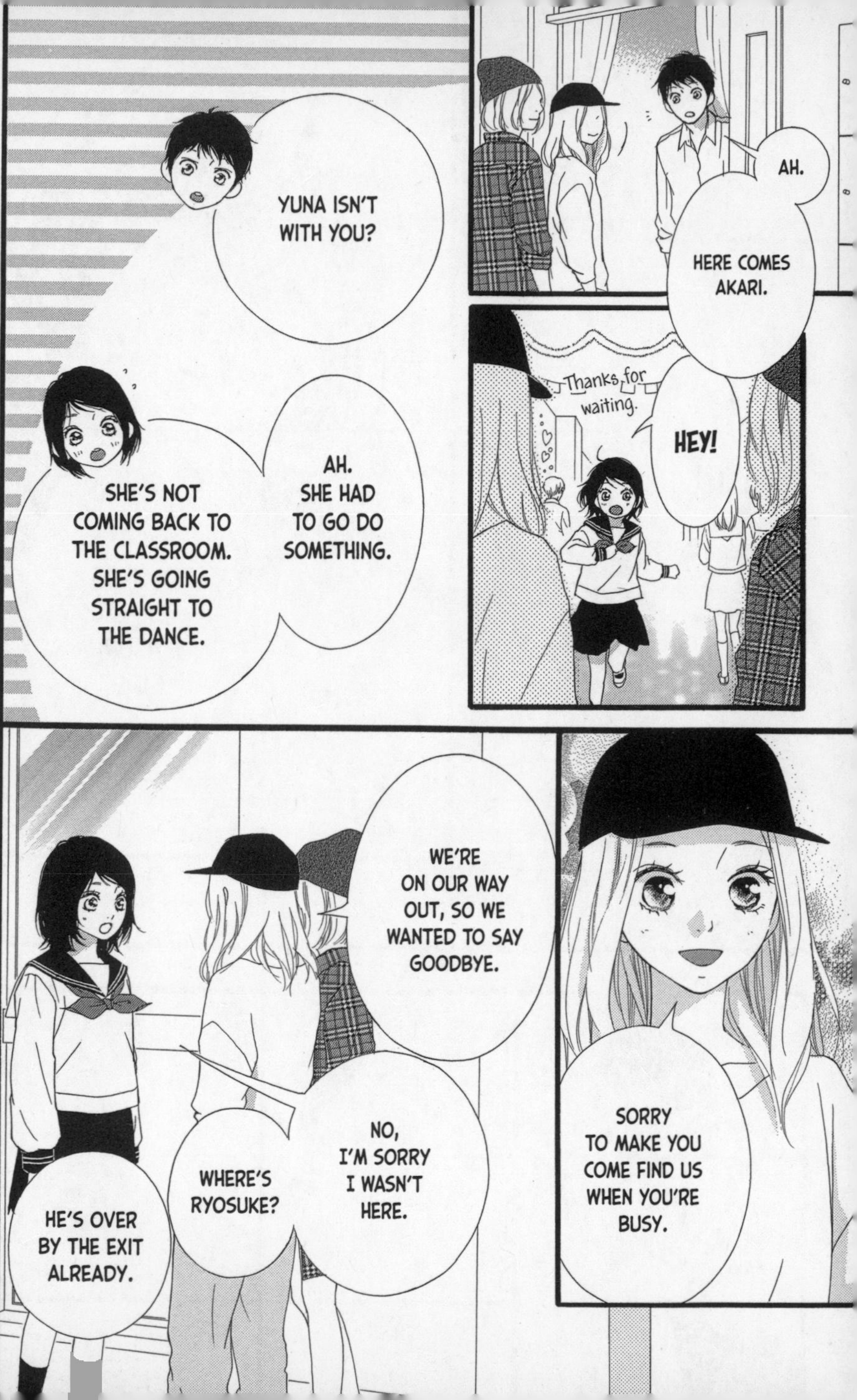
AH.
HERE COMES AKARI.
Thanks for waiting.
HEY!
YUNA ISN'T WITH YOU?
AH. SHE HAD TO GO DO SOMETHING.
SHE'S NOT COMING BACK TO THE CLASSROOM. SHE'S GOING STRAIGHT TO THE DANCE.
SORRY TO MAKE YOU COME FIND US WHEN YOU'RE BUSY.
WE'RE ON OUR WAY OUT, SO WE WANTED TO SAY GOODBYE.
NO, I'M SORRY I WASN'T HERE.
WHERE'S RYOSUKE?
HE'S OVER BY THE EXIT ALREADY.

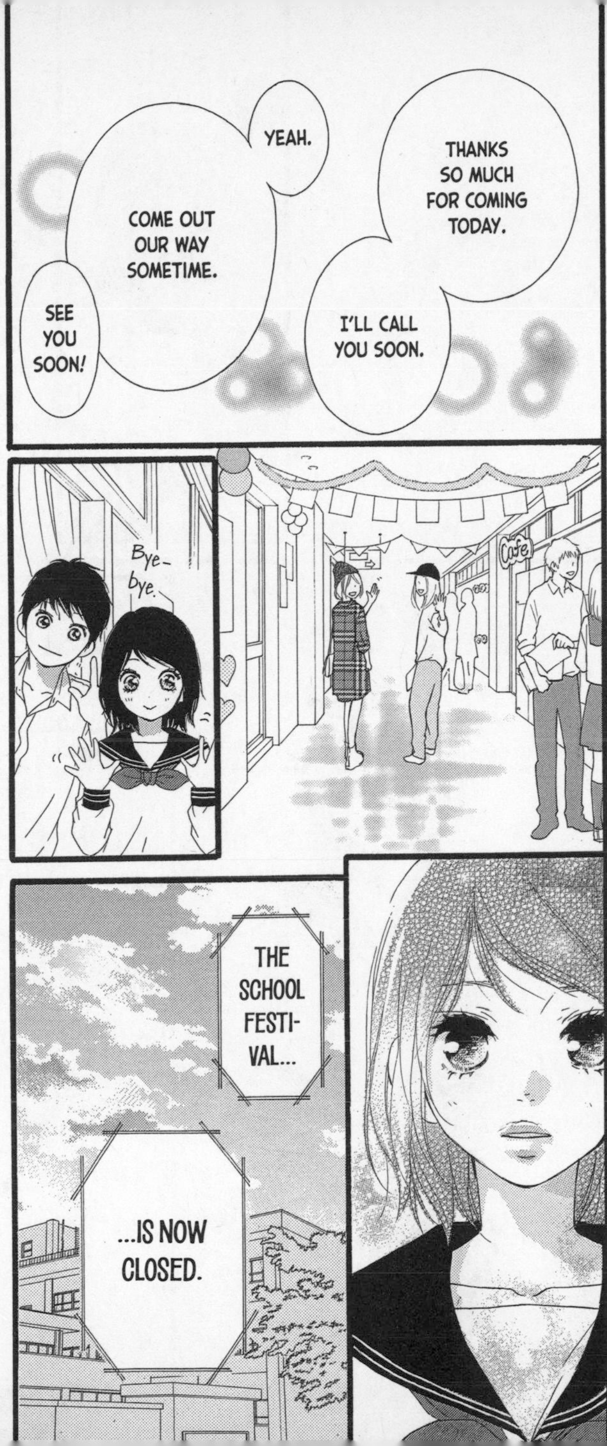
THANKS SO MUCH FOR COMING TODAY.
YEAH.
I'LL CALL YOU SOON.
COME OUT OUR WAY SOMETIME.
SEE YOU SOON!
Bye-bye.
THE SCHOOL FESTI-VAL...
...IS NOW CLOSED.

I wrote before about going to Disney Sea, but I usually don't go anywhere that has big crowds. Maybe that's why, even though I don't get sick very often, I caught a cold after being out in that crowd. I got a very sore throat, then a low fever and after that a runny nose that wouldn't stop. I've never appreci-ated tissues with lotion as much as then when I was sick. I had to blow my nose every couple of minutes. I don't even know how many boxes I went through. Afterwards I found out three of the four of us who went that day got sick with the same symptoms. Wow! But I was also a little amused. What I really wanted to say in conclusion is that the person who invented tissues with lotion is a true genius. Thank you very much.

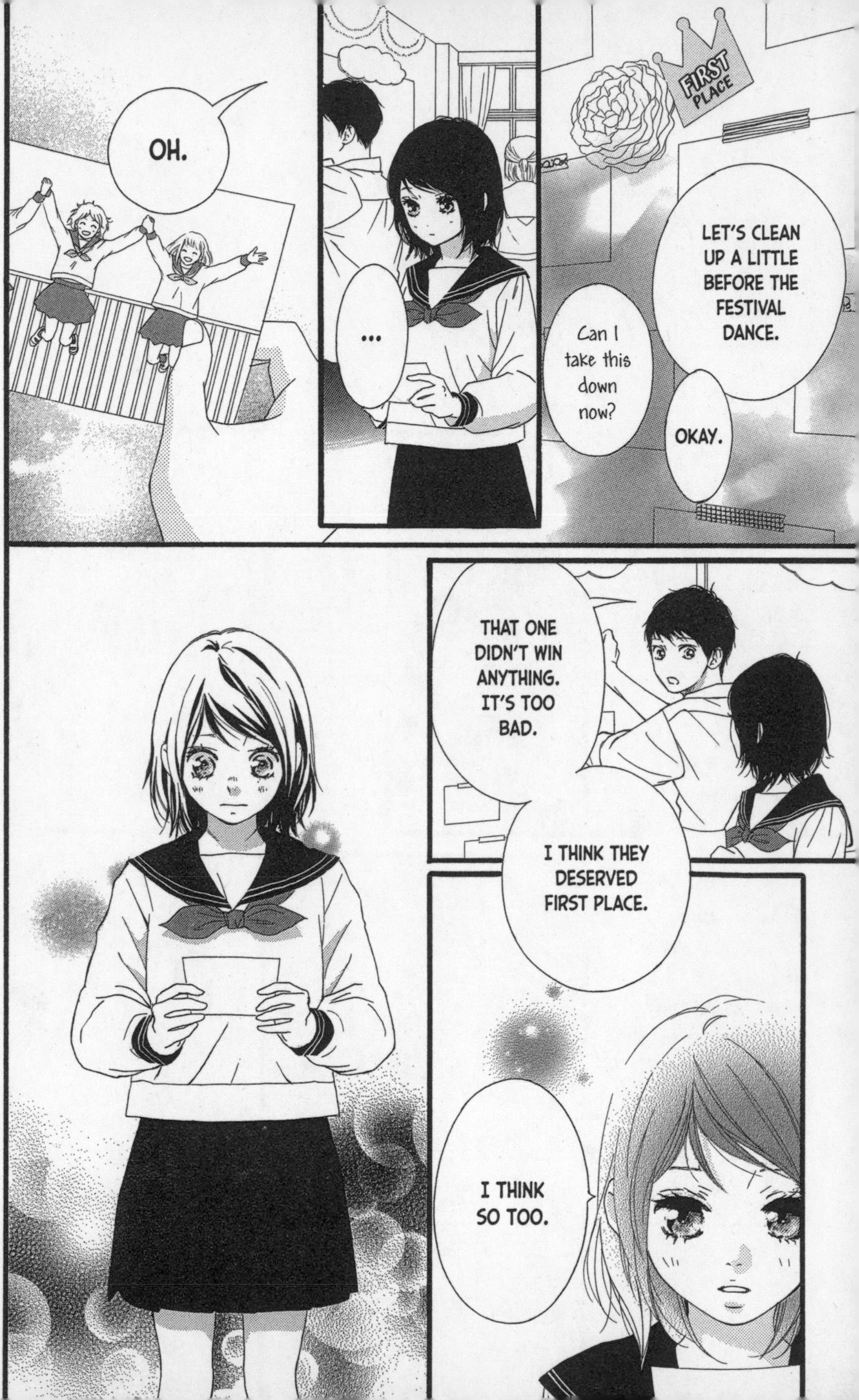
FIRST PLACE
LET'S CLEAN UP A LITTLE BEFORE THE FESTIVAL DANCE.
Can I take this down now?
OKAY.
...
OH.
THAT ONE DIDN'T WIN ANYTHING. IT'S TOO BAD.
I THINK THEY DESERVED FIRST PLACE.
I THINK SO TOO.

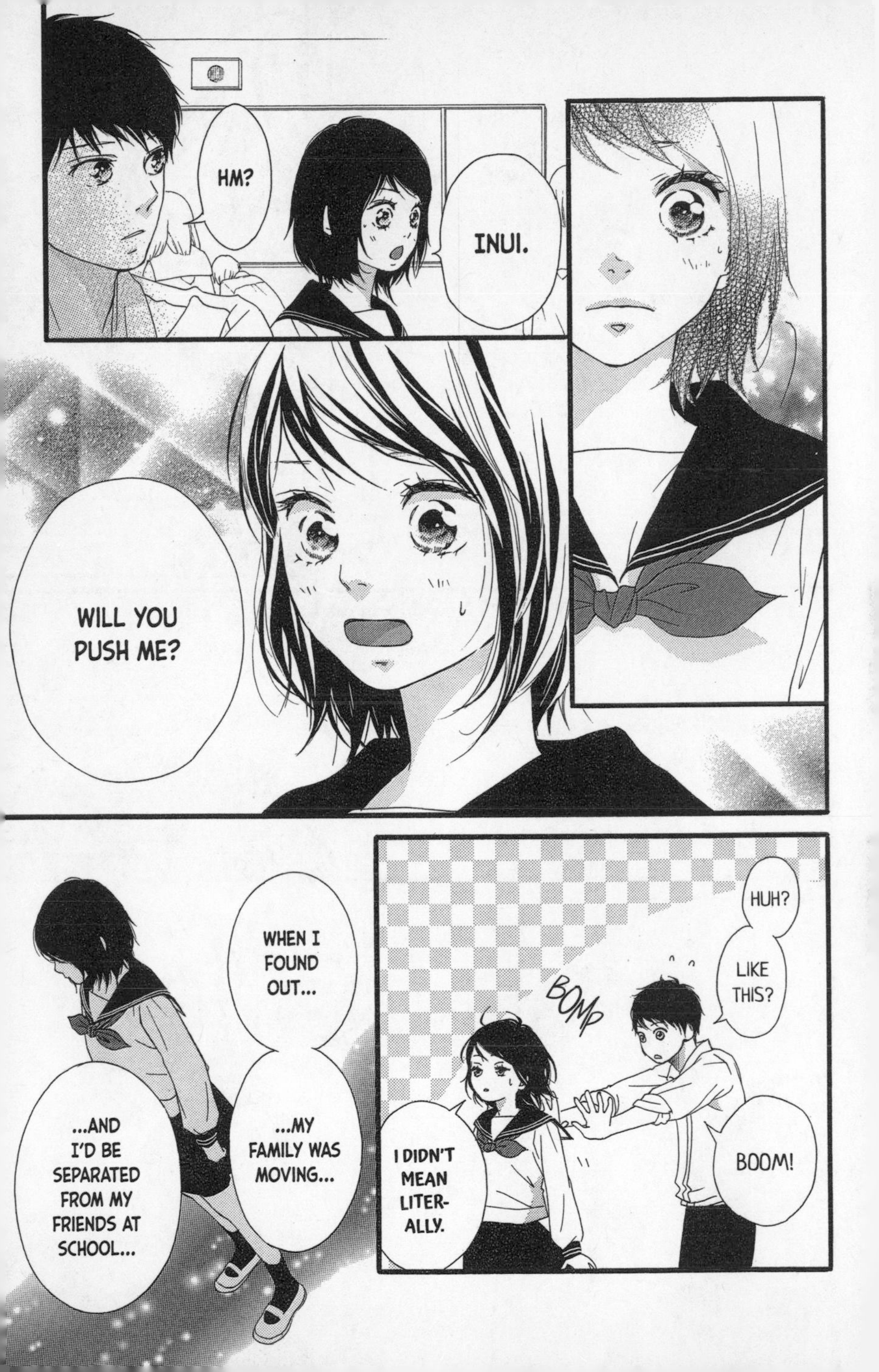
INUI.
HM?
WILL YOU PUSH ME?
HUH?
LIKE THIS?
BOMP
BOOM!
I DIDN'T MEAN LITER-ALLY.
WHEN I FOUND OUT...
...MY FAMILY WAS MOVING...
...AND I'D BE SEPARATED FROM MY FRIENDS AT SCHOOL...

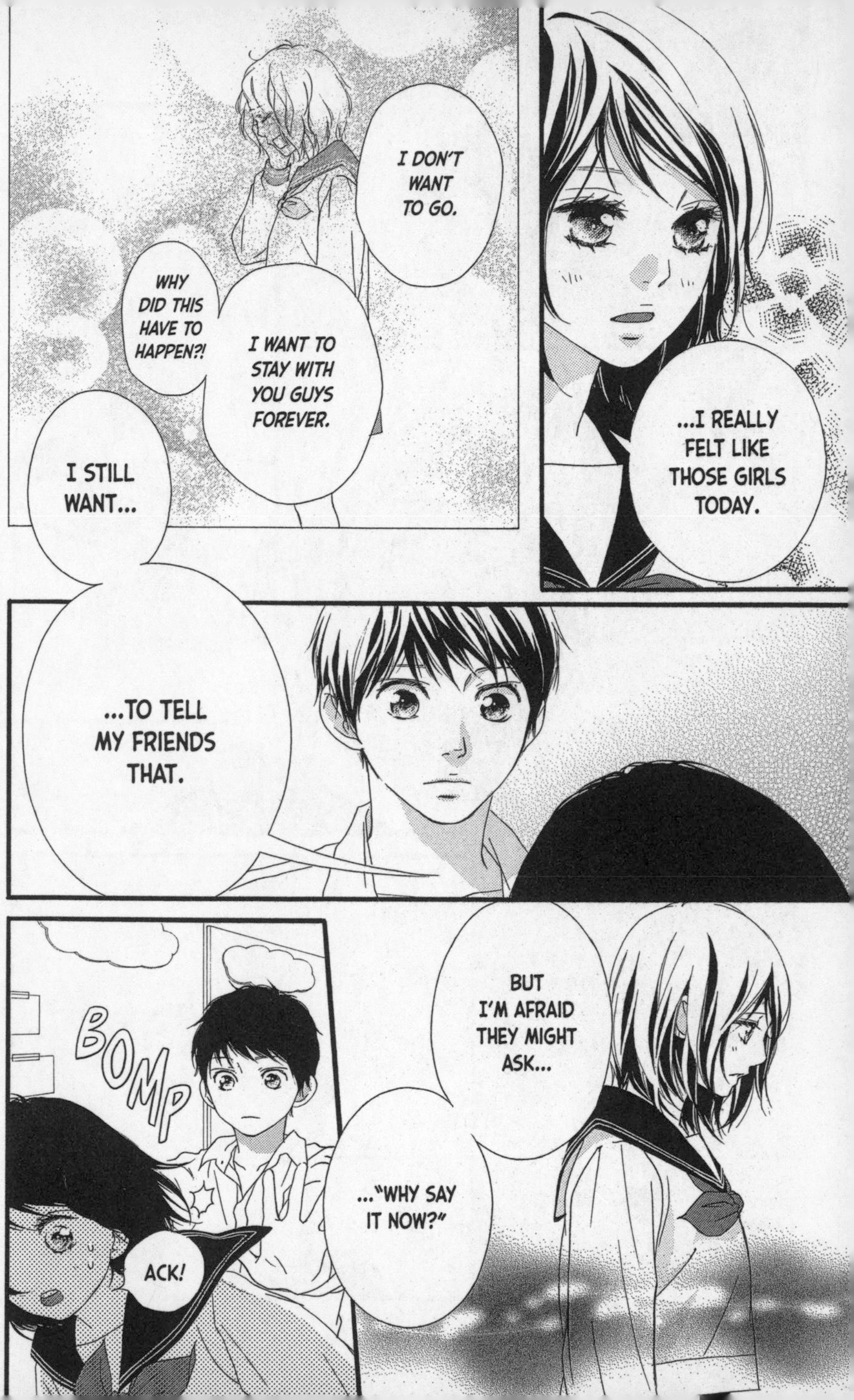
...I REALLY FELT LIKE THOSE GIRLS TODAY.
I DON'T WANT TO GO.
I WANT TO STAY WITH YOU GUYS FOREVER.
WHY DID THIS HAVE TO HAPPEN?!
I STILL WANT...
...TO TELL MY FRIENDS THAT.
BUT I'M AFRAID THEY MIGHT ASK...
..."WHY SAY IT NOW?"
BOMP
ACK!

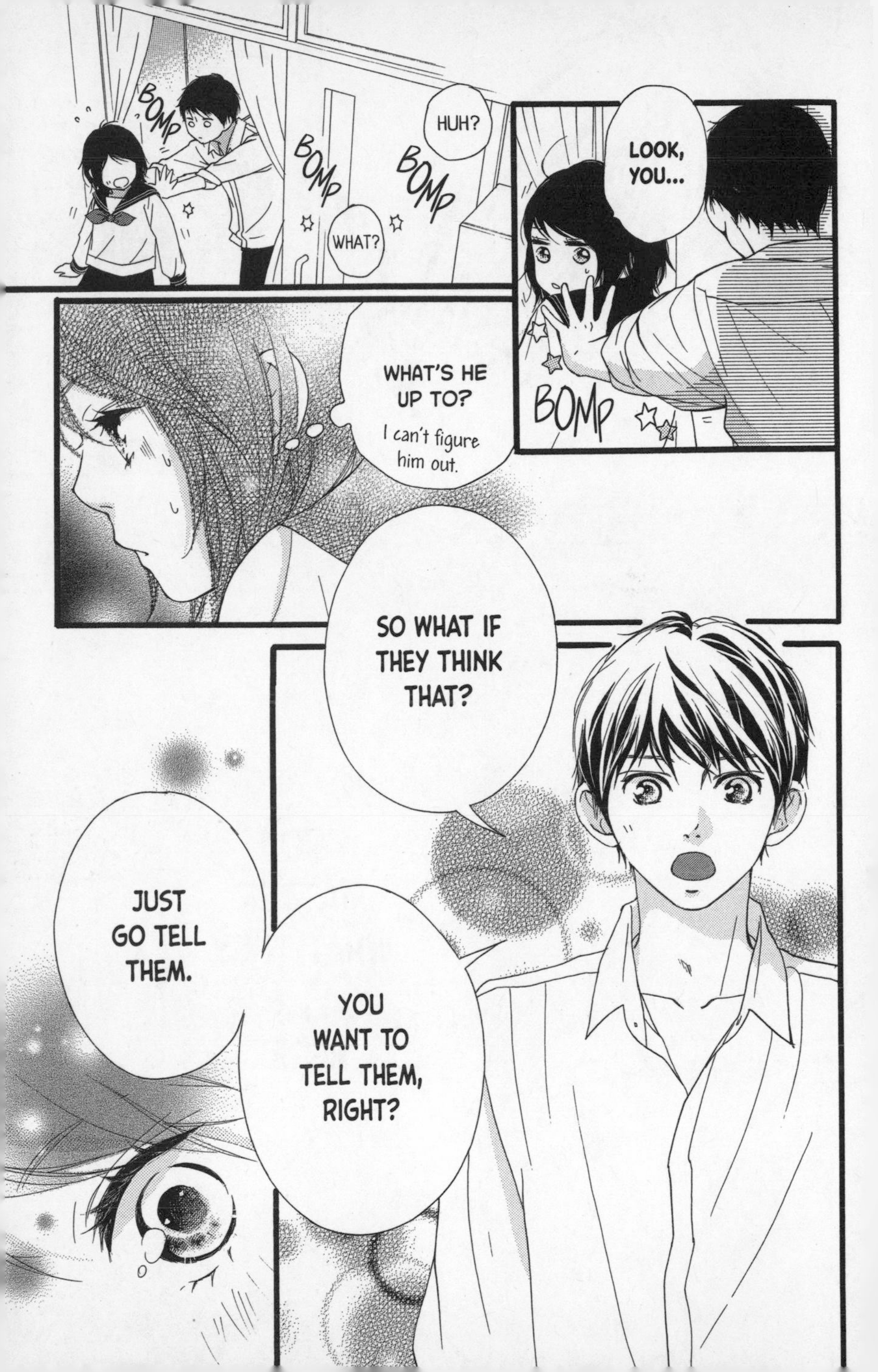
BOMP
HUH?
BOMP
BOMP
WHAT?
LOOK, YOU...
BOMP
WHAT'S HE UP TO?
I can't figure him out.
SO WHAT IF THEY THINK THAT?
YOU WANT TO TELL THEM, RIGHT?
JUST GO TELL THEM.

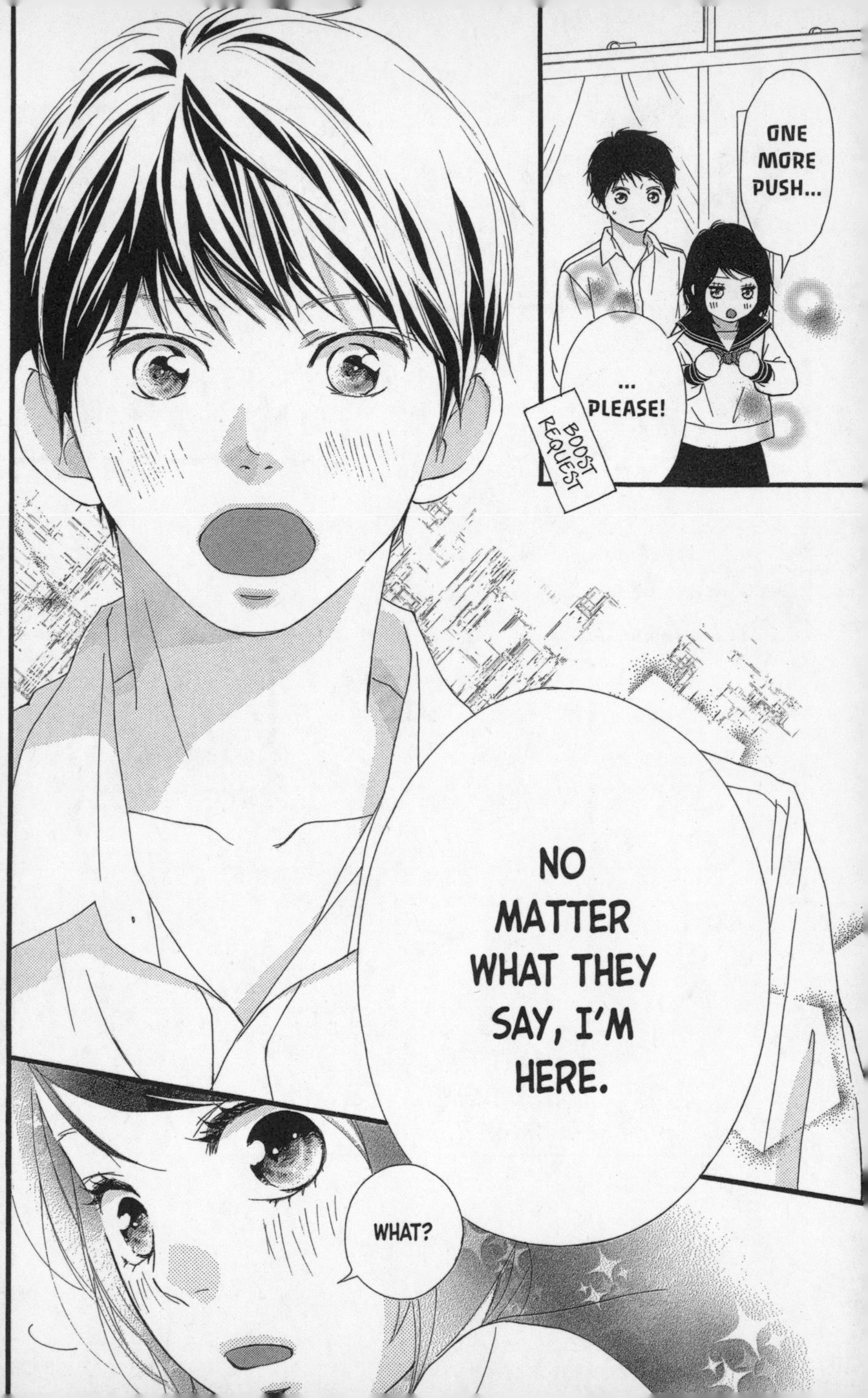
ONE MORE PUSH...
... PLEASE!
BOOST REQUEST
NO MATTER WHAT THEY SAY, I'M HERE.
WHAT?

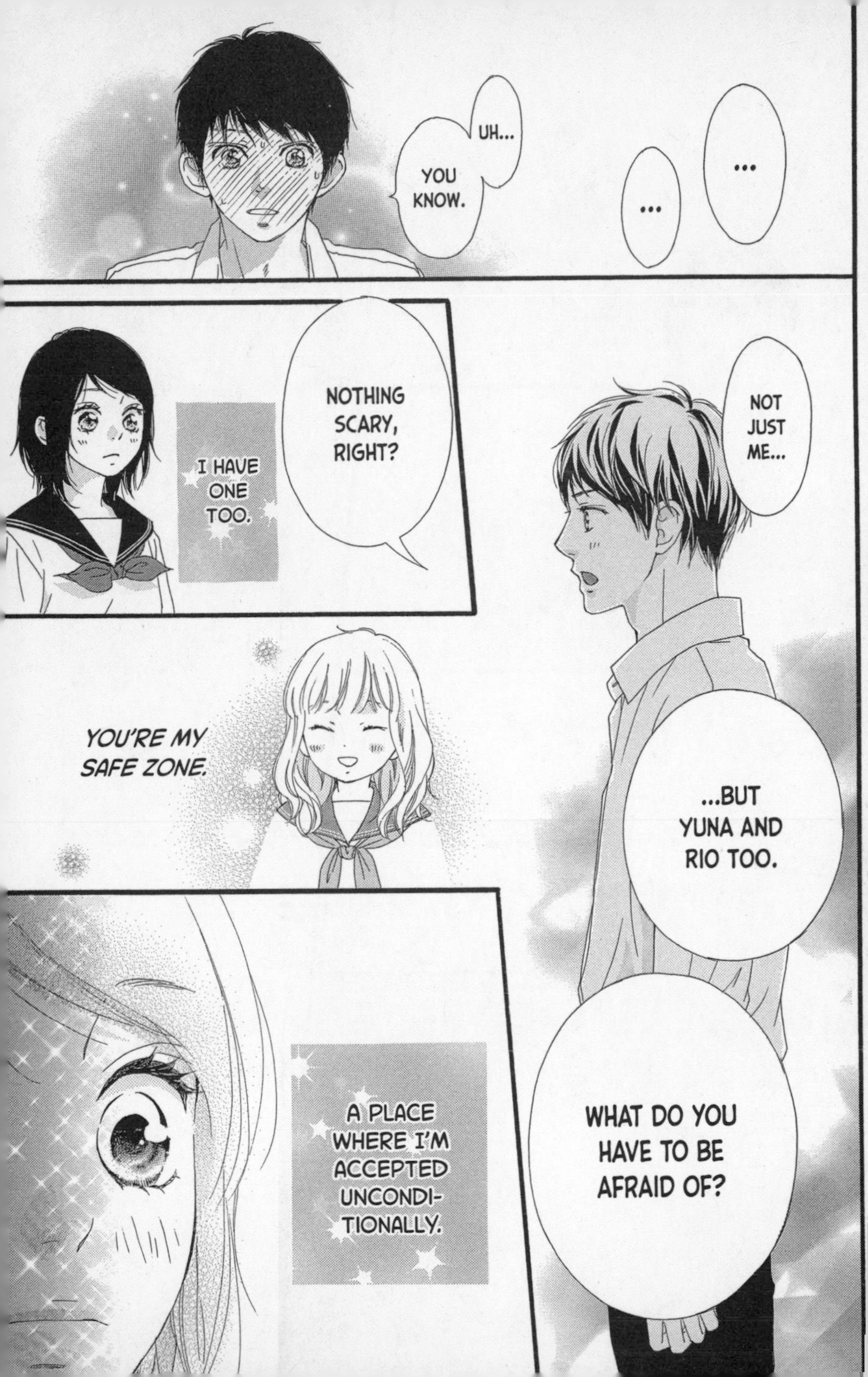
...
...
UH...
YOU KNOW.
NOT JUST ME...
...BUT YUNA AND RIO TOO.
WHAT DO YOU HAVE TO BE AFRAID OF?
NOTHING SCARY, RIGHT?
I HAVE ONE TOO.
YOU'RE MY SAFE ZONE.
A PLACE WHERE I'M ACCEPTED UNCONDITIONALLY.

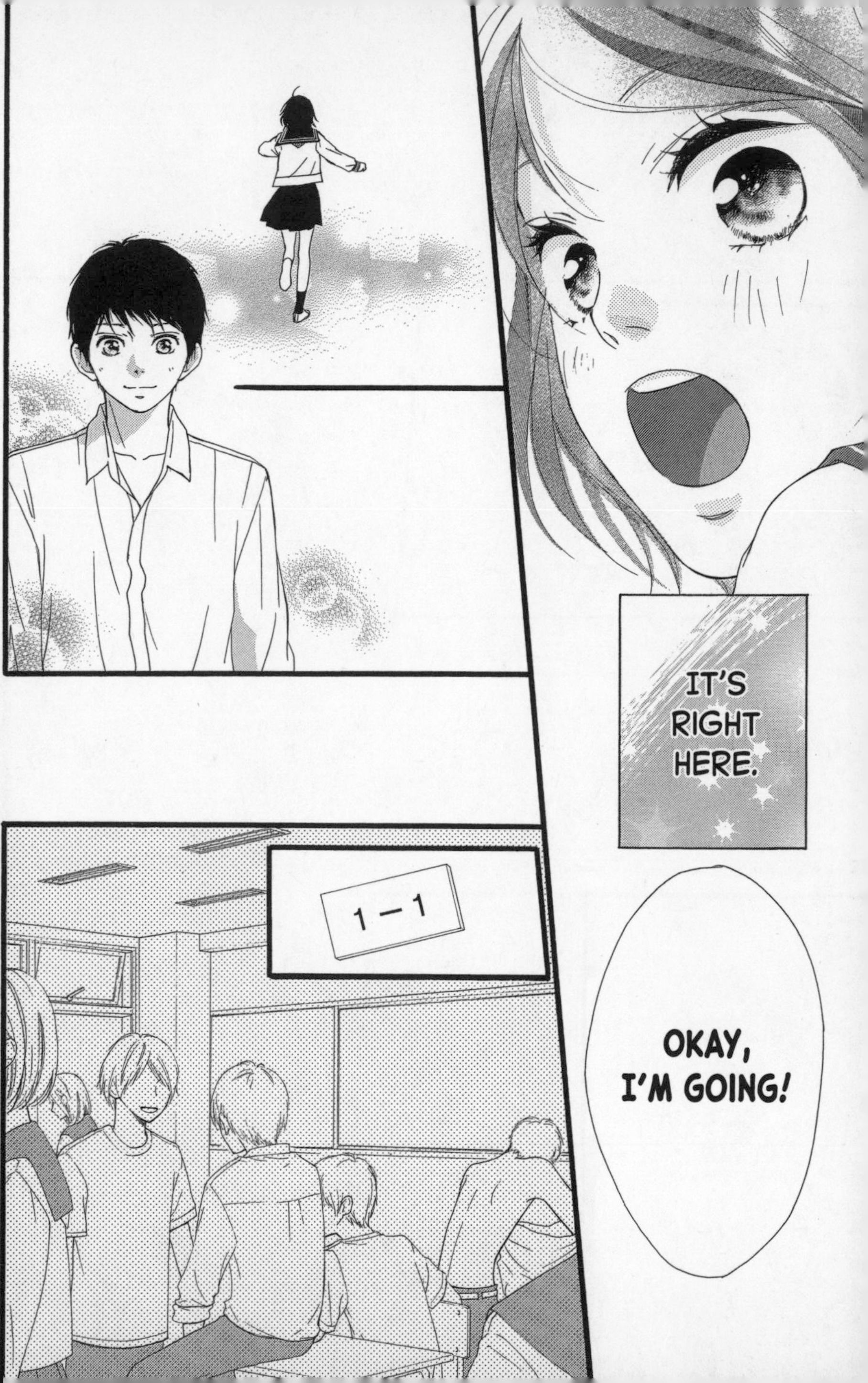
IT'S RIGHT HERE.
OKAY, I'M GOING!
1 — 1

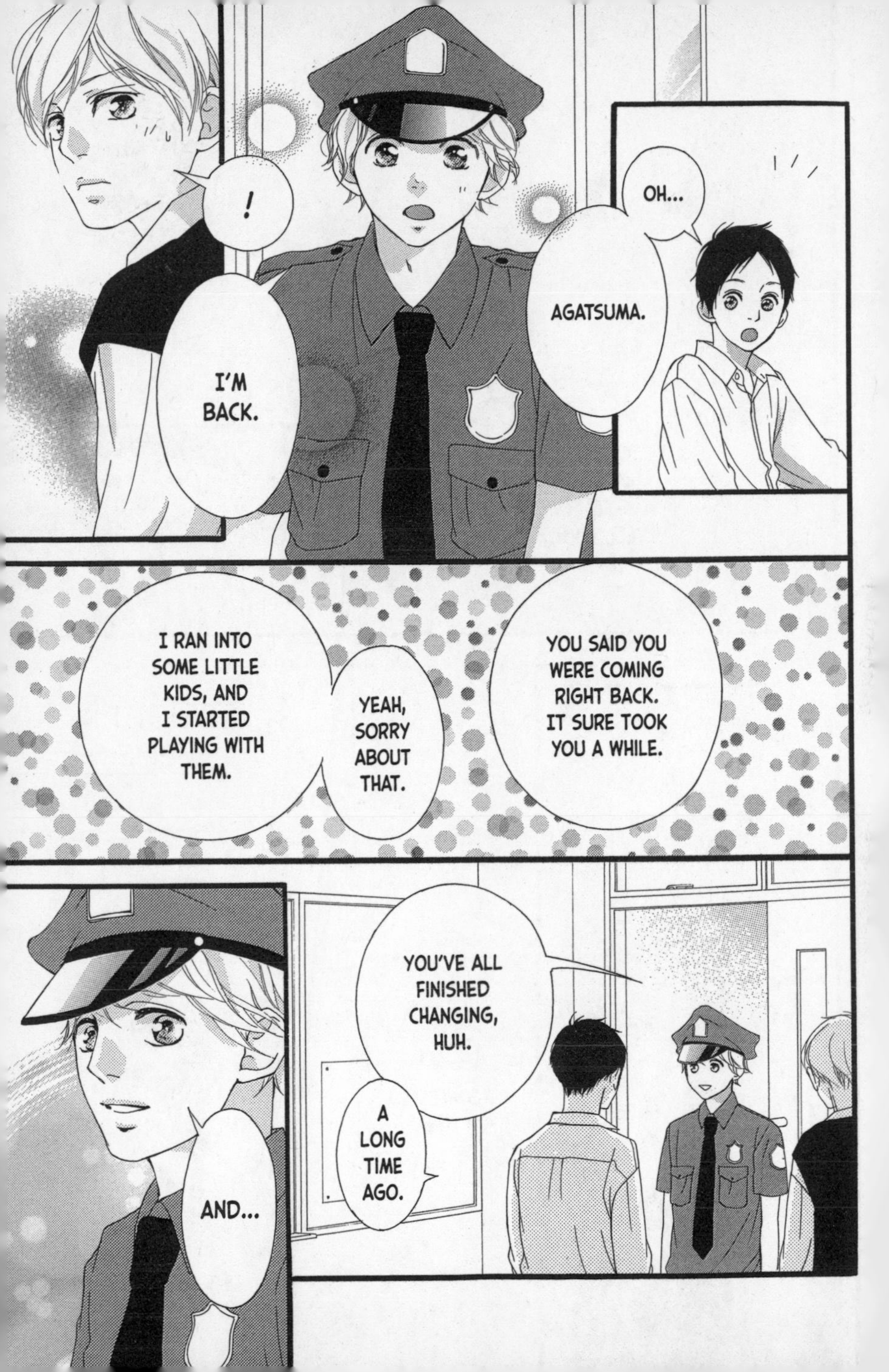
OH...
AGATSUMA.
!
I'M BACK.
YOU SAID YOU WERE COMING RIGHT BACK. IT SURE TOOK YOU A WHILE.
YEAH, SORRY ABOUT THAT.
I RAN INTO SOME LITTLE KIDS, AND I STARTED PLAYING WITH THEM.
YOU'VE ALL FINISHED CHANGING, HUH.
A LONG TIME AGO.
AND...

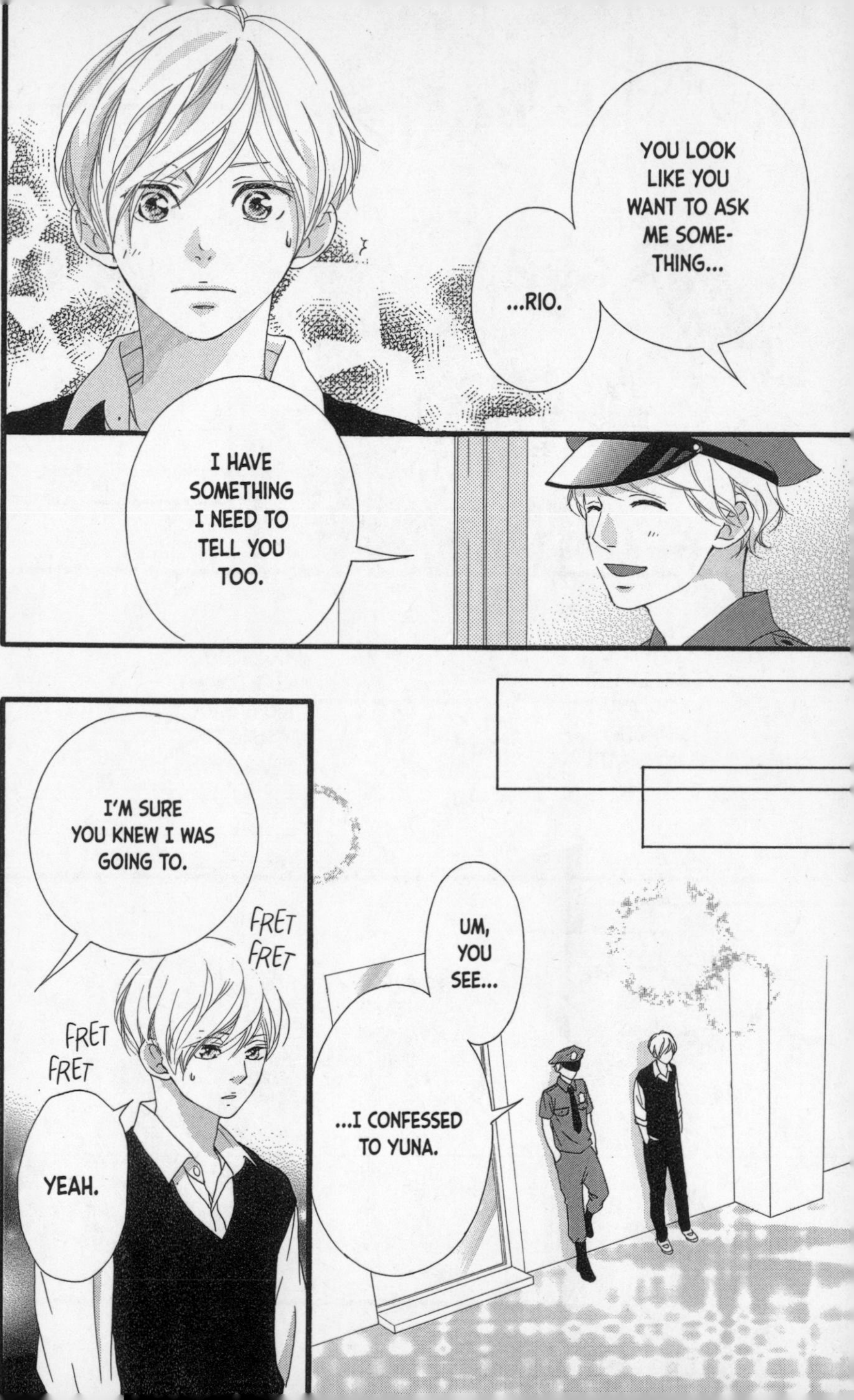
YOU LOOK LIKE YOU WANT TO ASK ME SOME-THING...
...RIO.
I HAVE SOMETHING I NEED TO TELL YOU TOO.
UM, YOU SEE...
...I CONFESSED TO YUNA.
I'M SURE YOU KNEW I WAS GOING TO.
FRET FRET
FRET FRET
YEAH.

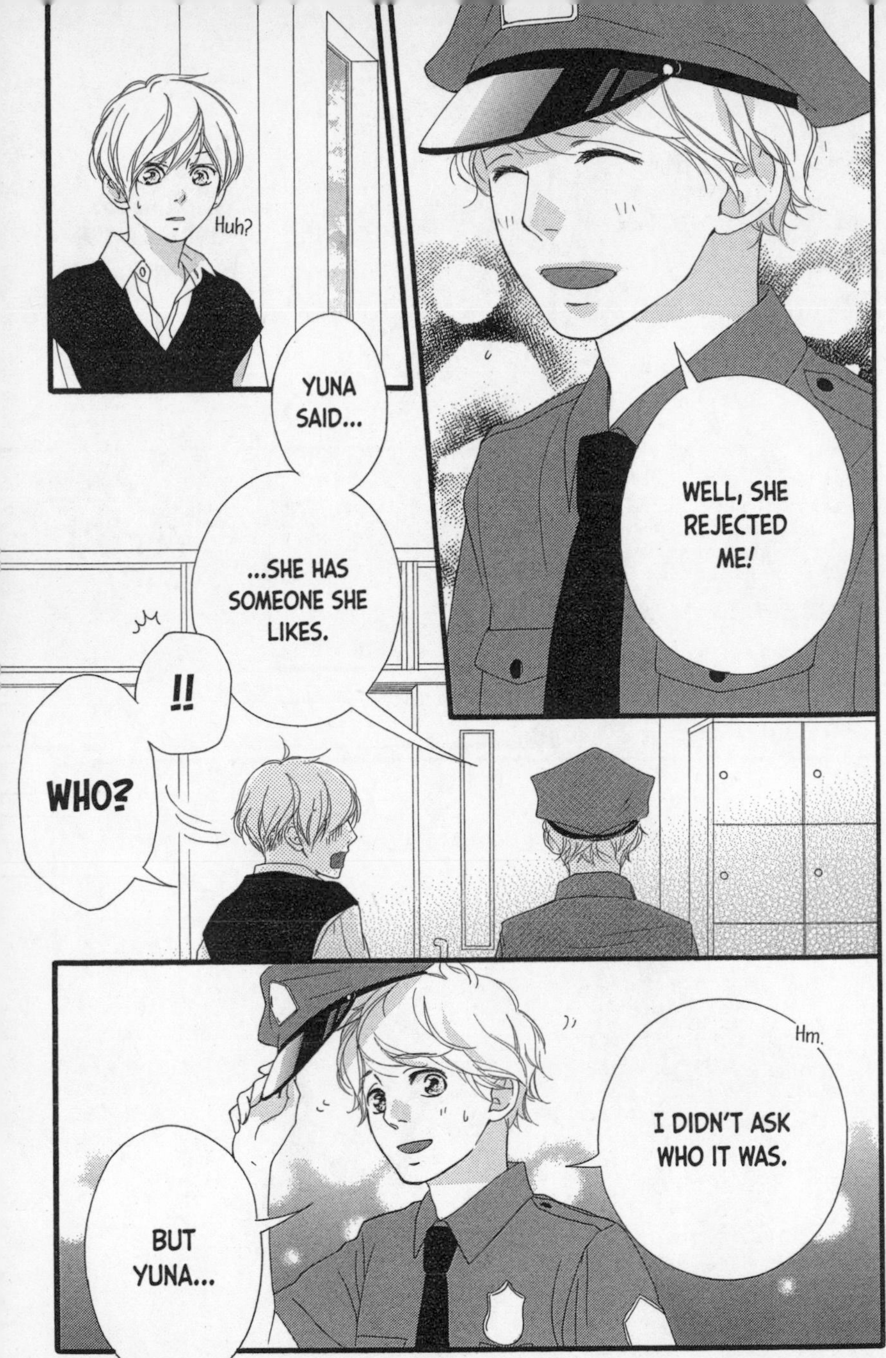
WELL, SHE REJECTED ME!
Huh?
YUNA SAID...
...SHE HAS SOMEONE SHE LIKES.
!!
WHO?
Hm.
I DIDN'T ASK WHO IT WAS.
BUT YUNA...

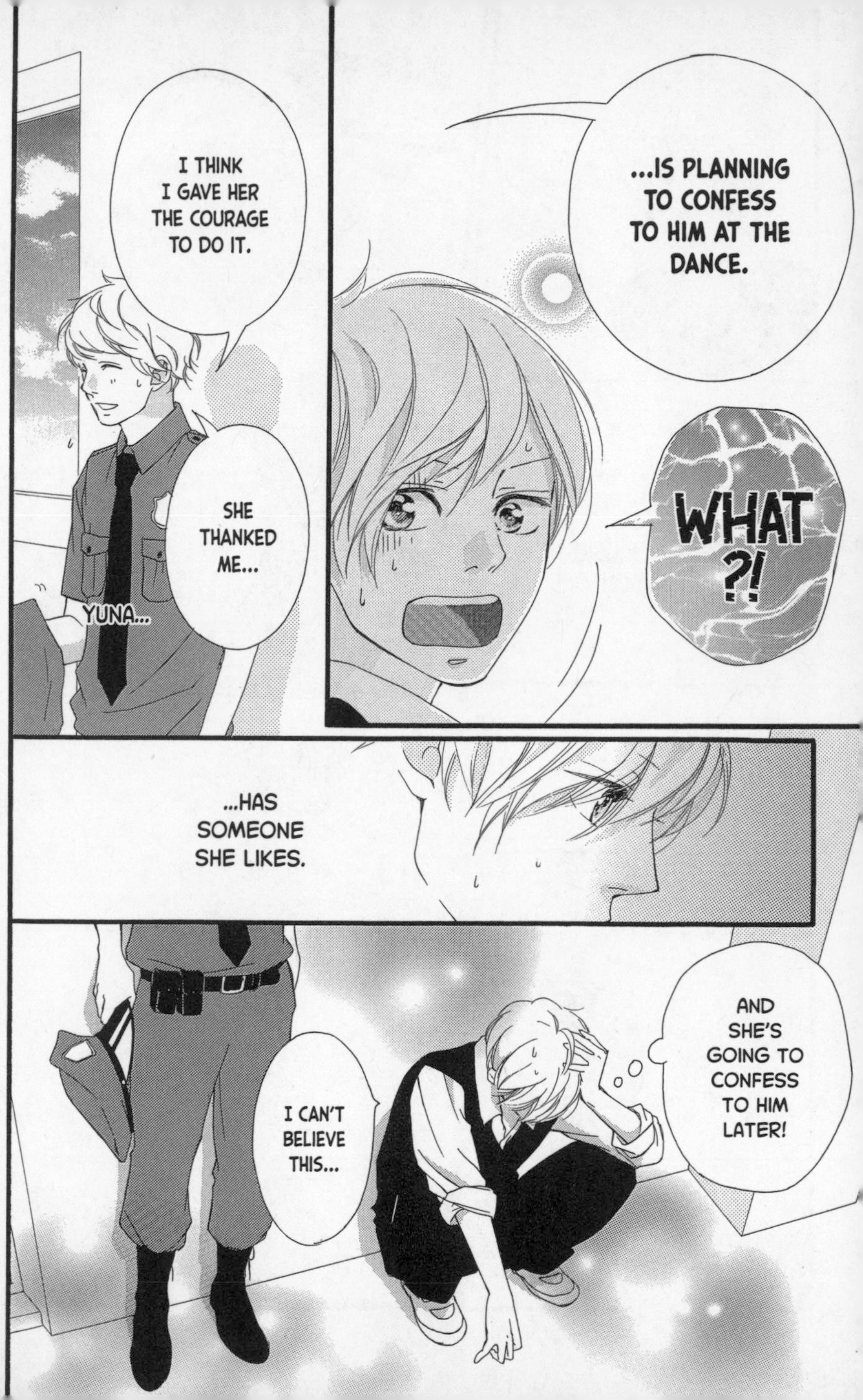
...IS PLANNING TO CONFESS TO HIM AT THE DANCE.
WHAT ?!
I THINK I GAVE HER THE COURAGE TO DO IT.
SHE THANKED ME...
YUNA...
...HAS SOMEONE SHE LIKES.
AND SHE'S GOING TO CONFESS TO HIM LATER!
I CAN'T BELIEVE THIS...

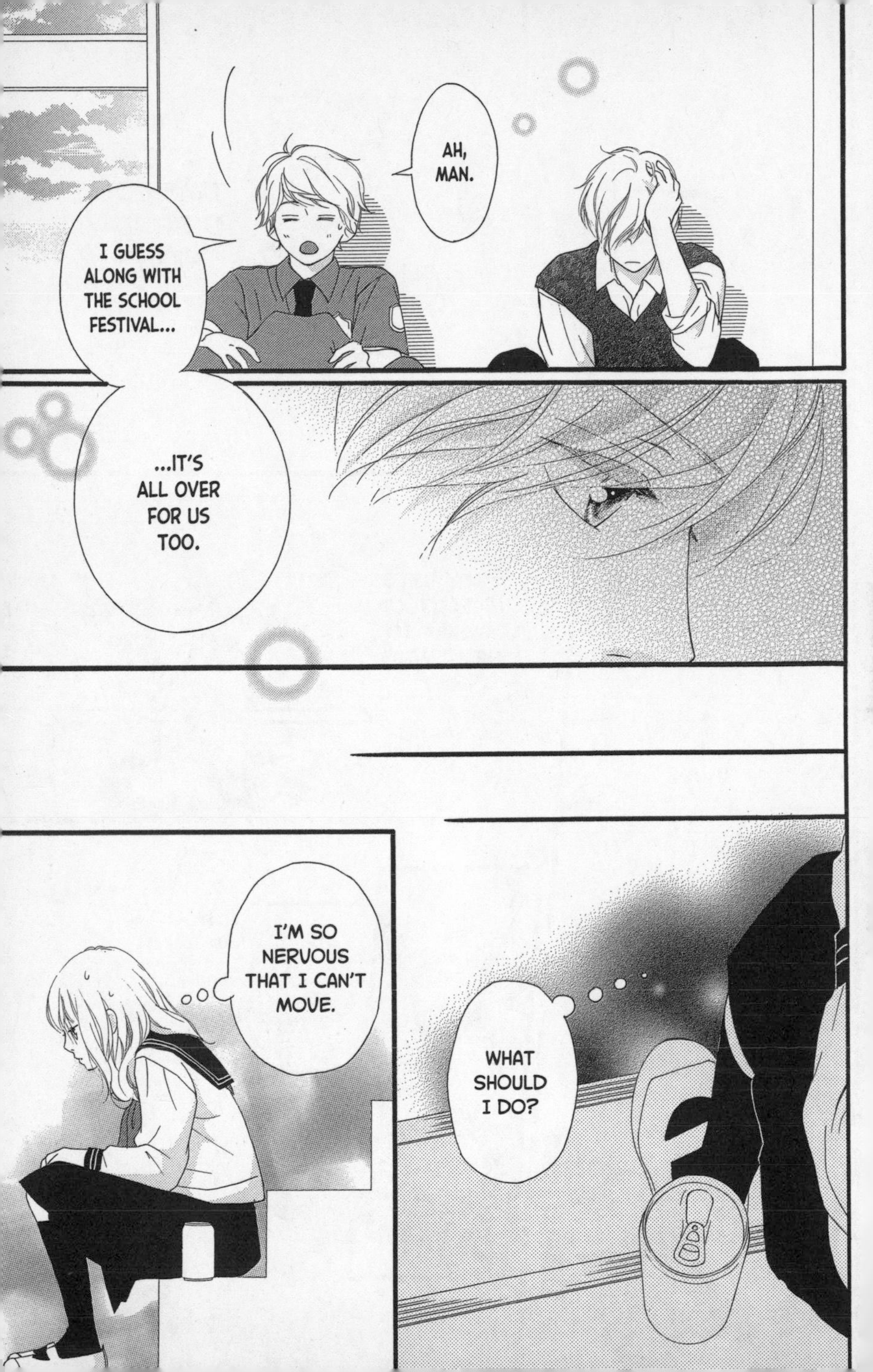
AH, MAN.
I GUESS ALONG WITH THE SCHOOL FESTIVAL...
...IT'S ALL OVER FOR US TOO.
WHAT SHOULD I DO?
I'M SO NERVOUS THAT I CAN'T MOVE.

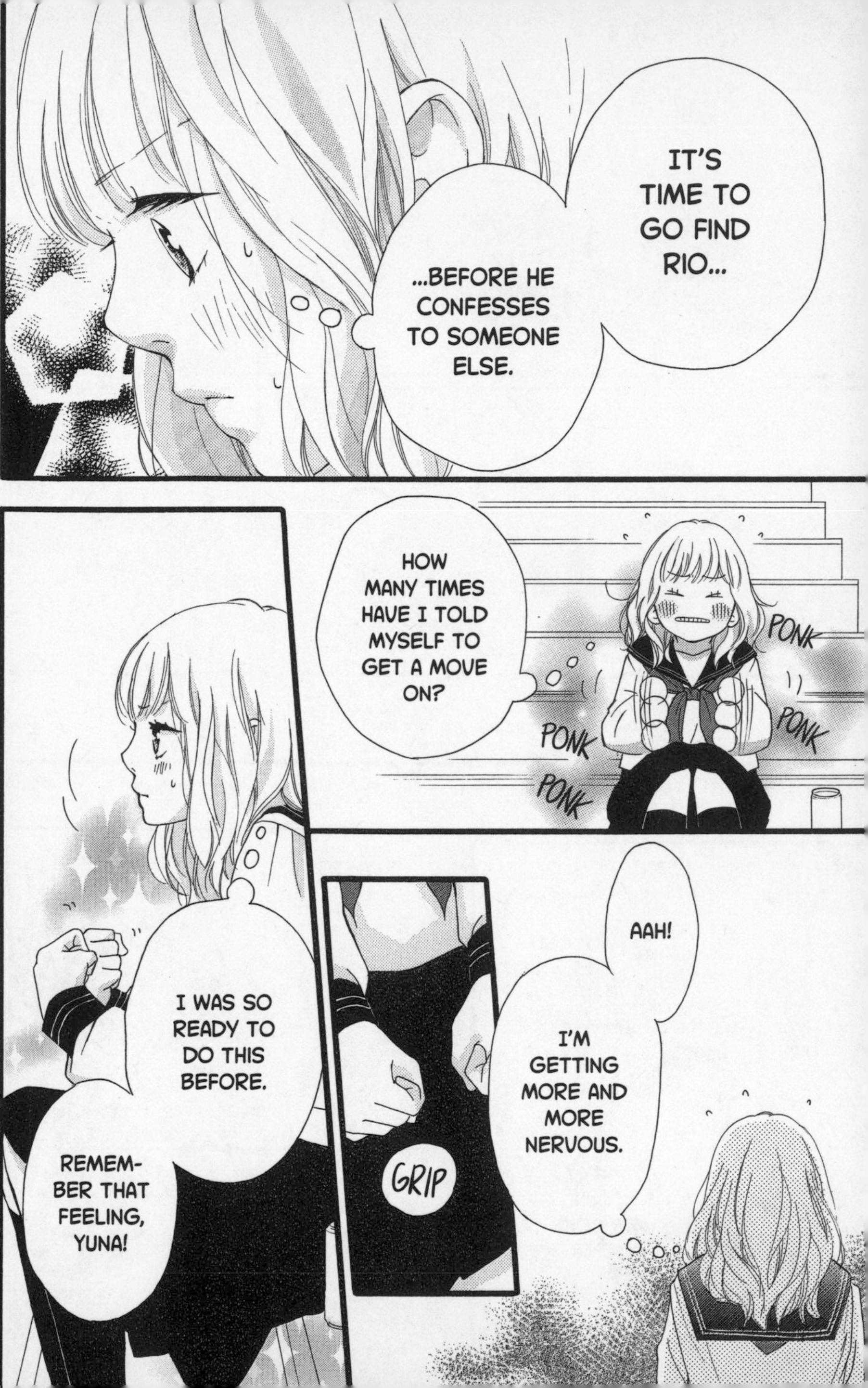
IT'S TIME TO GO FIND RIO...
...BEFORE HE CONFESSES TO SOMEONE ELSE.
HOW MANY TIMES HAVE I TOLD MYSELF TO GET A MOVE ON?
PONK
PONK
PONK
PONK
AAH!
I'M GETTING MORE AND MORE NERVOUS.
GRIP
I WAS SO READY TO DO THIS BEFORE.
REMEM-BER THAT FEELING, YUNA!

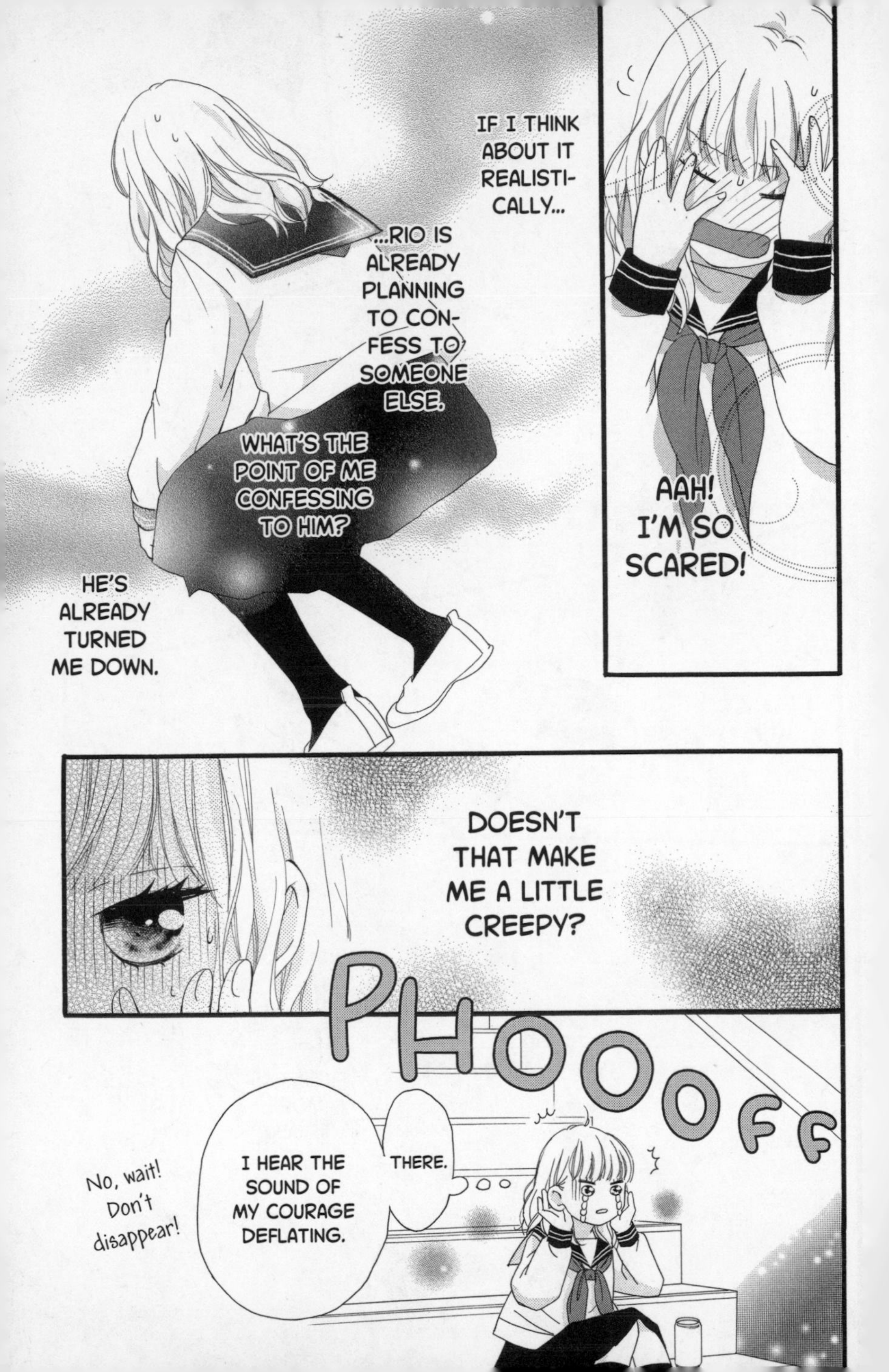
AAH! I'M SO SCARED!
IF I THINK ABOUT IT REALISTICALLY...
...RIO IS ALREADY PLANNING TO CONFESS TO SOMEONE ELSE.
WHAT'S THE POINT OF ME CONFESSING TO HIM?
HE'S ALREADY TURNED ME DOWN.
DOESN'T THAT MAKE ME A LITTLE CREEPY?
PHOOOFF
THERE.
I HEAR THE SOUND OF MY COURAGE DEFLATING.
No, wait! Don't disappear!

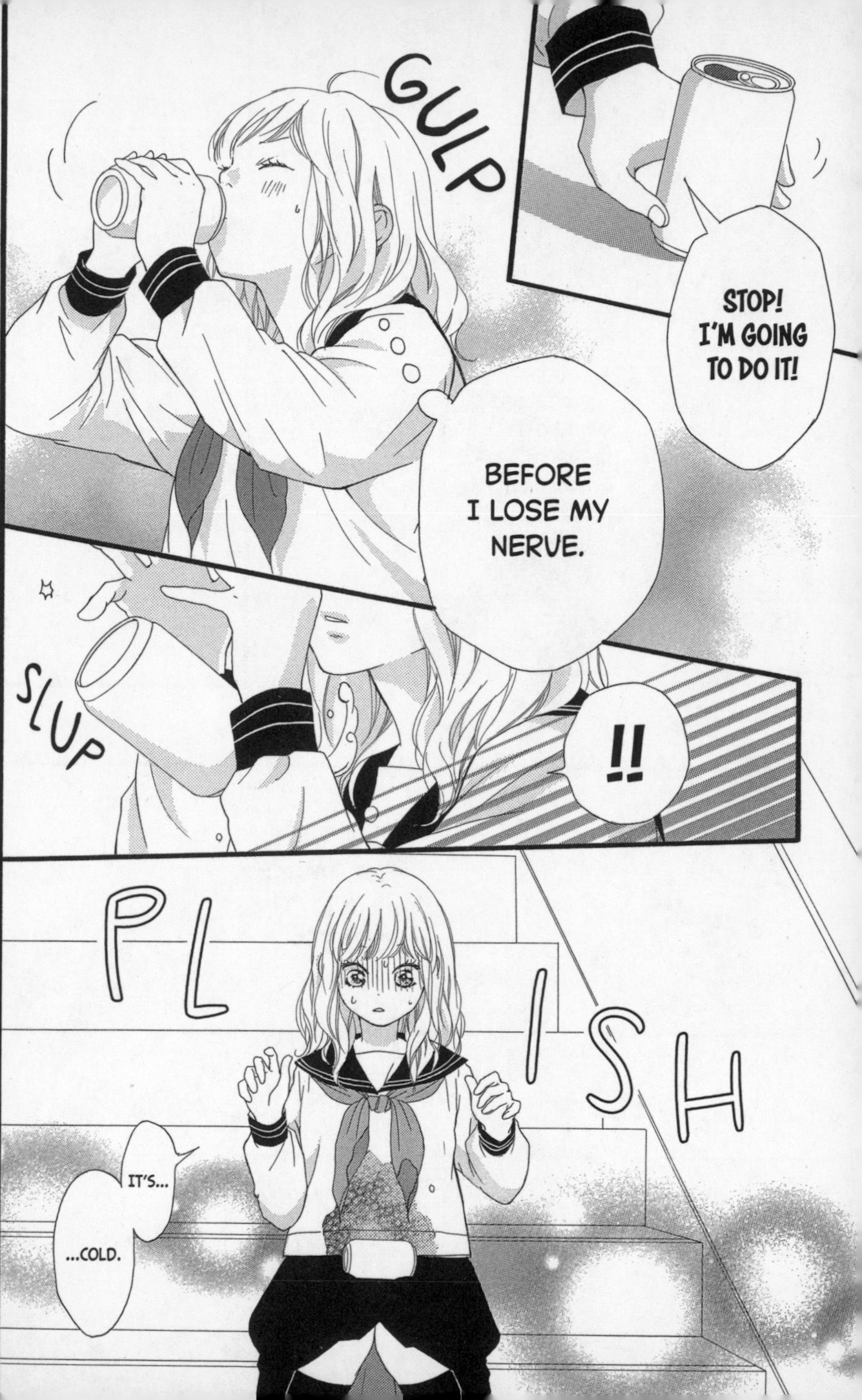
STOP! I'M GOING TO DO IT!
GULP
BEFORE I LOSE MY NERVE.
!!
SLUP
PLISH
IT'S...
...COLD.

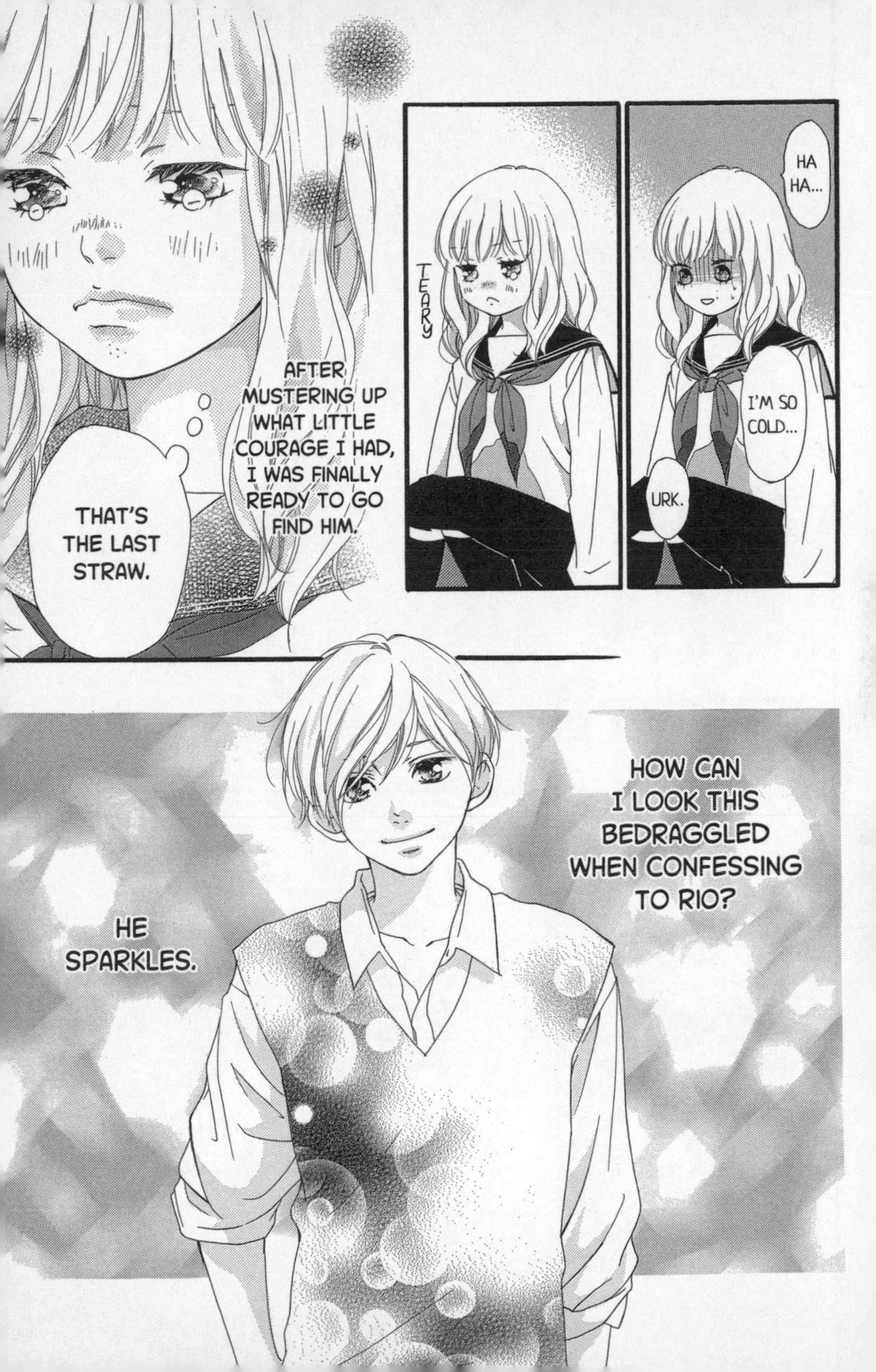
HA HA...
I'M SO COLD...
URK.
TEARY
AFTER MUSTERING UP WHAT LITTLE COURAGE I HAD, I WAS FINALLY READY TO GO FIND HIM.
THAT'S THE LAST STRAW.
HOW CAN I LOOK THIS BEDRAGGLED WHEN CONFESSING TO RIO?
HE SPARKLES.

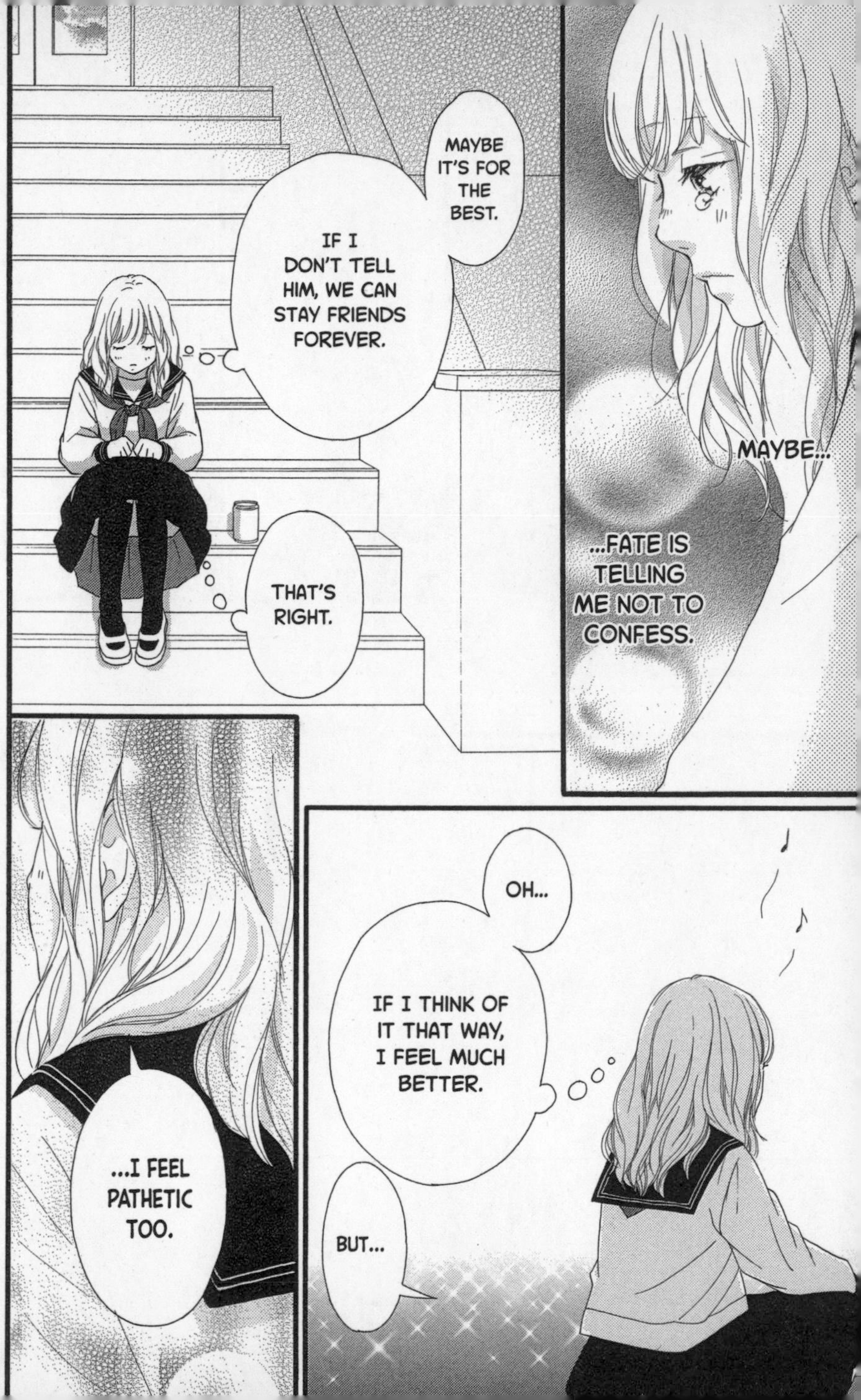
MAYBE...
...FATE IS TELLING ME NOT TO CONFESS.
MAYBE IT'S FOR THE BEST.
IF I DON'T TELL HIM, WE CAN STAY FRIENDS FOREVER.
THAT'S RIGHT.
OH...
IF I THINK OF IT THAT WAY, I FEEL MUCH BETTER.
BUT...
...I FEEL PATHETIC TOO.

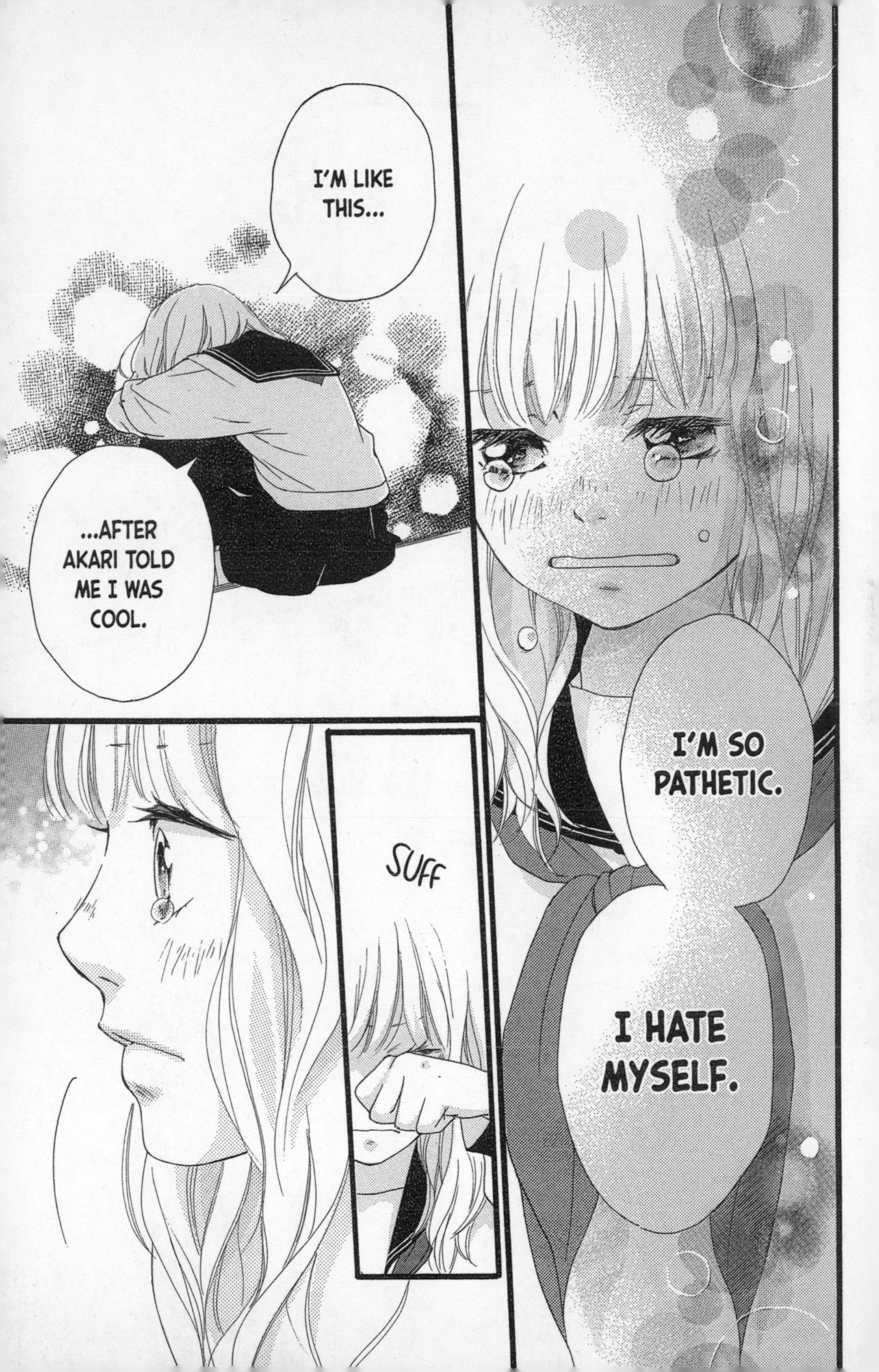
I'M LIKE THIS...
...AFTER AKARI TOLD ME I WAS COOL.
I'M SO PATHETIC.
I HATE MYSELF.
SUFF

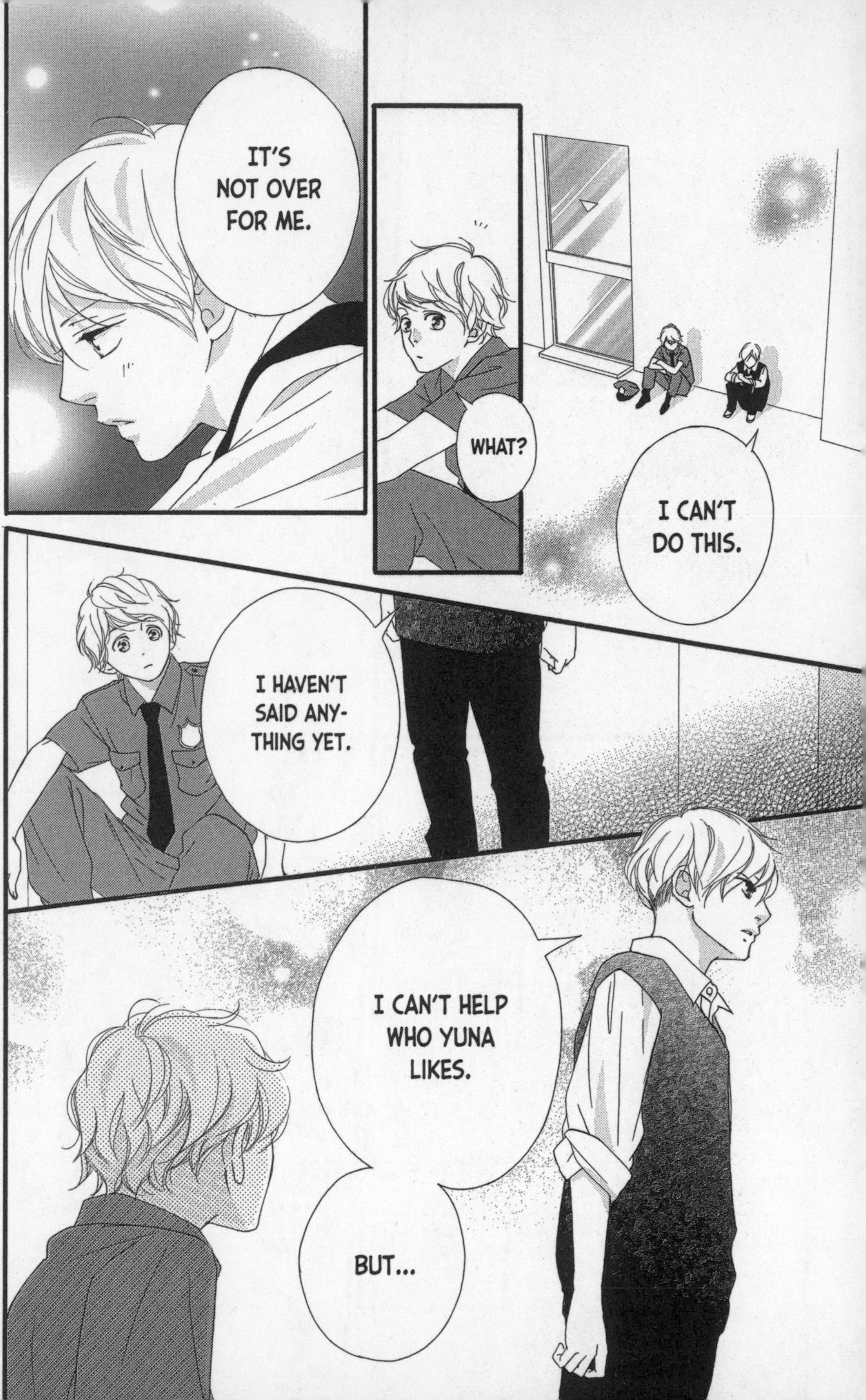
I CAN'T DO THIS.
WHAT?
IT'S NOT OVER FOR ME.
I HAVEN'T SAID ANY-THING YET.
I CAN'T HELP WHO YUNA LIKES.
BUT...

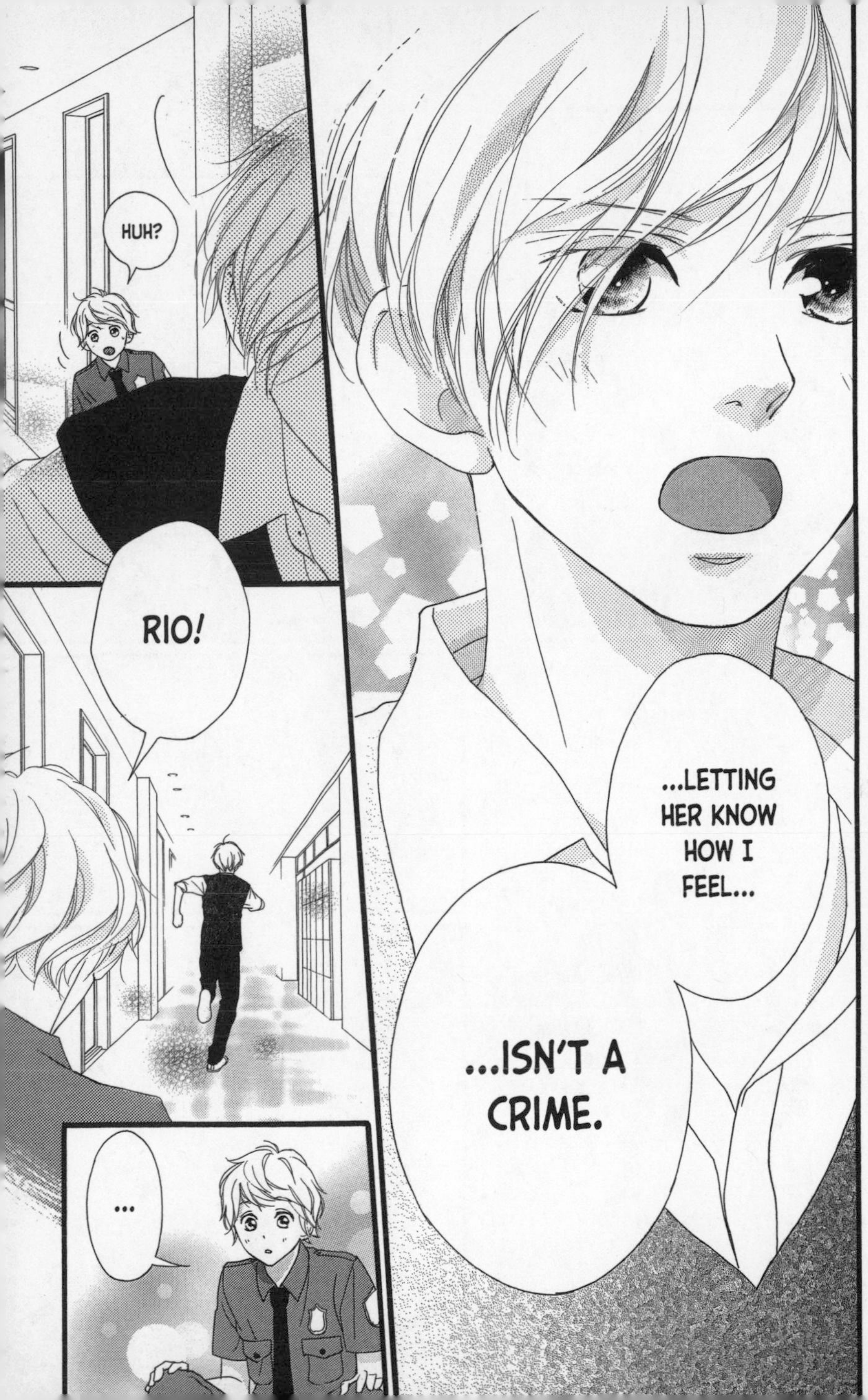
...LETTING HER KNOW HOW I FEEL...
...ISN'T A CRIME.
HUH?
RIO!
...

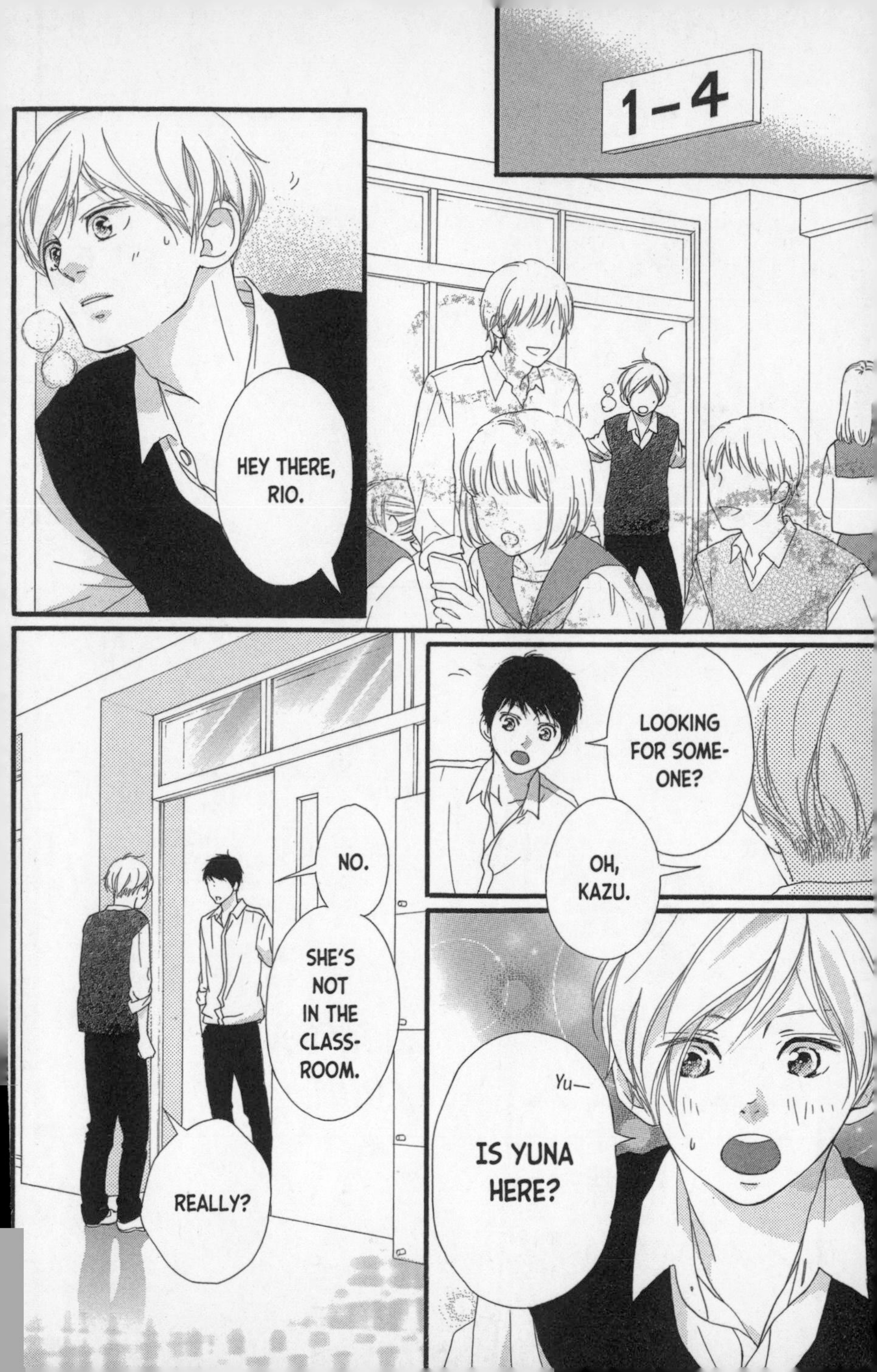
1-4
HEY THERE, RIO.
LOOKING FOR SOME-ONE?
OH, KAZU.
Yu—
IS YUNA HERE?
NO.
SHE'S NOT IN THE CLASS-ROOM.
REALLY?

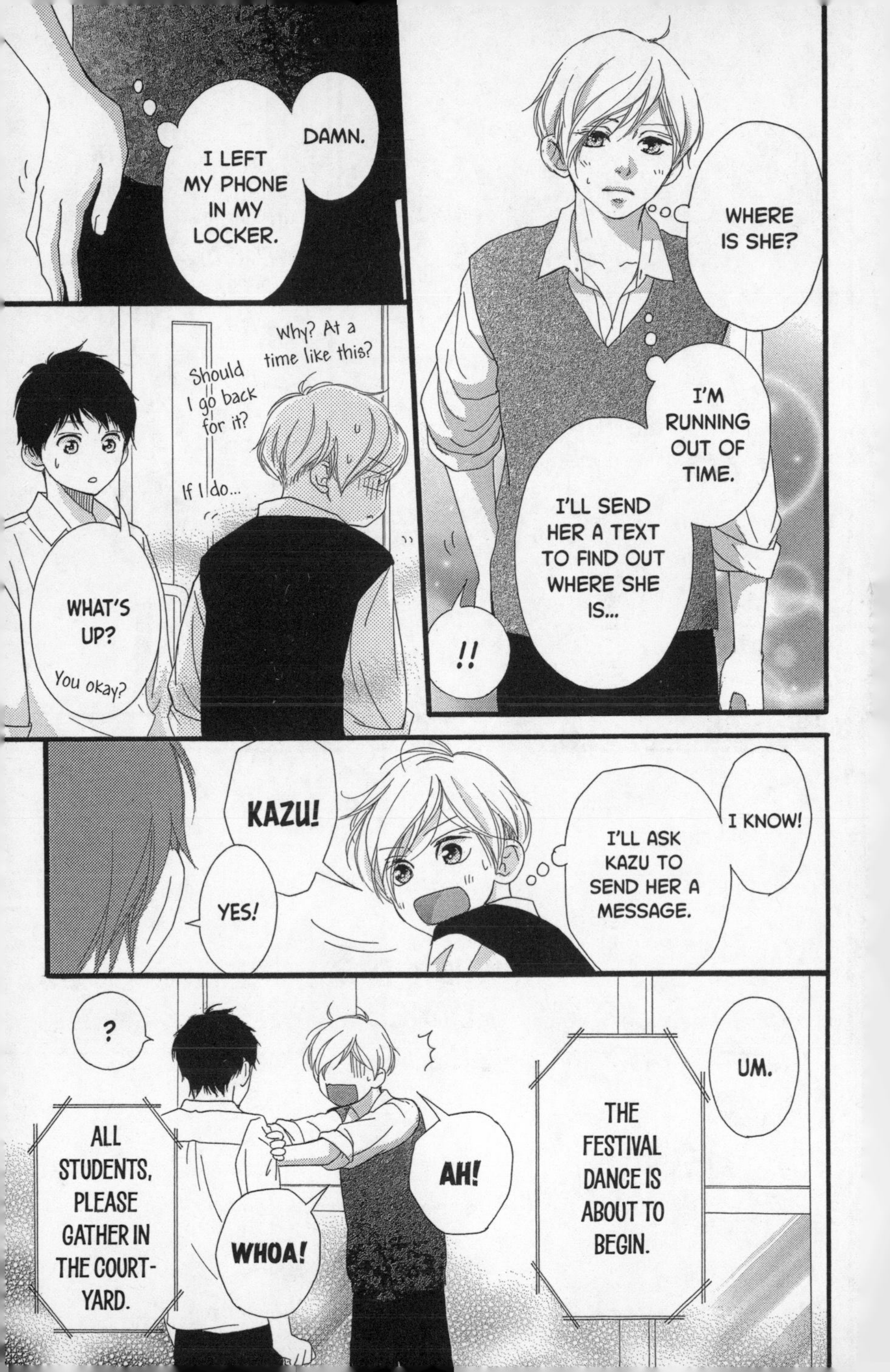
WHERE IS SHE?
I'M RUNNING OUT OF TIME.
I'LL SEND HER A TEXT TO FIND OUT WHERE SHE IS...
!!
DAMN.
I LEFT MY PHONE IN MY LOCKER.
Why? At a time like this?
Should I go back for it?
If I do...
WHAT'S UP?
You okay?
I KNOW!
I'LL ASK KAZU TO SEND HER A MESSAGE.
KAZU!
YES!
UM.
THE FESTIVAL DANCE IS ABOUT TO BEGIN.
AH!
?
WHOA!
ALL STUDENTS, PLEASE GATHER IN THE COURT-YARD.

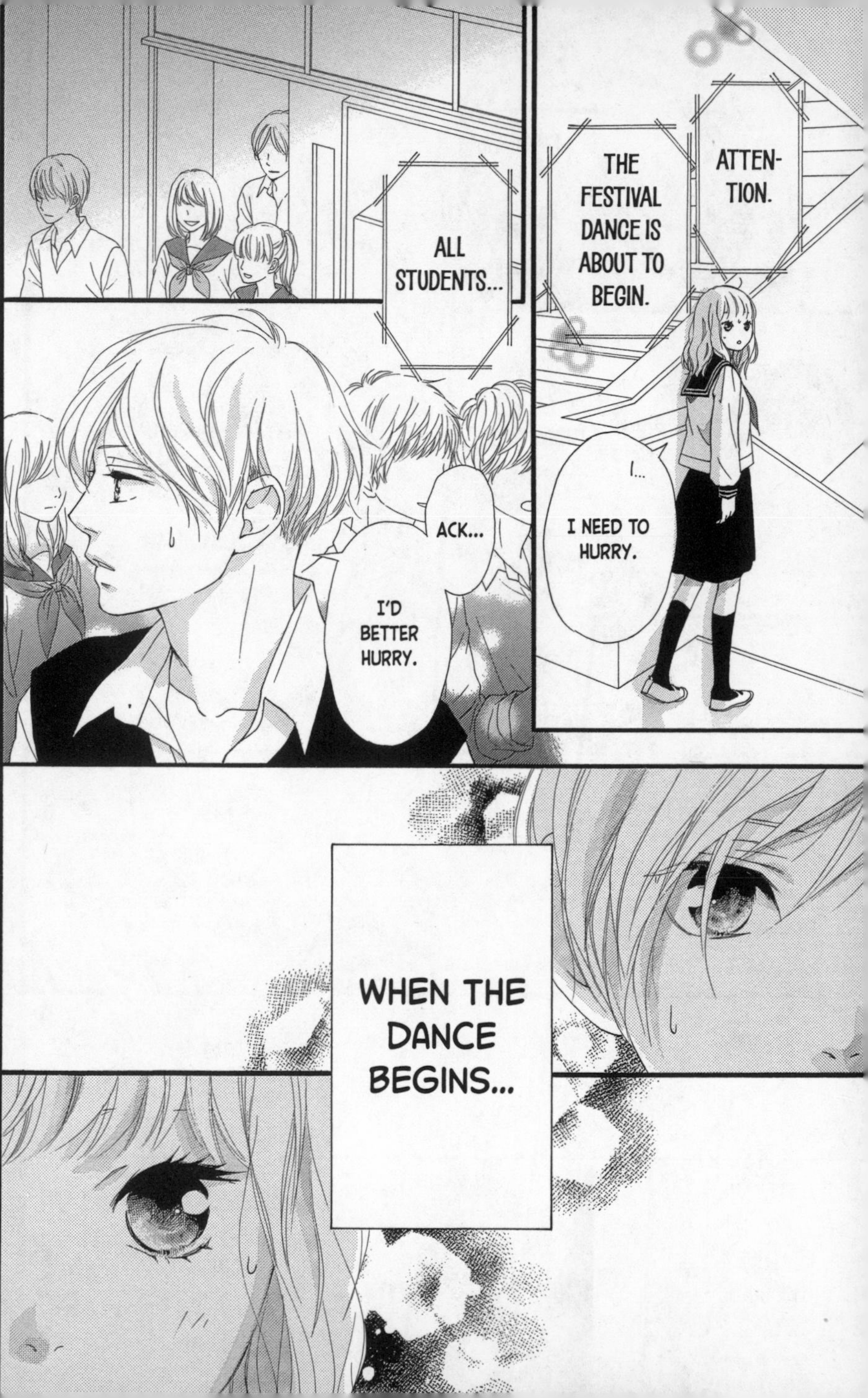
ATTEN-TION.
THE FESTIVAL DANCE IS ABOUT TO BEGIN.
I...
I NEED TO HURRY.
ALL STUDENTS...
ACK...
I'D BETTER HURRY.
WHEN THE DANCE BEGINS...

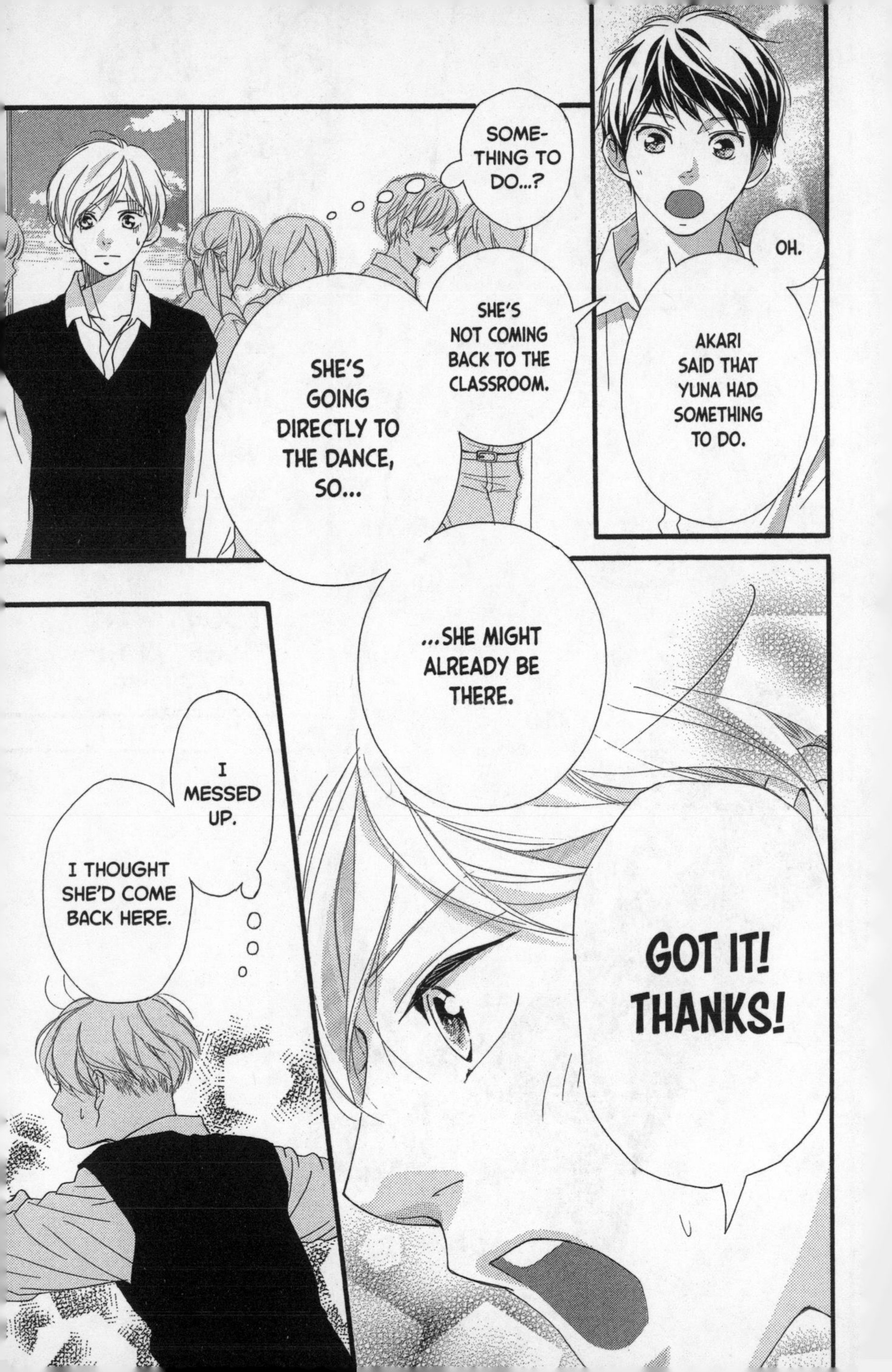
OH.
AKARI SAID THAT YUNA HAD SOMETHING TO DO.
SOME-THING TO DO...?
SHE'S NOT COMING BACK TO THE CLASSROOM.
SHE'S GOING DIRECTLY TO THE DANCE, SO...
...SHE MIGHT ALREADY BE THERE.
GOT IT! THANKS!
I MESSED UP.
I THOUGHT SHE'D COME BACK HERE.

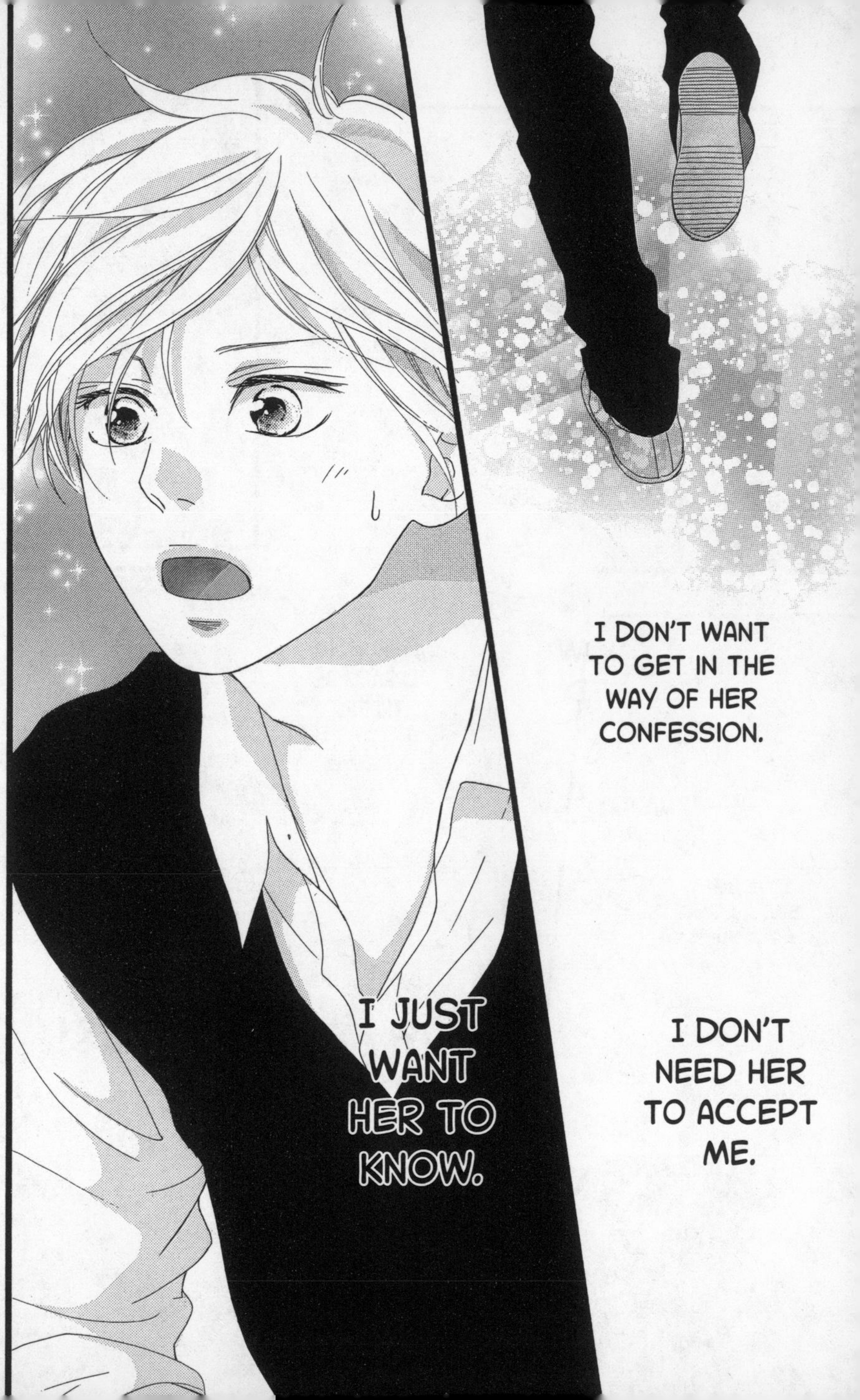
I DON'T WANT TO GET IN THE WAY OF HER CONFESSION.
I DON'T NEED HER TO ACCEPT ME.
I JUST WANT HER TO KNOW.

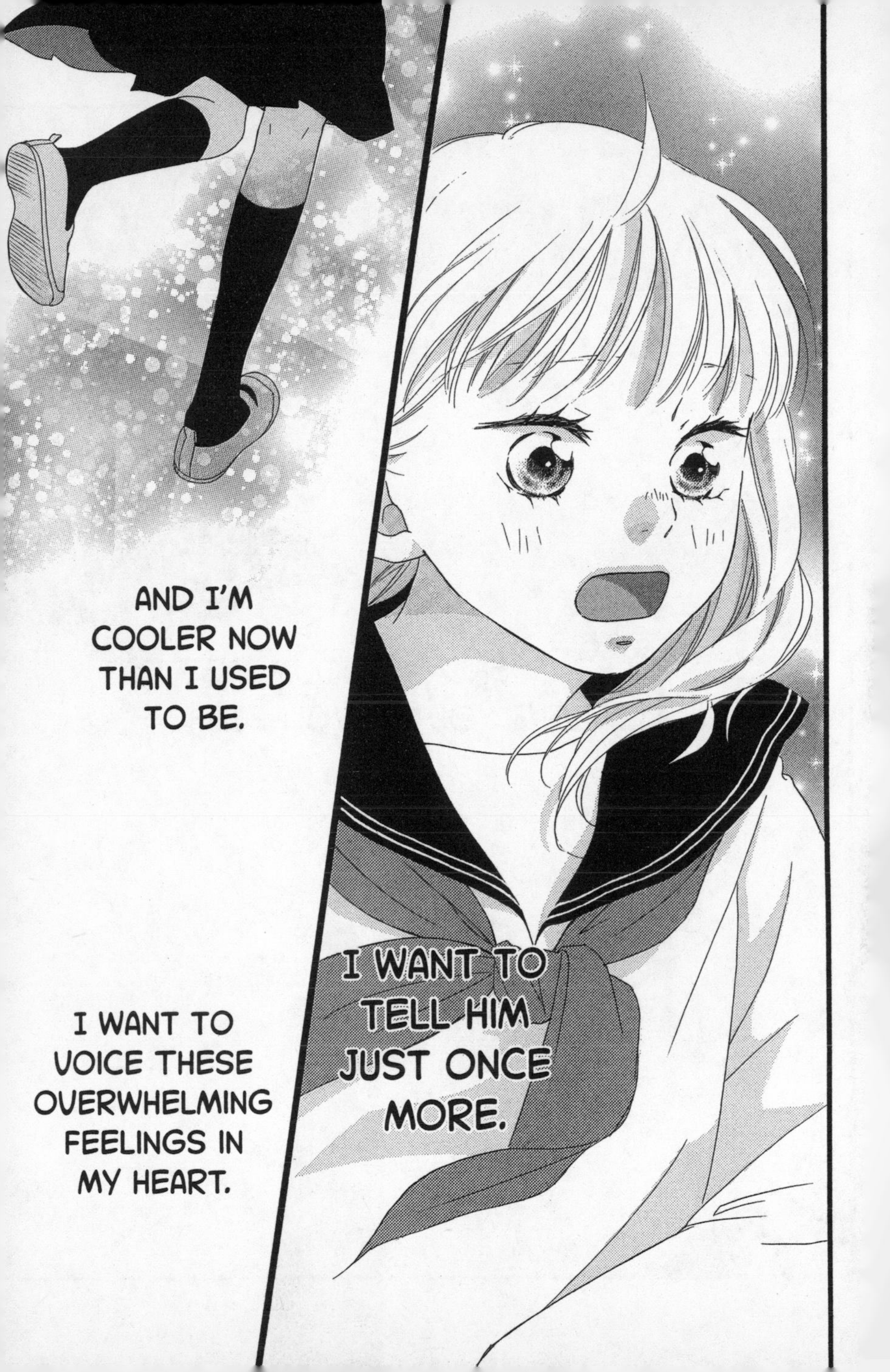
AND I'M COOLER NOW THAN I USED TO BE.
I WANT TO VOICE THESE OVERWHELMING FEELINGS IN MY HEART.
I WANT TO TELL HIM JUST ONCE MORE.

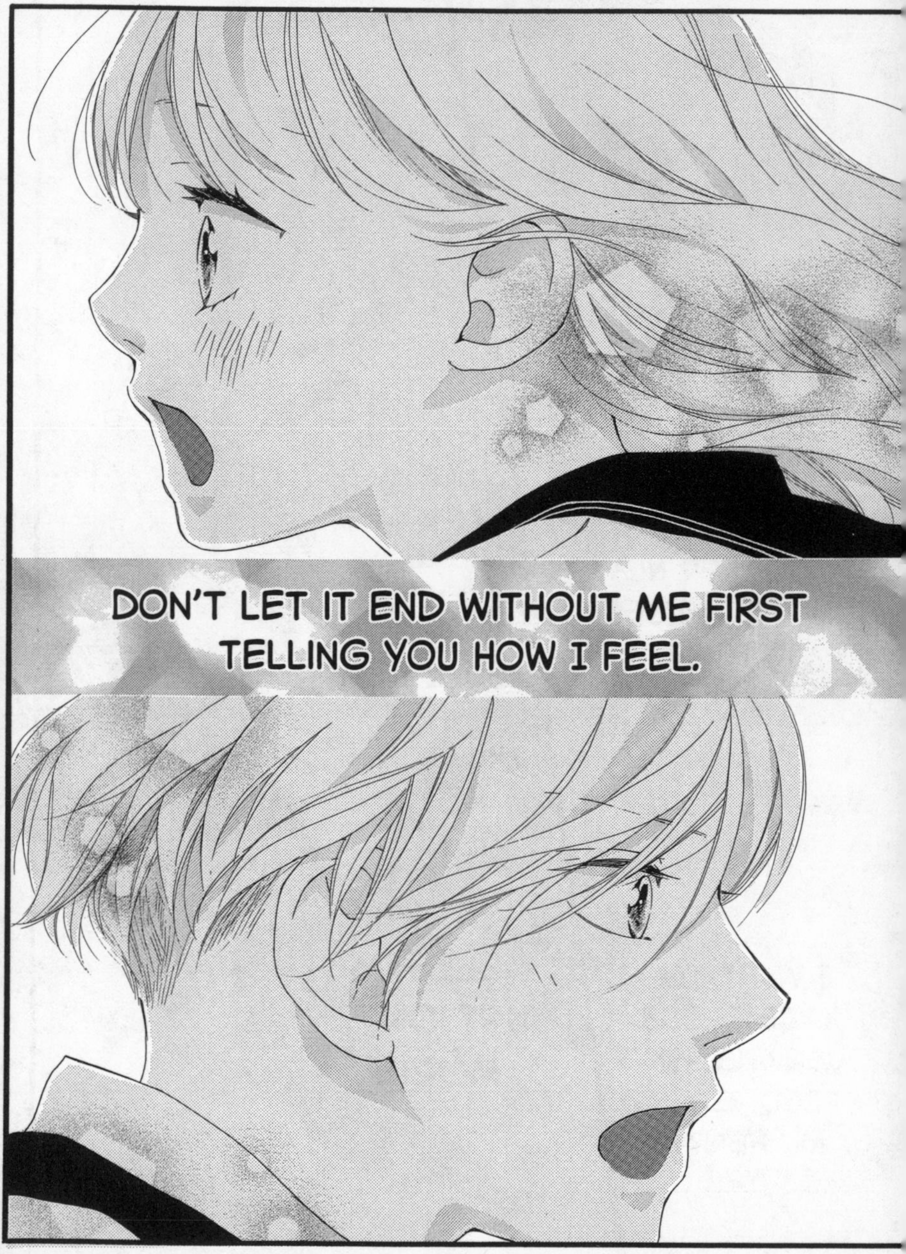
DON'T LET IT END WITHOUT ME FIRST TELLING YOU HOW I FEEL.

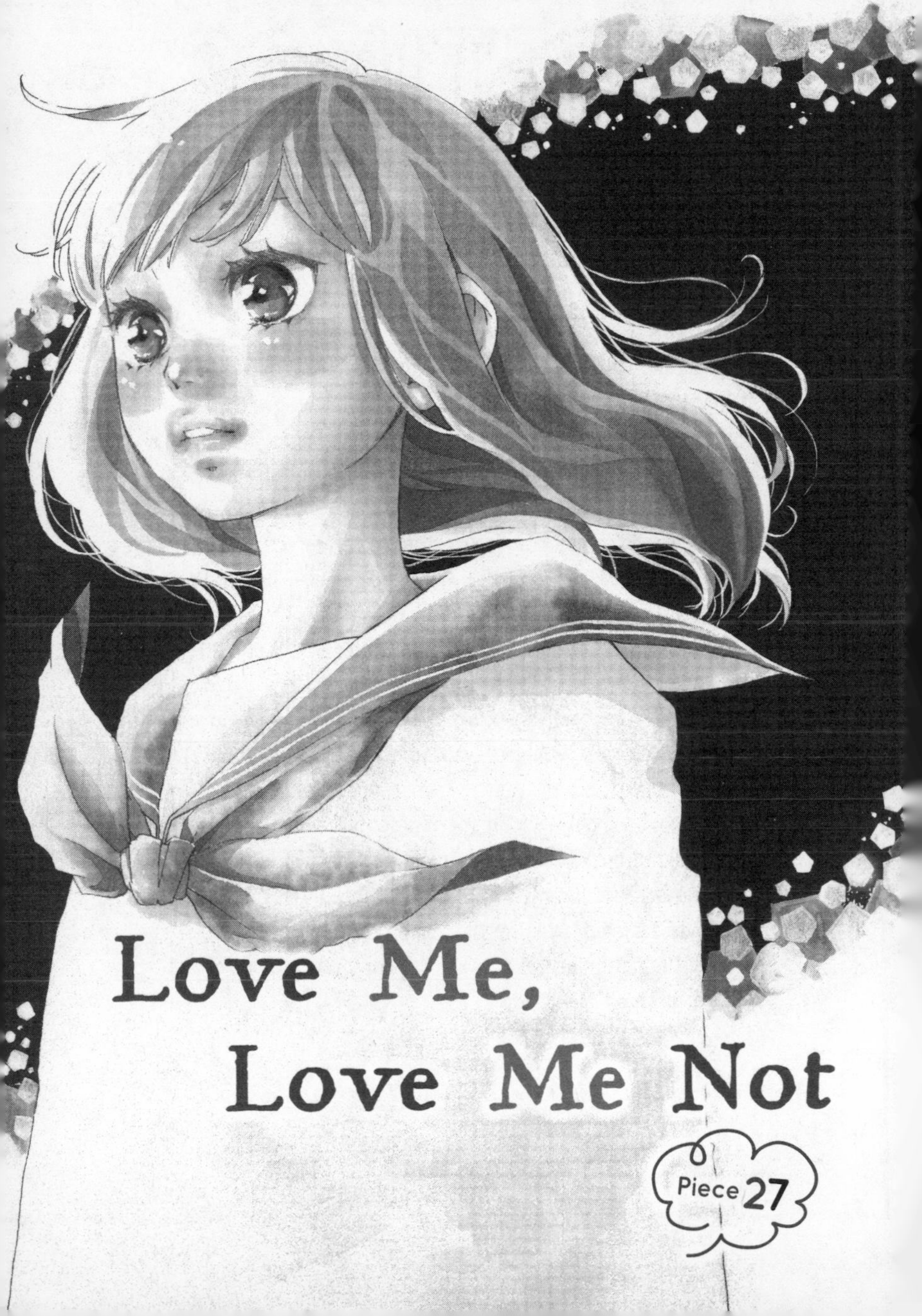
Love Me,
Love Me Not
Piece 27

GREETINGS

Hello. I'm Io Sakisaka. Thank you very much for picking up volume 7 of *Love Me, Love Me Not*.

I've recently acquired an iPad Pro. For some reason, everyone at the studio bought one around the same time. I thought, "If I ride this wave, I may learn how to use it along with everyone else. If I miss this opportunity, I may never get one." A few days later, I got the good news that Clip Studio Paint, a wonderful software for drawing, was available for iPad. Yay! (But I haven't learned how to use that program yet!) I'm scheming to have everyone who's learned to use Clip Studio Paint teach me the useful parts. (I'm terrible at it.) Once I learn to use it, I can travel without having to worry about how long I'm away because I'll be able to work anywhere. I think that might be the best way to work. But it gave me pause when my assistant asked, "Will you work while you're travelling?" I've never once taken out my work kit while travelling. I always bring my old-school work kit (pen, notebook, loose leaf) travelling, but once I get to my destination, I think, "I'm travelling because I wanted to do something different." So I never take out my kit. Well, that's no good. But with an iPad, I might be inspired to work... I'm kind of looking forward to what I might do.

Io Sakisaka

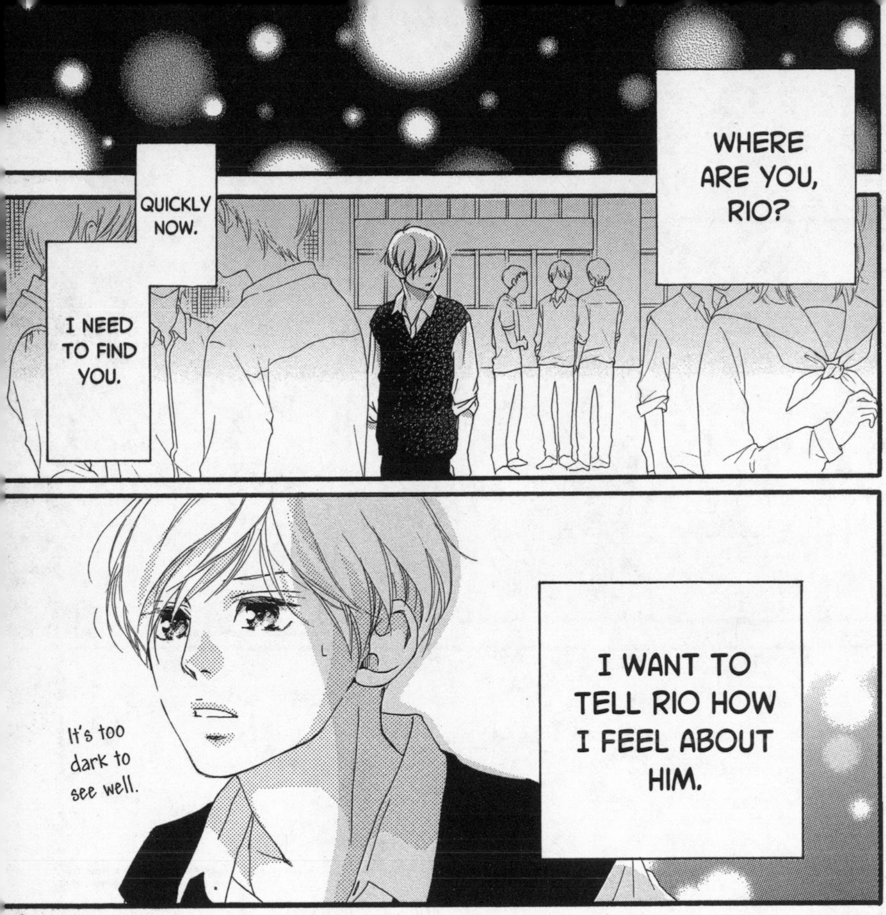
WHERE ARE YOU, RIO?
QUICKLY NOW.
I NEED TO FIND YOU.
I WANT TO TELL RIO HOW I FEEL ABOUT HIM.
It's too dark to see well.

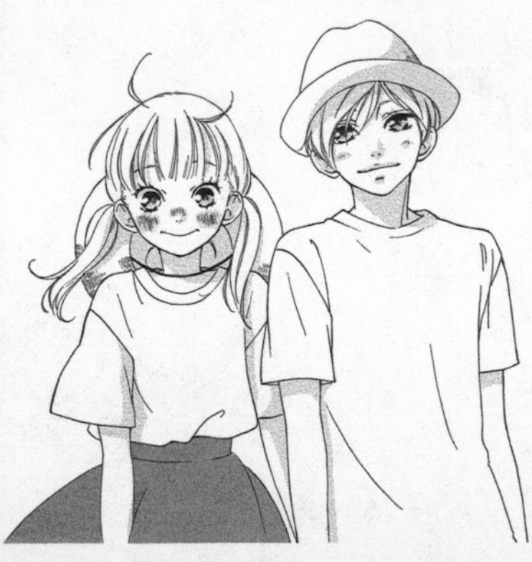

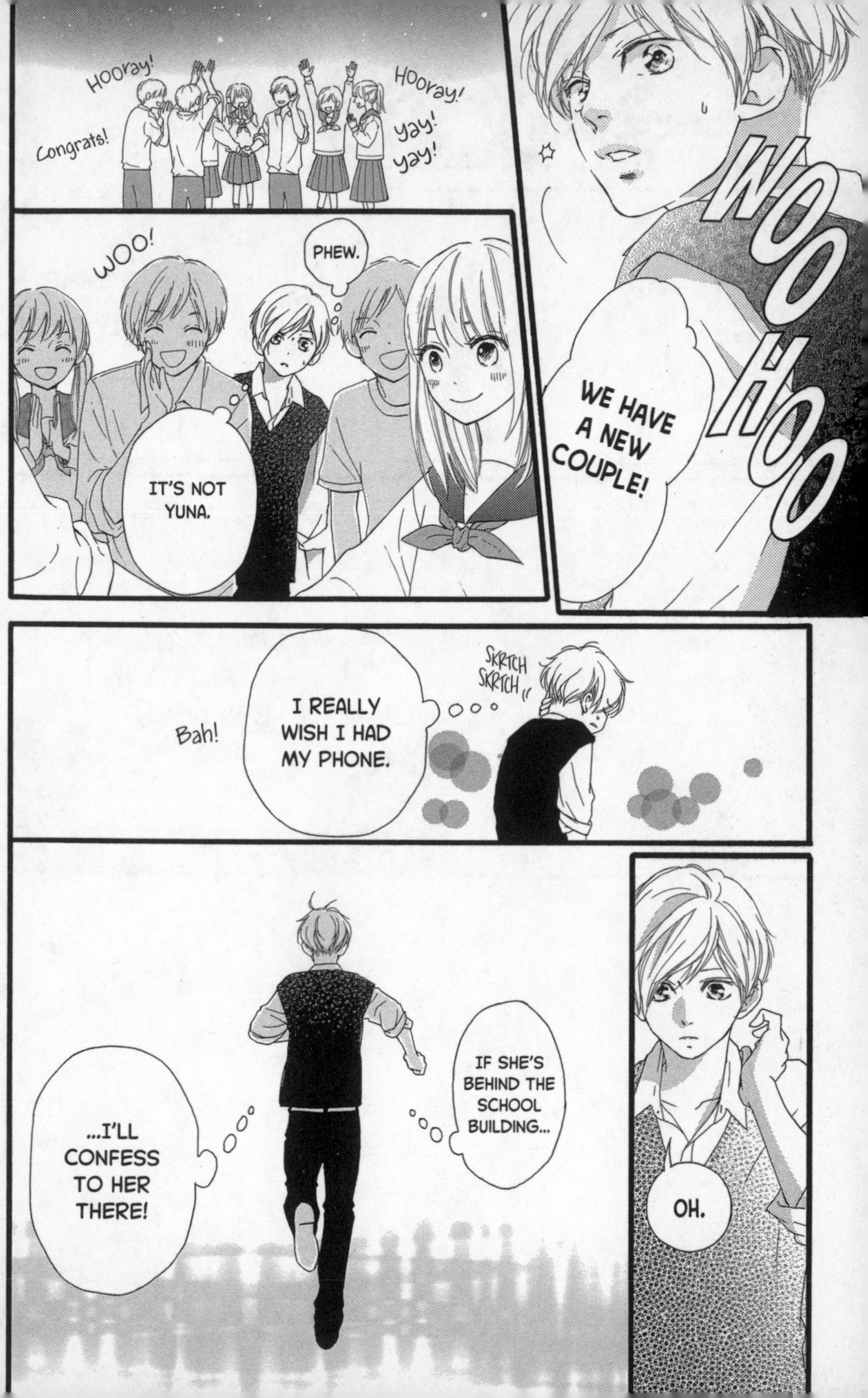
WOO HOO
WE HAVE A NEW COUPLE!
Hooray!
yay! yay!
Hooray!
Congrats!
PHEW.
WOO!
IT'S NOT YUNA.
SKRTCH SKRTCH
I REALLY WISH I HAD MY PHONE.
Bah!
OH.
IF SHE'S BEHIND THE SCHOOL BUILDING...
...I'LL CONFESS TO HER THERE!

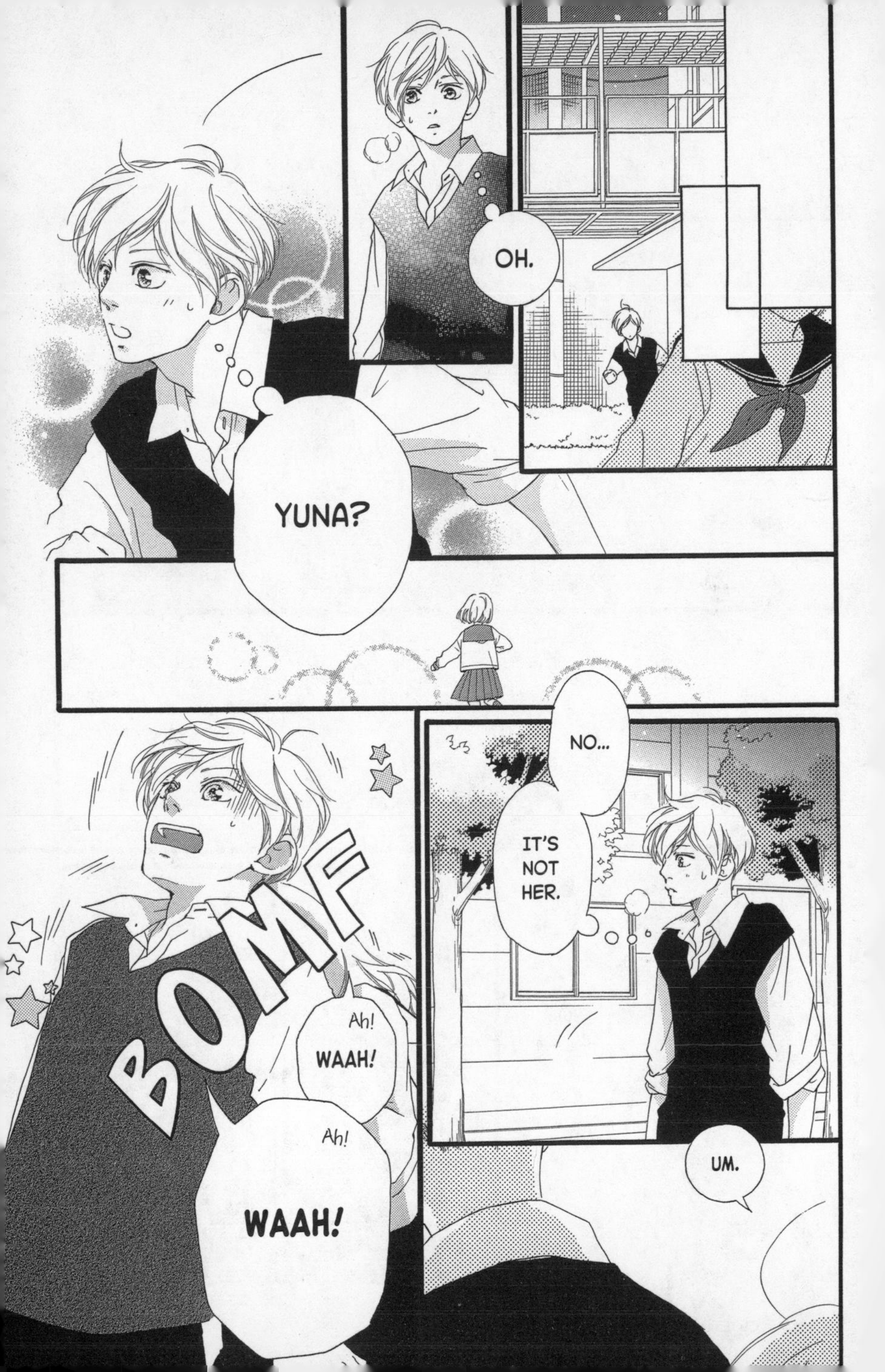
OH.
YUNA?
NO...
IT'S NOT HER.
UM.
BOMF
Ah! WAAH!
Ah! WAAH!

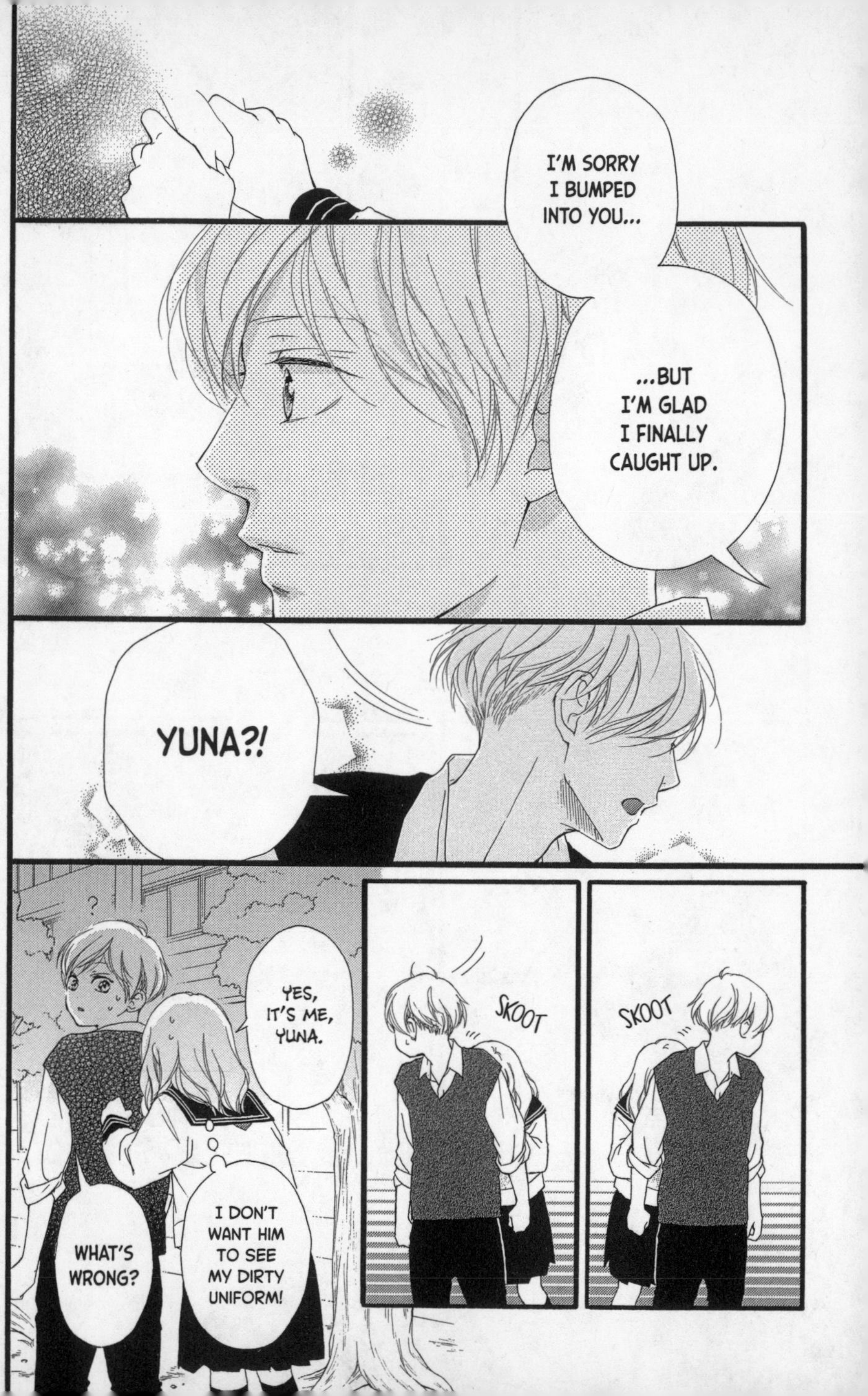
I'M SORRY I BUMPED INTO YOU...
...BUT I'M GLAD I FINALLY CAUGHT UP.
YUNA?!
SKOOT
SKOOT
YES, IT'S ME, YUNA.
I DON'T WANT HIM TO SEE MY DIRTY UNIFORM!
WHAT'S WRONG?

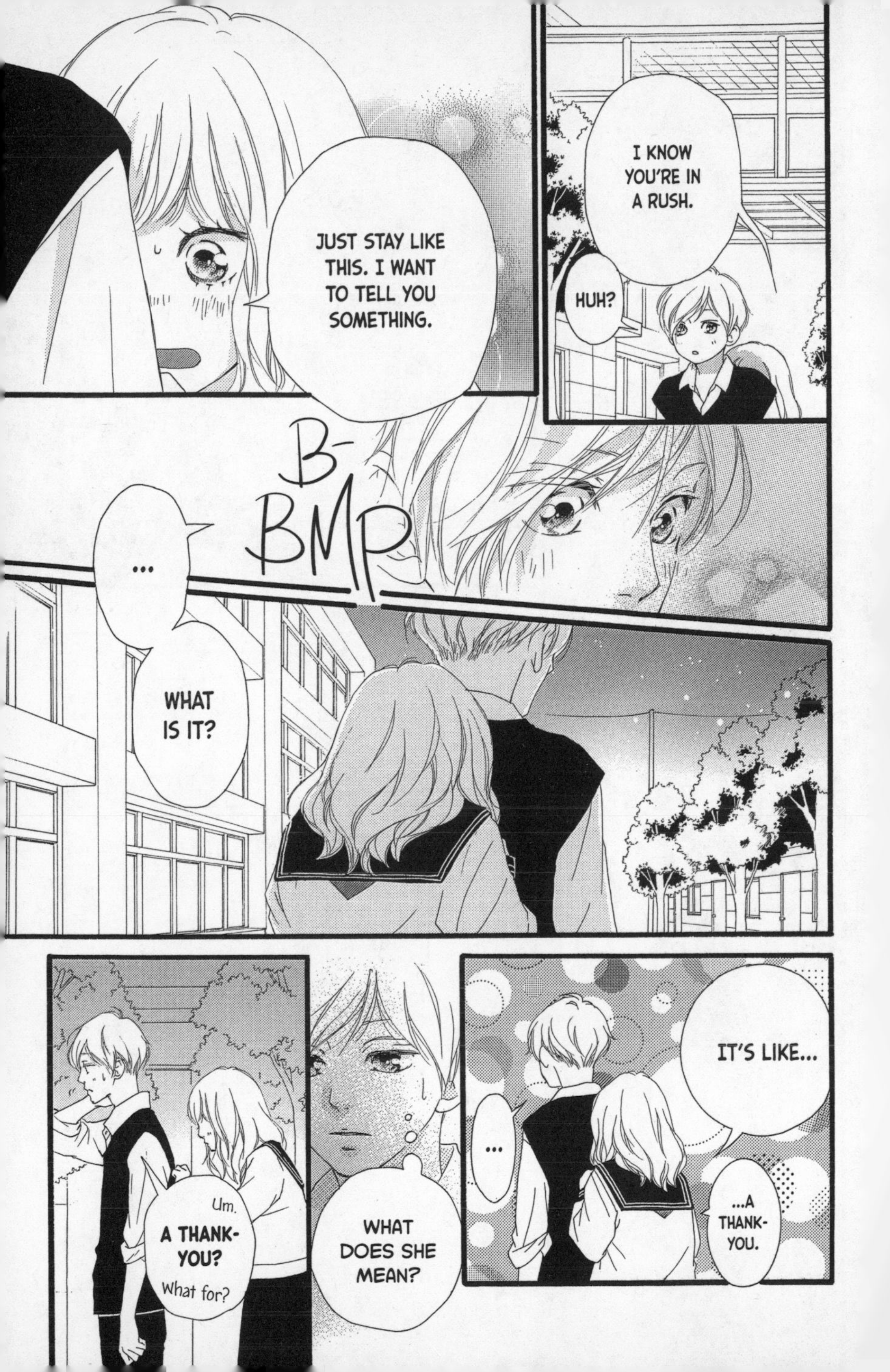
I KNOW YOU'RE IN A RUSH.
HUH?
JUST STAY LIKE THIS. I WANT TO TELL YOU SOMETHING.
B-BMP
...
WHAT IS IT?
IT'S LIKE...
...A THANK-YOU.
...
WHAT DOES SHE MEAN?
Um.
A THANK-YOU?
What for?

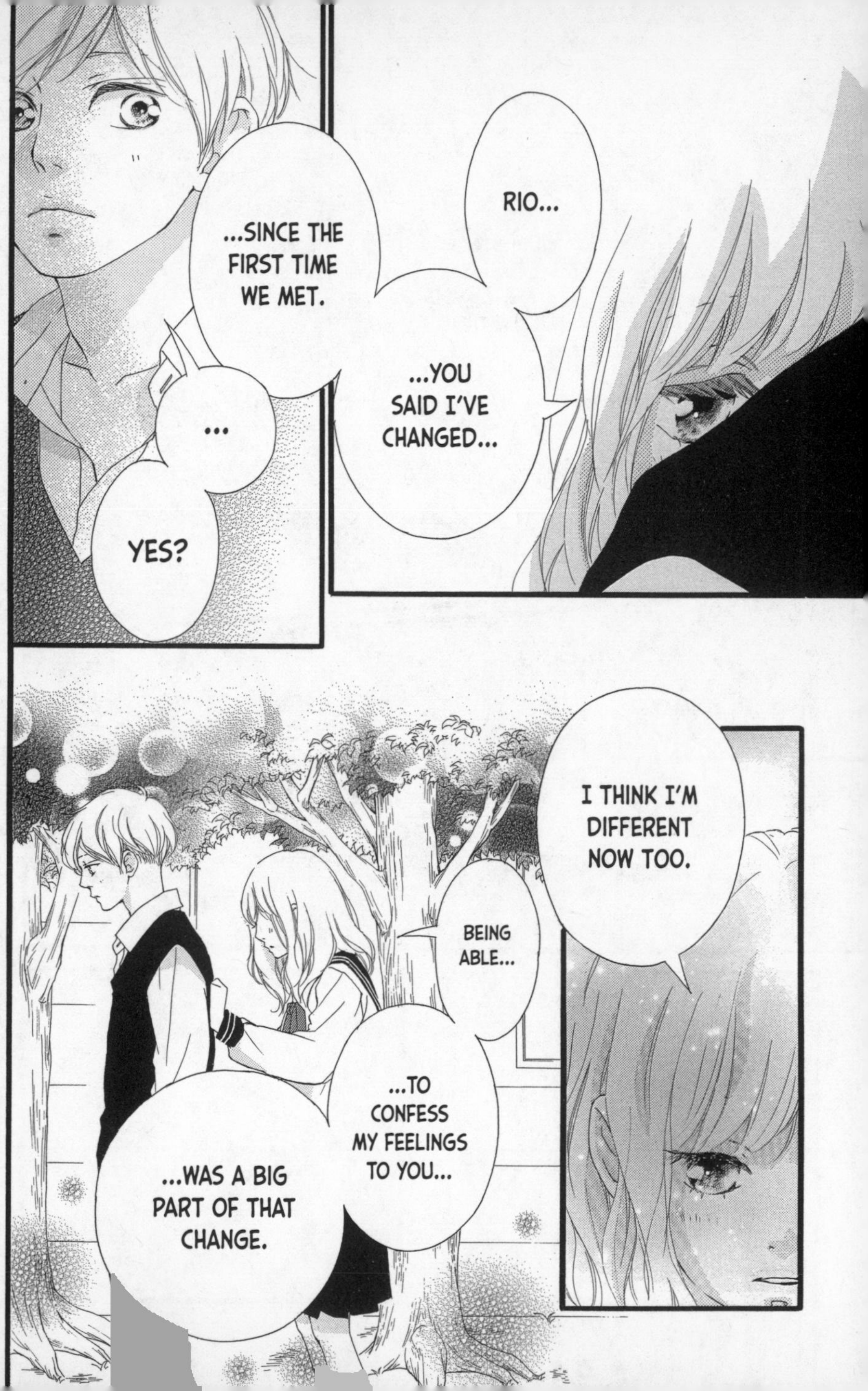
RIO...
...YOU SAID I'VE CHANGED...
...SINCE THE FIRST TIME WE MET.
...
YES?
I THINK I'M DIFFERENT NOW TOO.
BEING ABLE...
...TO CONFESS MY FEELINGS TO YOU...
...WAS A BIG PART OF THAT CHANGE.

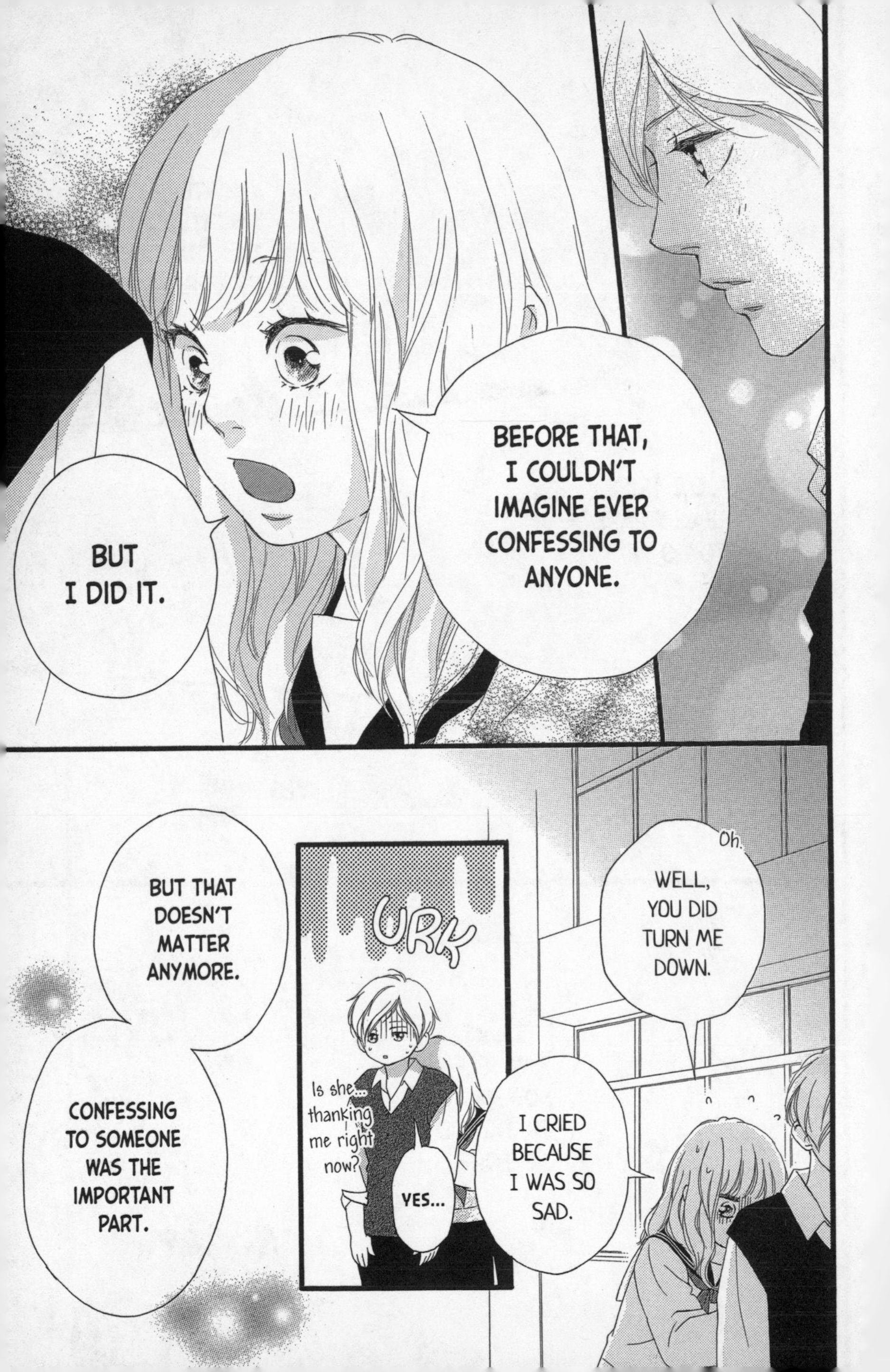
BEFORE THAT, I COULDN'T IMAGINE EVER CONFESSING TO ANYONE.
BUT I DID IT.
Oh.
WELL, YOU DID TURN ME DOWN.
I CRIED BECAUSE I WAS SO SAD.
URK
Is she... thanking me right now?
YES...
BUT THAT DOESN'T MATTER ANYMORE.
CONFESSING TO SOMEONE WAS THE IMPORTANT PART.

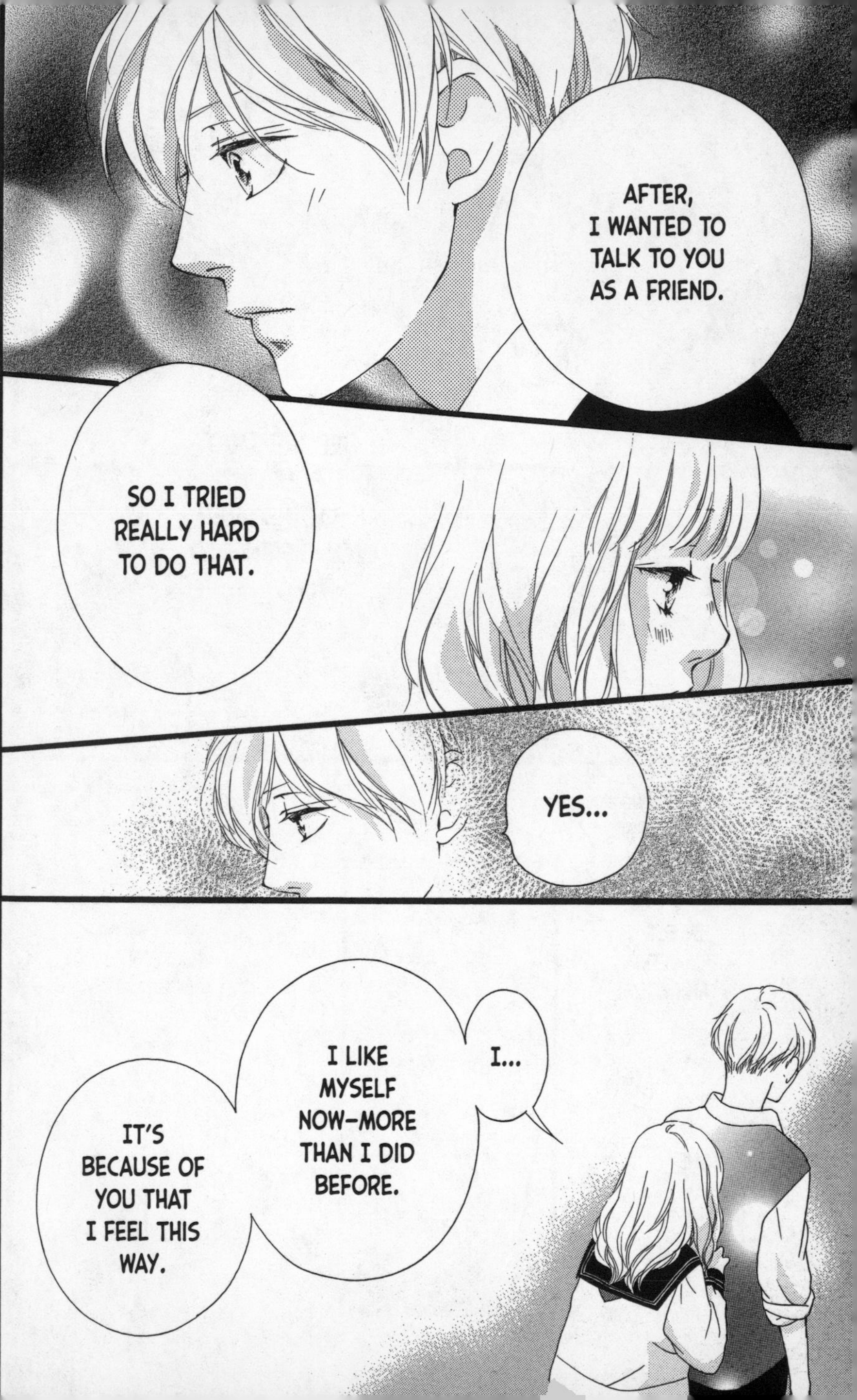
AFTER, I WANTED TO TALK TO YOU AS A FRIEND.
SO I TRIED REALLY HARD TO DO THAT.
YES...
I...
I LIKE MYSELF NOW—MORE THAN I DID BEFORE.
IT'S BECAUSE OF YOU THAT I FEEL THIS WAY.

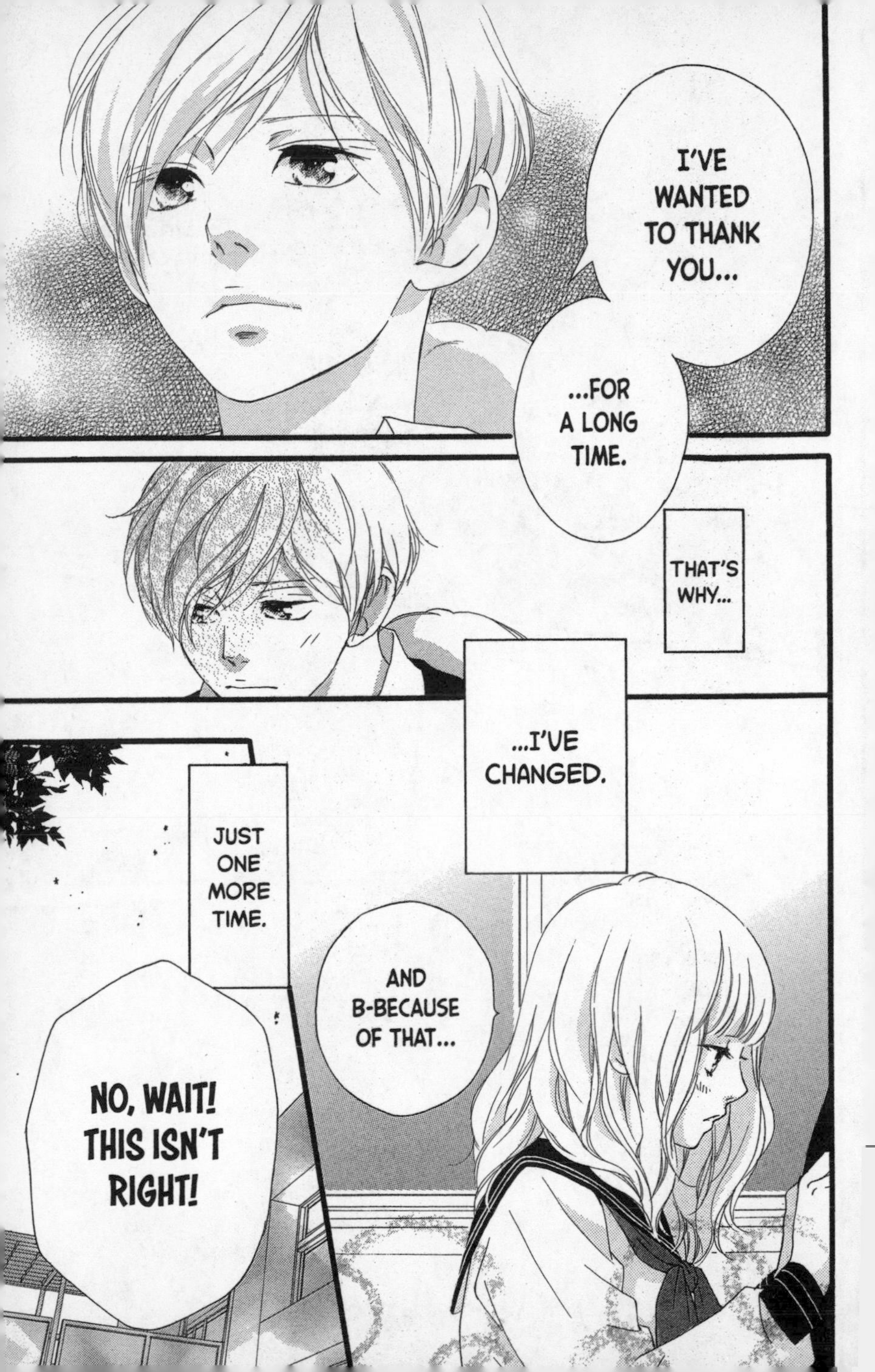
I'VE WANTED TO THANK YOU...
...FOR A LONG TIME.
THAT'S WHY...
...I'VE CHANGED.
AND B-BECAUSE OF THAT...
JUST ONE MORE TIME.
NO, WAIT! THIS ISN'T RIGHT!

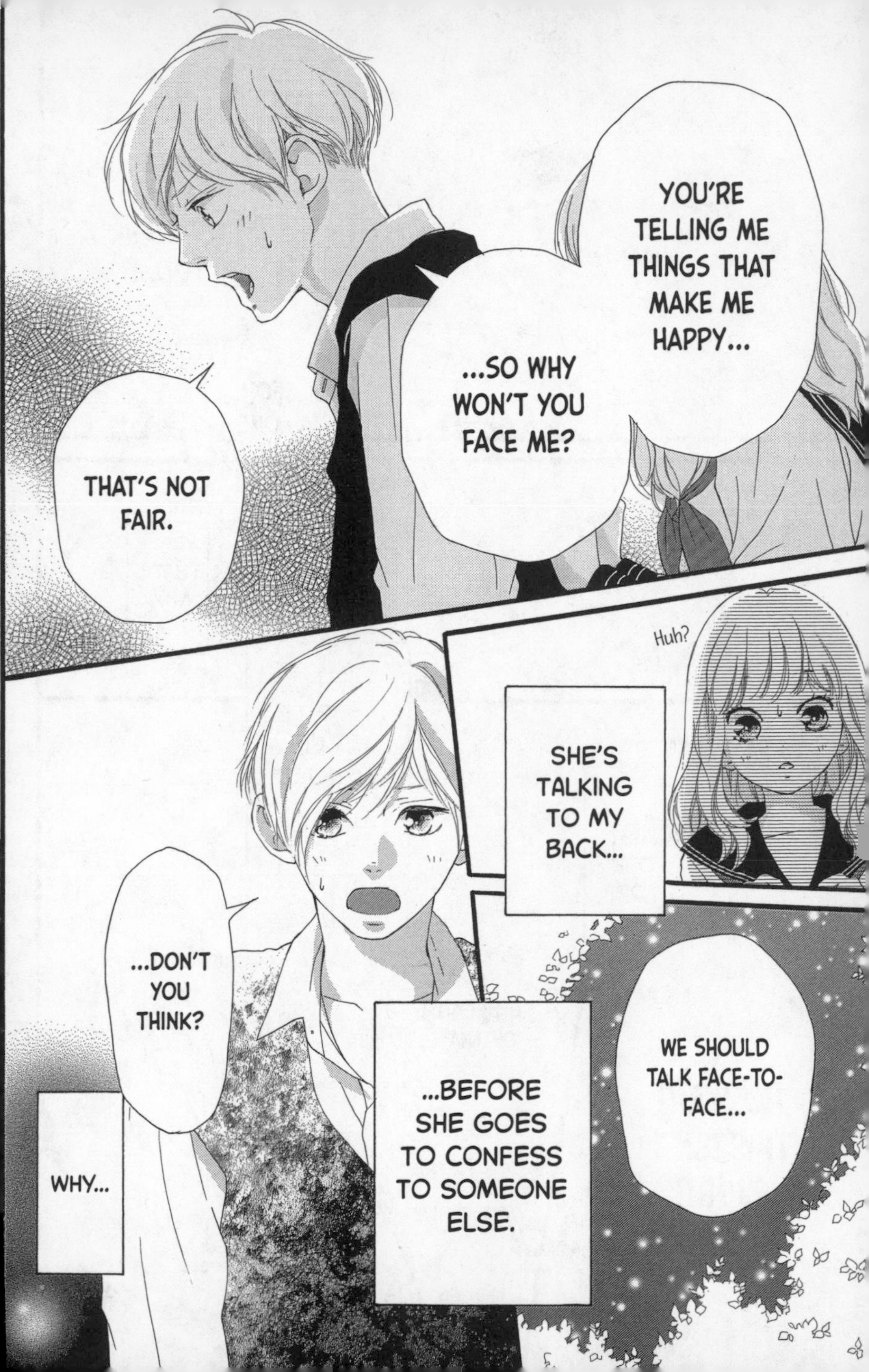
YOU'RE TELLING ME THINGS THAT MAKE ME HAPPY...
...SO WHY WON'T YOU FACE ME?
THAT'S NOT FAIR.
Huh?
SHE'S TALKING TO MY BACK...
WE SHOULD TALK FACE-TO-FACE...
...DON'T YOU THINK?
...BEFORE SHE GOES TO CONFESS TO SOMEONE ELSE.
WHY...

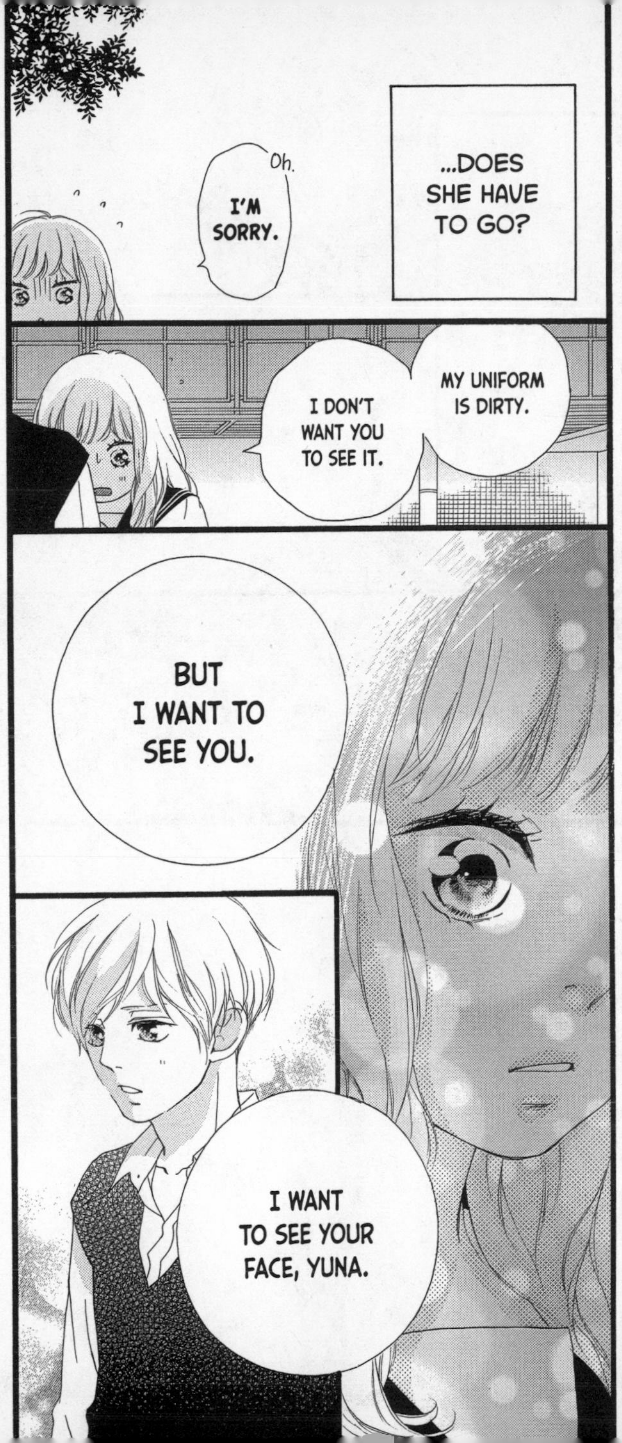
...DOES SHE HAVE TO GO?
Oh.
I'M SORRY.
MY UNIFORM IS DIRTY.
I DON'T WANT YOU TO SEE IT.
BUT I WANT TO SEE YOU.
I WANT TO SEE YOUR FACE, YUNA.

When I'm working, the closer I get to the deadline, the less I sleep. By the time the deadline is two or three days away, I can't think straight. I have many conversations with my assistants that don't make sense. I think, "Oh, I bet I'm not being clear right now, but I don't know which part isn't making sense..." The one thing I do know is that they're very good at anticipating what I mean. I'm always very grateful for their maturity in dealing with me. Thank you, thank you. And when the sleep deprivation worsens, I have auditory hallucinations. It's like that tinny sound you hear from other people's headphones, so it's (probably) music. When I hear this, I know I'm completely maxed out, so I give in and take a nap. By the way, what is that music?

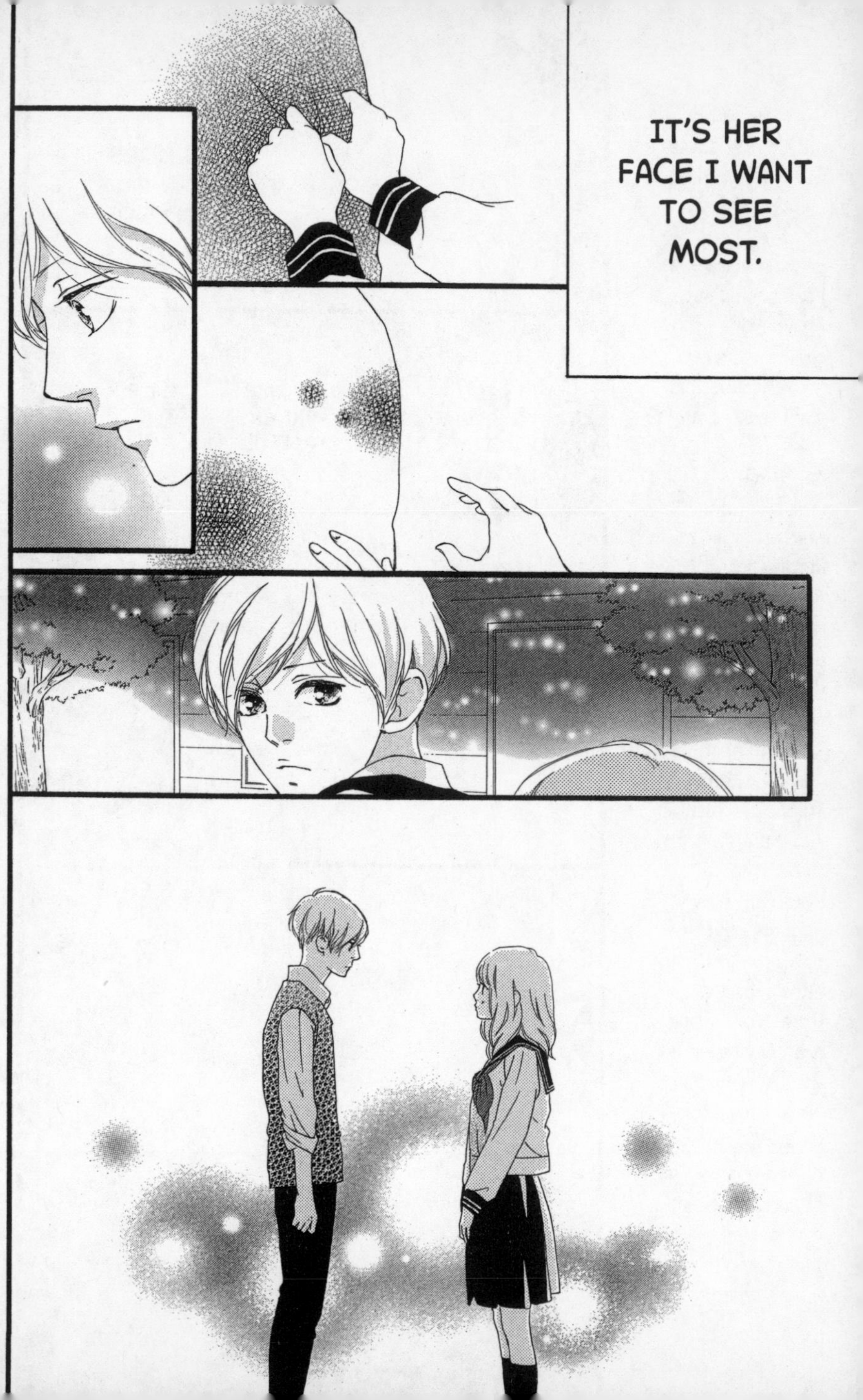
IT'S HER FACE I WANT TO SEE MOST.

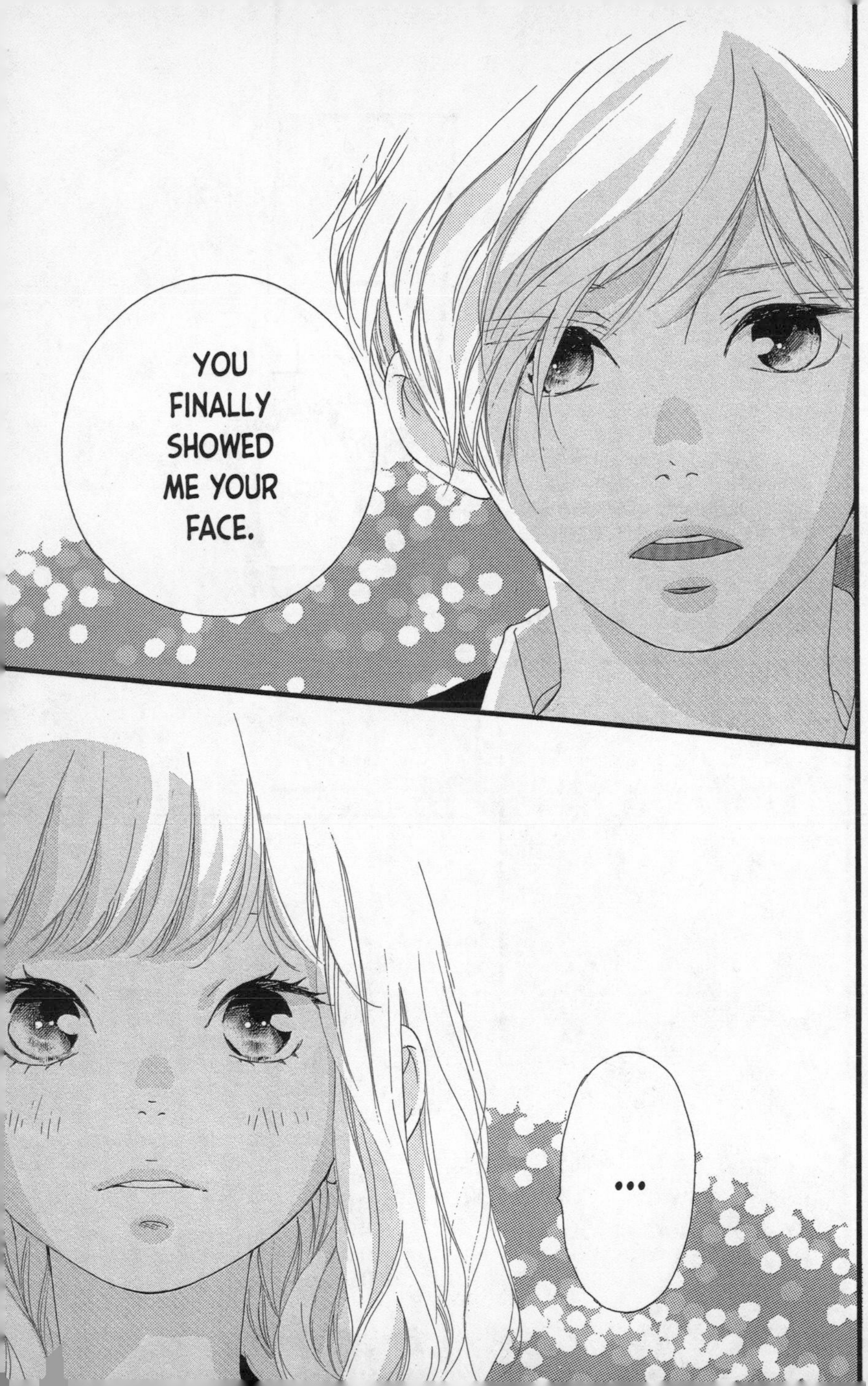
YOU FINALLY SHOWED ME YOUR FACE.
...

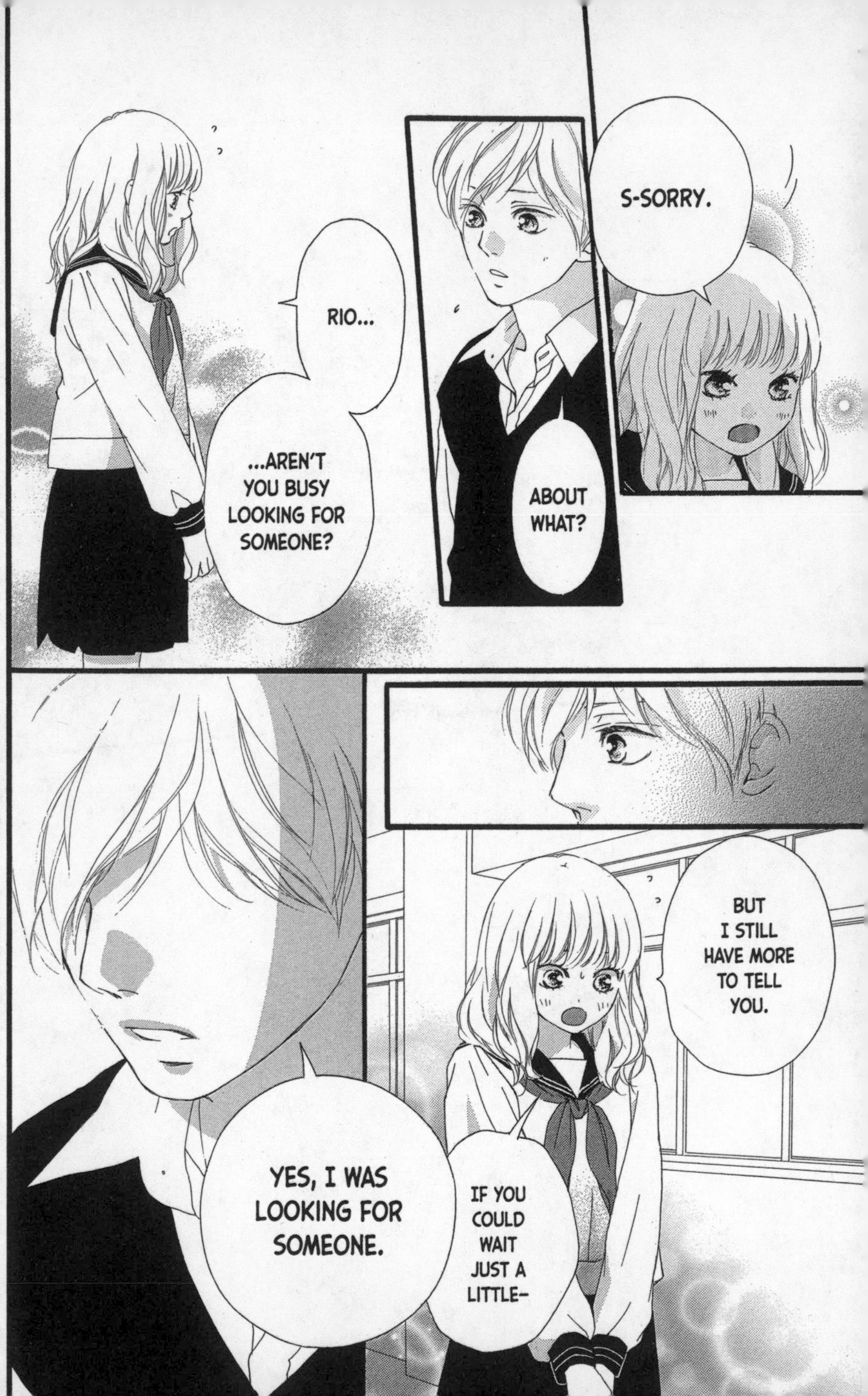
S-SORRY.
ABOUT WHAT?
RIO...
...AREN'T YOU BUSY LOOKING FOR SOMEONE?
BUT I STILL HAVE MORE TO TELL YOU.
IF YOU COULD WAIT JUST A LITTLE-
YES, I WAS LOOKING FOR SOMEONE.

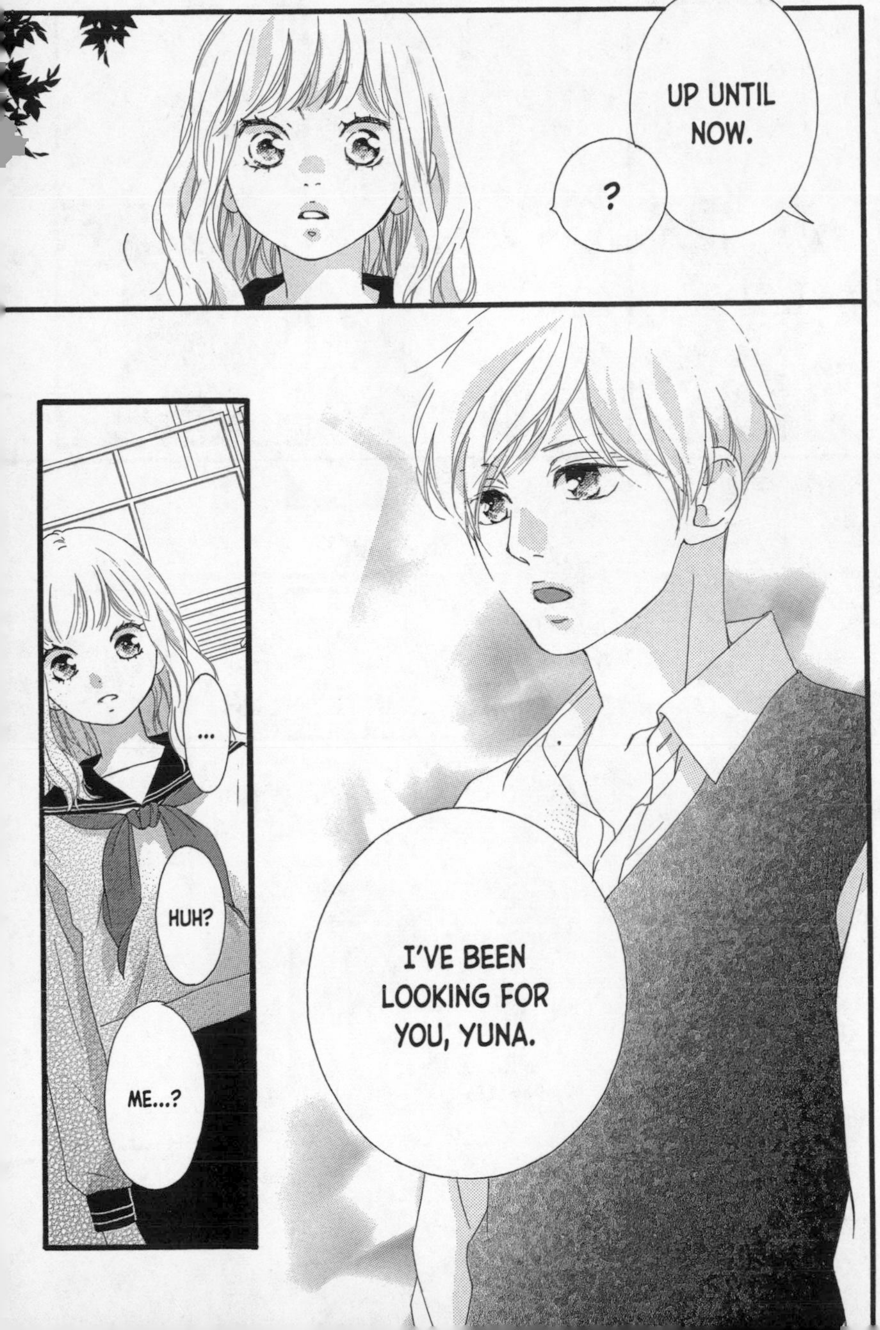
UP UNTIL NOW.
?
I'VE BEEN LOOKING FOR YOU, YUNA.
...
HUH?
ME...?

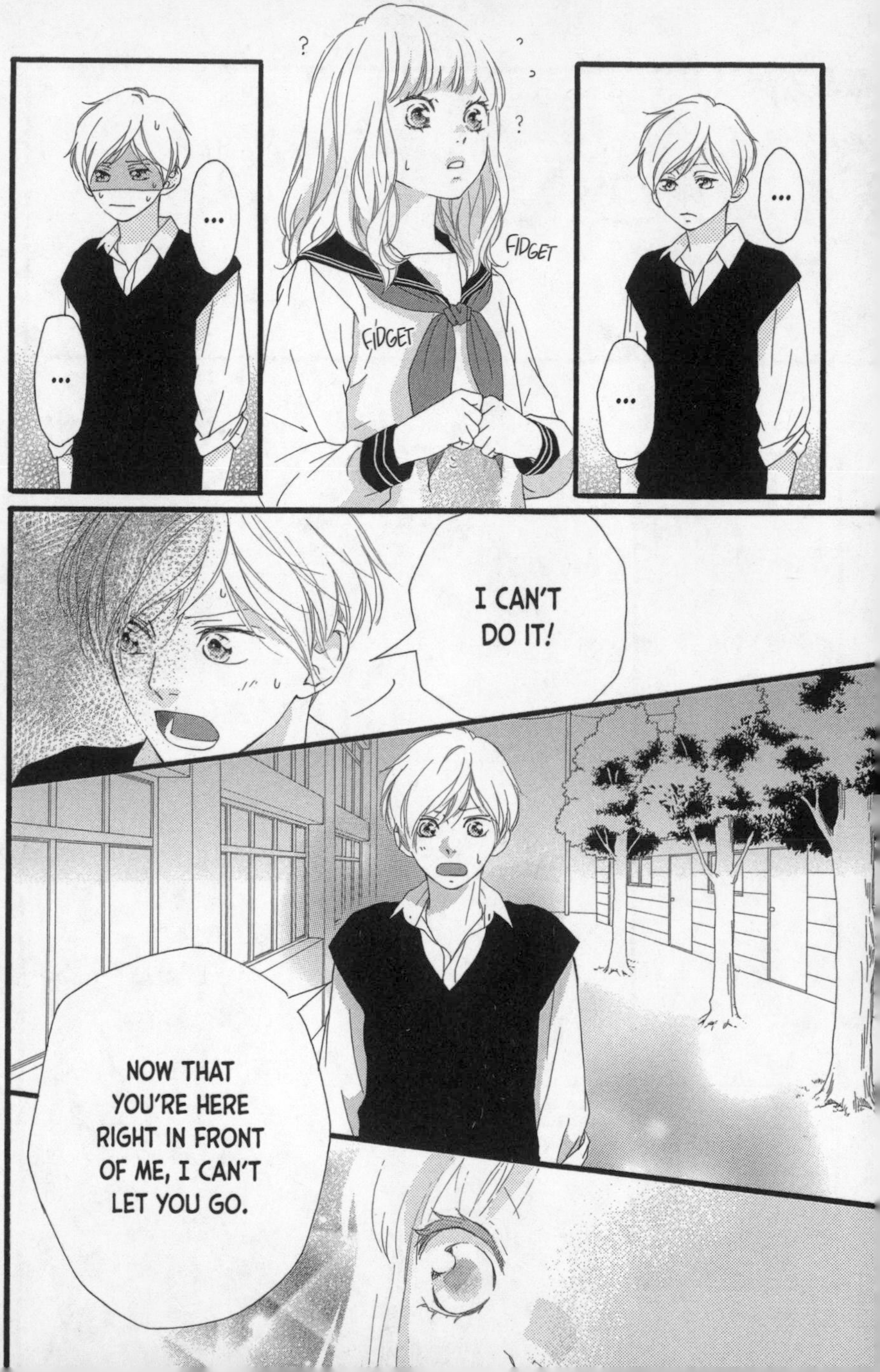
...
...
FIDGET
FIDGET
...
...
I CAN'T DO IT!
NOW THAT YOU'RE HERE RIGHT IN FRONT OF ME, I CAN'T LET YOU GO.

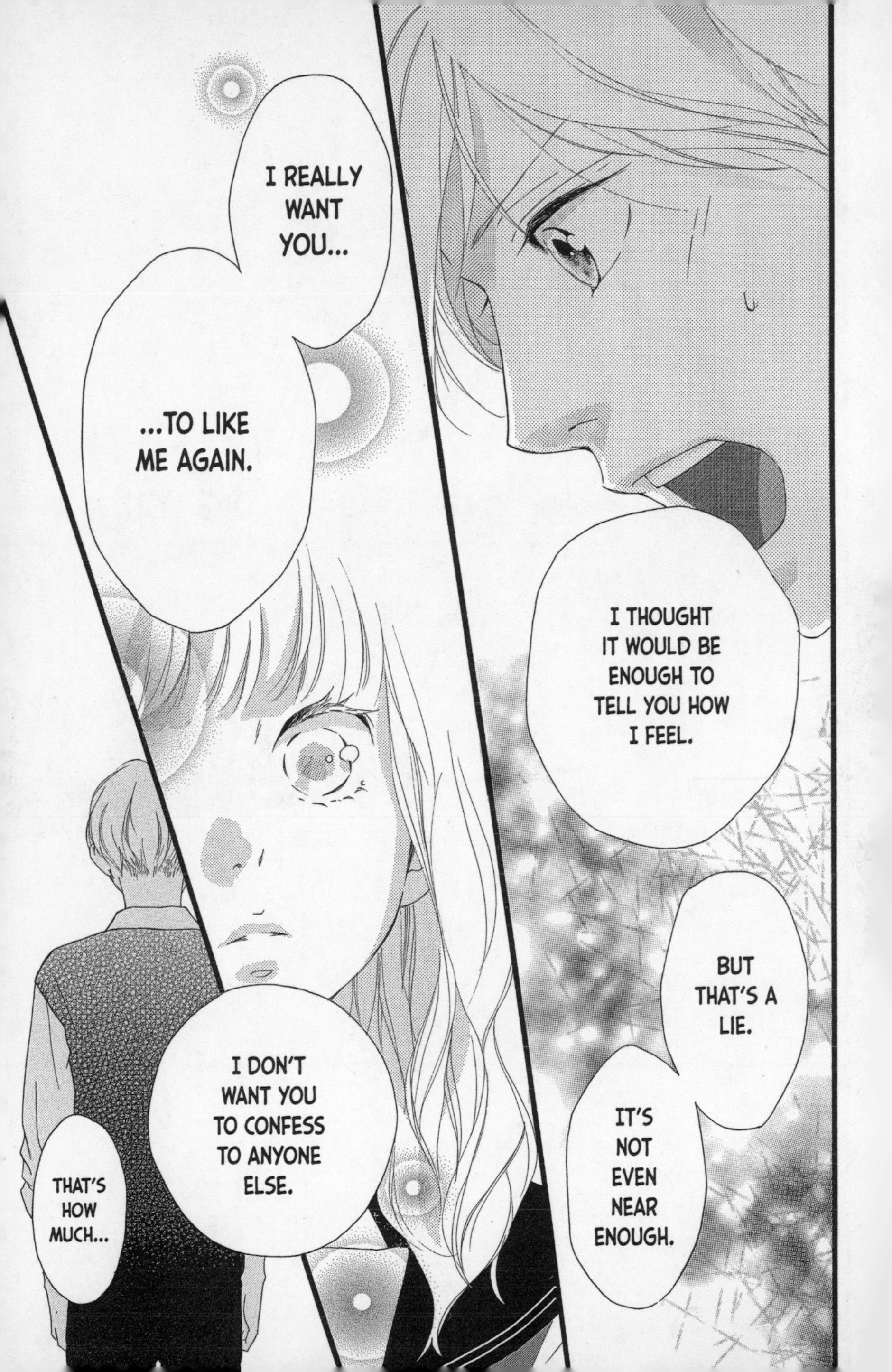
I THOUGHT IT WOULD BE ENOUGH TO TELL YOU HOW I FEEL.
BUT THAT'S A LIE.
IT'S NOT EVEN NEAR ENOUGH.
I REALLY WANT YOU...
...TO LIKE ME AGAIN.
I DON'T WANT YOU TO CONFESS TO ANYONE ELSE.
THAT'S HOW MUCH...

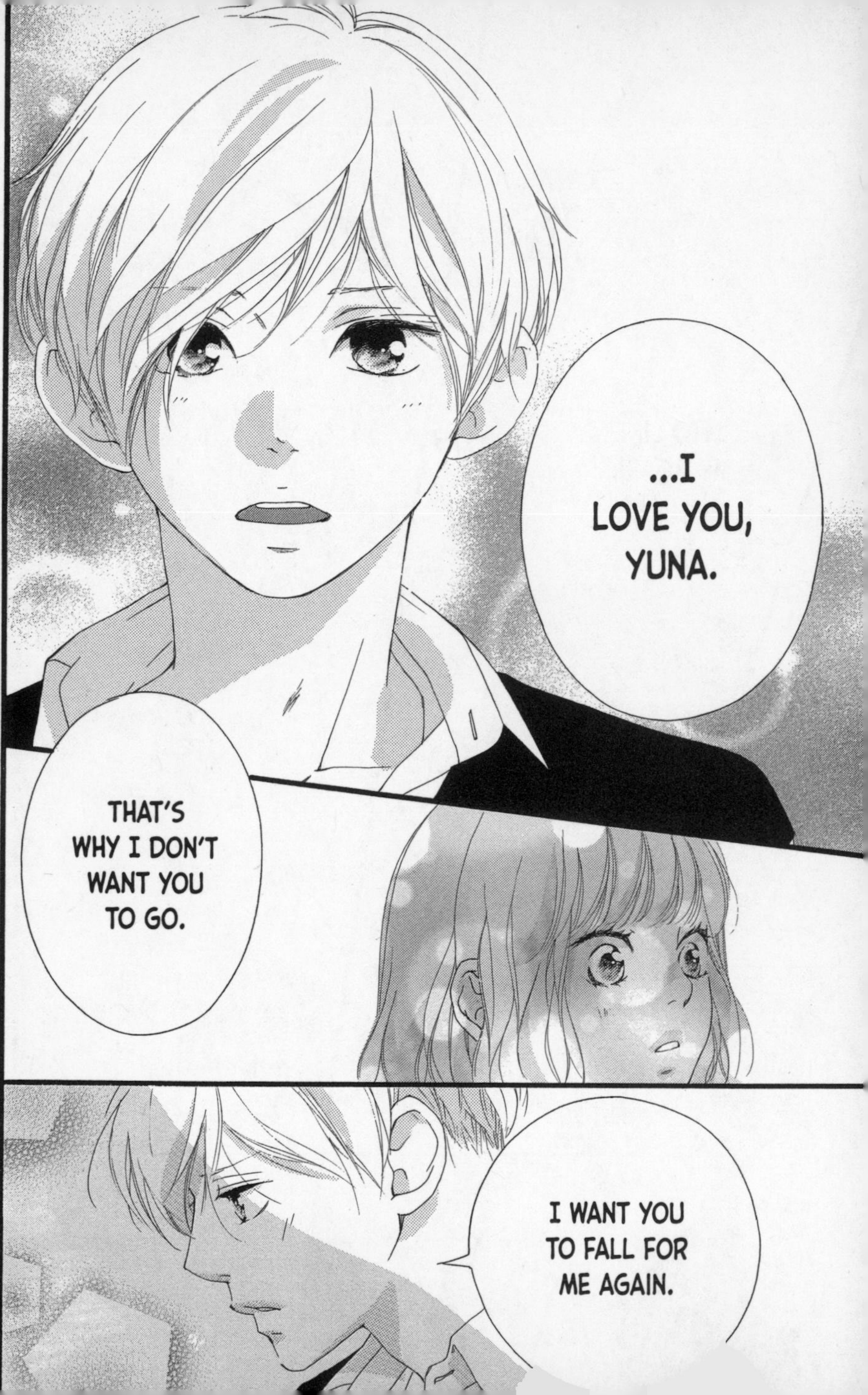
...I LOVE YOU, YUNA.
THAT'S WHY I DON'T WANT YOU TO GO.
I WANT YOU TO FALL FOR ME AGAIN.

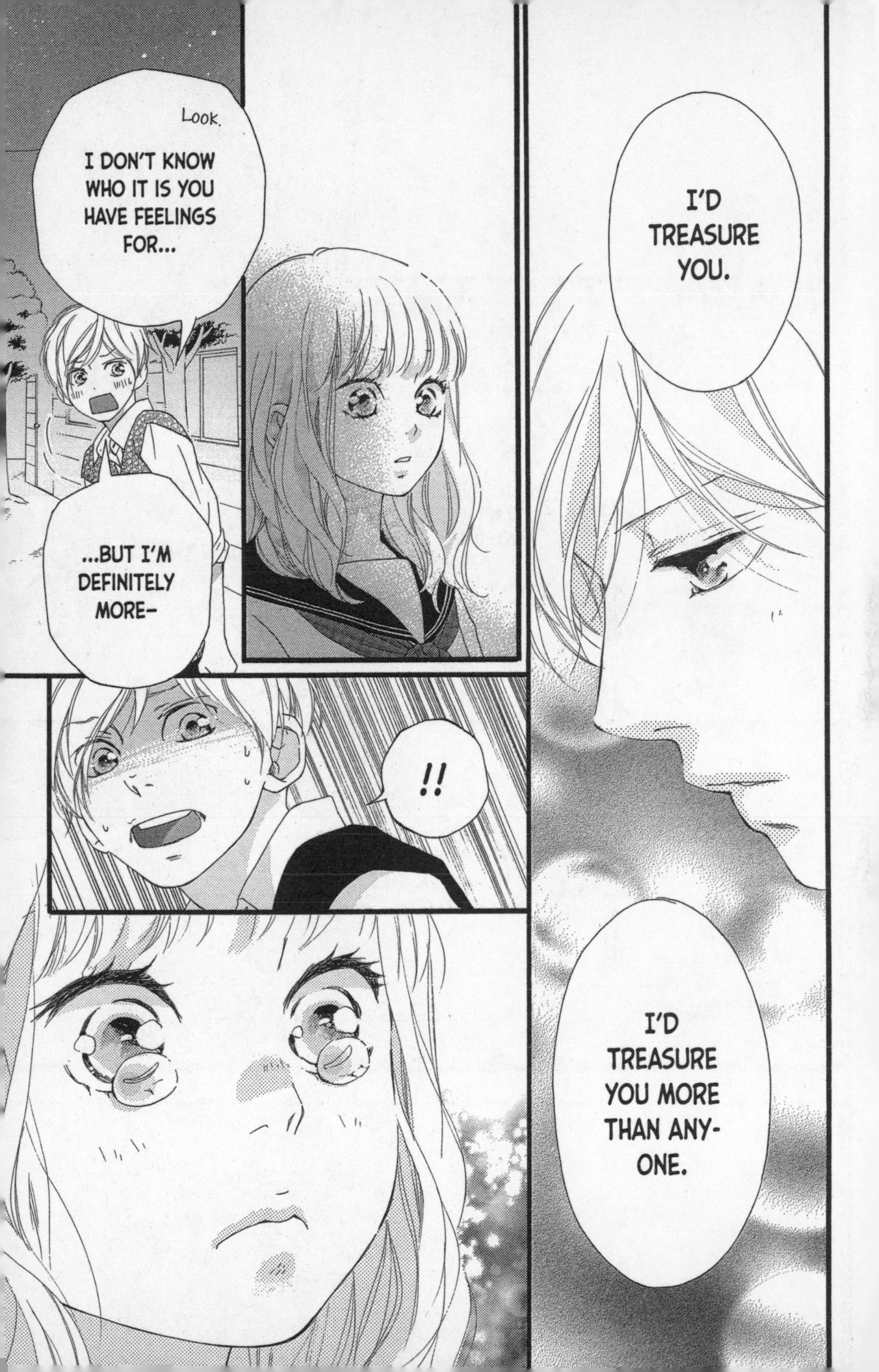
I'D TREASURE YOU.
I'D TREASURE YOU MORE THAN ANY-ONE.
Look.
I DON'T KNOW WHO IT IS YOU HAVE FEELINGS FOR...
...BUT I'M DEFINITELY MORE-
!!

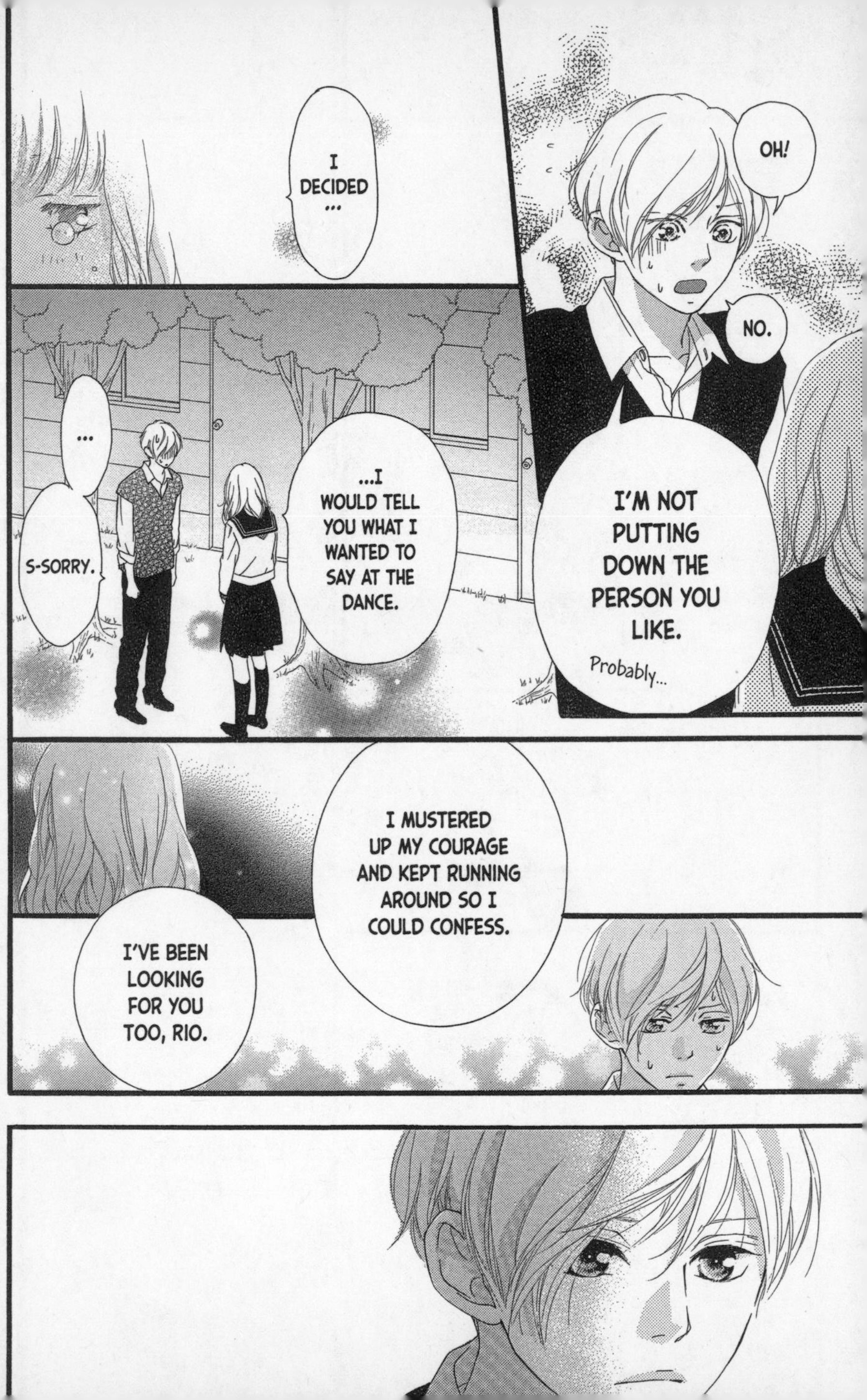
OH!
NO.
I'M NOT PUTTING DOWN THE PERSON YOU LIKE.
Probably...
I DECIDED ...
...I WOULD TELL YOU WHAT I WANTED TO SAY AT THE DANCE.
...
S-SORRY.
I MUSTERED UP MY COURAGE AND KEPT RUNNING AROUND SO I COULD CONFESS.
I'VE BEEN LOOKING FOR YOU TOO, RIO.

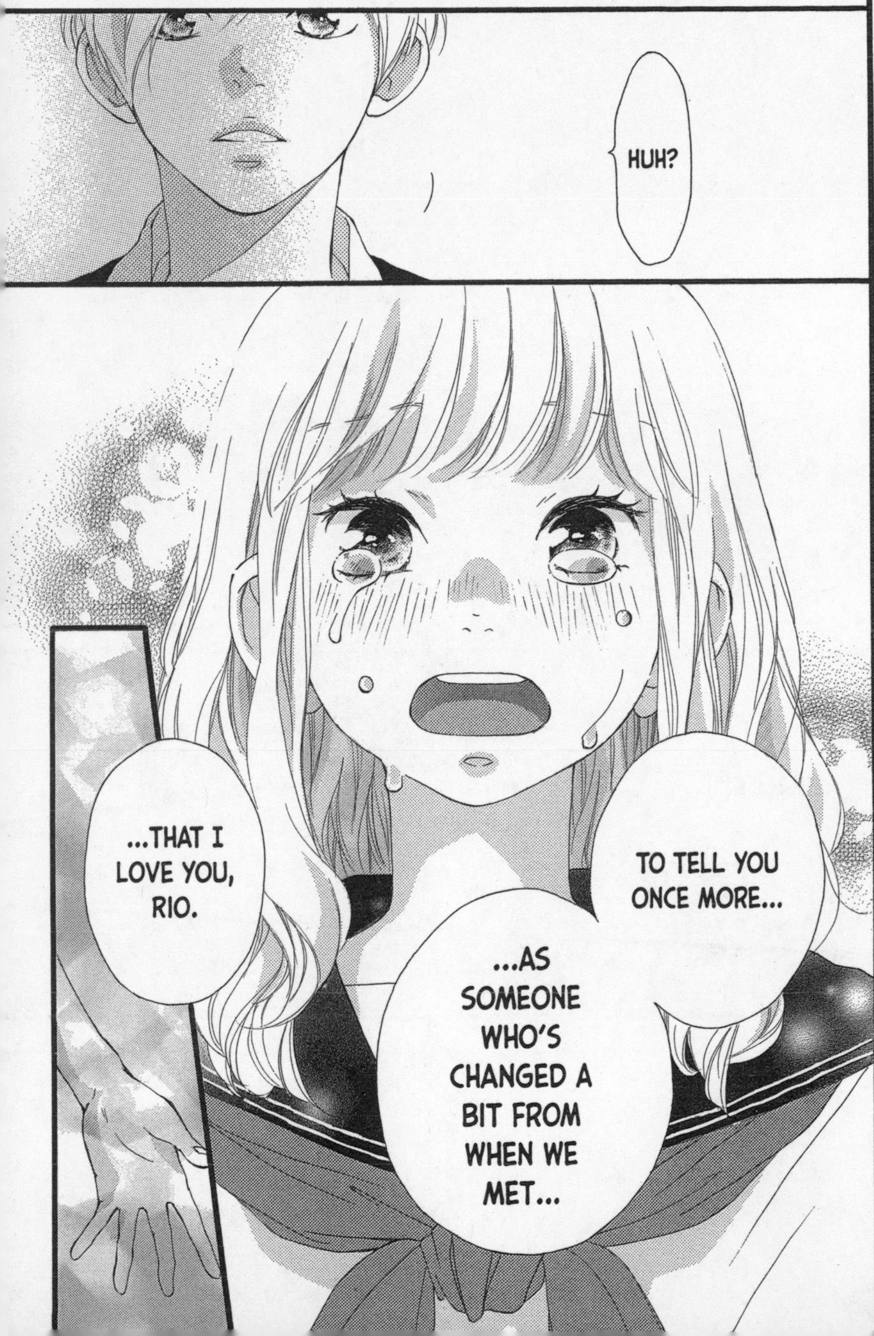
HUH?
TO TELL YOU ONCE MORE...
...AS SOMEONE WHO'S CHANGED A BIT FROM WHEN WE MET...
...THAT I LOVE YOU, RIO.

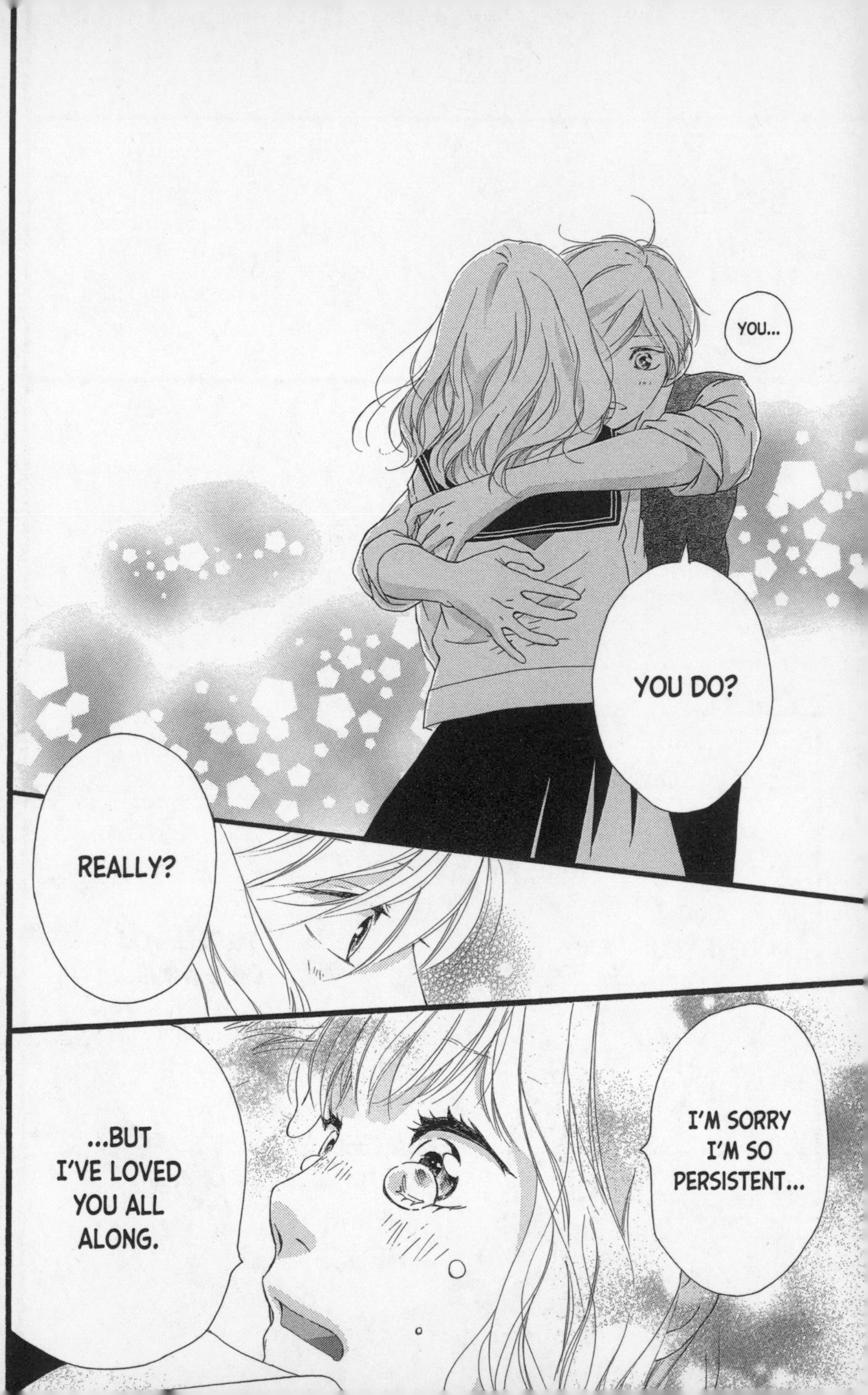
YOU...
YOU DO?
REALLY?
I'M SORRY I'M SO PERSISTENT...
...BUT I'VE LOVED YOU ALL ALONG.

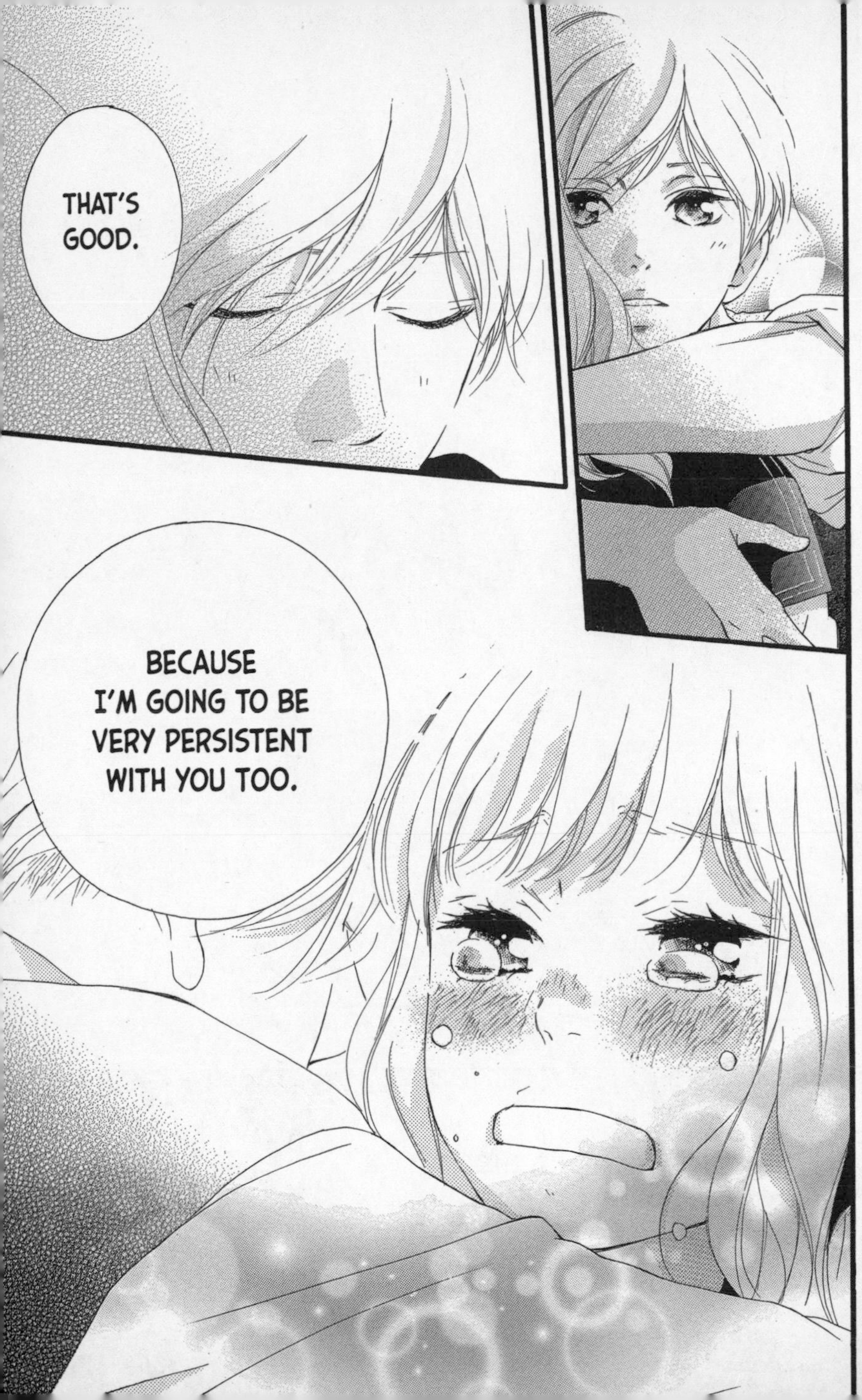
THAT'S GOOD.
BECAUSE I'M GOING TO BE VERY PERSISTENT WITH YOU TOO.

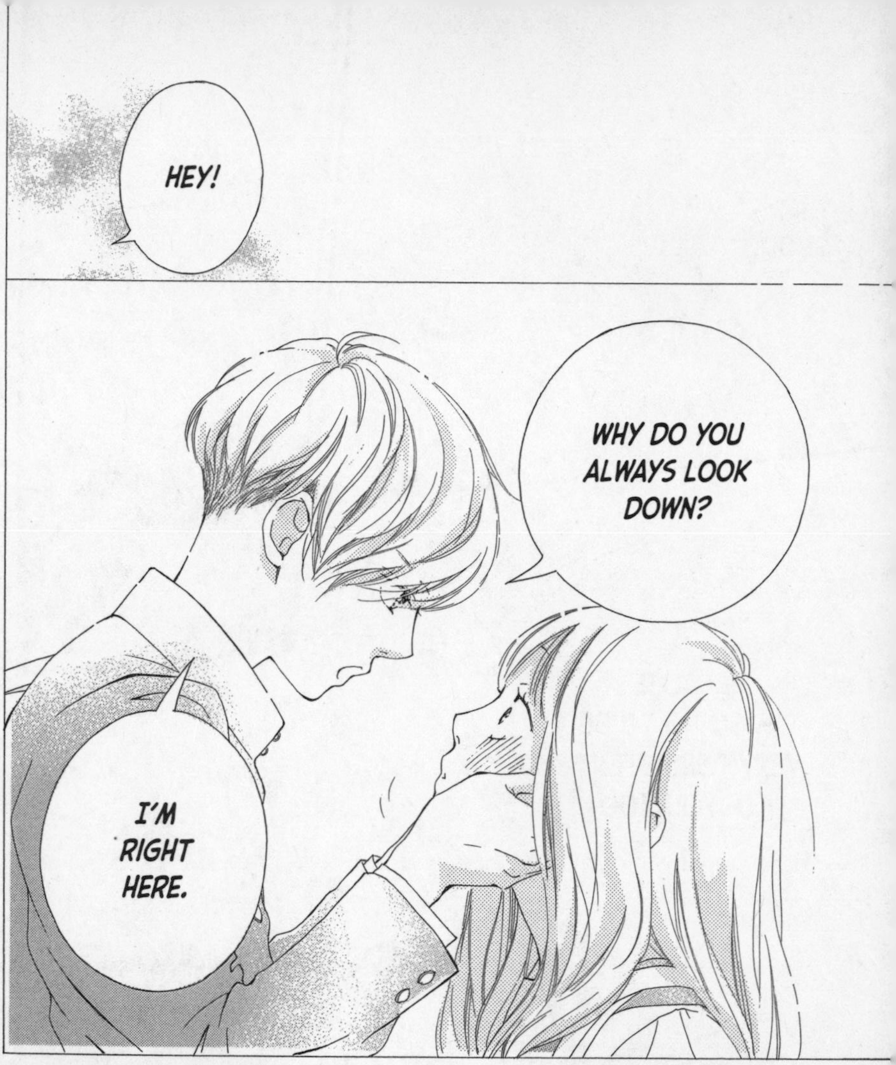
HEY!
WHY DO YOU ALWAYS LOOK DOWN?
I'M RIGHT HERE.

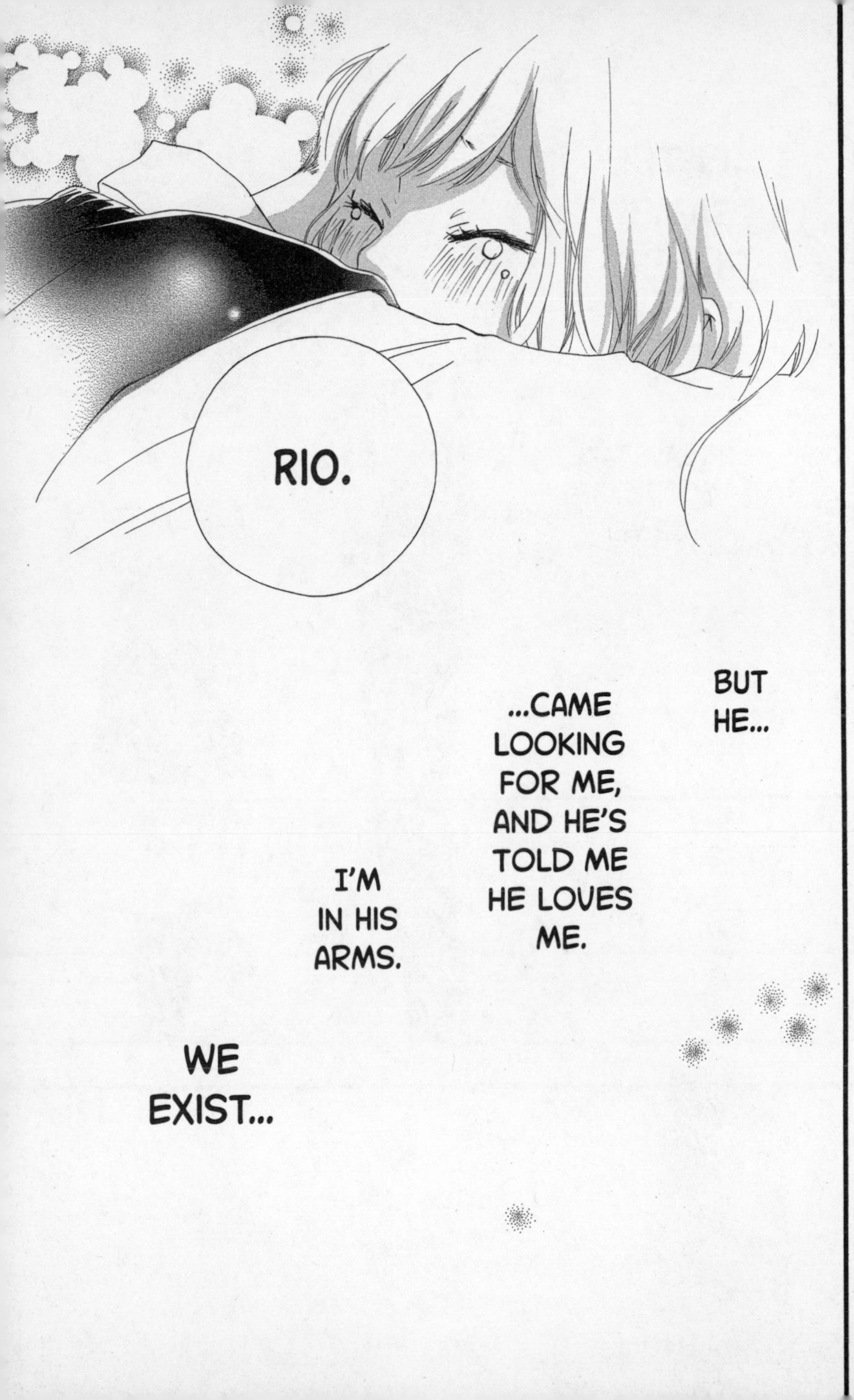
RIO.
BUT HE...
...CAME LOOKING FOR ME, AND HE'S TOLD ME HE LOVES ME.
I'M IN HIS ARMS.
WE EXIST...

...IN THE SAME PLACE.

PLEASE TAKE GOOD CARE OF ME.

DITTO...

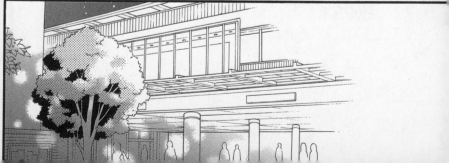

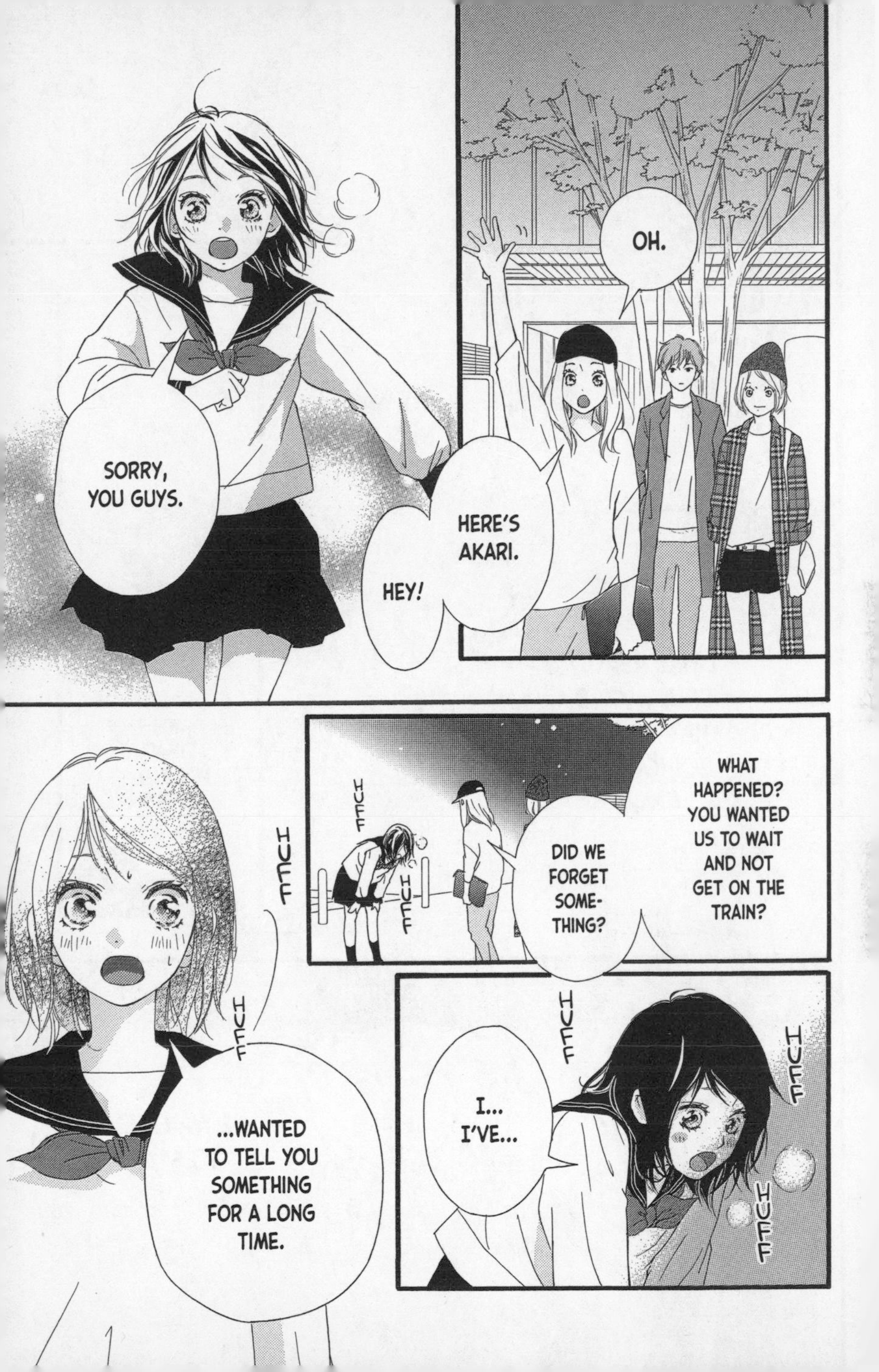
OH.
HERE'S AKARI.
HEY!
SORRY, YOU GUYS.
WHAT HAPPENED? YOU WANTED US TO WAIT AND NOT GET ON THE TRAIN?
DID WE FORGET SOME-THING?
HUFF
HUFF
HUFF
HUFF
I... I'VE...
HUFF
HUFF
...WANTED TO TELL YOU SOMETHING FOR A LONG TIME.

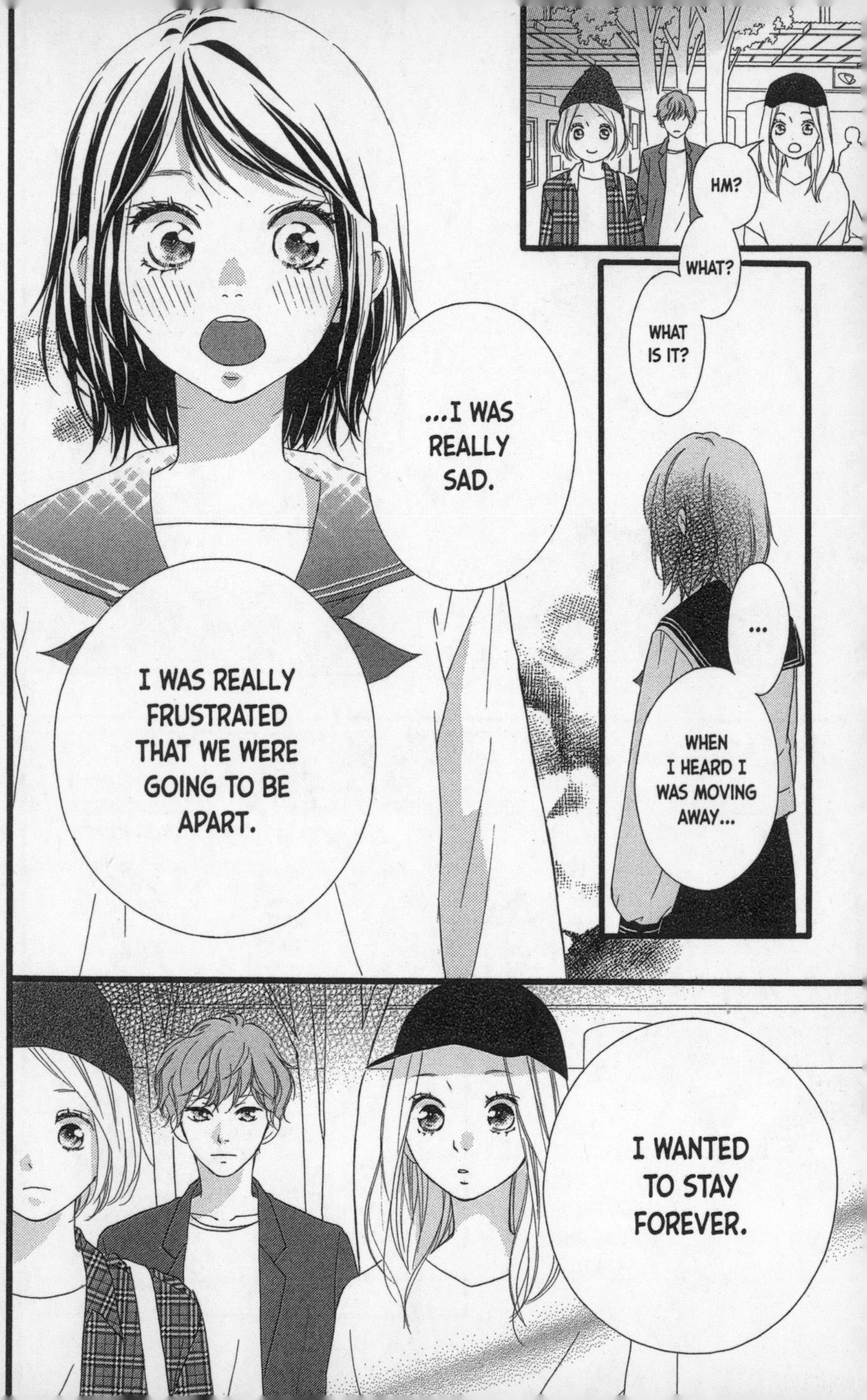
HM?
WHAT?
WHAT IS IT?
...
WHEN I HEARD I WAS MOVING AWAY...
...I WAS REALLY SAD.
I WAS REALLY FRUSTRATED THAT WE WERE GOING TO BE APART.
I WANTED TO STAY FOREVER.

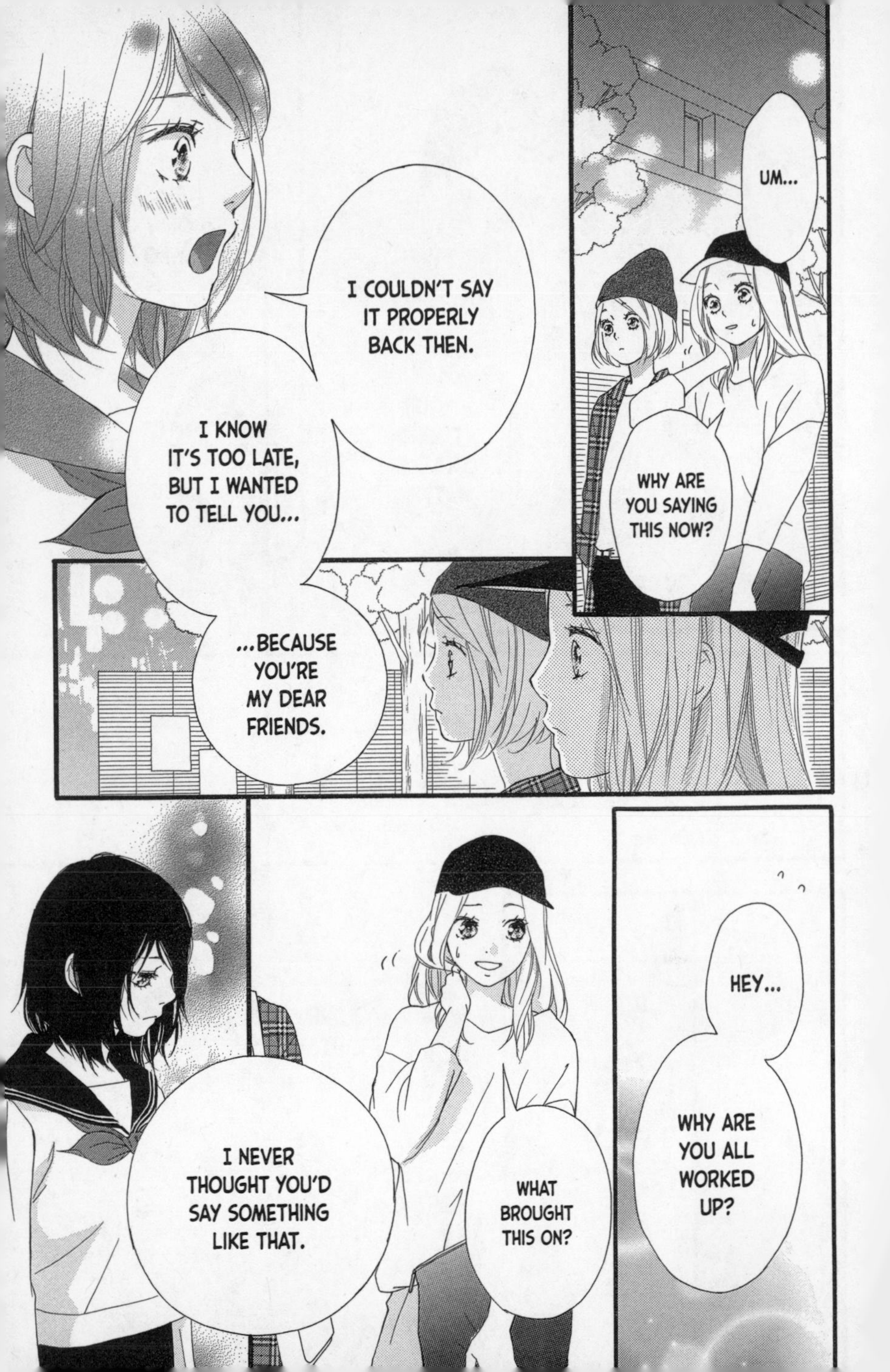
UM...
WHY ARE YOU SAYING THIS NOW?
I COULDN'T SAY IT PROPERLY BACK THEN.
I KNOW IT'S TOO LATE, BUT I WANTED TO TELL YOU...
...BECAUSE YOU'RE MY DEAR FRIENDS.
HEY...
WHY ARE YOU ALL WORKED UP?
WHAT BROUGHT THIS ON?
I NEVER THOUGHT YOU'D SAY SOMETHING LIKE THAT.

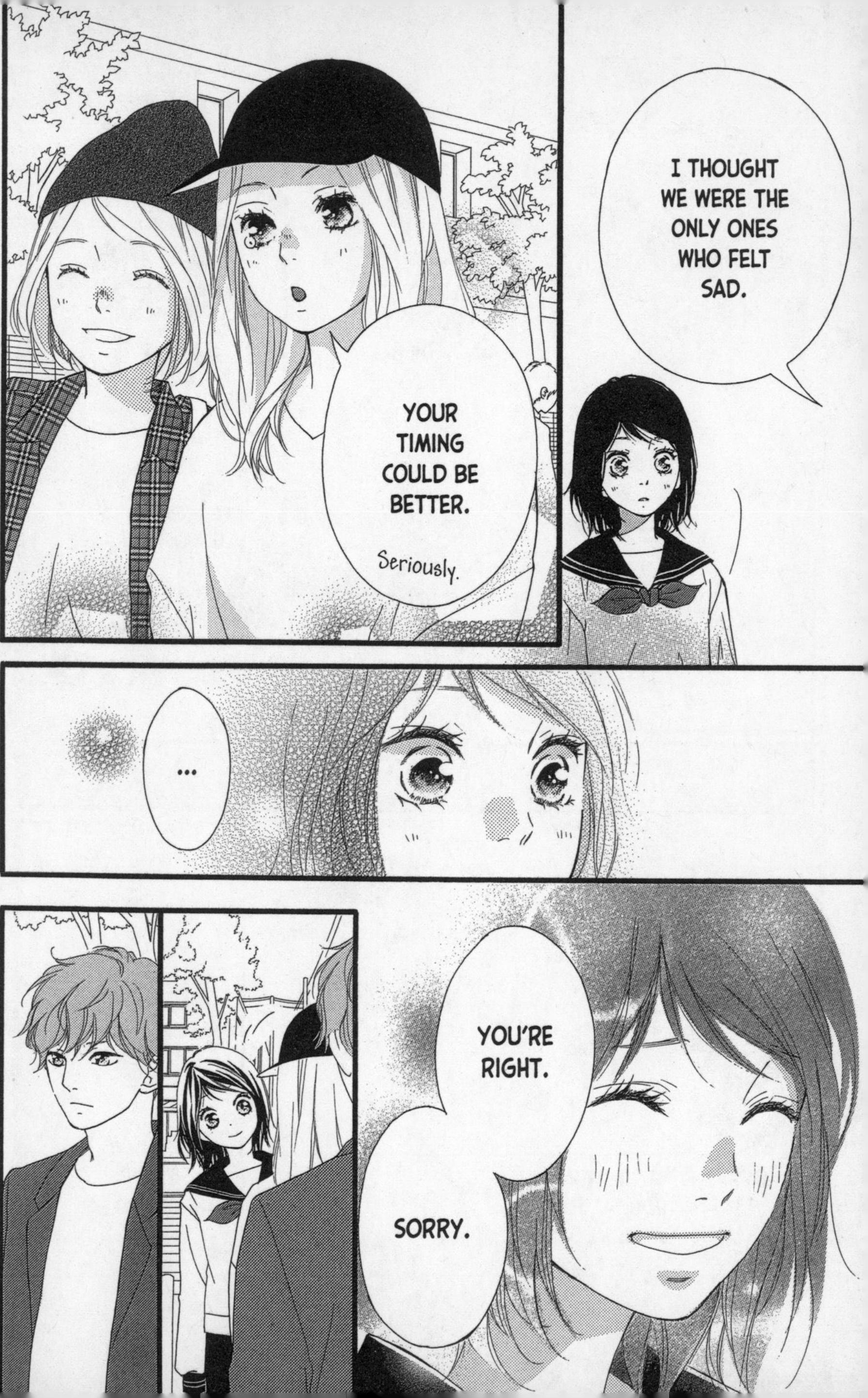
I THOUGHT WE WERE THE ONLY ONES WHO FELT SAD.
YOUR TIMING COULD BE BETTER.
Seriously.
...
YOU'RE RIGHT.
SORRY.

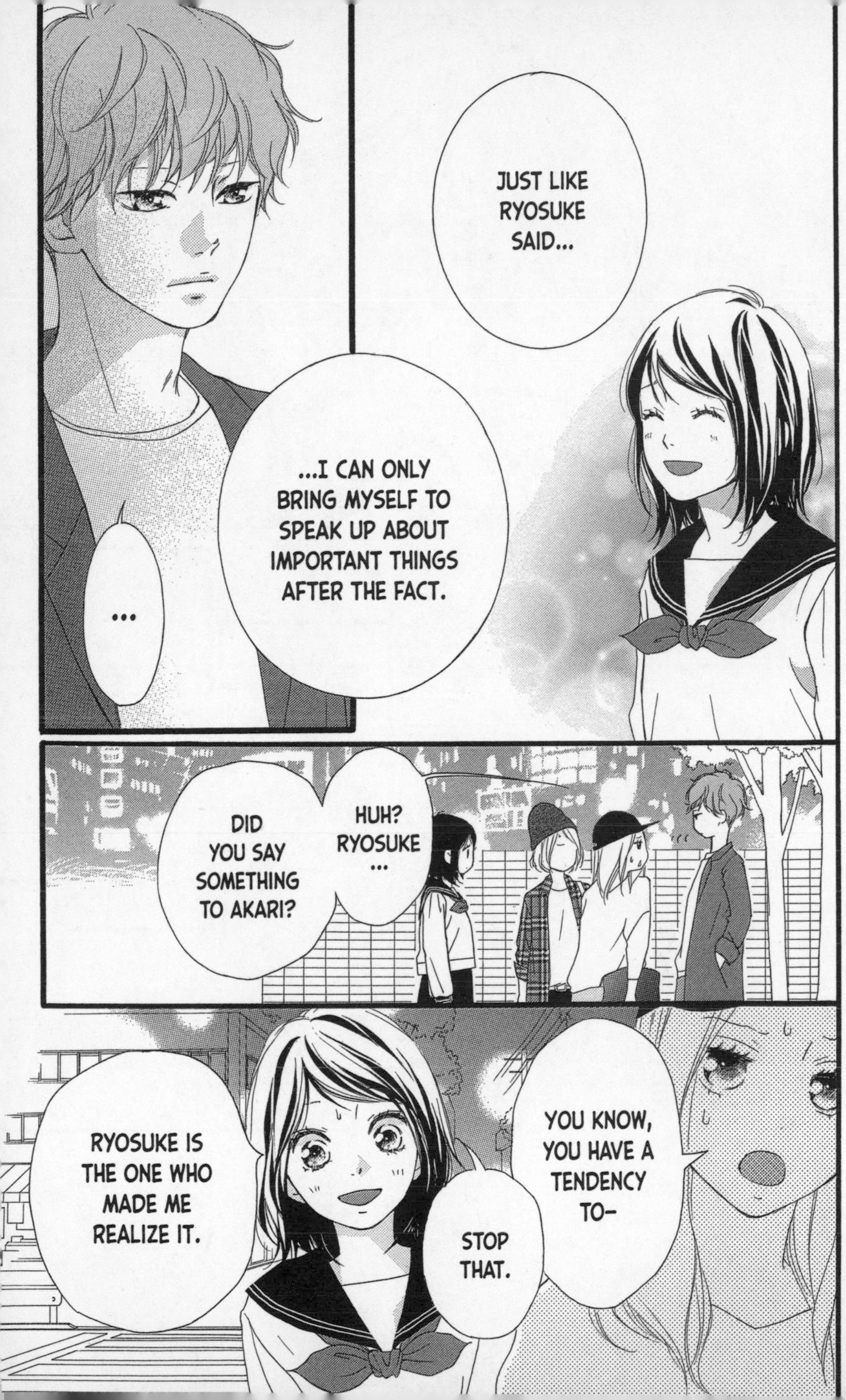
JUST LIKE RYOSUKE SAID...
...I CAN ONLY BRING MYSELF TO SPEAK UP ABOUT IMPORTANT THINGS AFTER THE FACT.
...
HUH? RYOSUKE ...
DID YOU SAY SOMETHING TO AKARI?
YOU KNOW, YOU HAVE A TENDENCY TO–
STOP THAT.
RYOSUKE IS THE ONE WHO MADE ME REALIZE IT.

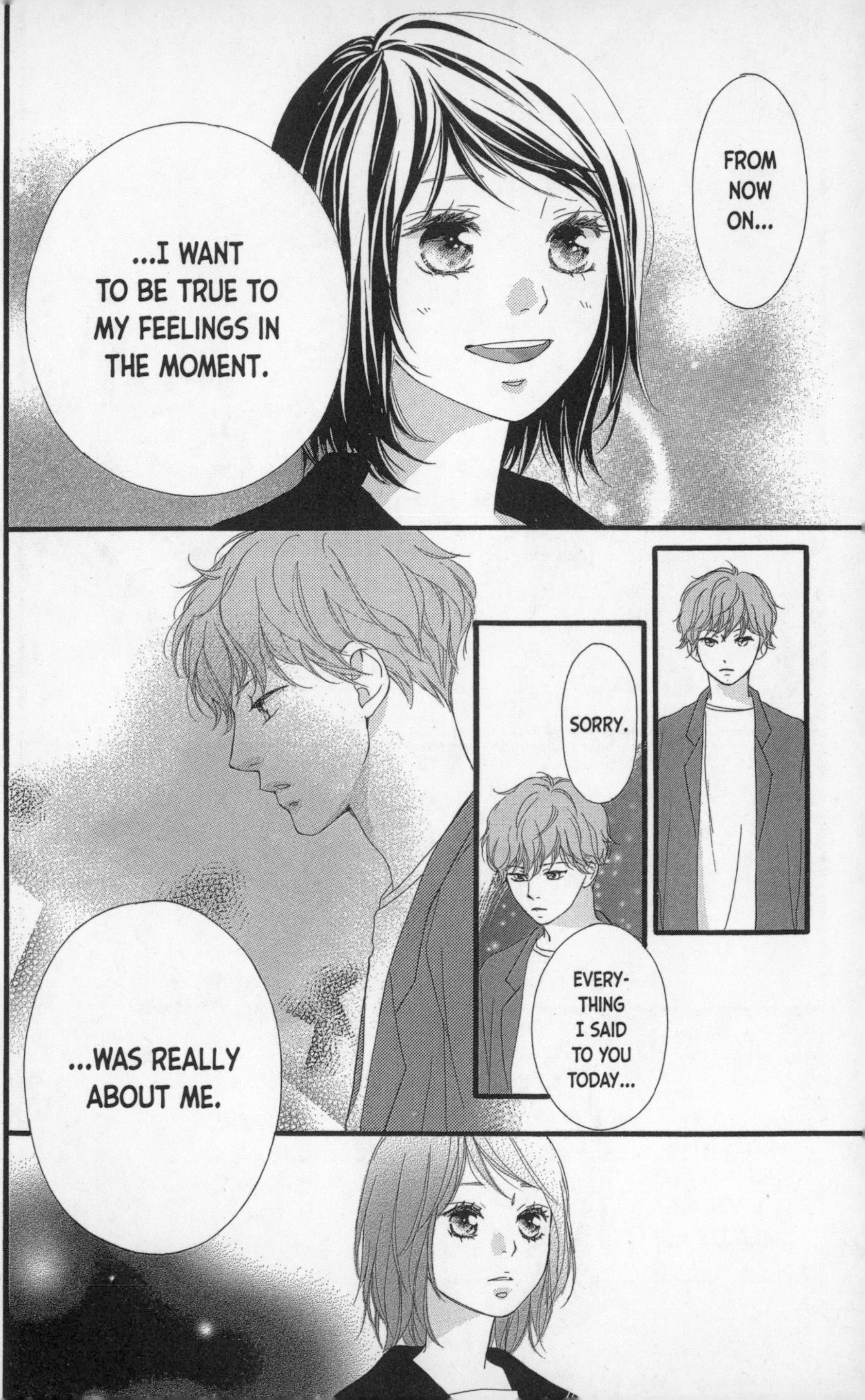
FROM NOW ON...
...I WANT TO BE TRUE TO MY FEELINGS IN THE MOMENT.
SORRY.
EVERY-THING I SAID TO YOU TODAY...
...WAS REALLY ABOUT ME.

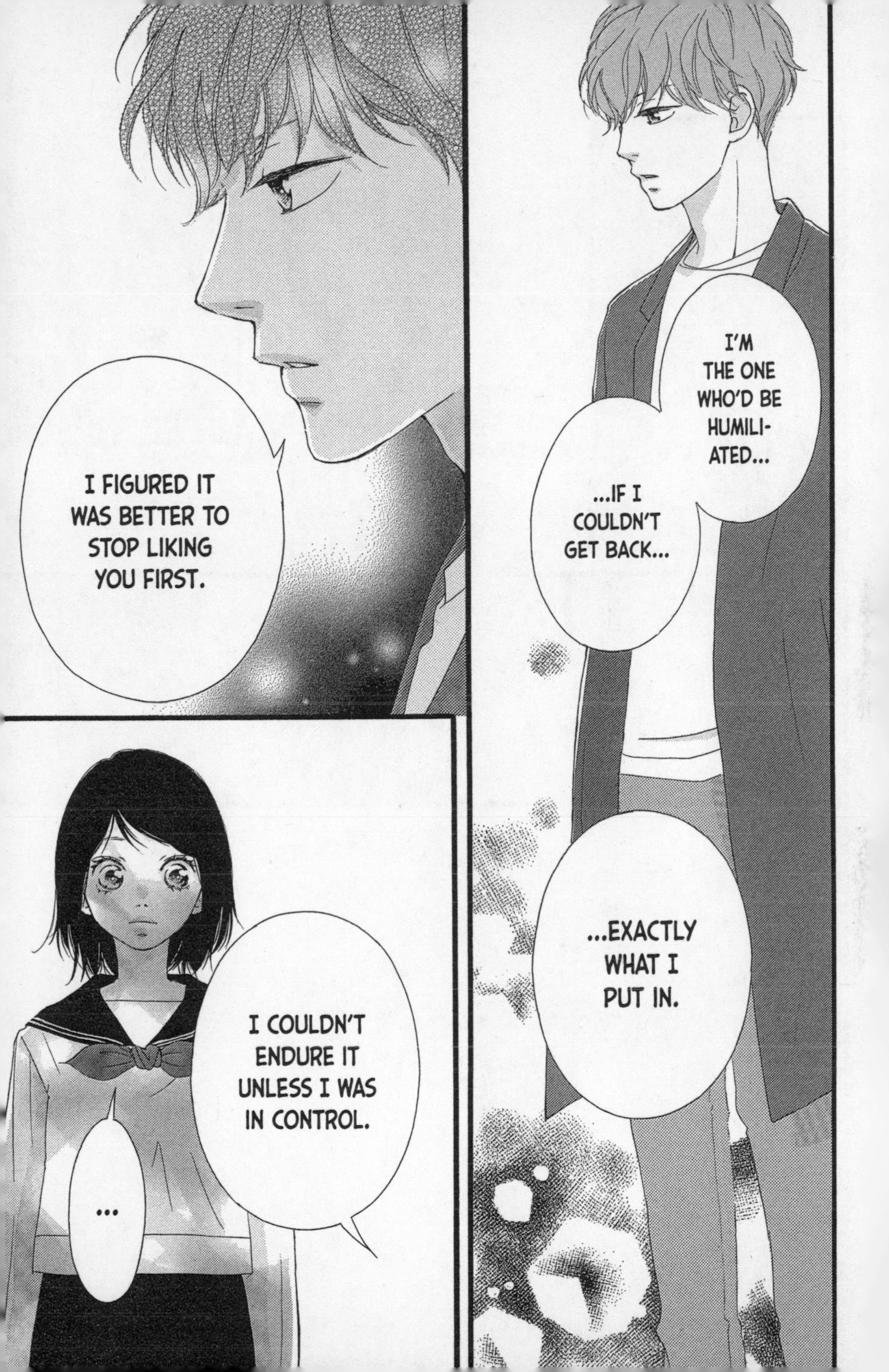
I'M THE ONE WHO'D BE HUMILI- ATED...
...IF I COULDN'T GET BACK...
...EXACTLY WHAT I PUT IN.
I FIGURED IT WAS BETTER TO STOP LIKING YOU FIRST.
I COULDN'T ENDURE IT UNLESS I WAS IN CONTROL.
...

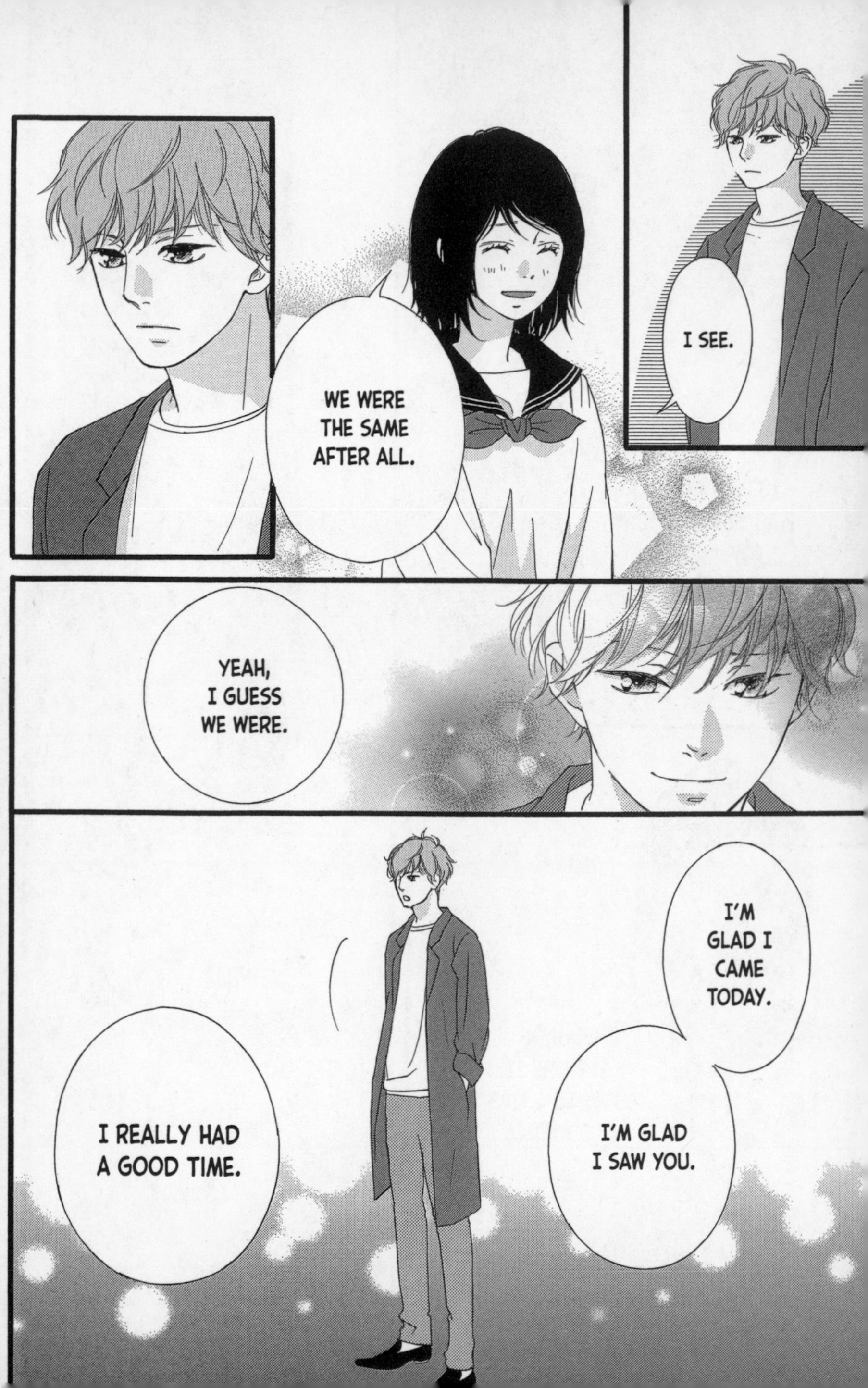
I SEE.
WE WERE THE SAME AFTER ALL.
YEAH, I GUESS WE WERE.
I'M GLAD I CAME TODAY.
I'M GLAD I SAW YOU.
I REALLY HAD A GOOD TIME.

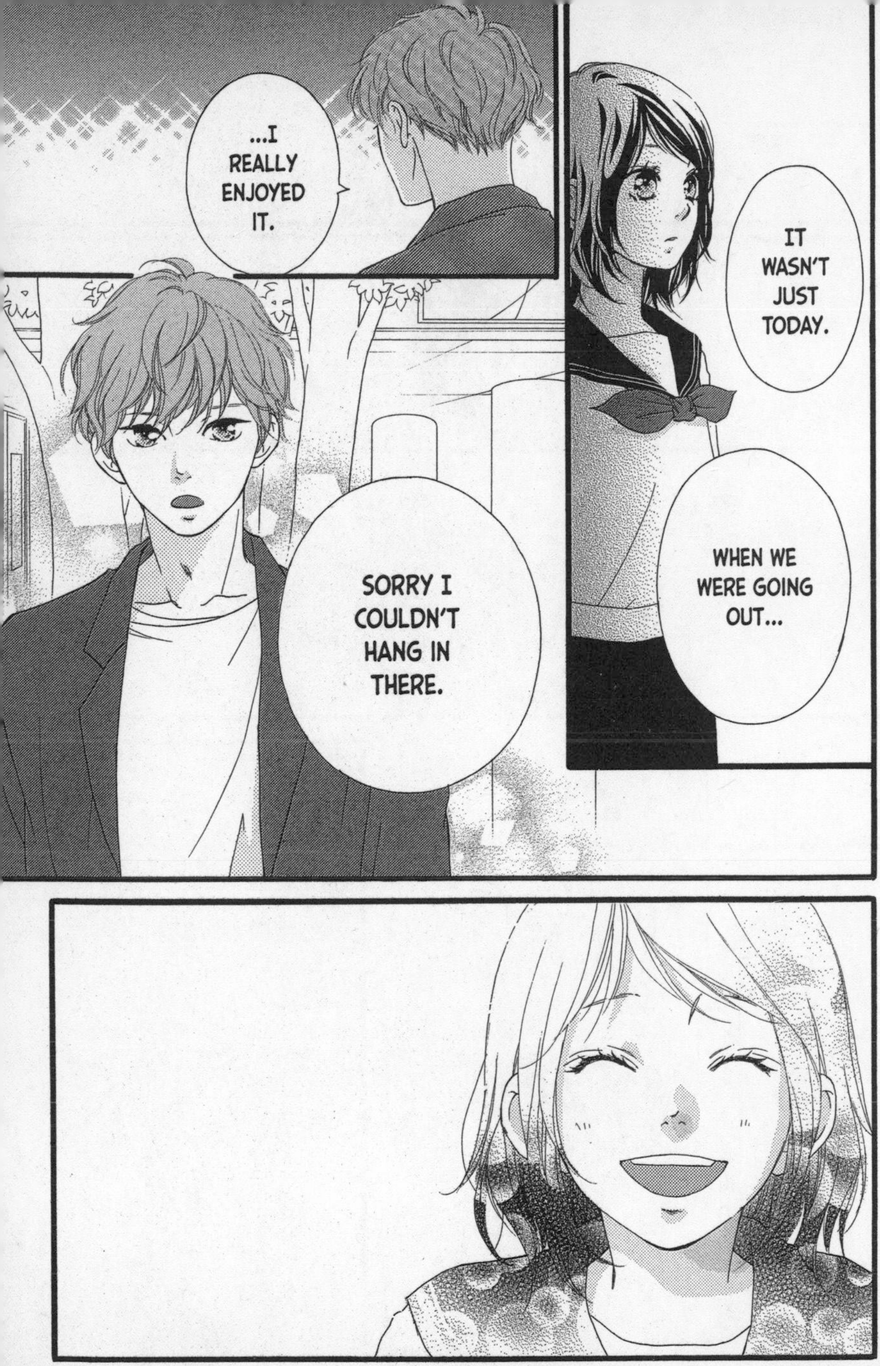
IT WASN'T JUST TODAY.
WHEN WE WERE GOING OUT...
...I REALLY ENJOYED IT.
SORRY I COULDN'T HANG IN THERE.

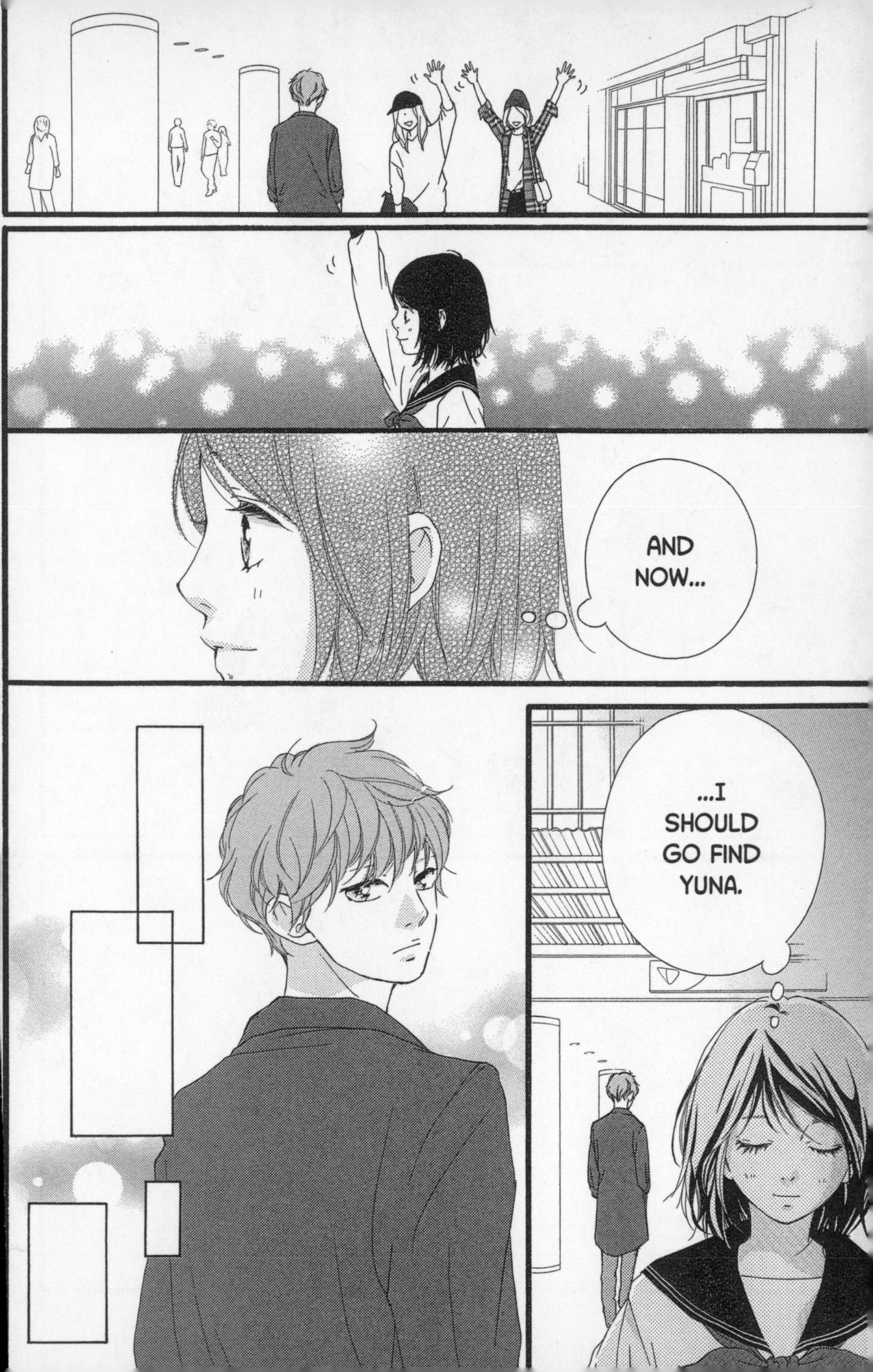
AND NOW...
...I SHOULD GO FIND YUNA.

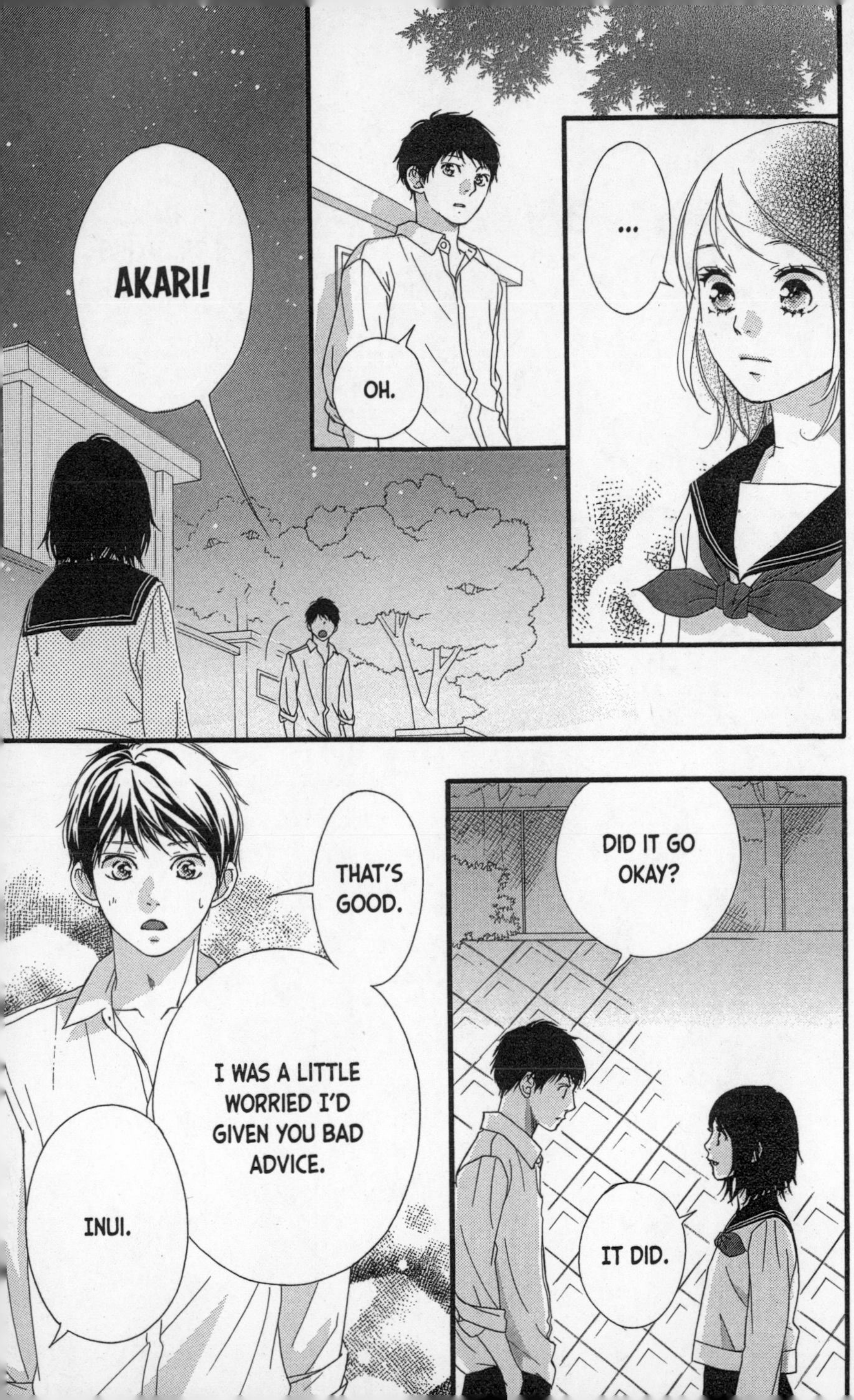
...
OH.
AKARI!
DID IT GO OKAY?
IT DID.
THAT'S GOOD.
I WAS A LITTLE WORRIED I'D GIVEN YOU BAD ADVICE.
INUI.

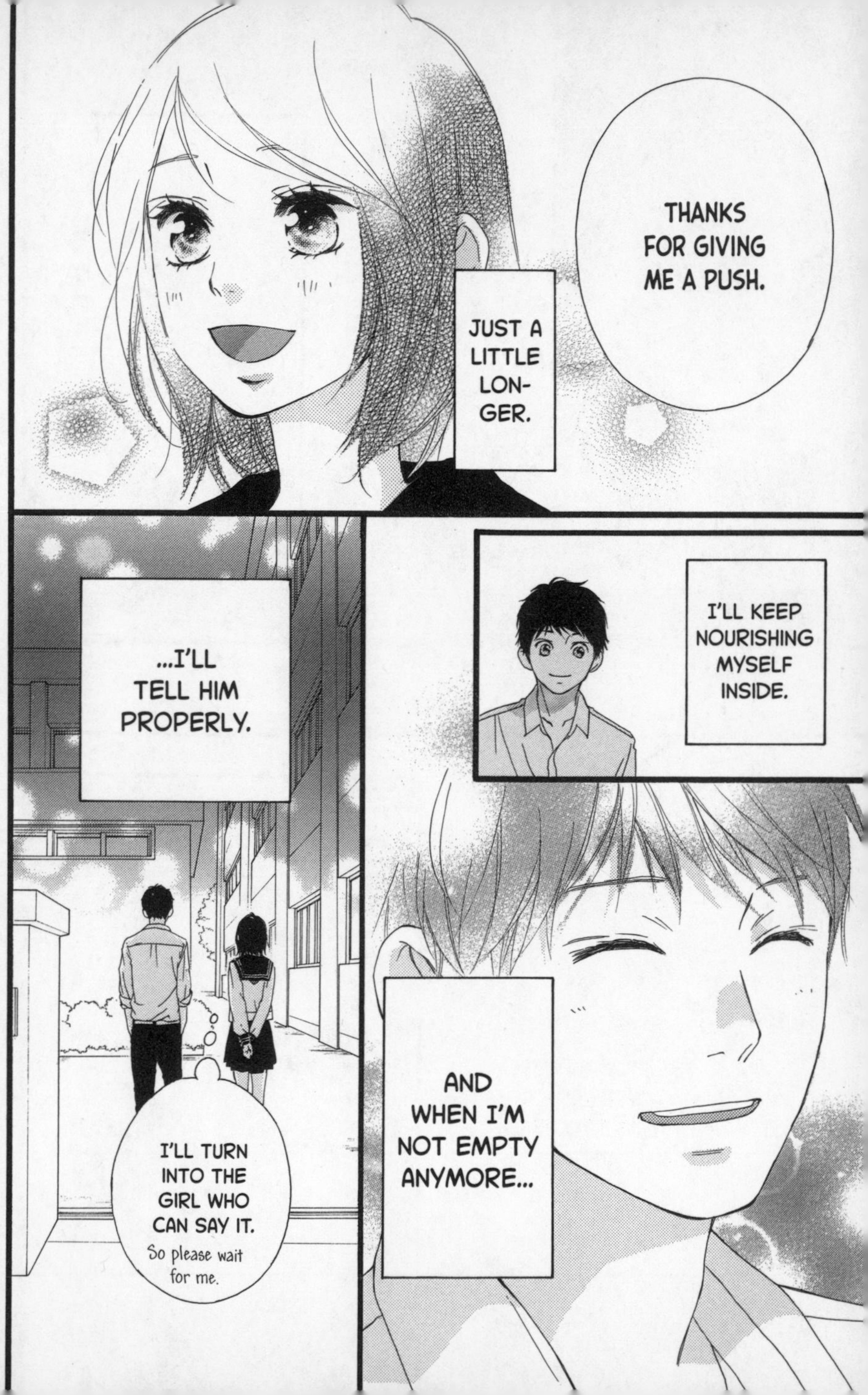
THANKS FOR GIVING ME A PUSH.
JUST A LITTLE LON- GER.
I'LL KEEP NOURISHING MYSELF INSIDE.
AND WHEN I'M NOT EMPTY ANYMORE...
...I'LL TELL HIM PROPERLY.
I'LL TURN INTO THE GIRL WHO CAN SAY IT.
So please wait for me.

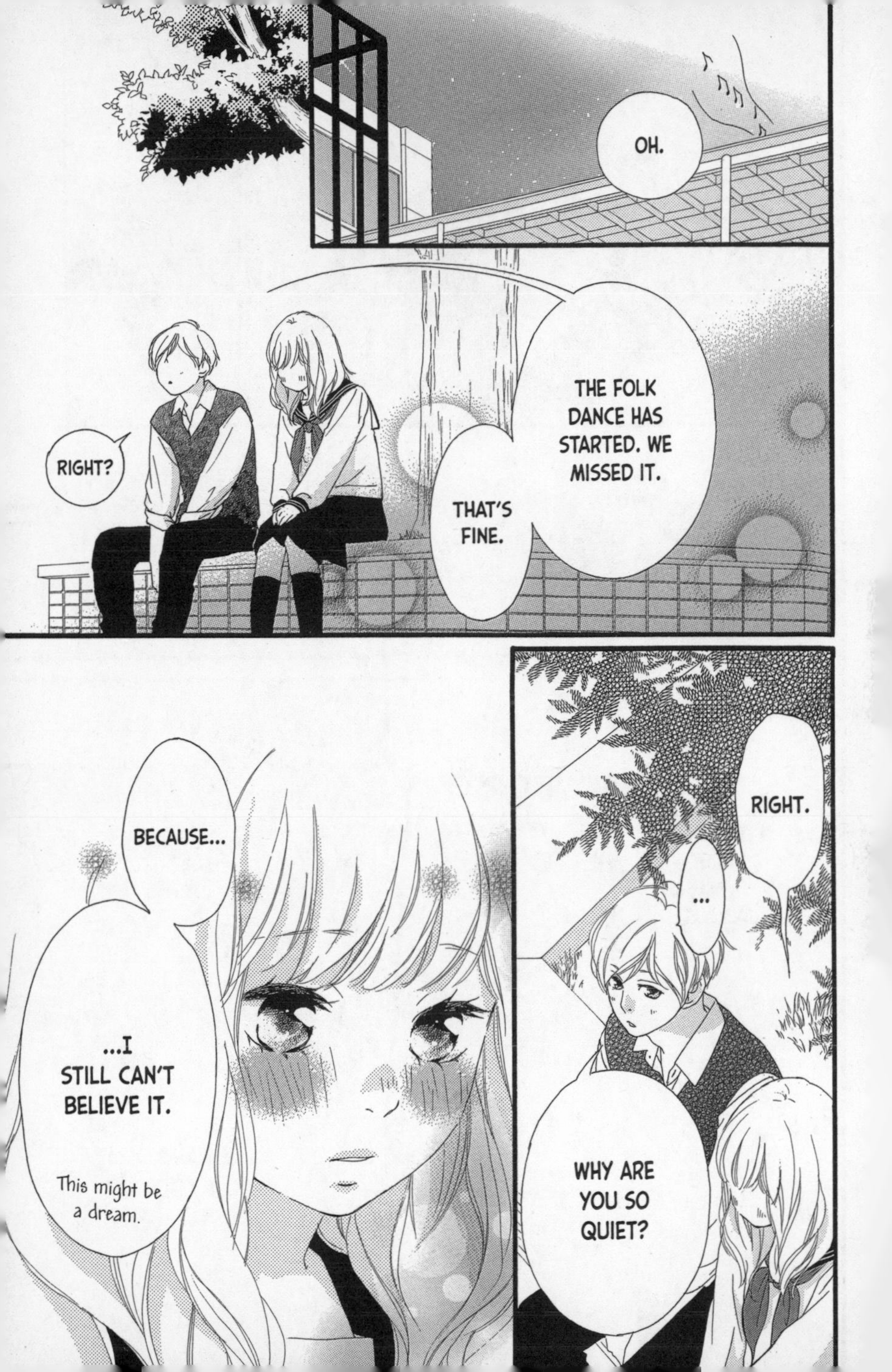
OH.
THE FOLK DANCE HAS STARTED. WE MISSED IT.
THAT'S FINE.
RIGHT?
RIGHT.
...
WHY ARE YOU SO QUIET?
BECAUSE...
...I STILL CAN'T BELIEVE IT.
This might be a dream.

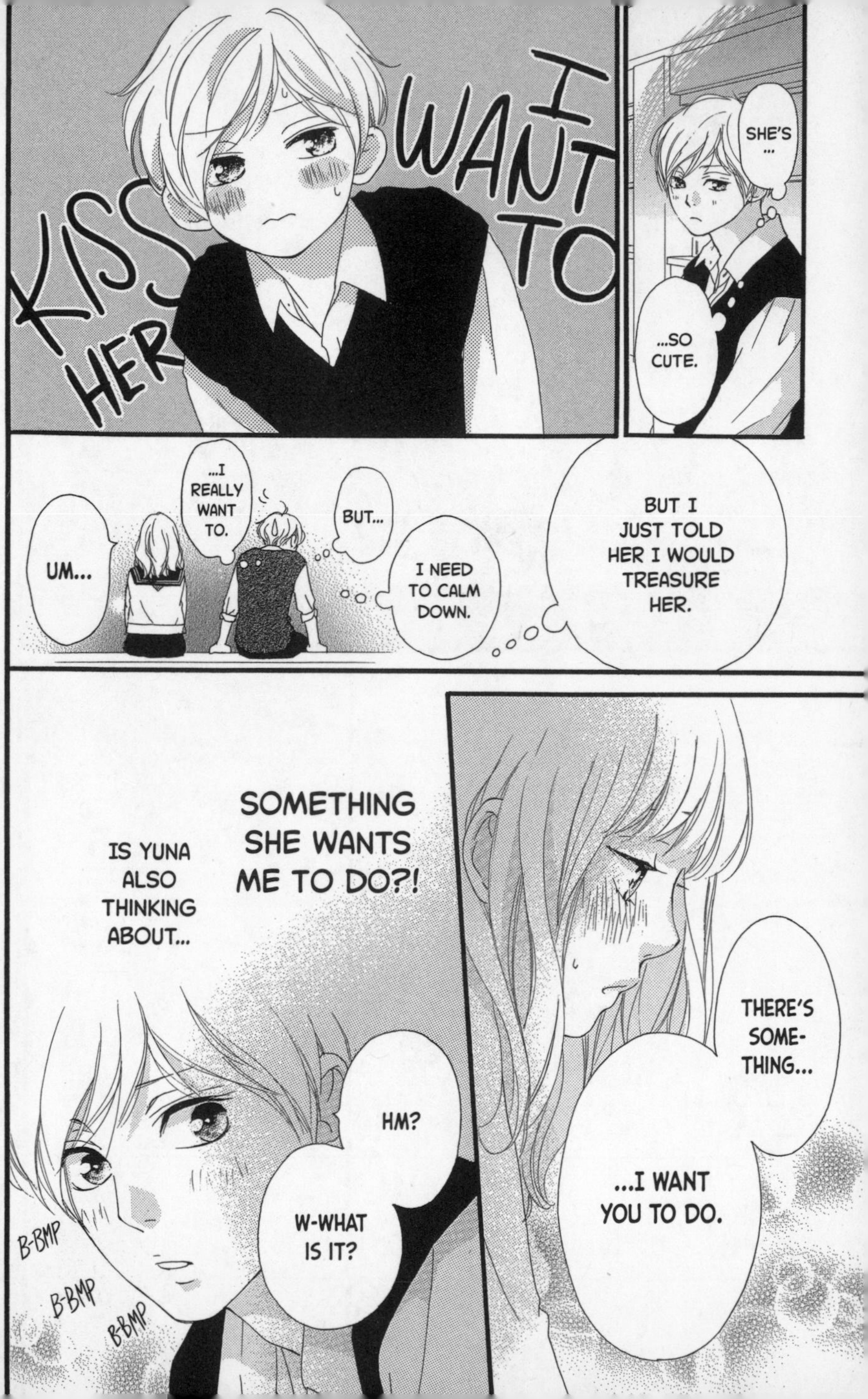
SHE'S...
...SO CUTE.
I WANT TO
KISS HER
BUT I JUST TOLD HER I WOULD TREASURE HER.
I NEED TO CALM DOWN.
BUT...
...I REALLY WANT TO.
UM...
THERE'S SOME-THING...
...I WANT YOU TO DO.
IS YUNA ALSO THINKING ABOUT...
SOMETHING SHE WANTS ME TO DO?!
HM?
W-WHAT IS IT?
B-BMP
B-BMP
B-BMP

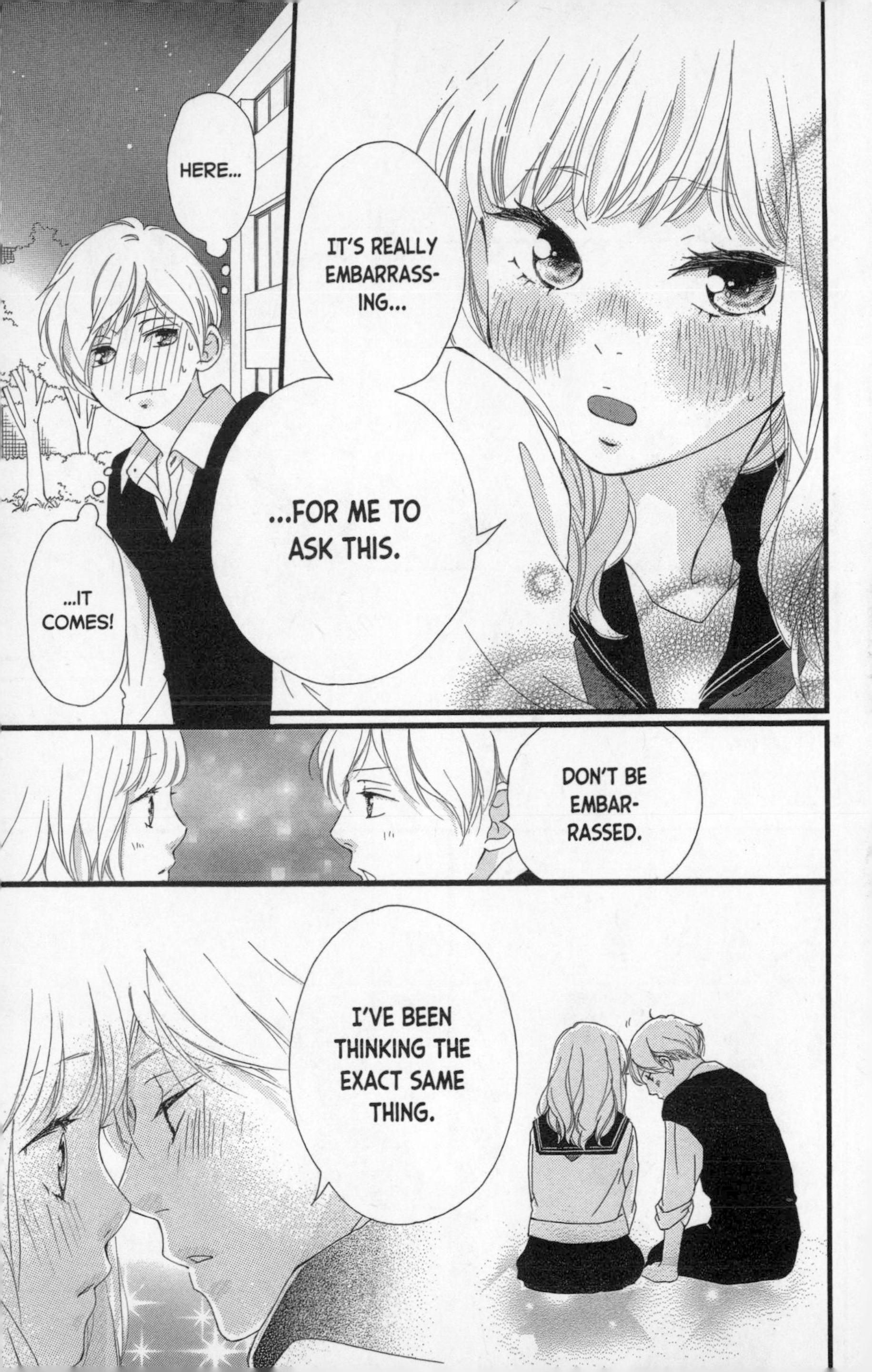
IT'S REALLY EMBARRASS-ING...
...FOR ME TO ASK THIS.
HERE...
...IT COMES!
DON'T BE EMBAR-RASSED.
I'VE BEEN THINKING THE EXACT SAME THING.

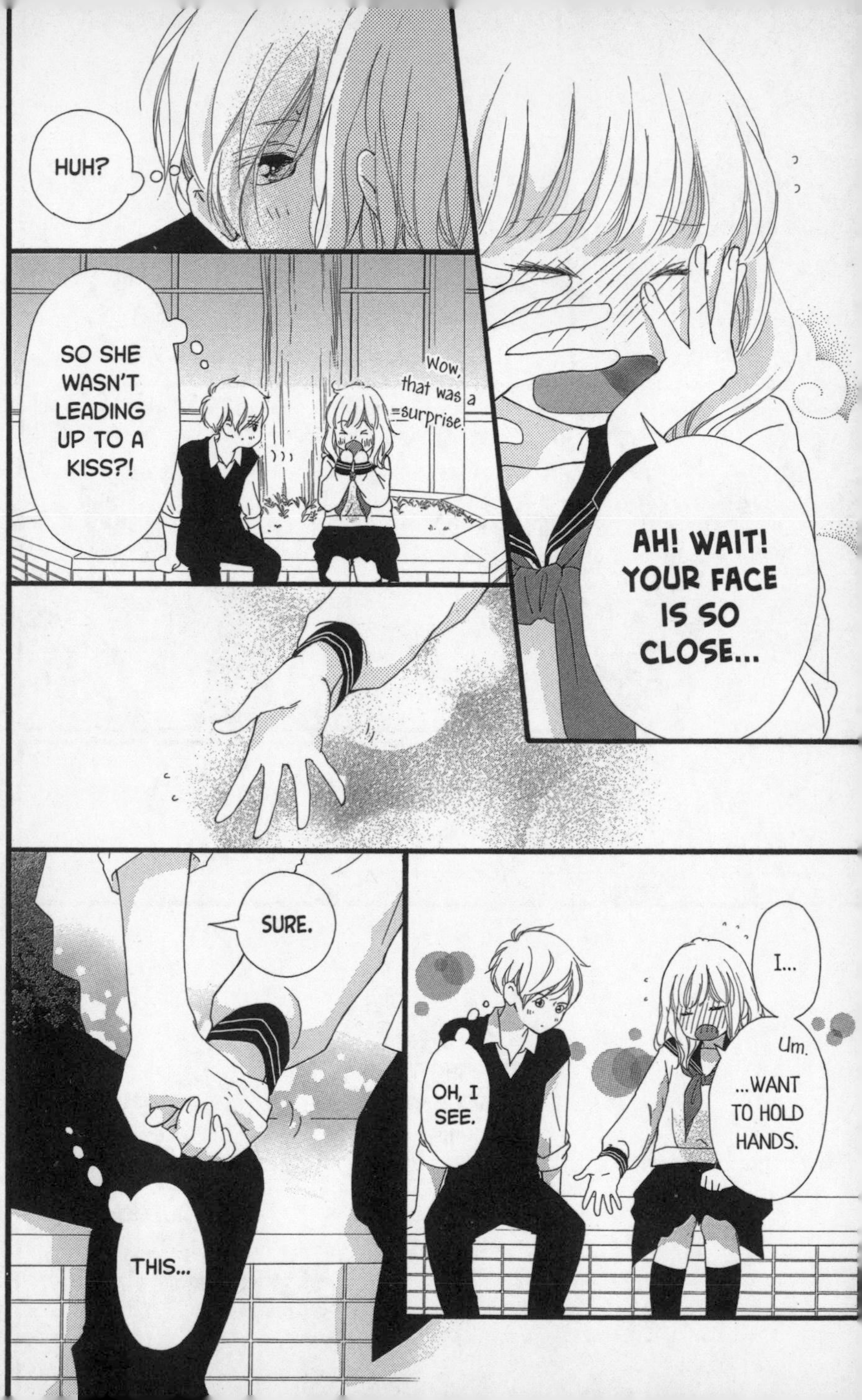
AH! WAIT! YOUR FACE IS SO CLOSE...
HUH?
Wow, that was a surprise.
SO SHE WASN'T LEADING UP TO A KISS?!
I...
Um.
...WANT TO HOLD HANDS.
OH, I SEE.
SURE.
THIS...

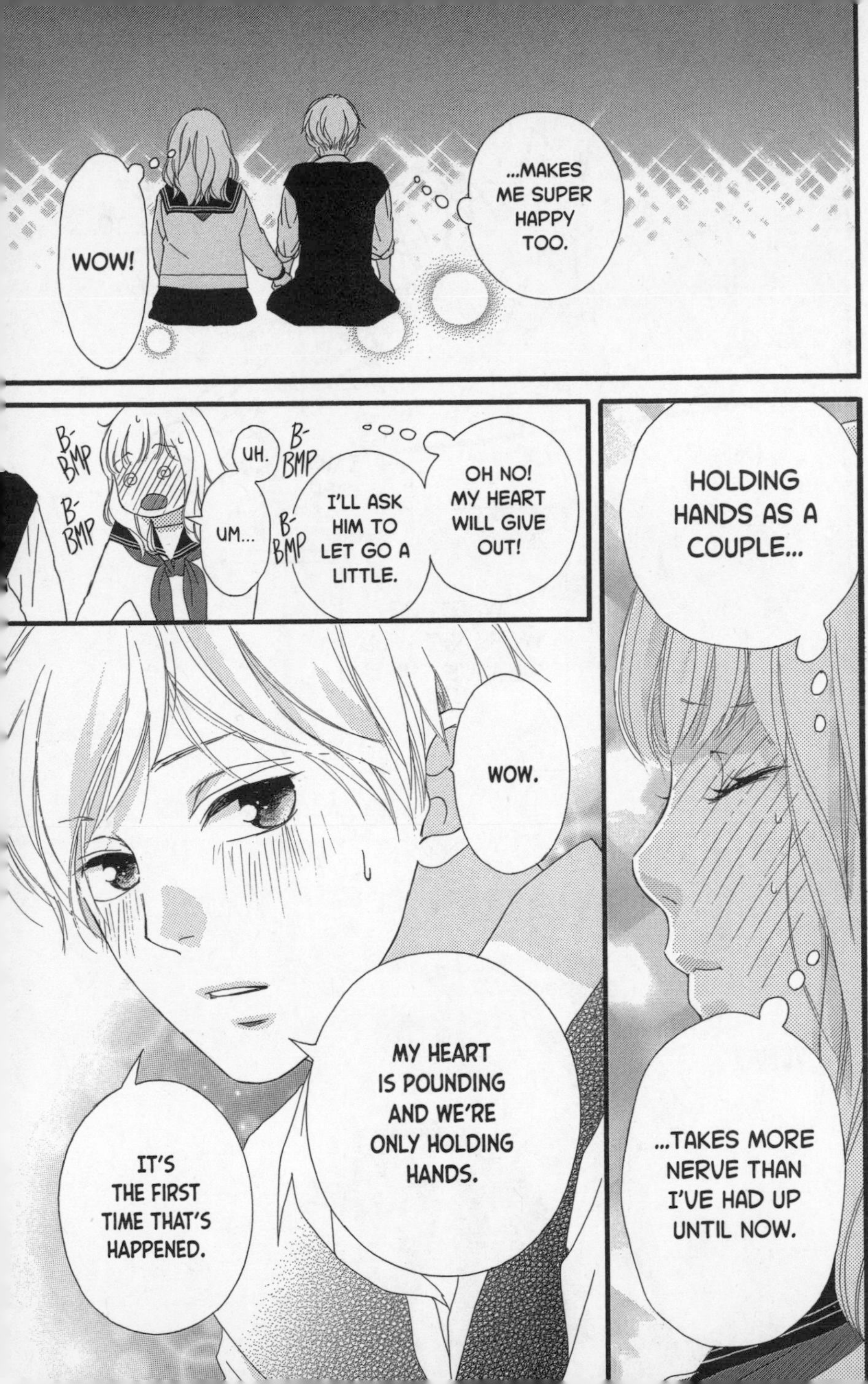
...MAKES ME SUPER HAPPY TOO.
WOW!
HOLDING HANDS AS A COUPLE...
...TAKES MORE NERVE THAN I'VE HAD UP UNTIL NOW.
OH NO! MY HEART WILL GIVE OUT!
I'LL ASK HIM TO LET GO A LITTLE.
B-BMP
UH.
B-BMP
UM...
B-BMP
B-BMP
WOW.
MY HEART IS POUNDING AND WE'RE ONLY HOLDING HANDS.
IT'S THE FIRST TIME THAT'S HAPPENED.

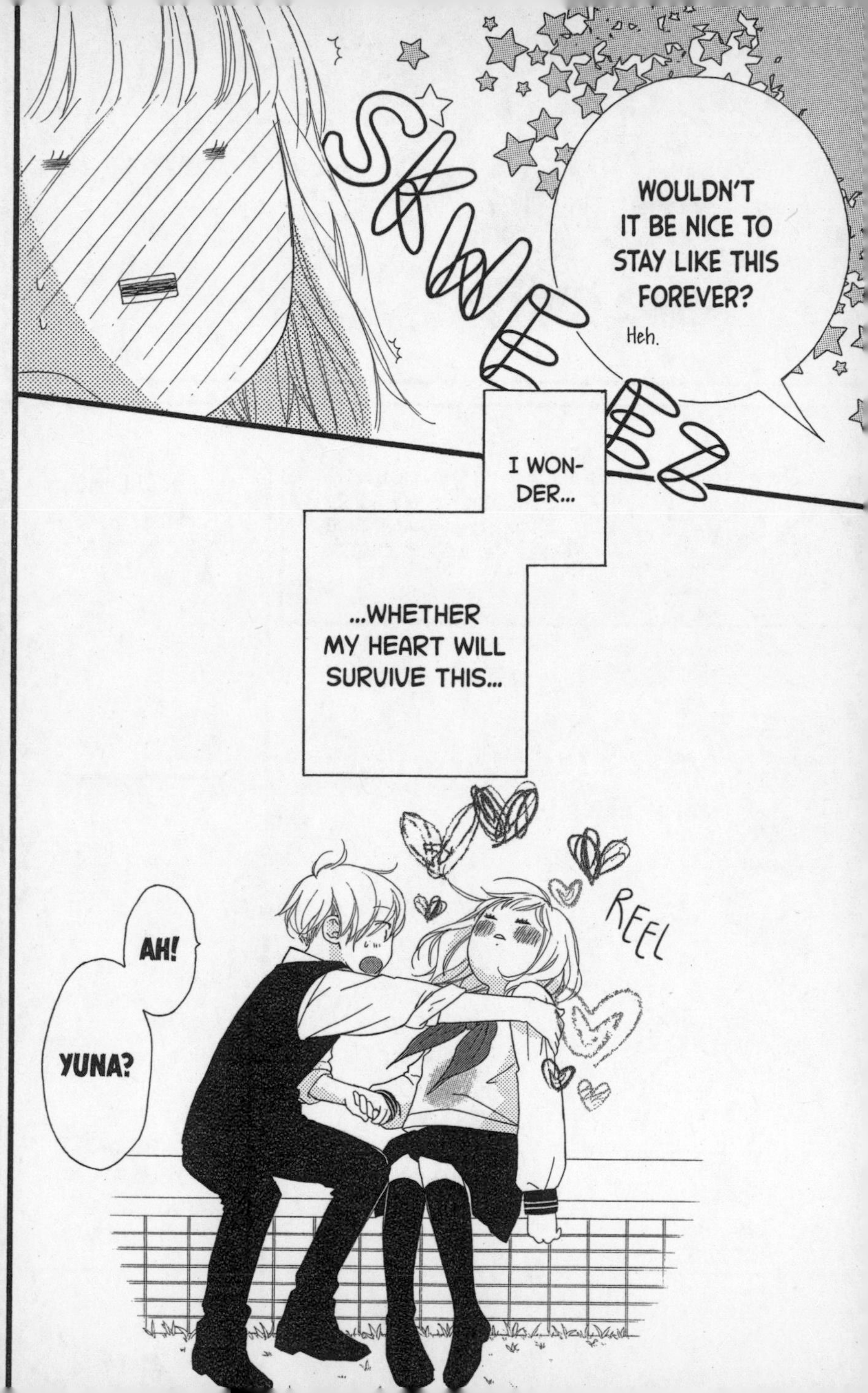
SKWEEZ
WOULDN'T IT BE NICE TO STAY LIKE THIS FOREVER?
Heh.
I WON-DER...
...WHETHER MY HEART WILL SURVIVE THIS...
REEL
AH!
YUNA?

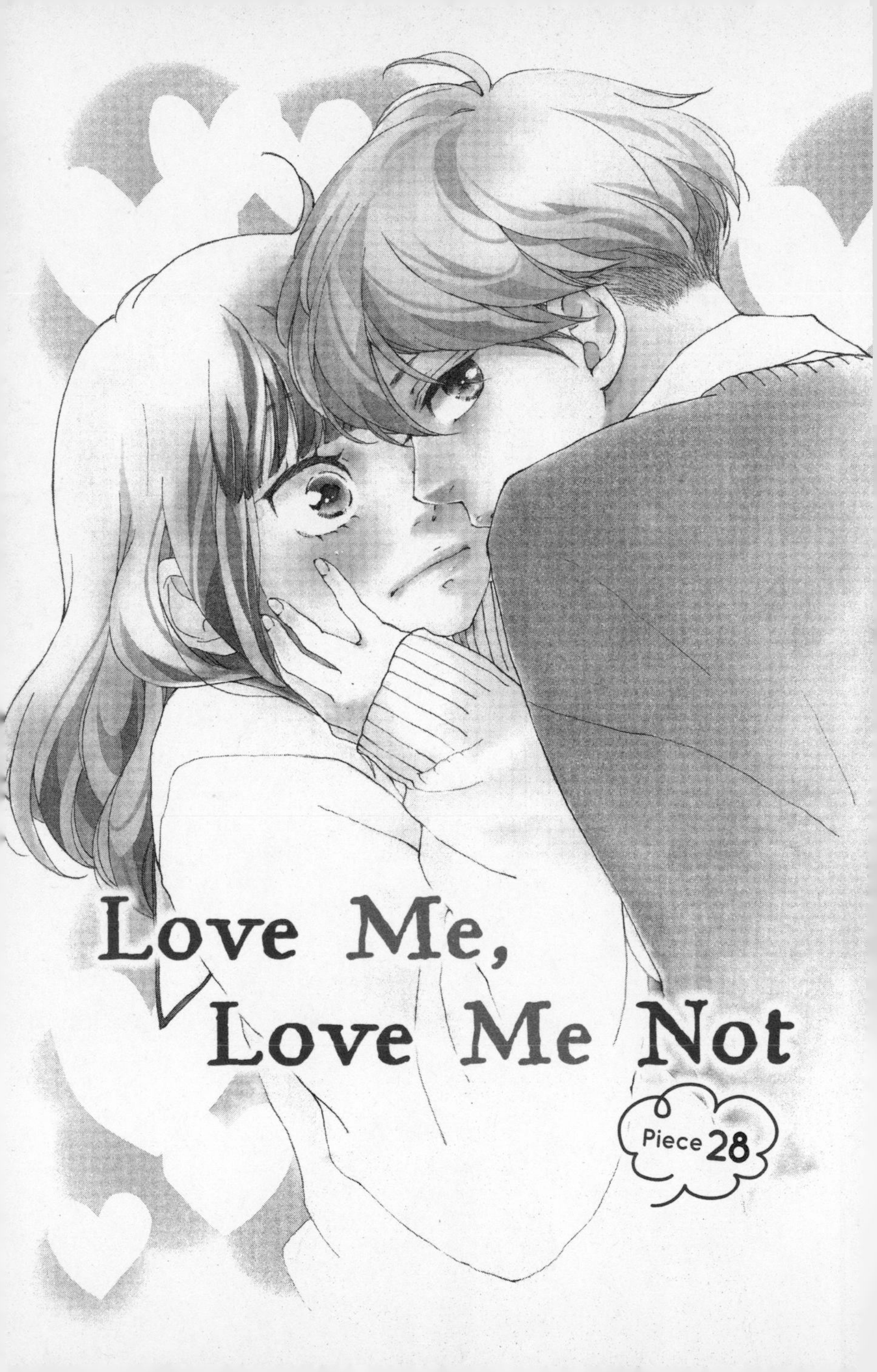
Love Me,
Love Me Not
Piece 28

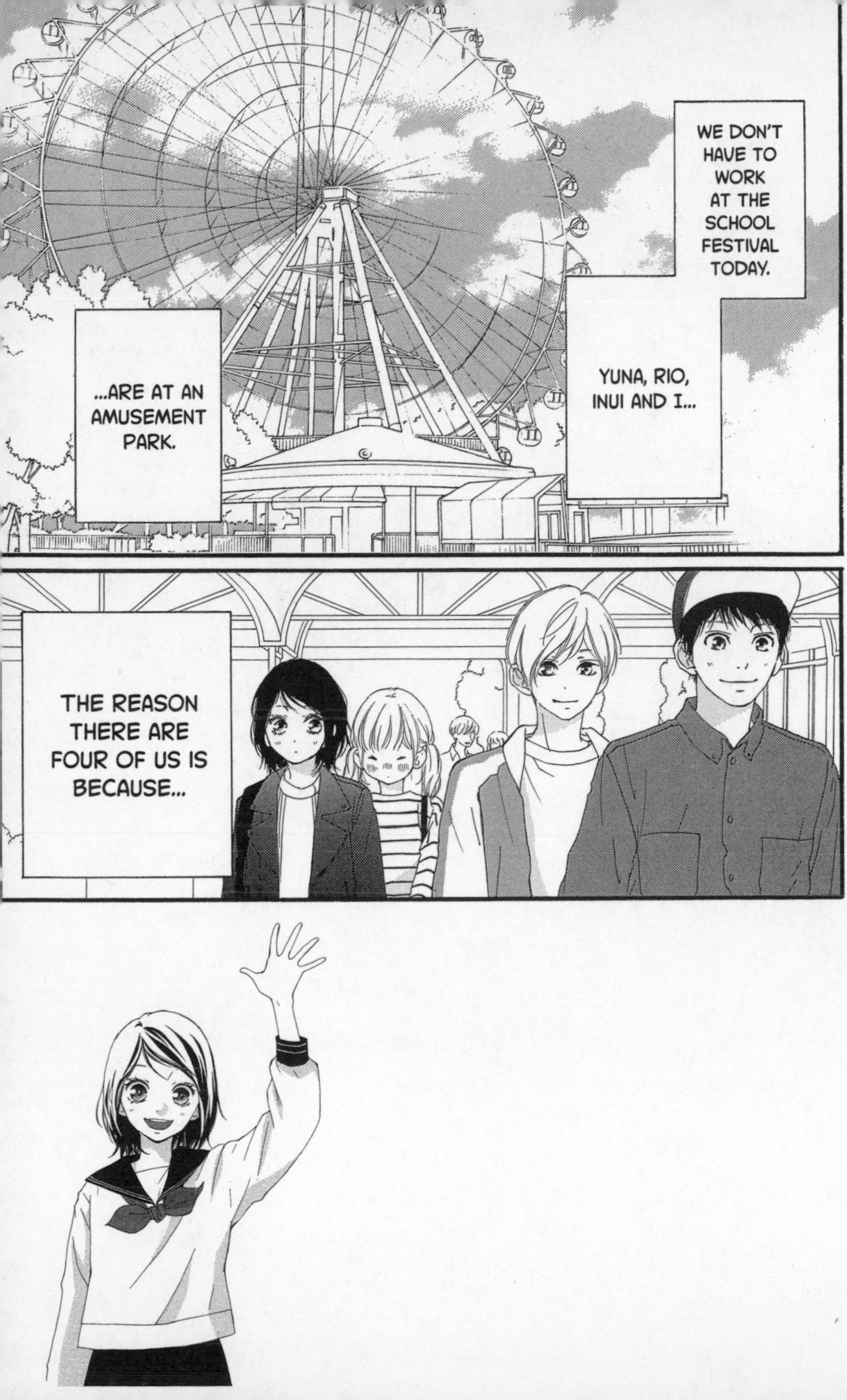
WE DON'T HAVE TO WORK AT THE SCHOOL FESTIVAL TODAY.
YUNA, RIO, INUI AND I...
...ARE AT AN AMUSEMENT PARK.
THE REASON THERE ARE FOUR OF US IS BECAUSE...

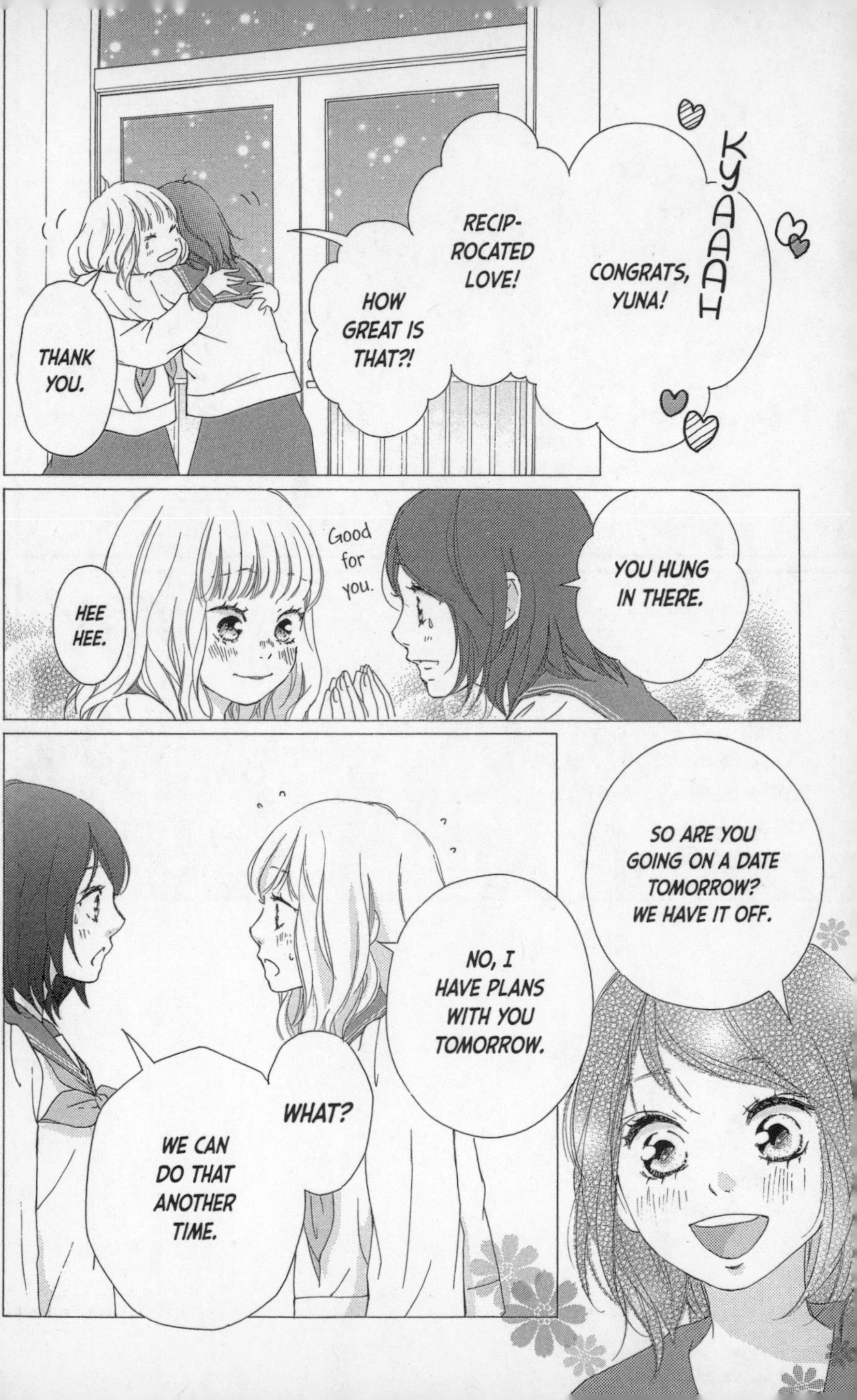
KYAAAH
CONGRATS, YUNA!
RECIP-ROCATED LOVE!
HOW GREAT IS THAT?!
THANK YOU.
YOU HUNG IN THERE.
Good for you.
HEE HEE.
SO ARE YOU GOING ON A DATE TOMORROW? WE HAVE IT OFF.
NO, I HAVE PLANS WITH YOU TOMORROW.
WHAT? WE CAN DO THAT ANOTHER TIME.

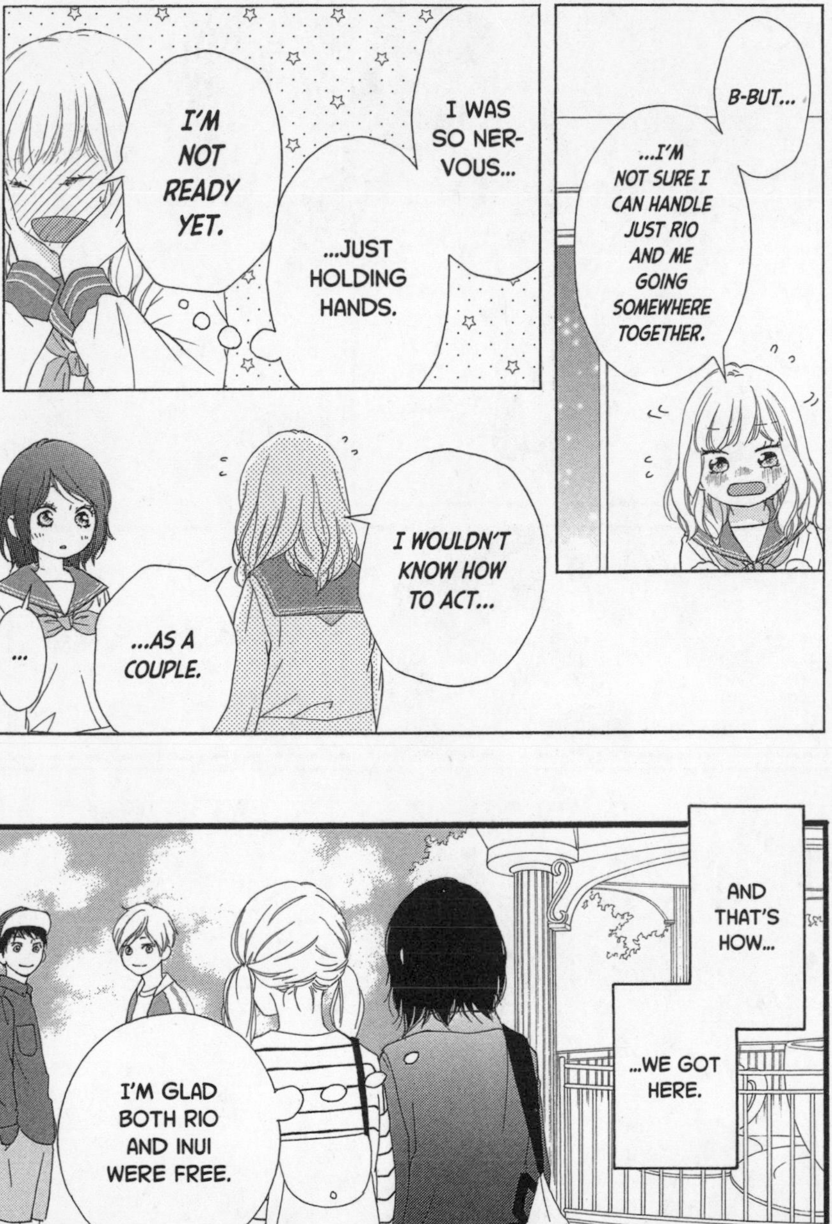
B-BUT...
...I'M NOT SURE I CAN HANDLE JUST RIO AND ME GOING SOMEWHERE TOGETHER.
I WAS SO NER-VOUS...
...JUST HOLDING HANDS.
I'M NOT READY YET.
I WOULDN'T KNOW HOW TO ACT...
...AS A COUPLE.
...
AND THAT'S HOW...
...WE GOT HERE.
I'M GLAD BOTH RIO AND INUI WERE FREE.

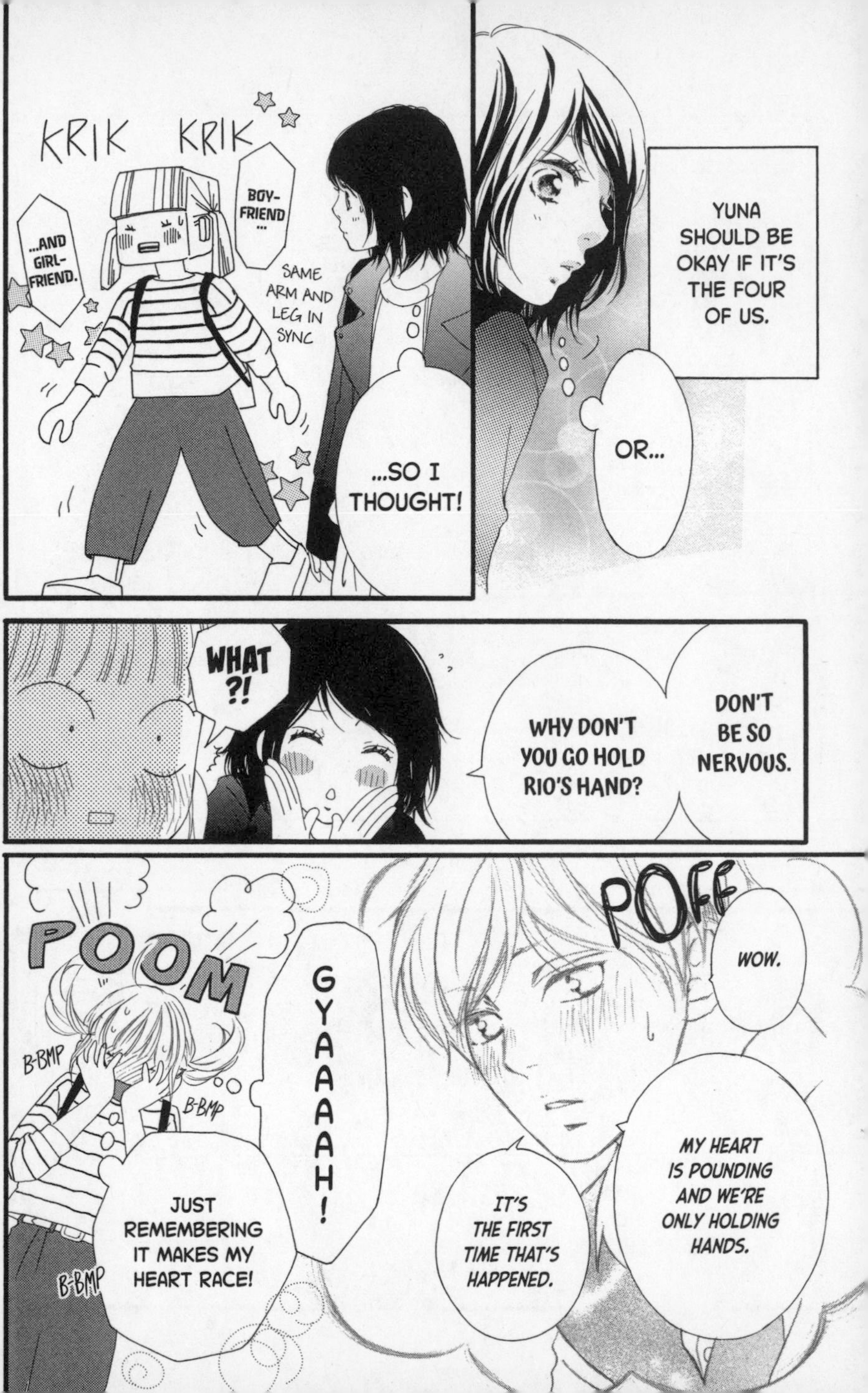
YUNA SHOULD BE OKAY IF IT'S THE FOUR OF US.
OR...
...SO I THOUGHT!
KRIK KRIK
BOY-FRIEND...
...AND GIRL-FRIEND.
SAME ARM AND LEG IN SYNC
DON'T BE SO NERVOUS.
WHY DON'T YOU GO HOLD RIO'S HAND?
WHAT?!
POFF
WOW.
MY HEART IS POUNDING AND WE'RE ONLY HOLDING HANDS.
IT'S THE FIRST TIME THAT'S HAPPENED.
GYAAAAAH!
POOM
B-BMP
B-BMP
JUST REMEMBERING IT MAKES MY HEART RACE!
B-BMP

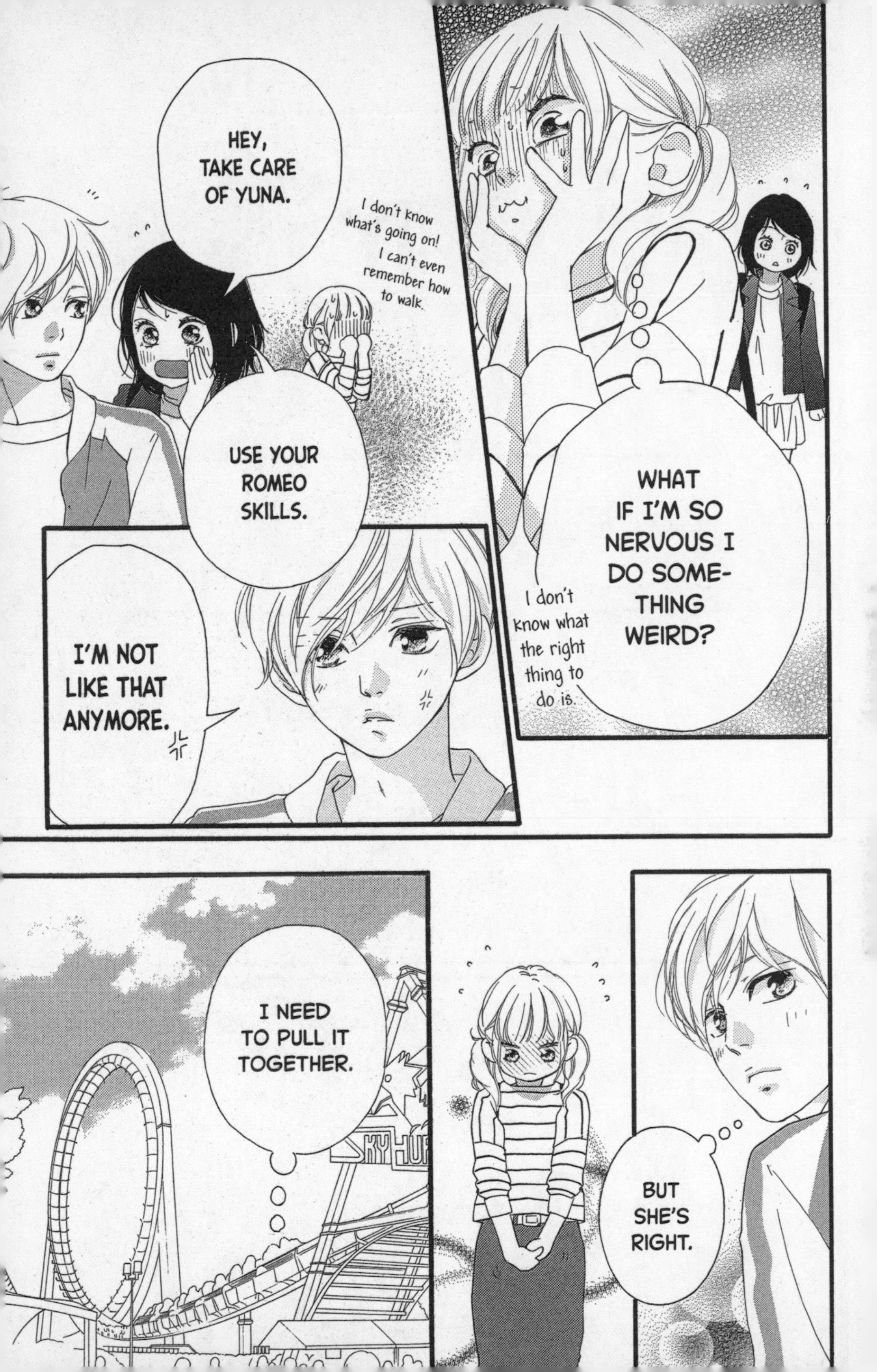
WHAT IF I'M SO NERVOUS I DO SOME-THING WEIRD?
I don't know what the right thing to do is.
HEY, TAKE CARE OF YUNA.
I don't know what's going on! I can't even remember how to walk.
USE YOUR ROMEO SKILLS.
I'M NOT LIKE THAT ANYMORE.
BUT SHE'S RIGHT.
I NEED TO PULL IT TOGETHER.

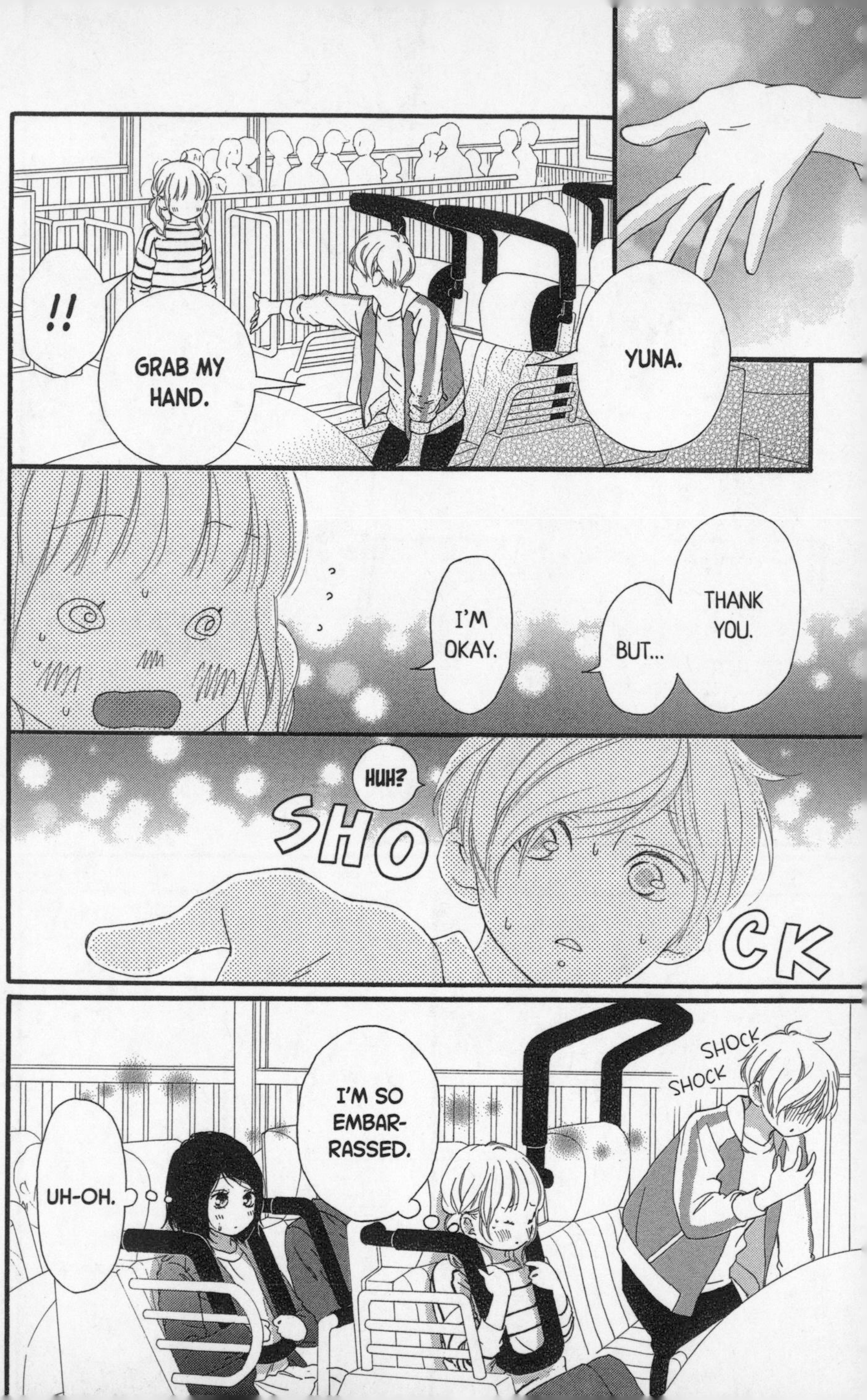
YUNA.
GRAB MY HAND.
!!
THANK YOU.
BUT...
I'M OKAY.
HUH?
SHOCK
SHOCK SHOCK
I'M SO EMBARRASSED.
UH-OH.

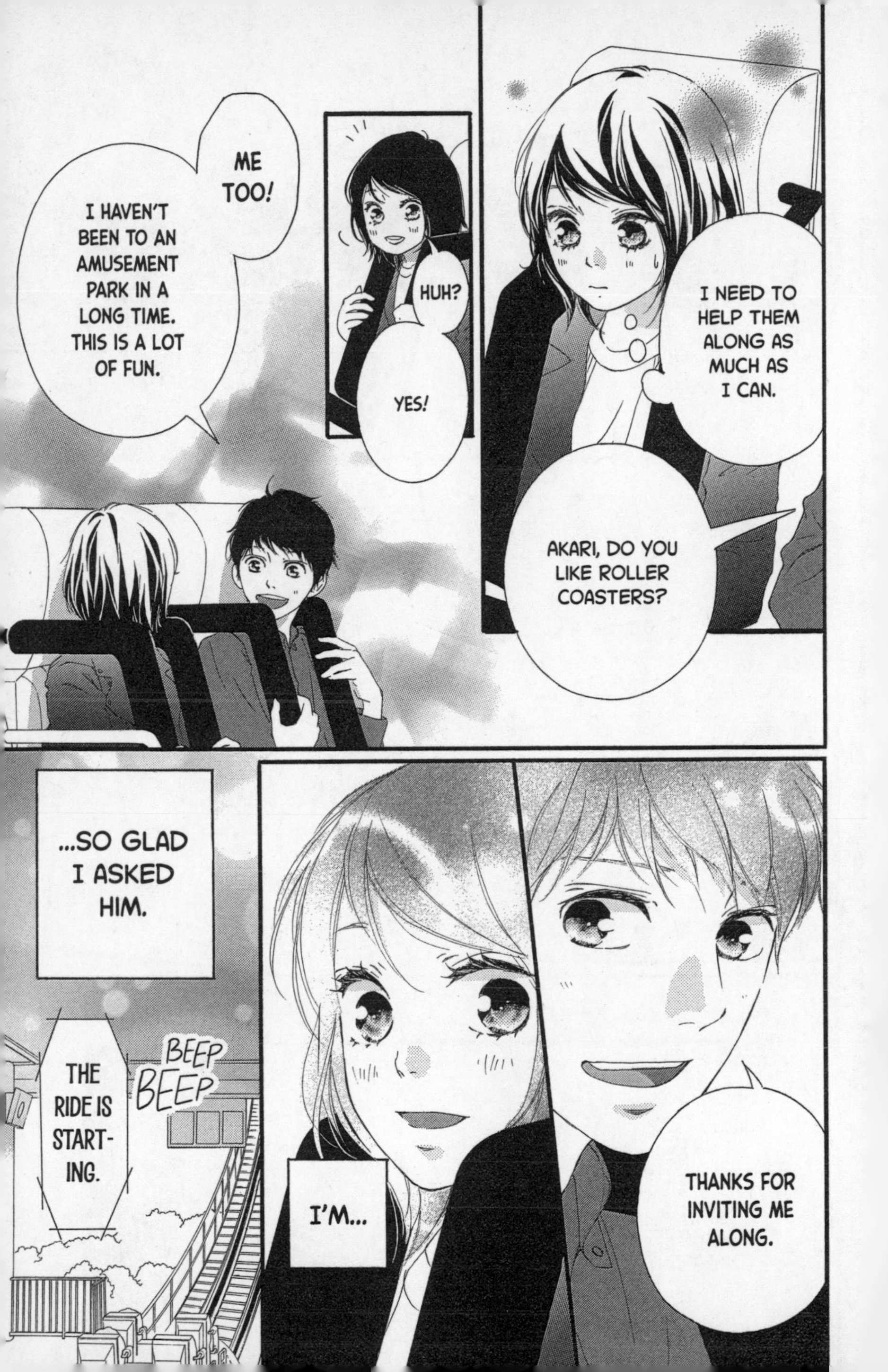
I NEED TO HELP THEM ALONG AS MUCH AS I CAN.
AKARI, DO YOU LIKE ROLLER COASTERS?
HUH?
YES!
ME TOO!
I HAVEN'T BEEN TO AN AMUSEMENT PARK IN A LONG TIME. THIS IS A LOT OF FUN.
THANKS FOR INVITING ME ALONG.
I'M...
...SO GLAD I ASKED HIM.
BEEP BEEP
THE RIDE IS START-ING.

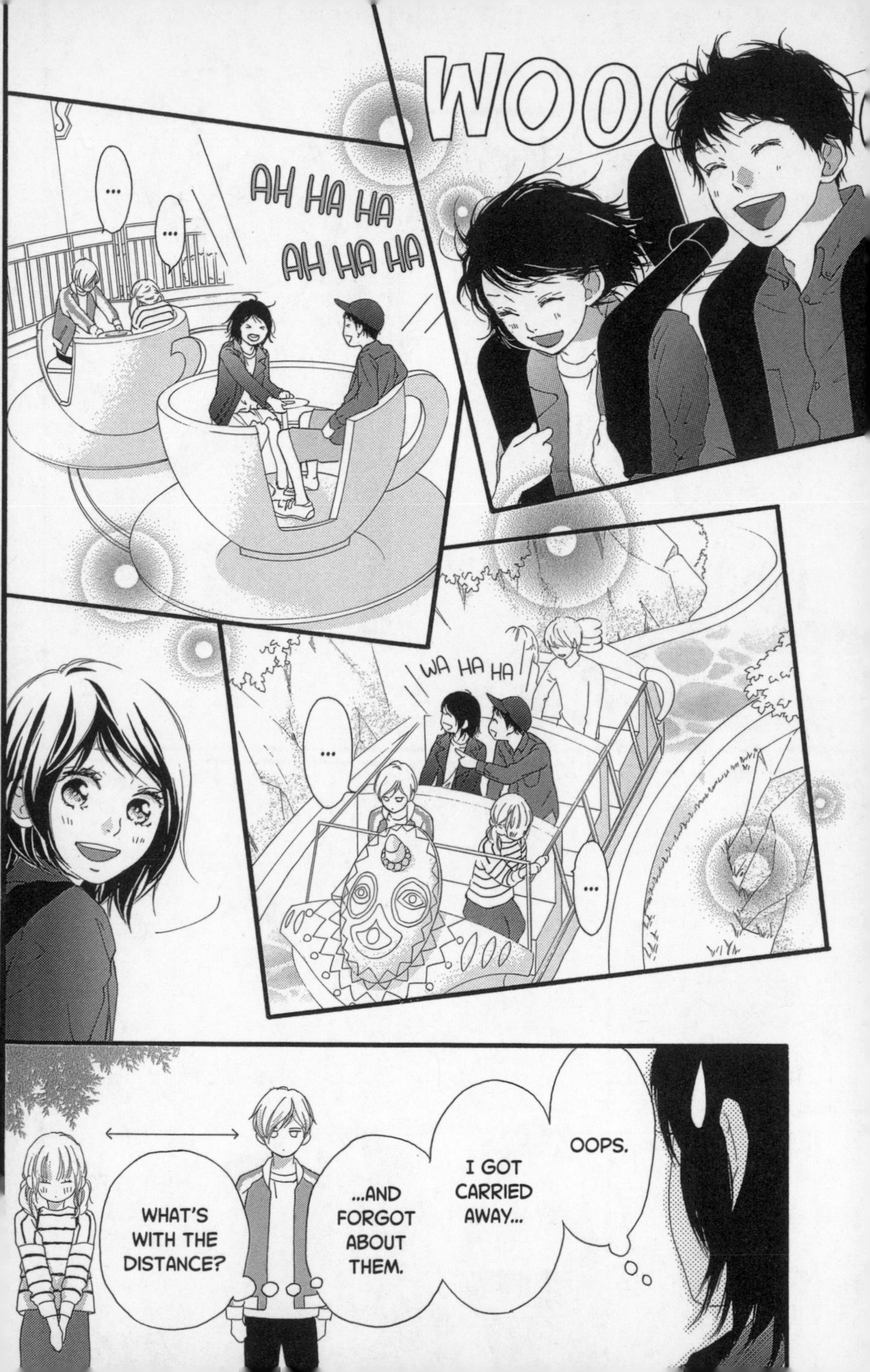

WOOO
AH HA HA
AH HA HA
...
...
WA HA HA
...
...
OOPS.
I GOT CARRIED AWAY...
...AND FORGOT ABOUT THEM.
WHAT'S WITH THE DISTANCE?

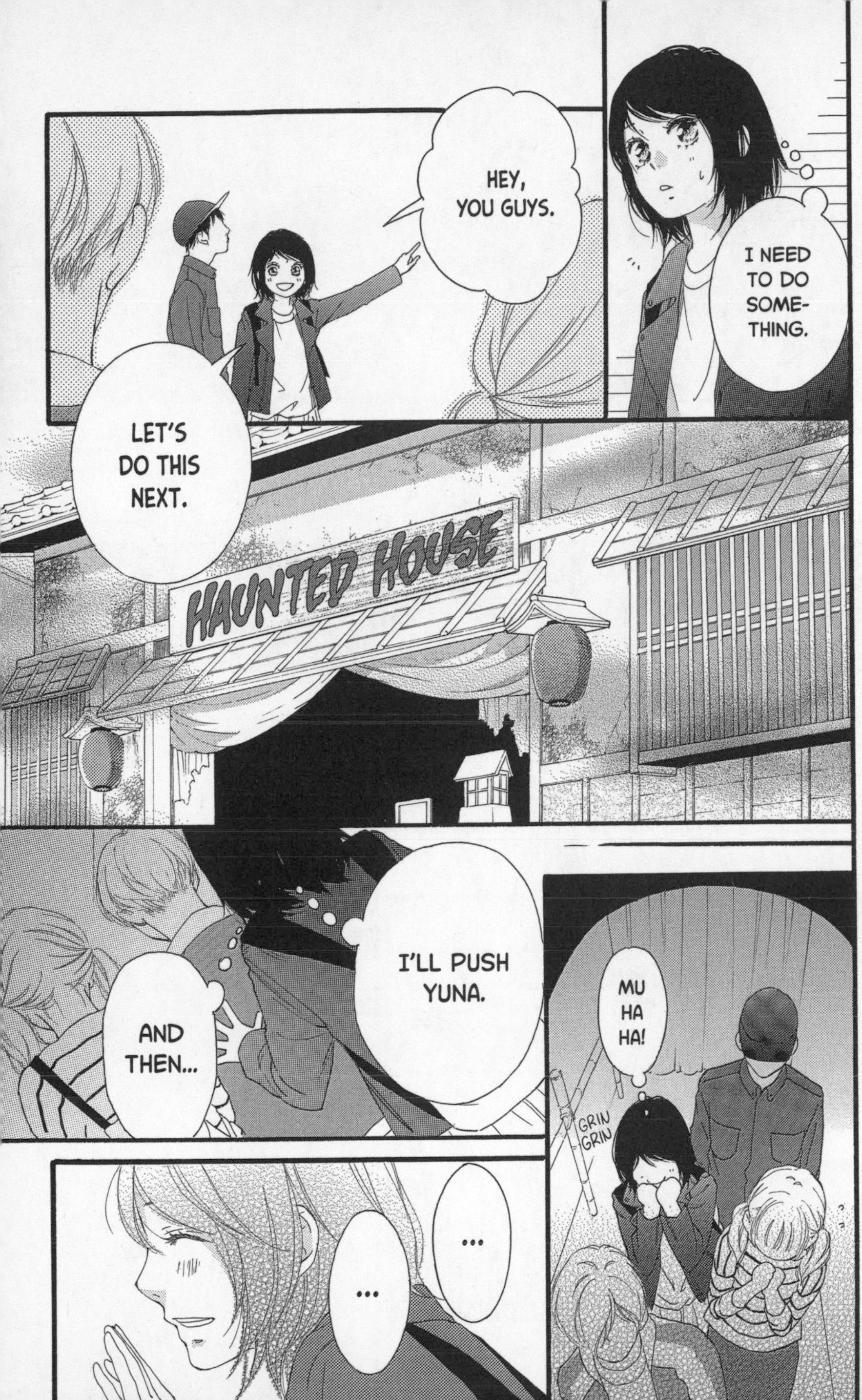
I NEED TO DO SOME-THING.
HEY, YOU GUYS.
LET'S DO THIS NEXT.
HAUNTED HOUSE
I'LL PUSH YUNA.
AND THEN...
MU HA HA!
GRIN GRIN
...
...

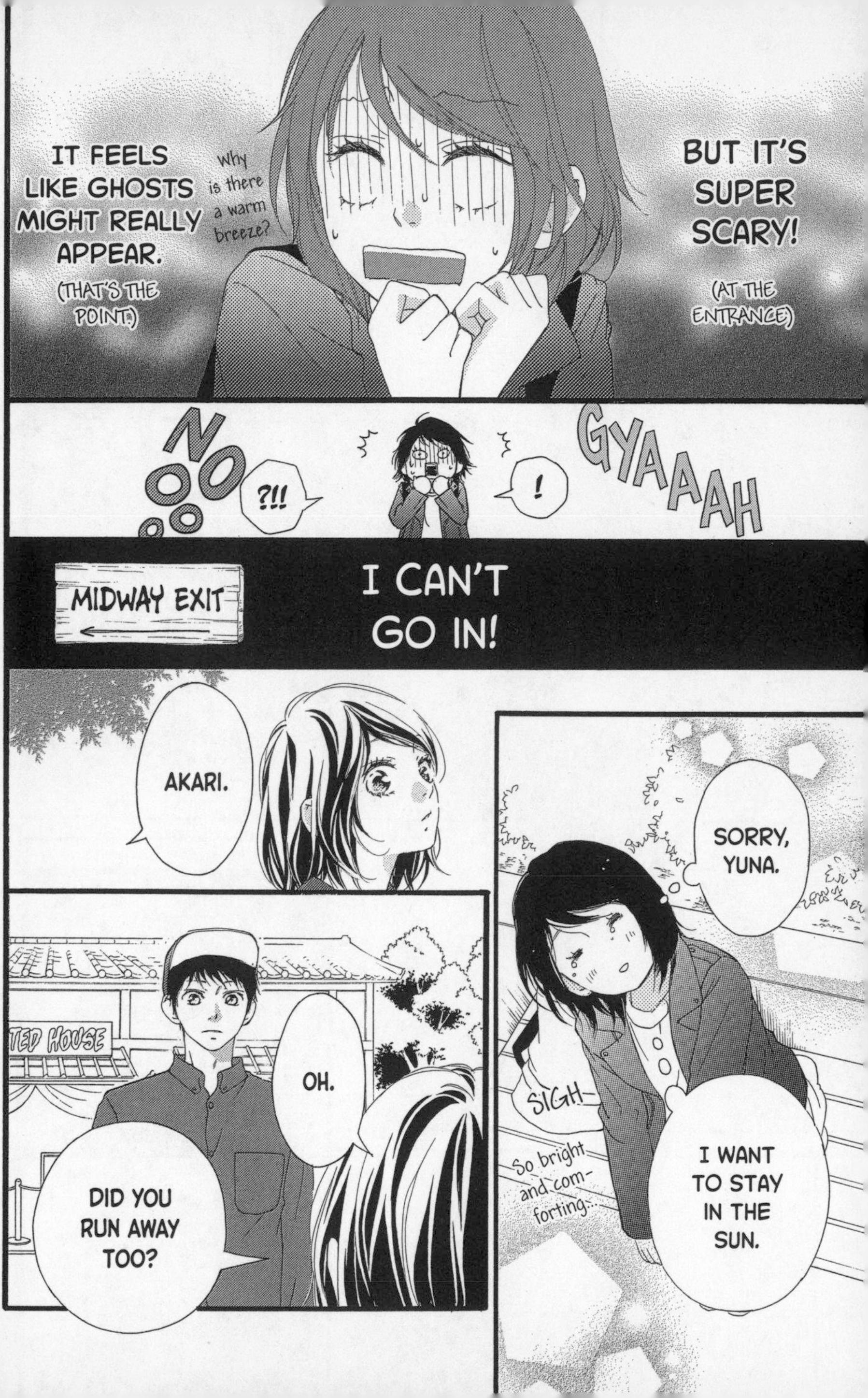
BUT IT'S SUPER SCARY!
(AT THE ENTRANCE)
Why is there a warm breeze?
IT FEELS LIKE GHOSTS MIGHT REALLY APPEAR.
(THAT'S THE POINT.)
GYAAAH
!
?!!
NOOOOO
I CAN'T GO IN!
MIDWAY EXIT
SORRY, YUNA.
SIGH—
I WANT TO STAY IN THE SUN.
So bright and com-forting...
AKARI.
OH.
TED HOUSE
DID YOU RUN AWAY TOO?

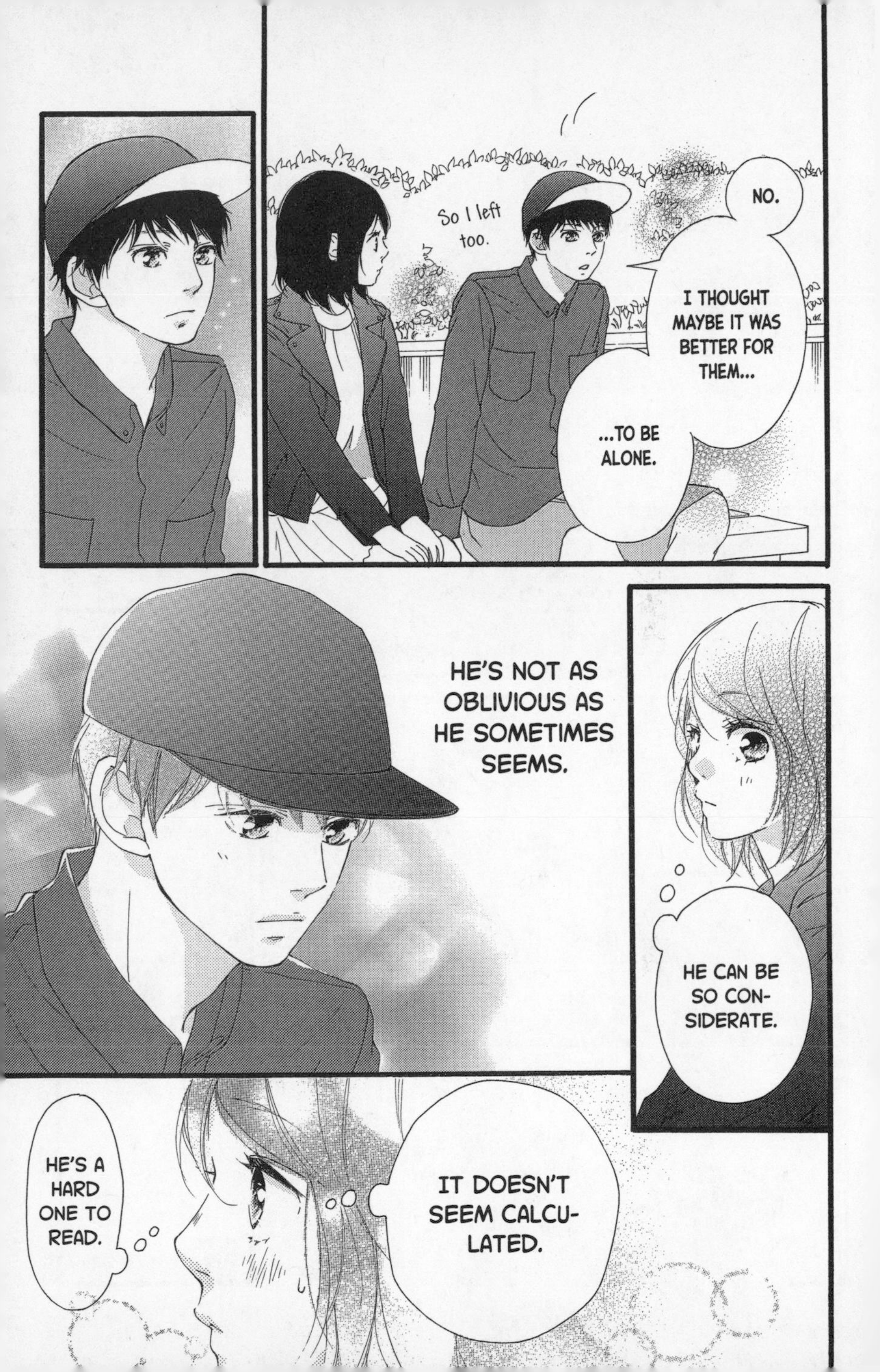
NO.
I THOUGHT MAYBE IT WAS BETTER FOR THEM...
...TO BE ALONE.
So I left too.
HE CAN BE SO CON-SIDERATE.
HE'S NOT AS OBLIVIOUS AS HE SOMETIMES SEEMS.
IT DOESN'T SEEM CALCU-LATED.
HE'S A HARD ONE TO READ.

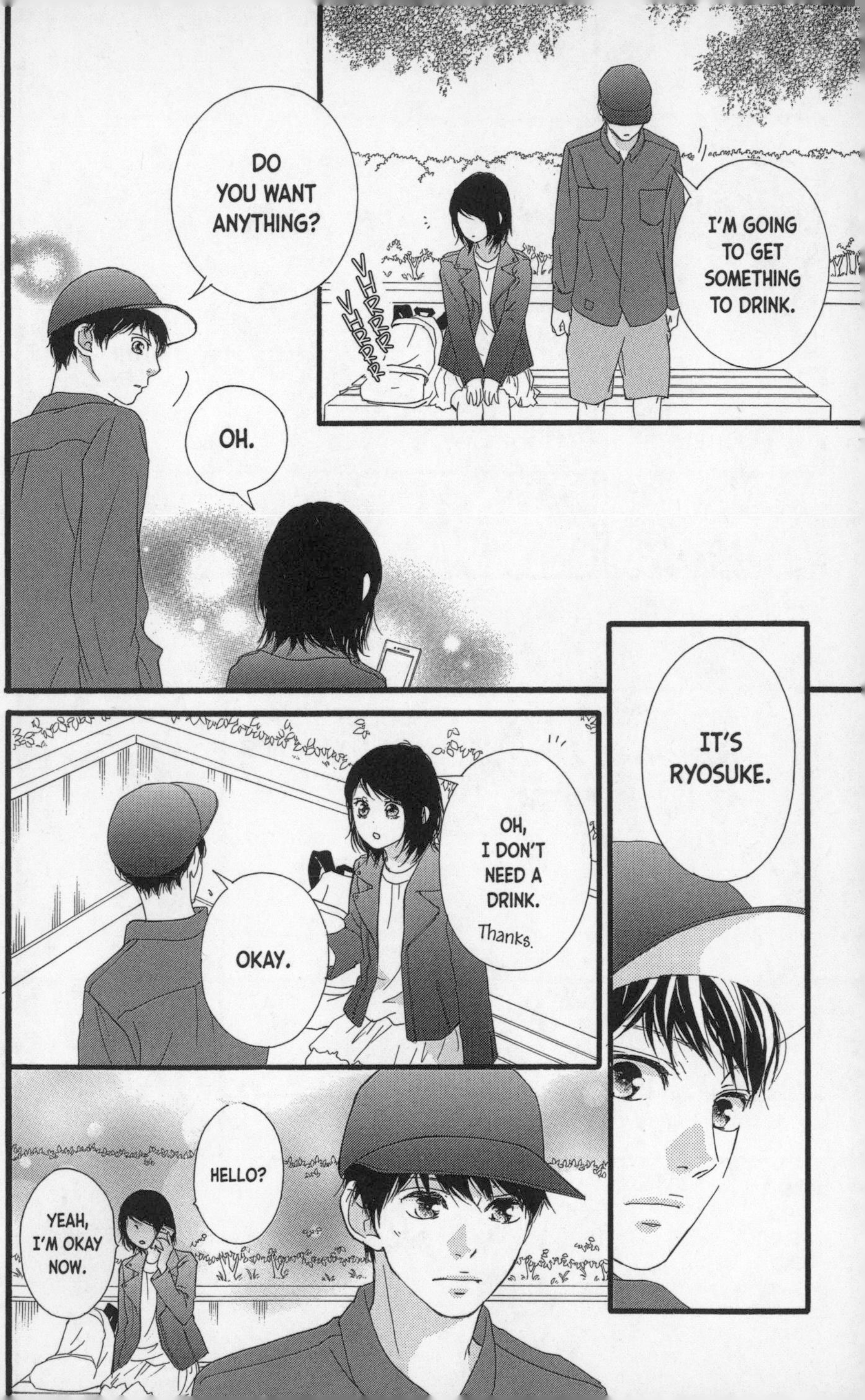
I'M GOING TO GET SOMETHING TO DRINK.
VHRRR
VHRRR
DO YOU WANT ANYTHING?
OH.
IT'S RYOSUKE.
OH, I DON'T NEED A DRINK.
Thanks.
OKAY.
HELLO?
YEAH, I'M OKAY NOW.

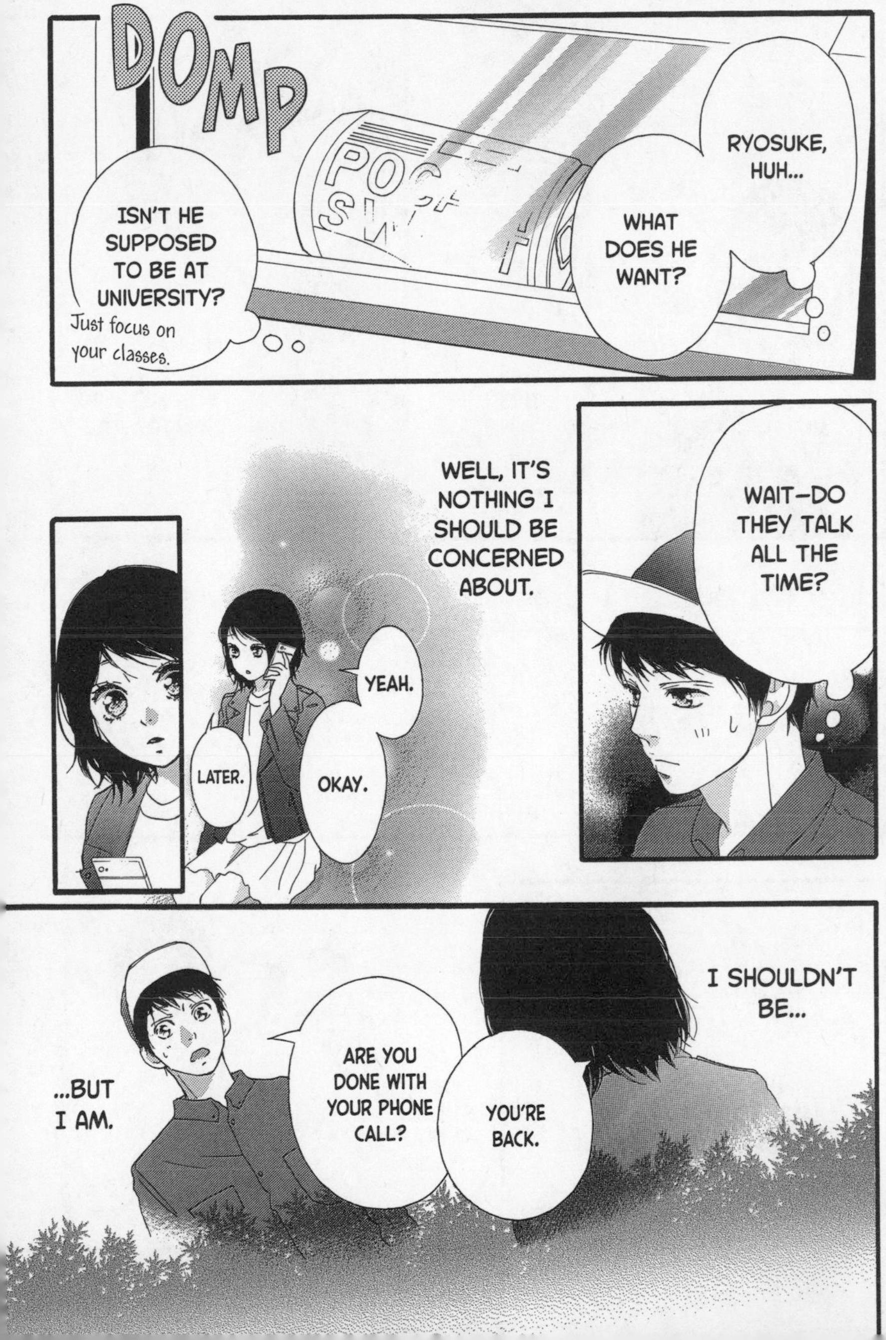
RYOSUKE, HUH...
WHAT DOES HE WANT?
DOMP
ISN'T HE SUPPOSED TO BE AT UNIVERSITY?
Just focus on your classes.
WAIT—DO THEY TALK ALL THE TIME?
WELL, IT'S NOTHING I SHOULD BE CONCERNED ABOUT.
YEAH.
OKAY.
LATER.
I SHOULDN'T BE...
YOU'RE BACK.
ARE YOU DONE WITH YOUR PHONE CALL?
...BUT I AM.

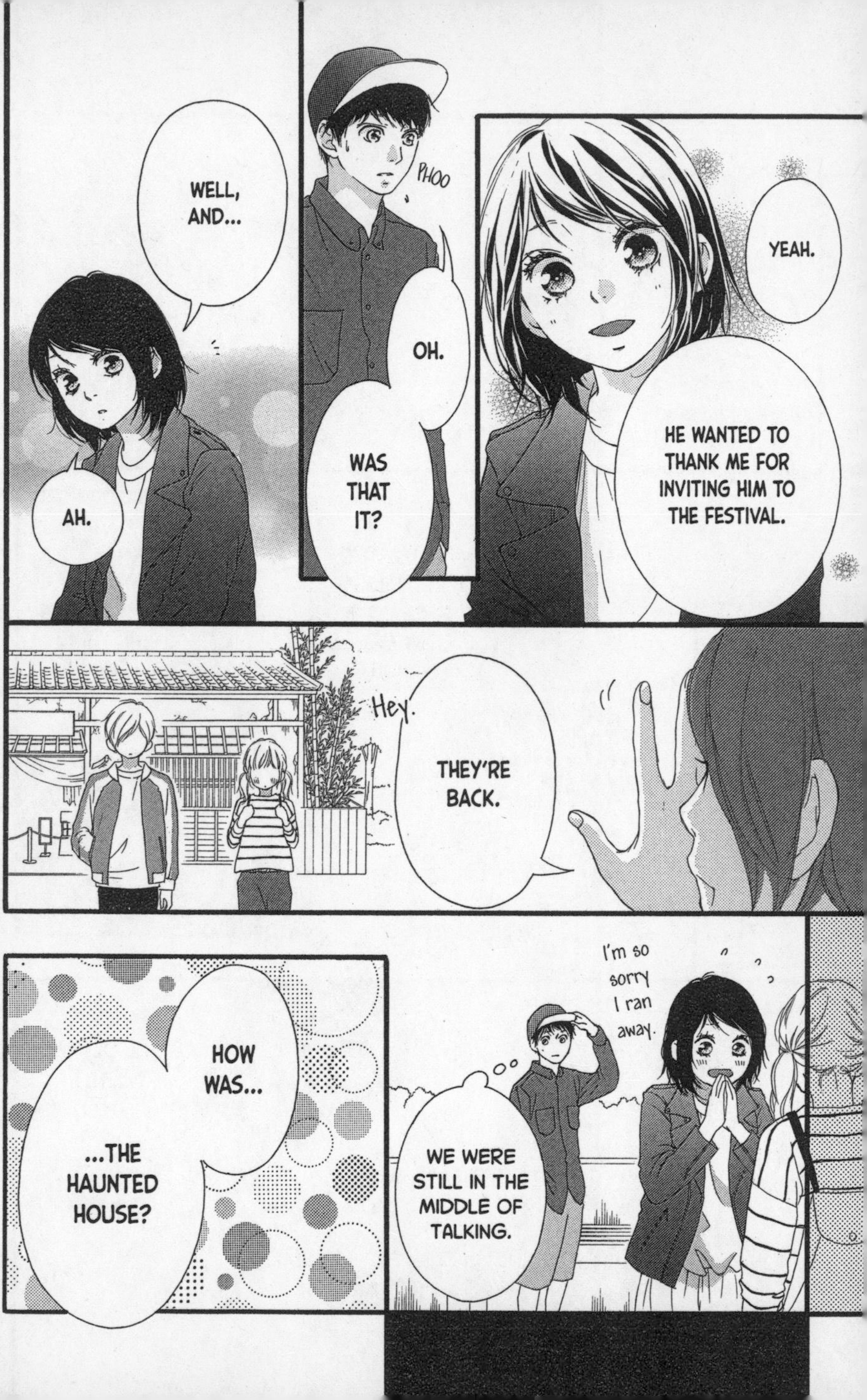
YEAH.
HE WANTED TO THANK ME FOR INVITING HIM TO THE FESTIVAL.
PHOO
OH.
WAS THAT IT?
WELL, AND...
AH.
Hey.
THEY'RE BACK.
I'm so sorry I ran away.
WE WERE STILL IN THE MIDDLE OF TALKING.
HOW WAS...
...THE HAUNTED HOUSE?

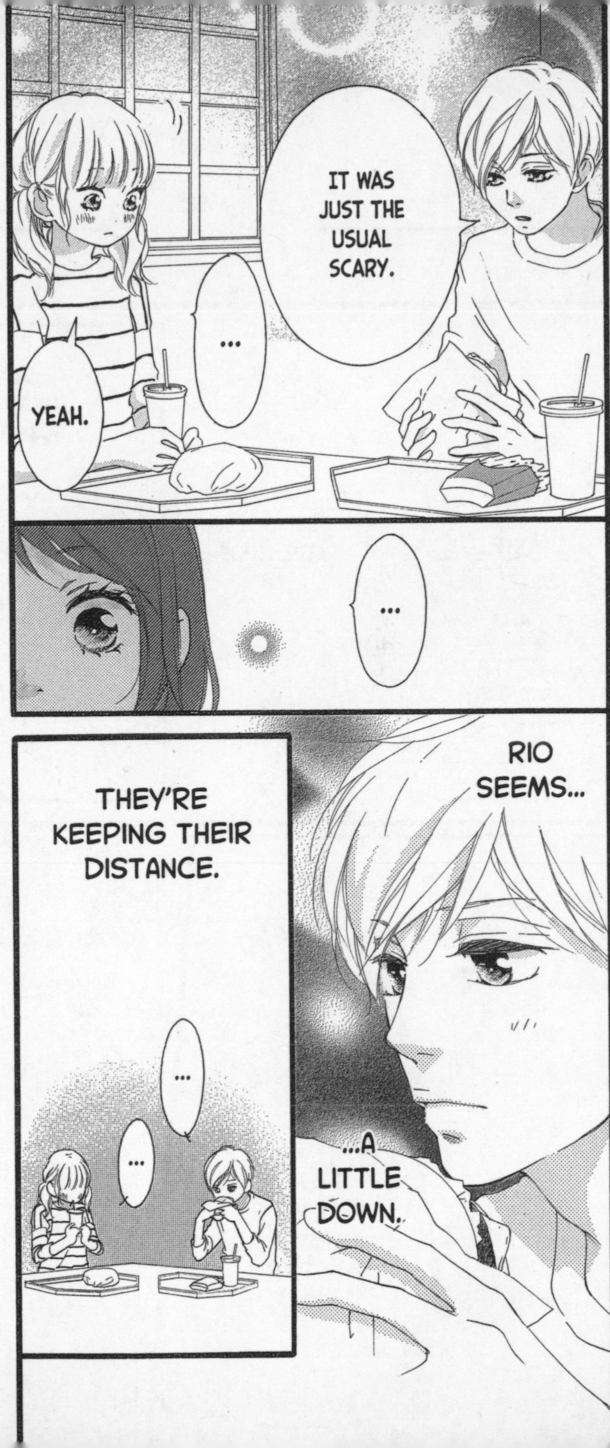
IT WAS JUST THE USUAL SCARY.
...
YEAH.
...
RIO SEEMS...
...A LITTLE DOWN.
THEY'RE KEEPING THEIR DISTANCE.
...
...

Up until now, every time a new volume came out, we used a song by Sonoko Inoue to make a promotional video for *Love Me, Love Me Not*. But this time, she's writing a song for it! It's too amazing. I have only respect and admiration for those who can write songs, and to have someone like Sonoko Inoue compose a song with this series in mind is truly a dream. "Love Song," which she created using *Love Me, Love Me Not* as inspiration, is packed with the cute feelings girls have. It's exciting just listening to it. It's a wonderful song. The song is for Yuna, Akari and all girls who are in love or who want to be. I'd love for everyone to listen to "Love Song" sung in her sweet voice.

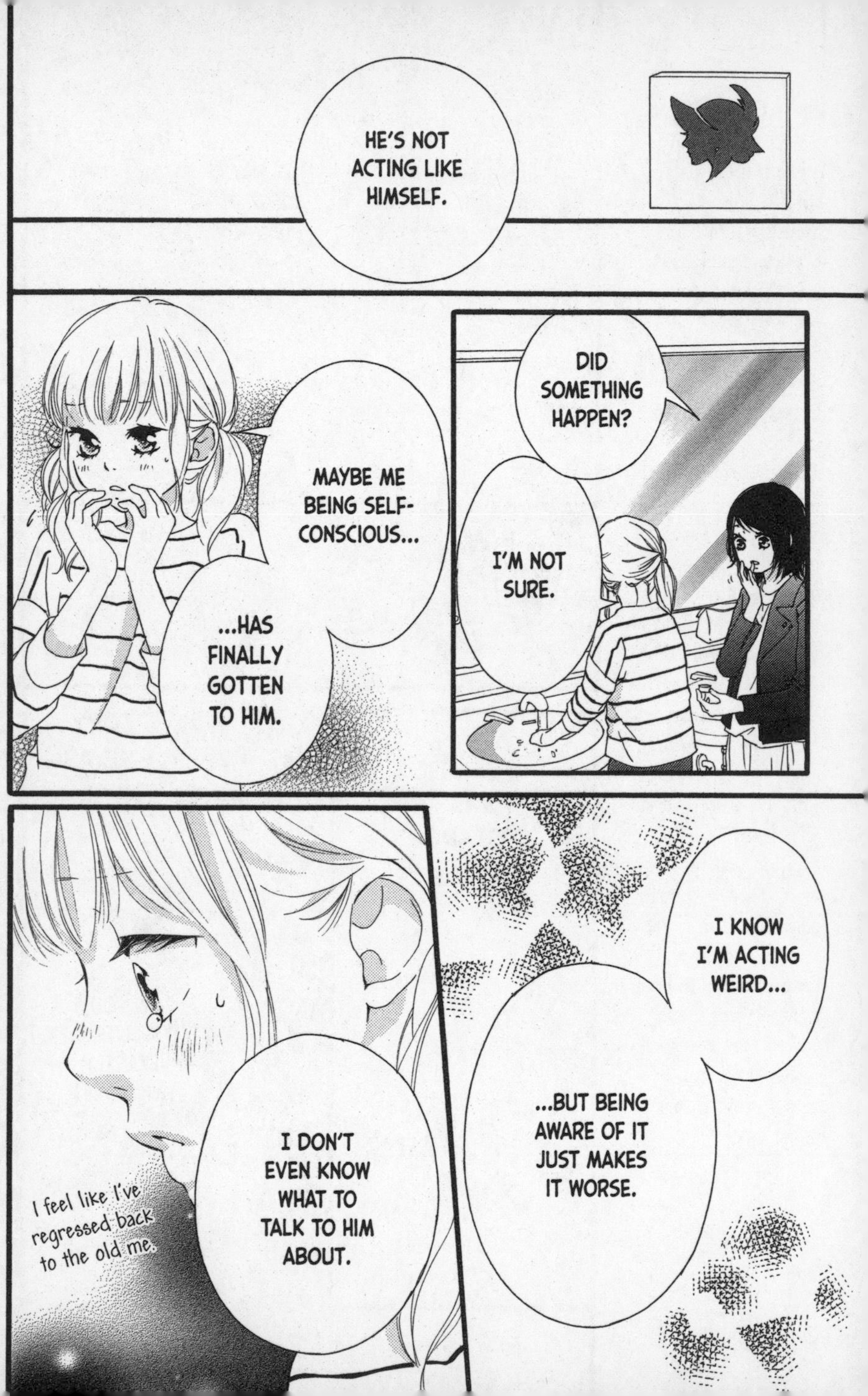
HE'S NOT ACTING LIKE HIMSELF.
DID SOMETHING HAPPEN?
I'M NOT SURE.
MAYBE ME BEING SELF-CONSCIOUS...
...HAS FINALLY GOTTEN TO HIM.
I KNOW I'M ACTING WEIRD...
...BUT BEING AWARE OF IT JUST MAKES IT WORSE.
I DON'T EVEN KNOW WHAT TO TALK TO HIM ABOUT.
I feel like I've regressed back to the old me.

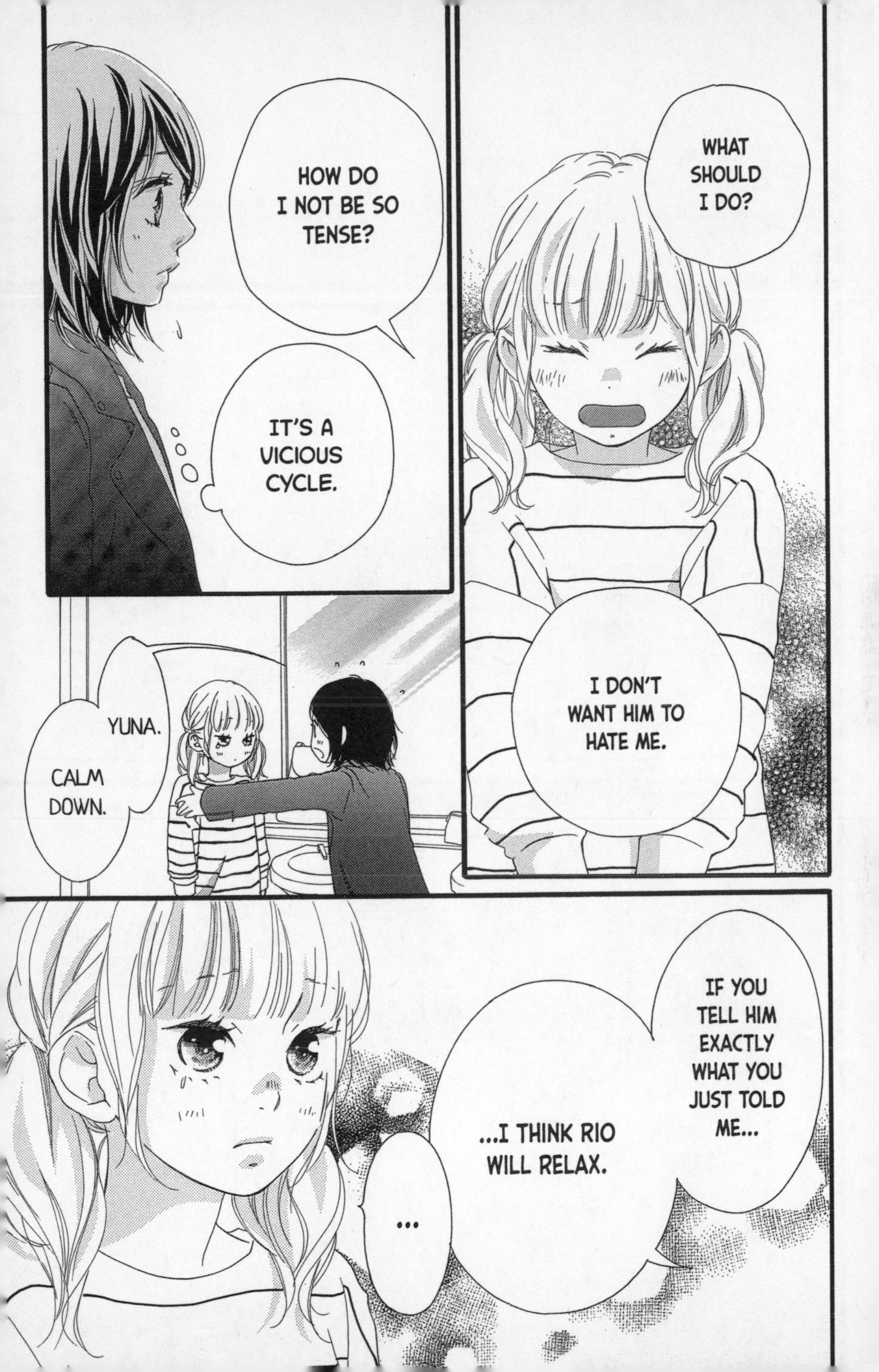
WHAT SHOULD I DO?
I DON'T WANT HIM TO HATE ME.
HOW DO I NOT BE SO TENSE?
IT'S A VICIOUS CYCLE.
YUNA.
CALM DOWN.
IF YOU TELL HIM EXACTLY WHAT YOU JUST TOLD ME...
...I THINK RIO WILL RELAX.
...

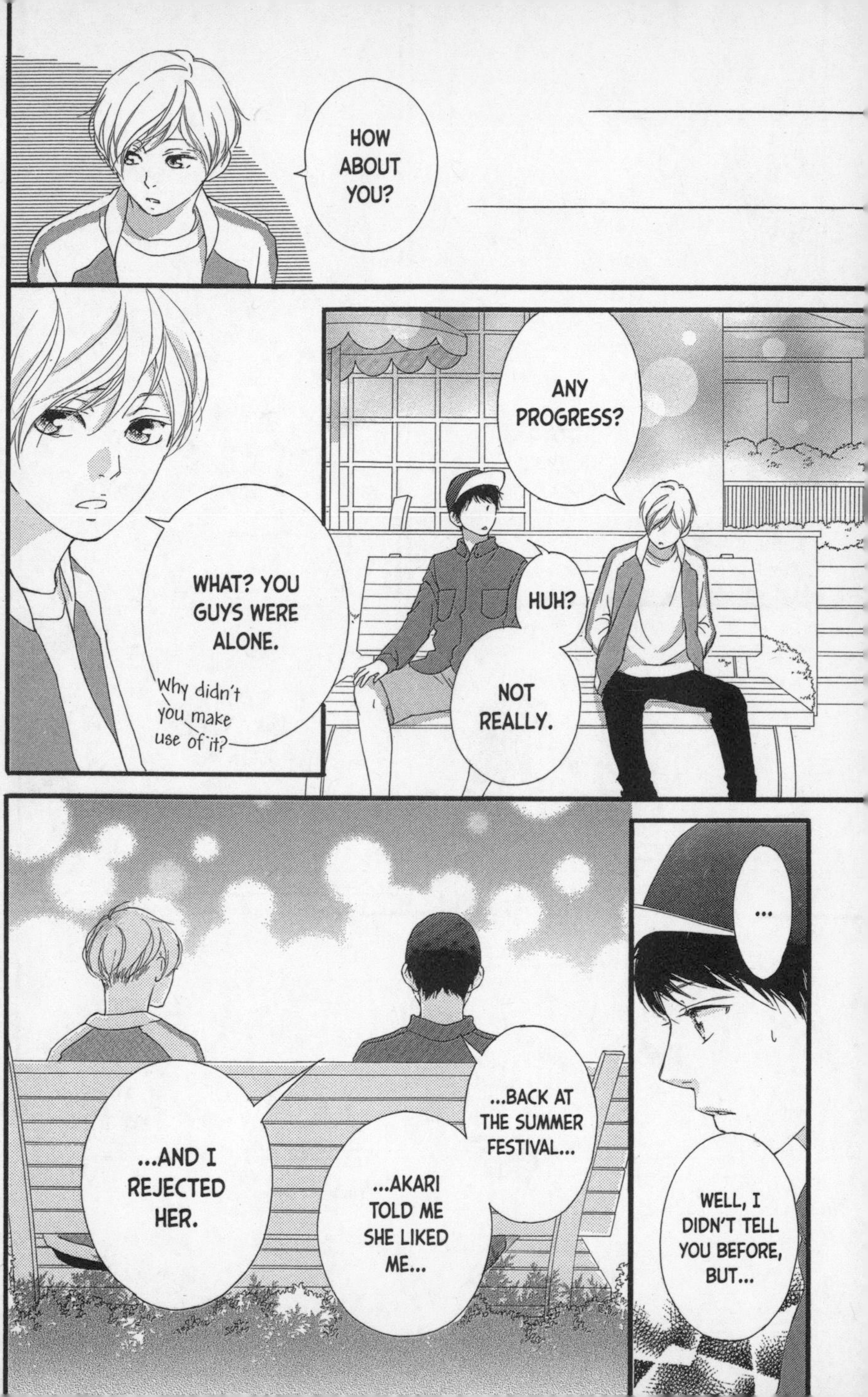
HOW ABOUT YOU?
ANY PROGRESS?
HUH?
NOT REALLY.
WHAT? YOU GUYS WERE ALONE.
Why didn't you make use of it?
...
WELL, I DIDN'T TELL YOU BEFORE, BUT...
...BACK AT THE SUMMER FESTIVAL...
...AKARI TOLD ME SHE LIKED ME...
...AND I REJECTED HER.

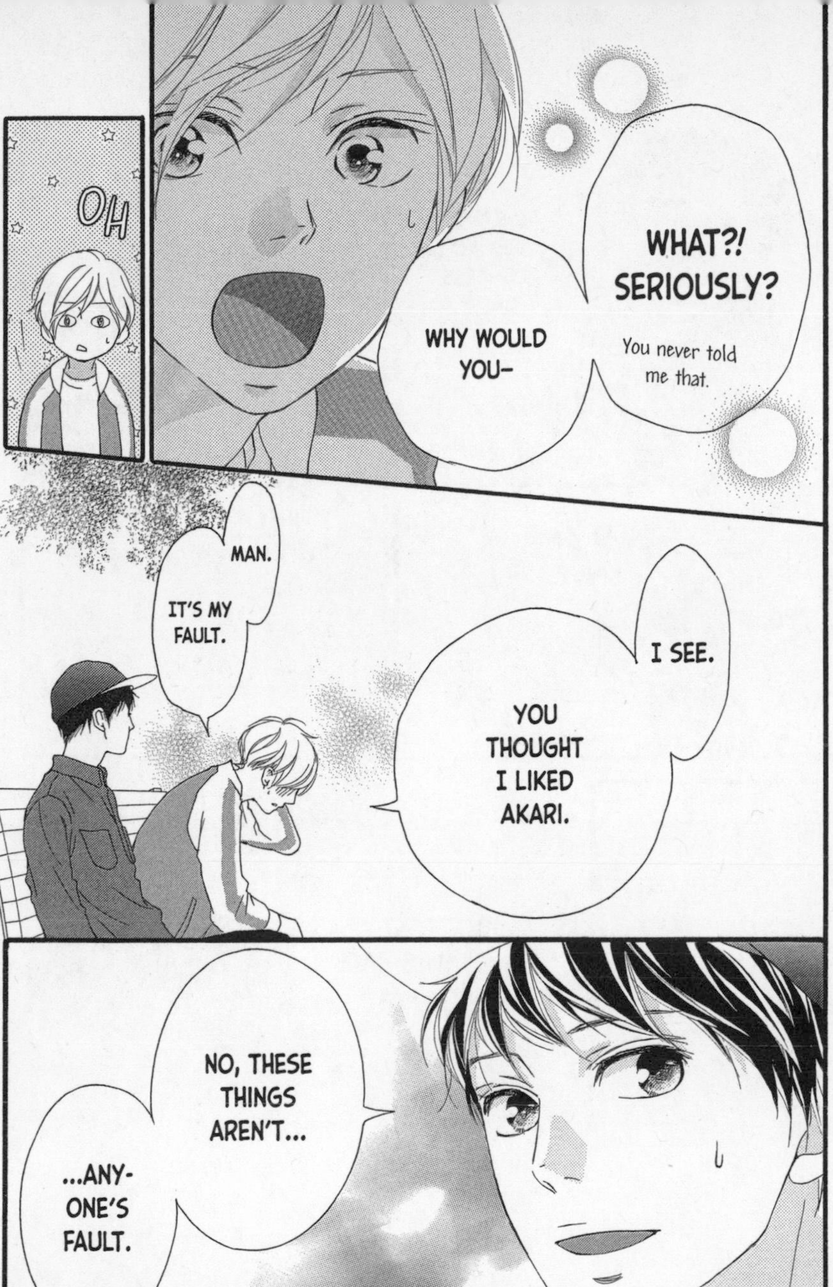
WHAT?! SERIOUSLY?
You never told me that.
WHY WOULD YOU–
OH
I SEE.
YOU THOUGHT I LIKED AKARI.
MAN.
IT'S MY FAULT.
NO, THESE THINGS AREN'T...
...ANY-ONE'S FAULT.

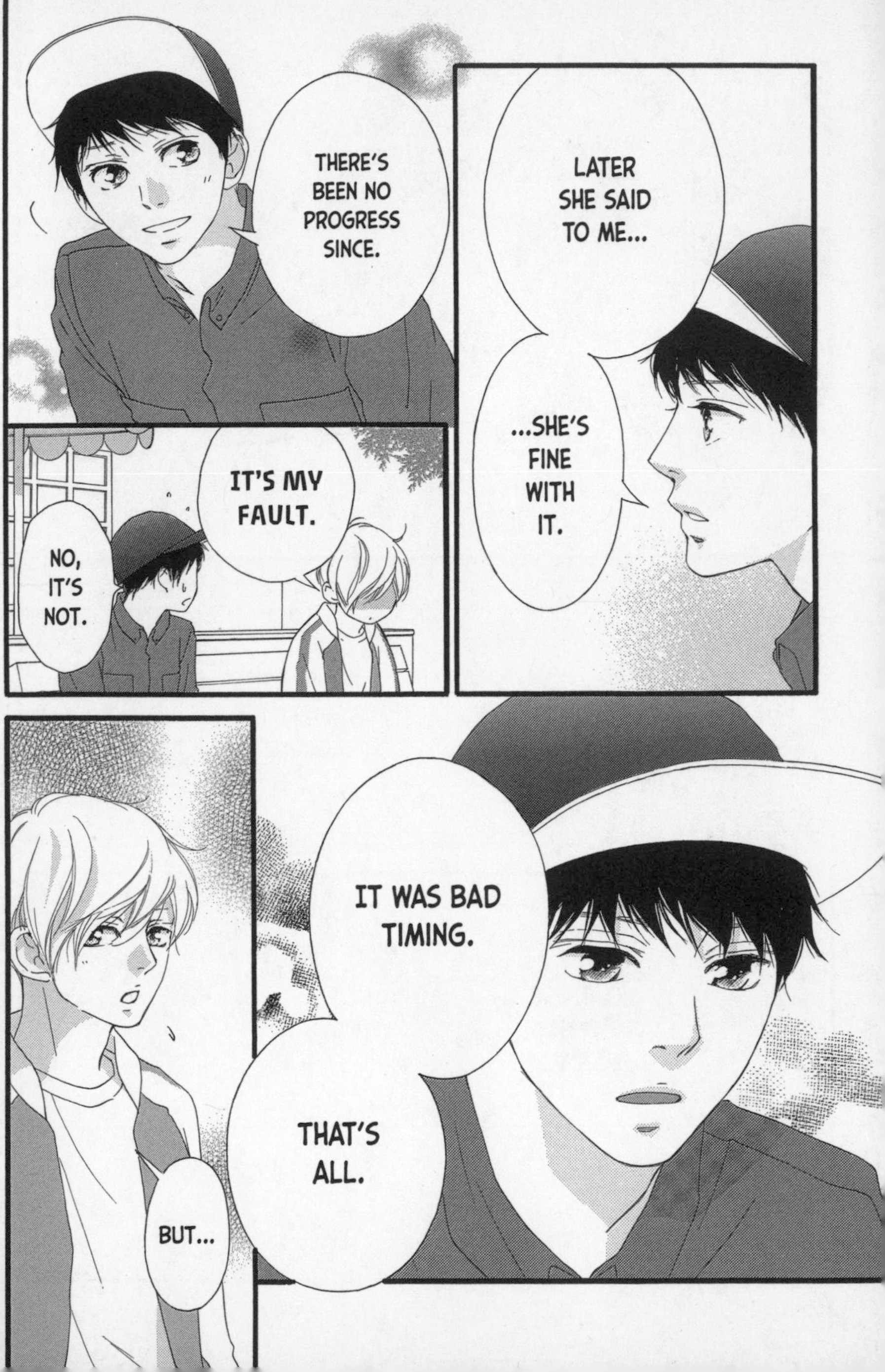
LATER SHE SAID TO ME...
...SHE'S FINE WITH IT.
THERE'S BEEN NO PROGRESS SINCE.
IT'S MY FAULT.
NO, IT'S NOT.
IT WAS BAD TIMING.
THAT'S ALL.
BUT...

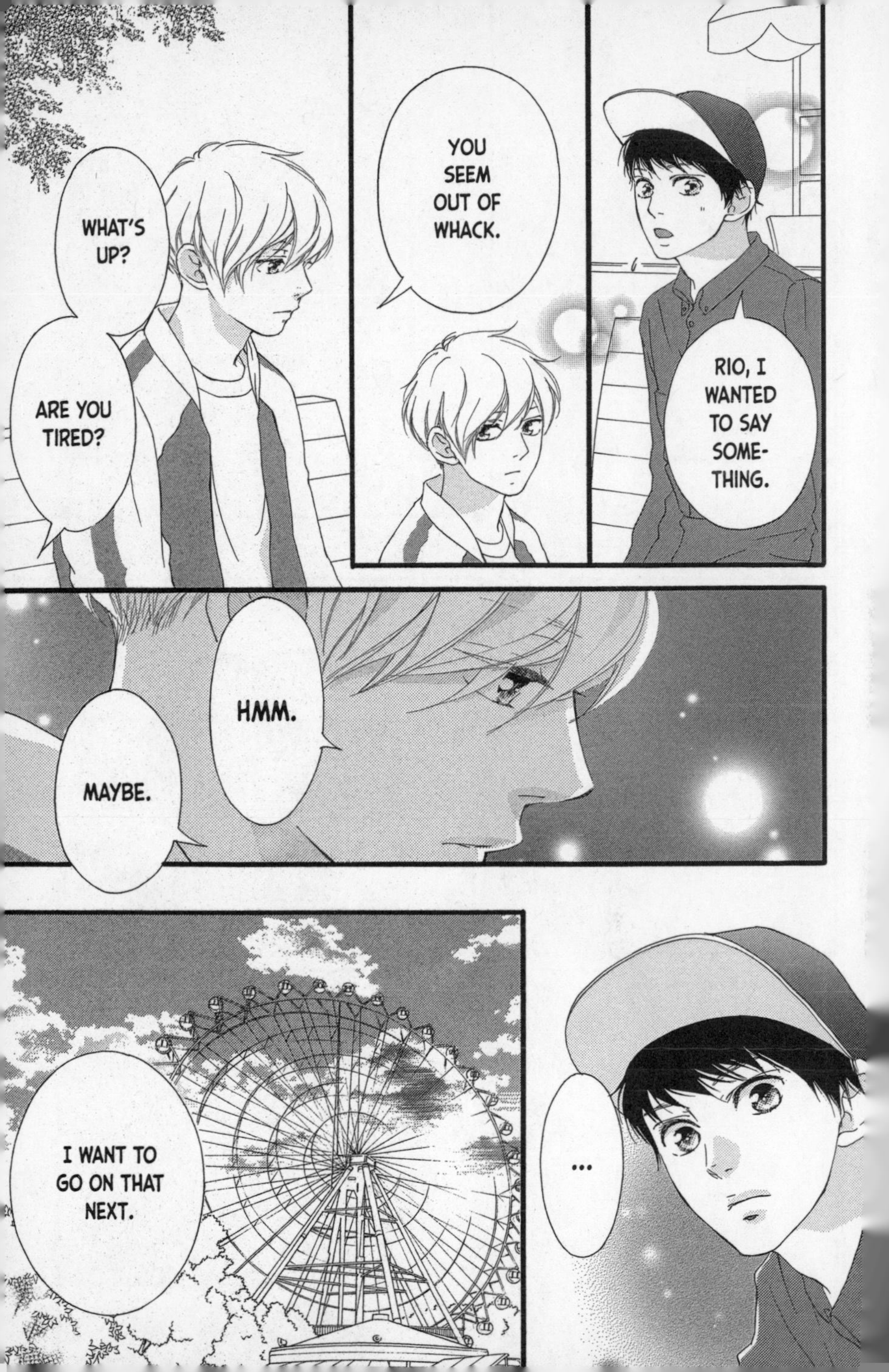
RIO, I WANTED TO SAY SOME-THING.
YOU SEEM OUT OF WHACK.
WHAT'S UP?
ARE YOU TIRED?
HMM.
MAYBE.
...
I WANT TO GO ON THAT NEXT.

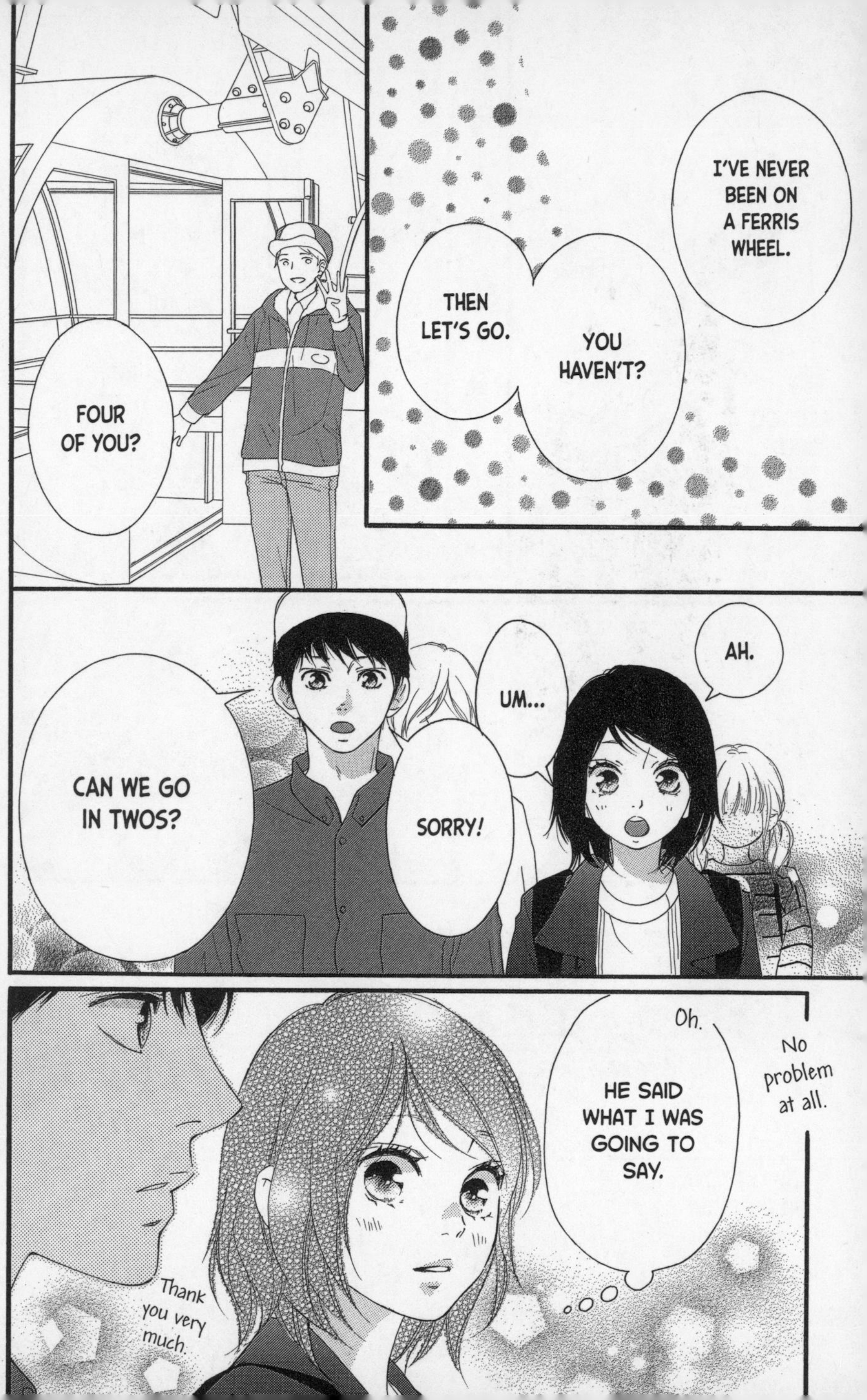
I'VE NEVER BEEN ON A FERRIS WHEEL.
YOU HAVEN'T?
THEN LET'S GO.
FOUR OF YOU?
AH.
UM...
SORRY!
CAN WE GO IN TWOS?
No problem at all.
Oh.
HE SAID WHAT I WAS GOING TO SAY.
Thank you very much.

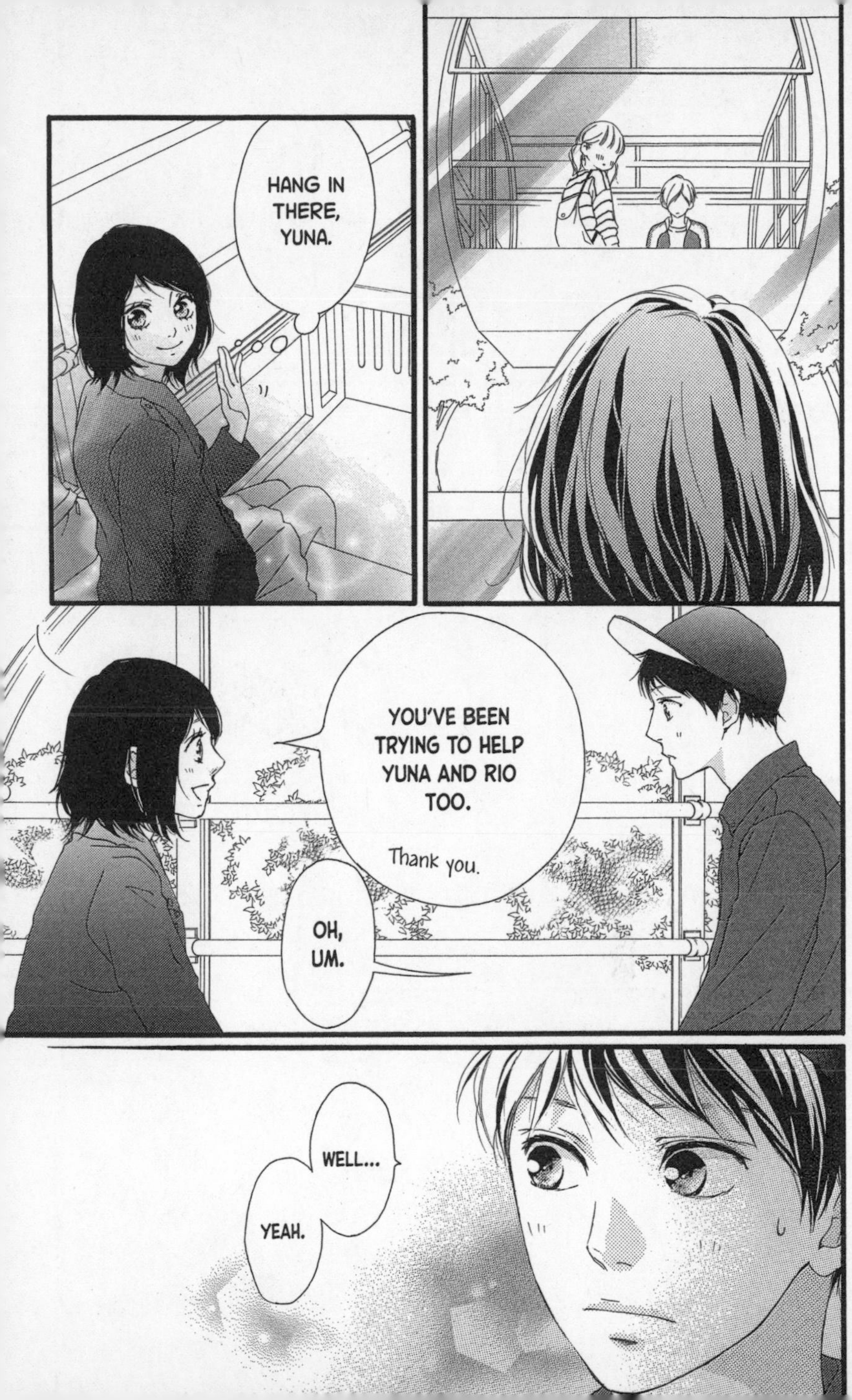
HANG IN THERE, YUNA.
YOU'VE BEEN TRYING TO HELP YUNA AND RIO TOO.
Thank you.
OH, UM.
WELL...
YEAH.

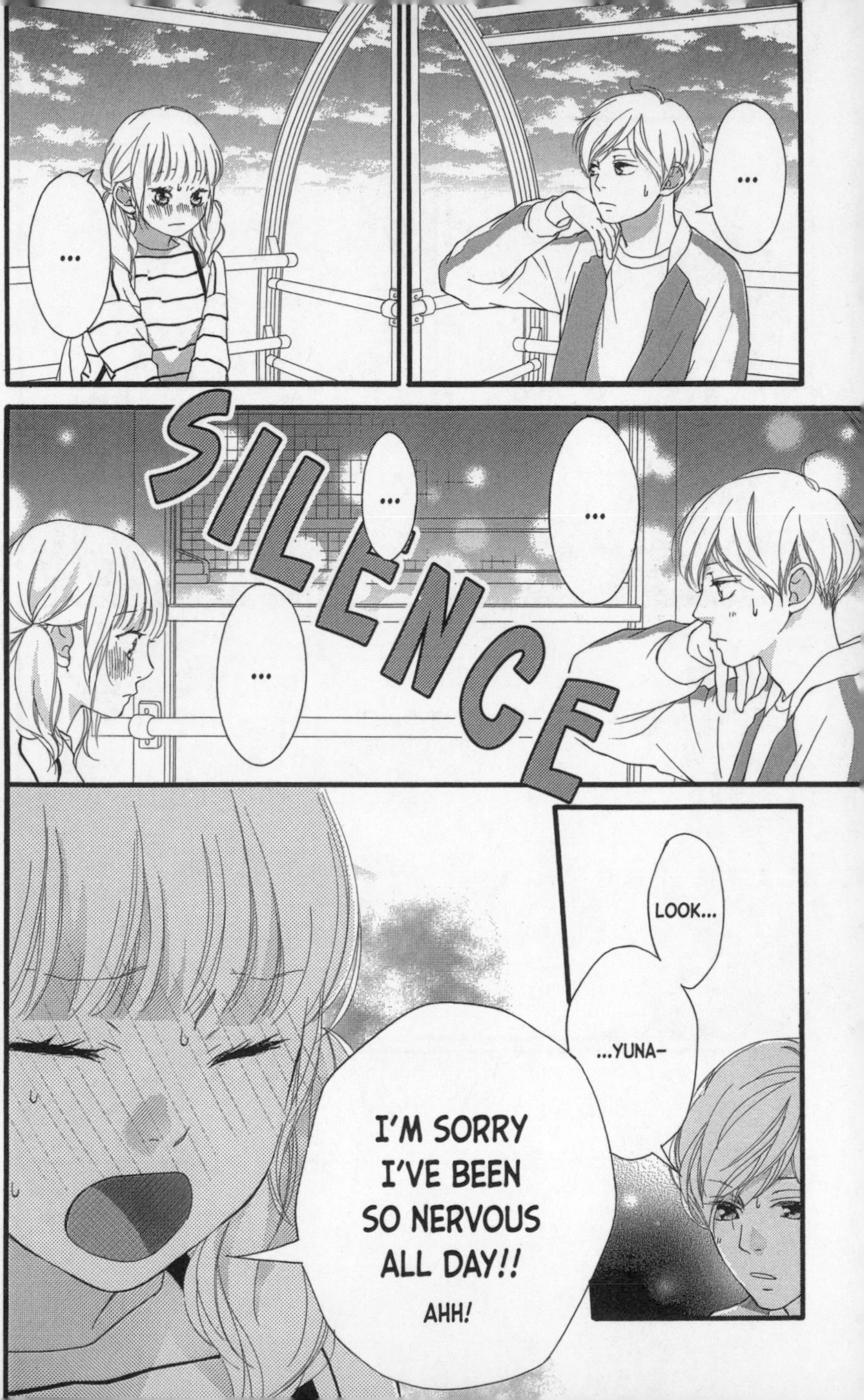
...
...
SILENCE
...
...
...
LOOK...
...YUNA–
I'M SORRY I'VE BEEN SO NERVOUS ALL DAY!!
AHH!

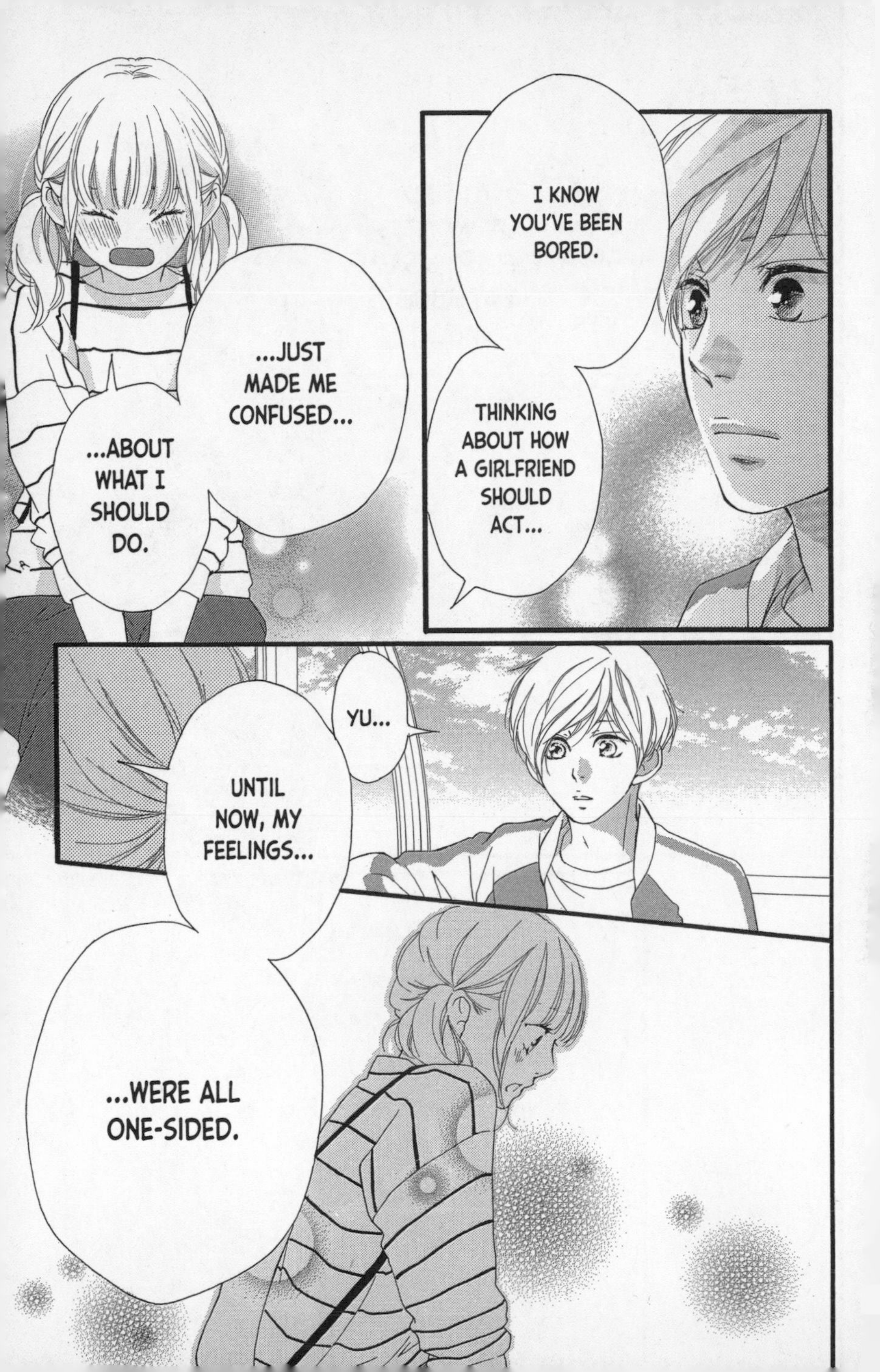
I KNOW YOU'VE BEEN BORED.
THINKING ABOUT HOW A GIRLFRIEND SHOULD ACT...
...JUST MADE ME CONFUSED...
...ABOUT WHAT I SHOULD DO.
YU...
UNTIL NOW, MY FEELINGS...
...WERE ALL ONE-SIDED.

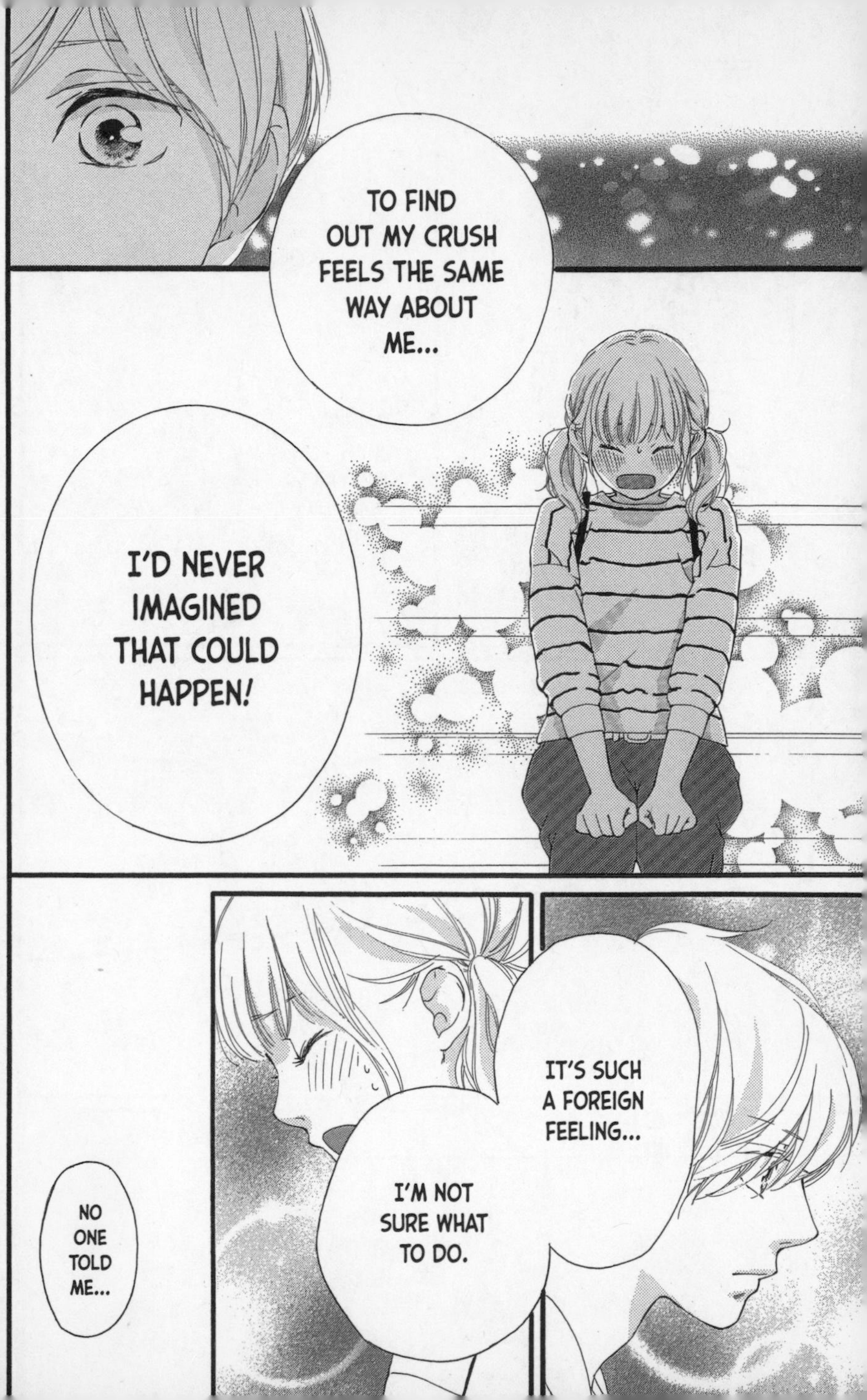
TO FIND OUT MY CRUSH FEELS THE SAME WAY ABOUT ME...
I'D NEVER IMAGINED THAT COULD HAPPEN!
IT'S SUCH A FOREIGN FEELING...
I'M NOT SURE WHAT TO DO.
NO ONE TOLD ME...

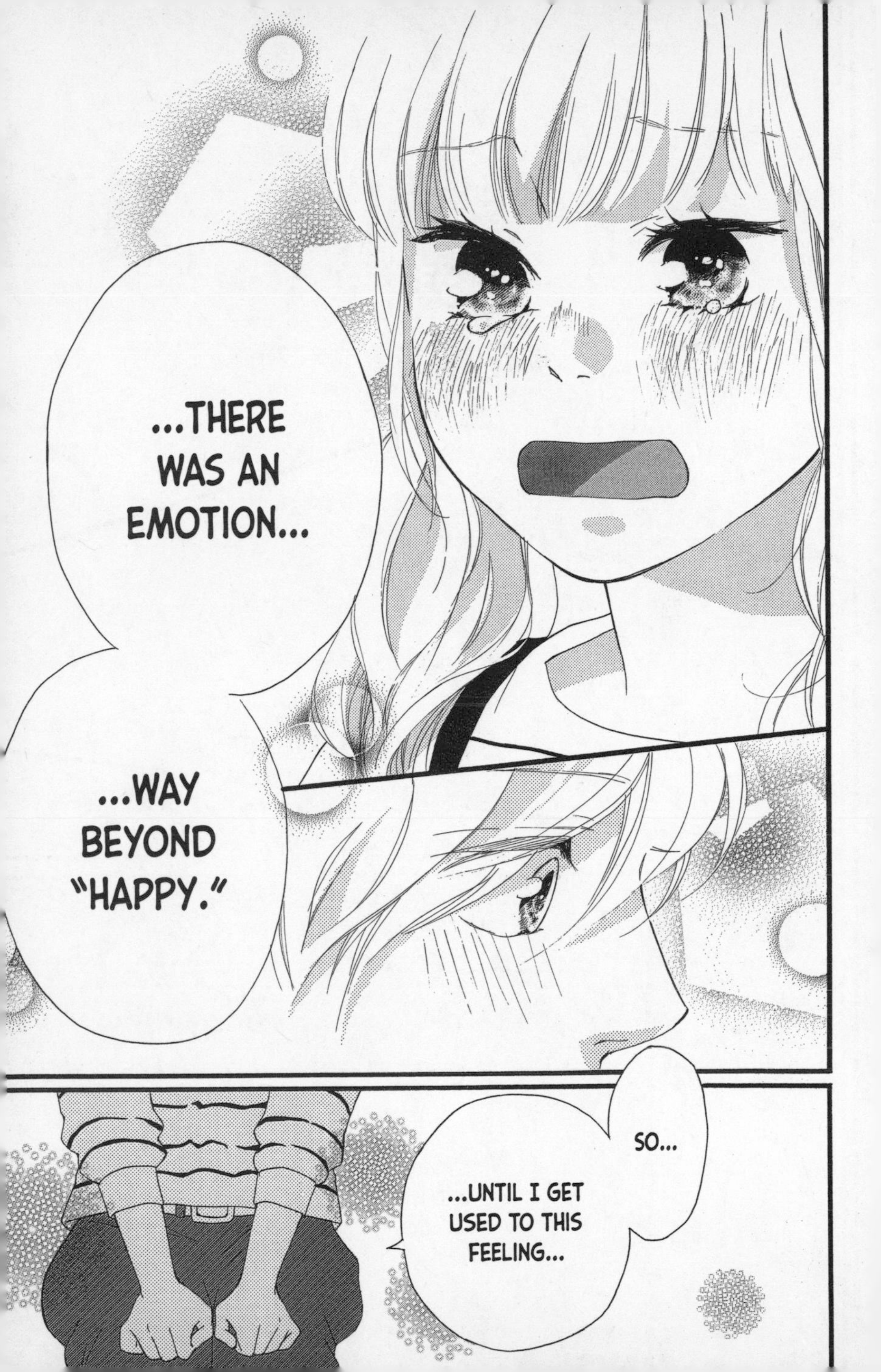
...THERE WAS AN EMOTION...
...WAY BEYOND "HAPPY."
SO...
...UNTIL I GET USED TO THIS FEELING...

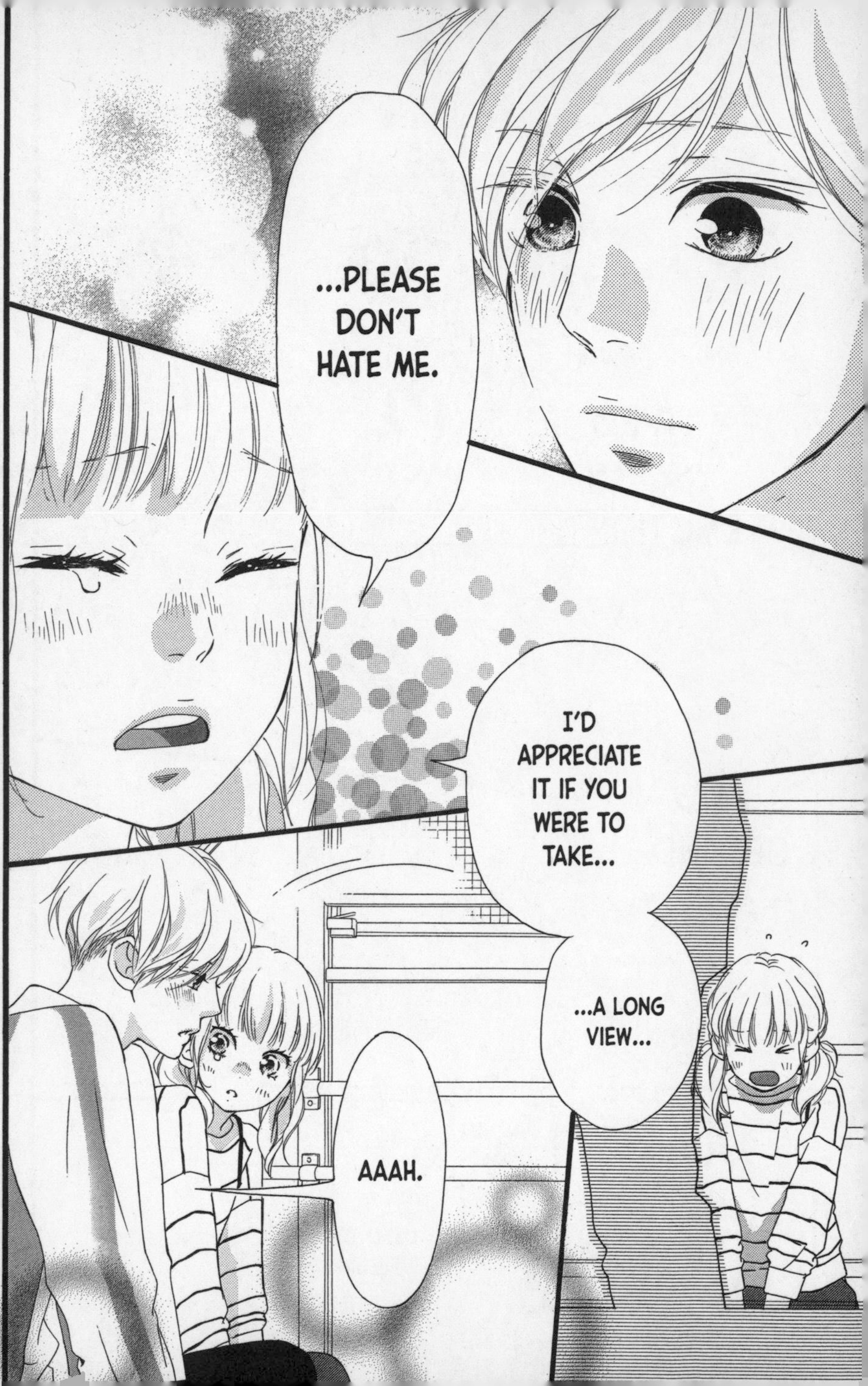
...PLEASE DON'T HATE ME.
I'D APPRECIATE IT IF YOU WERE TO TAKE...
...A LONG VIEW...
AAAH.

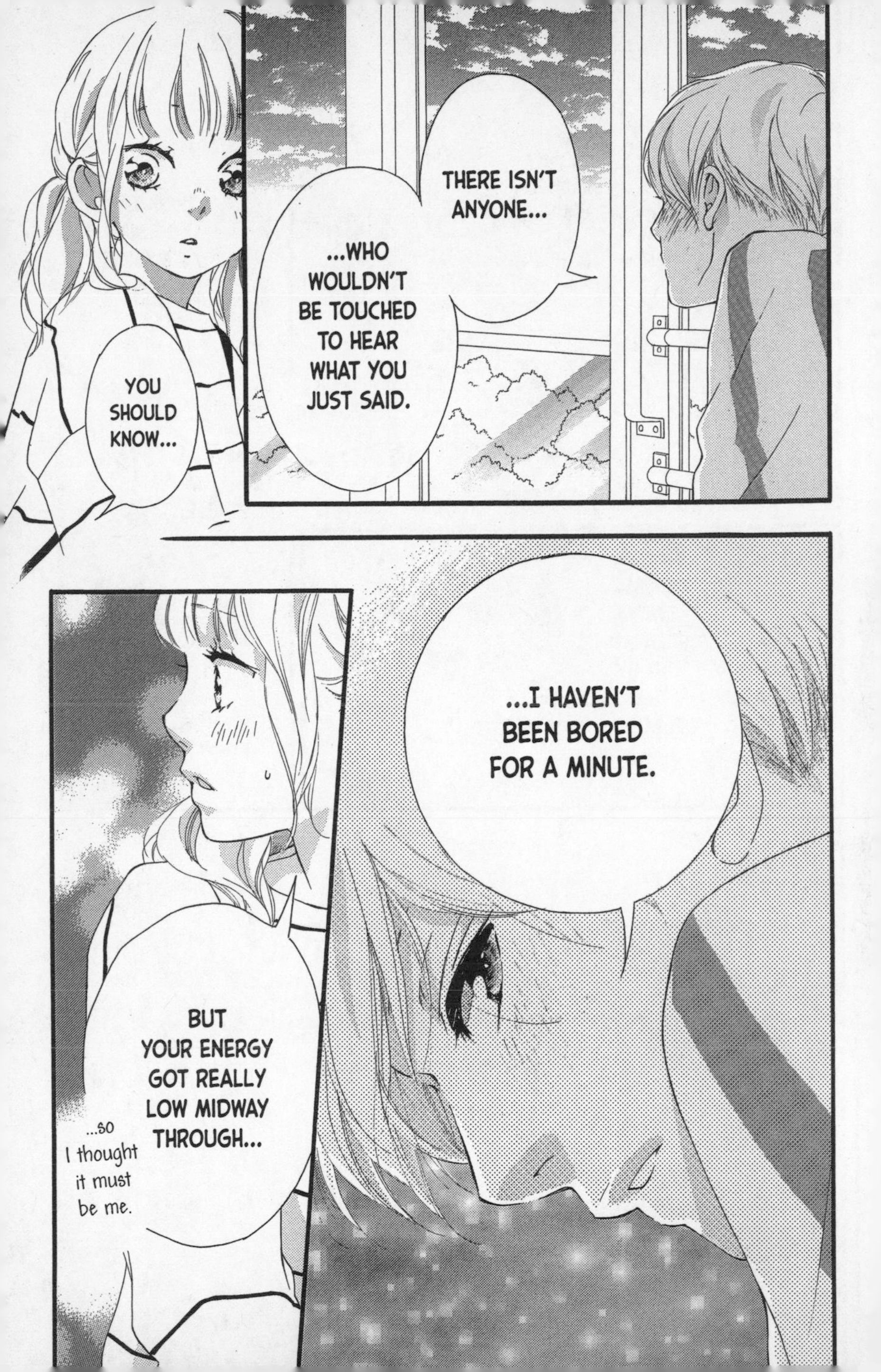
THERE ISN'T ANYONE...
...WHO WOULDN'T BE TOUCHED TO HEAR WHAT YOU JUST SAID.
YOU SHOULD KNOW...
...I HAVEN'T BEEN BORED FOR A MINUTE.
BUT YOUR ENERGY GOT REALLY LOW MIDWAY THROUGH...
...so I thought it must be me.

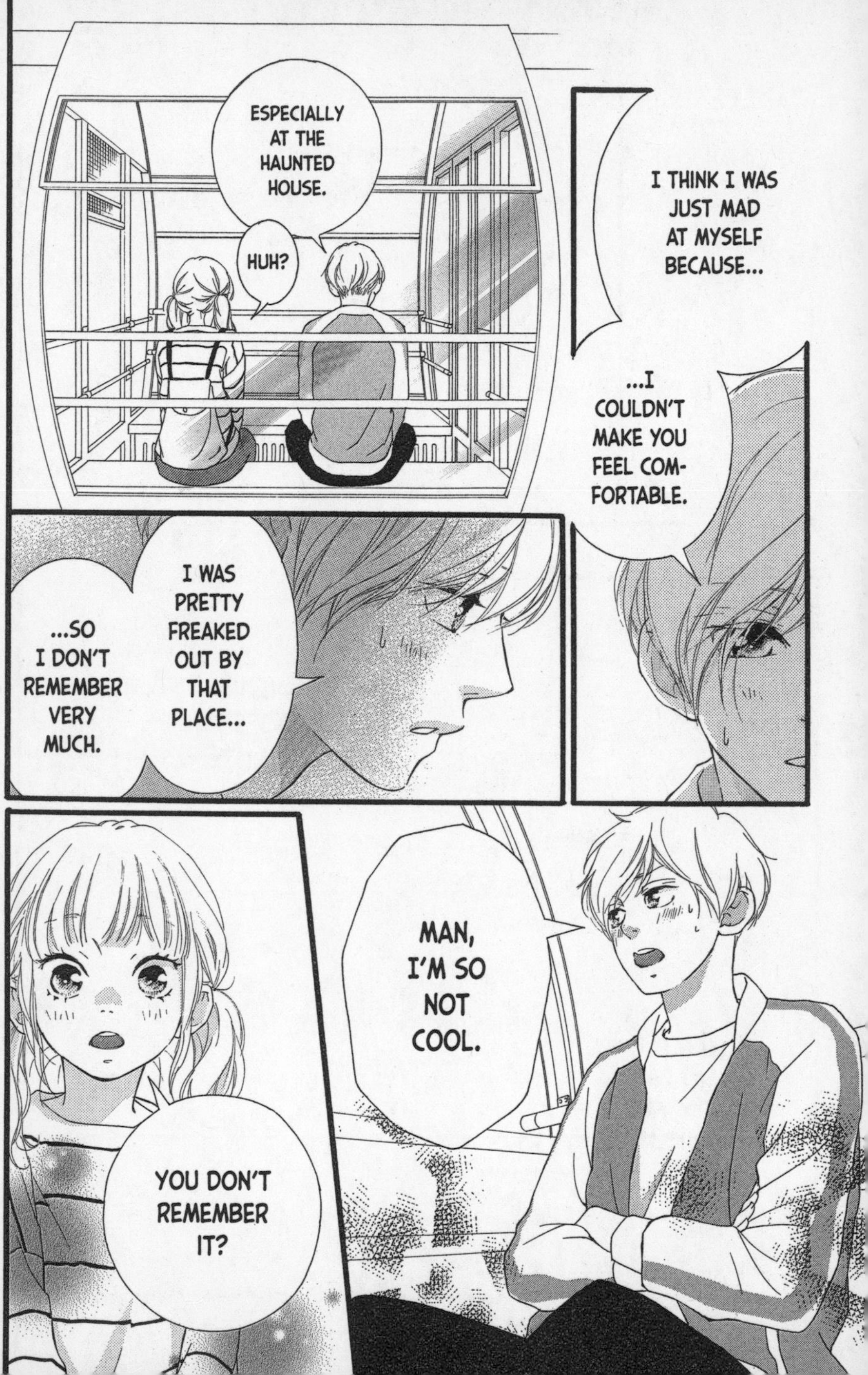
ESPECIALLY AT THE HAUNTED HOUSE.
HUH?
I THINK I WAS JUST MAD AT MYSELF BECAUSE...
...I COULDN'T MAKE YOU FEEL COM-FORTABLE.
I WAS PRETTY FREAKED OUT BY THAT PLACE...
...SO I DON'T REMEMBER VERY MUCH.
MAN, I'M SO NOT COOL.
YOU DON'T REMEMBER IT?

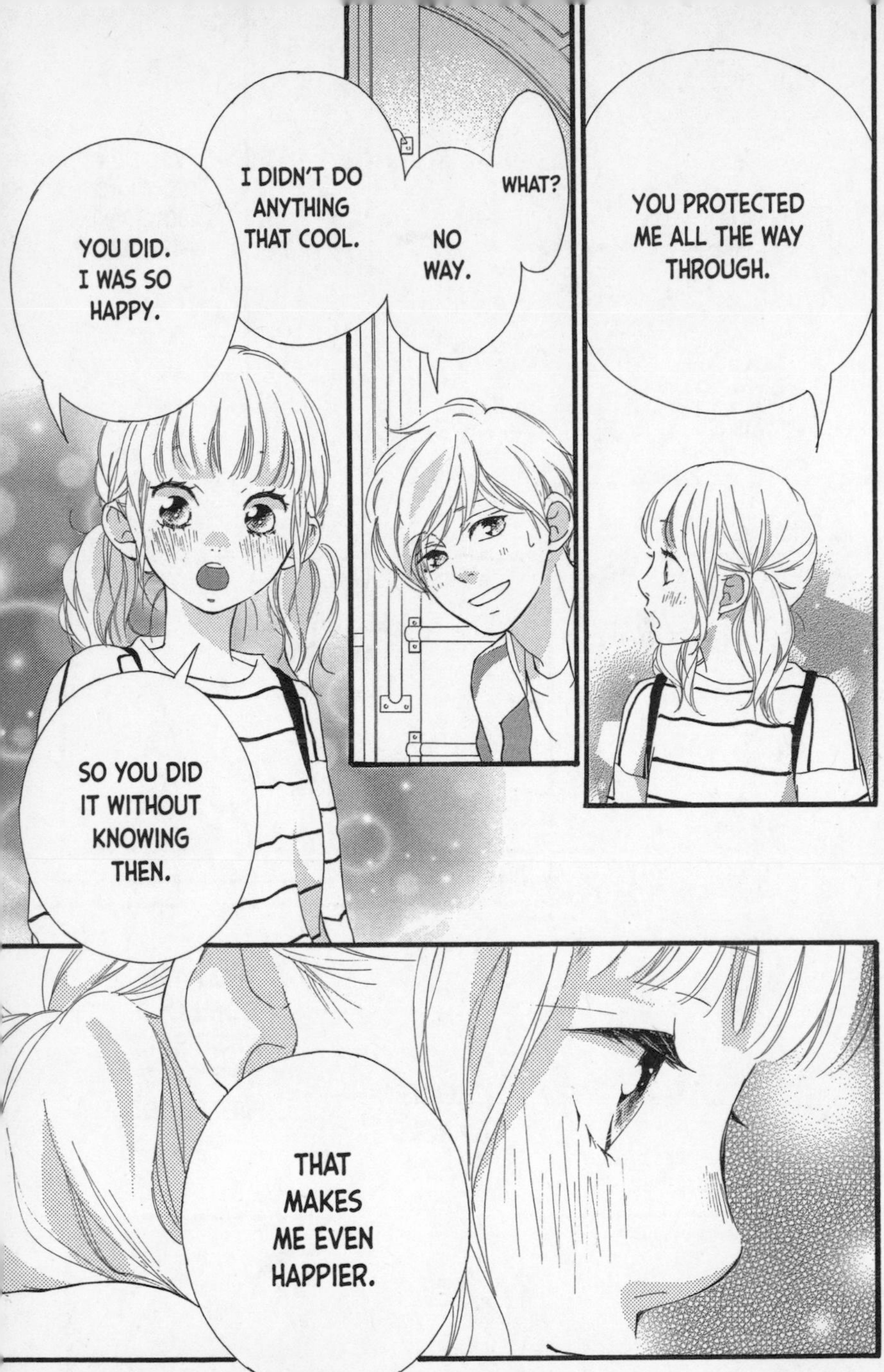
YOU PROTECTED ME ALL THE WAY THROUGH.
WHAT?
NO WAY.
I DIDN'T DO ANYTHING THAT COOL.
YOU DID. I WAS SO HAPPY.
SO YOU DID IT WITHOUT KNOWING THEN.
THAT MAKES ME EVEN HAPPIER.

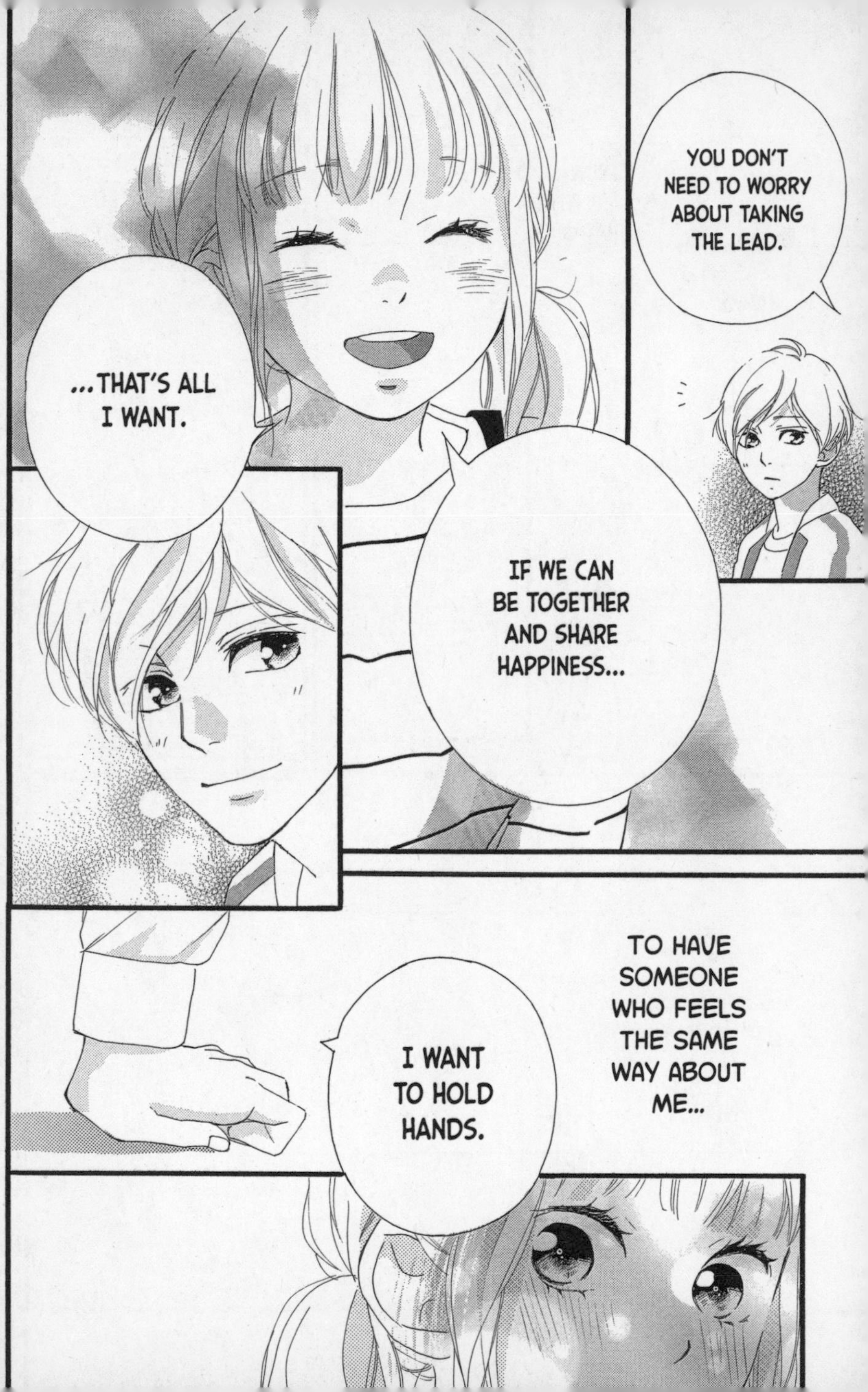
YOU DON'T NEED TO WORRY ABOUT TAKING THE LEAD.
IF WE CAN BE TOGETHER AND SHARE HAPPINESS...
...THAT'S ALL I WANT.
TO HAVE SOMEONE WHO FEELS THE SAME WAY ABOUT ME...
I WANT TO HOLD HANDS.

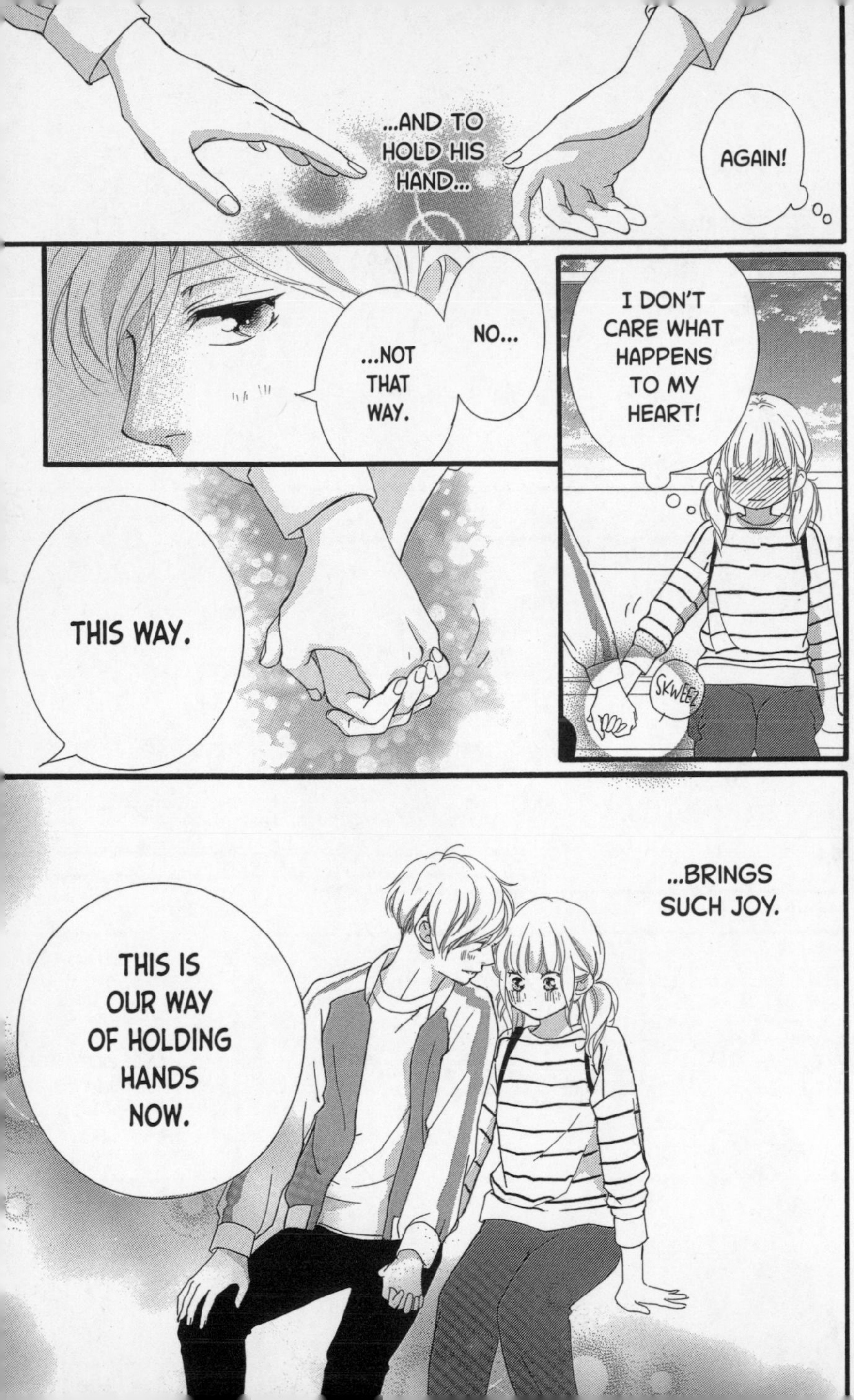
AGAIN!
...AND TO HOLD HIS HAND...
I DON'T CARE WHAT HAPPENS TO MY HEART!
SKWEEZ
NO...
...NOT THAT WAY.
THIS WAY.
...BRINGS SUCH JOY.
THIS IS OUR WAY OF HOLDING HANDS NOW.

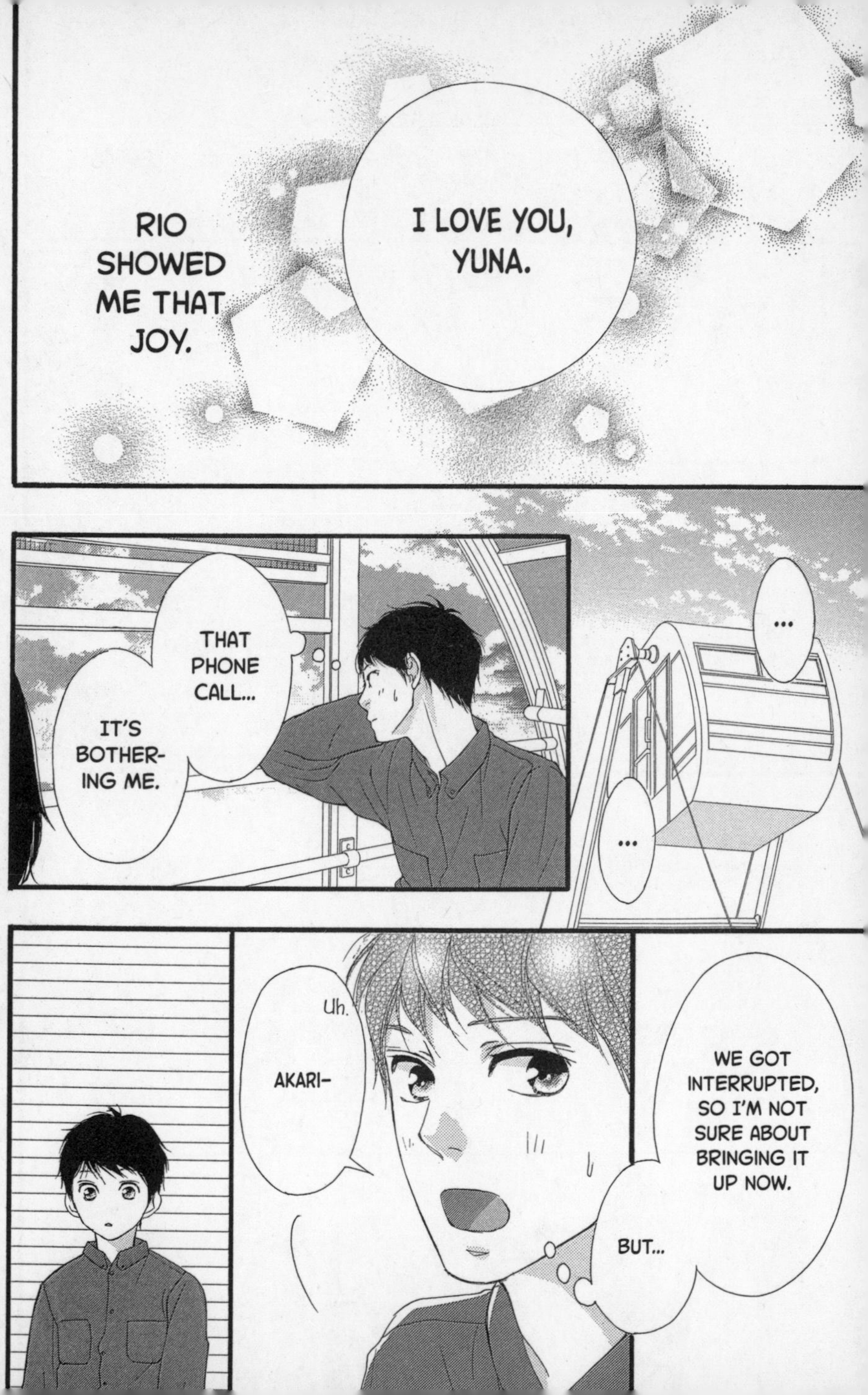
I LOVE YOU, YUNA.
RIO SHOWED ME THAT JOY.
...
...
THAT PHONE CALL...
IT'S BOTHERING ME.
WE GOT INTERRUPTED, SO I'M NOT SURE ABOUT BRINGING IT UP NOW.
BUT...
Uh.
AKARI-

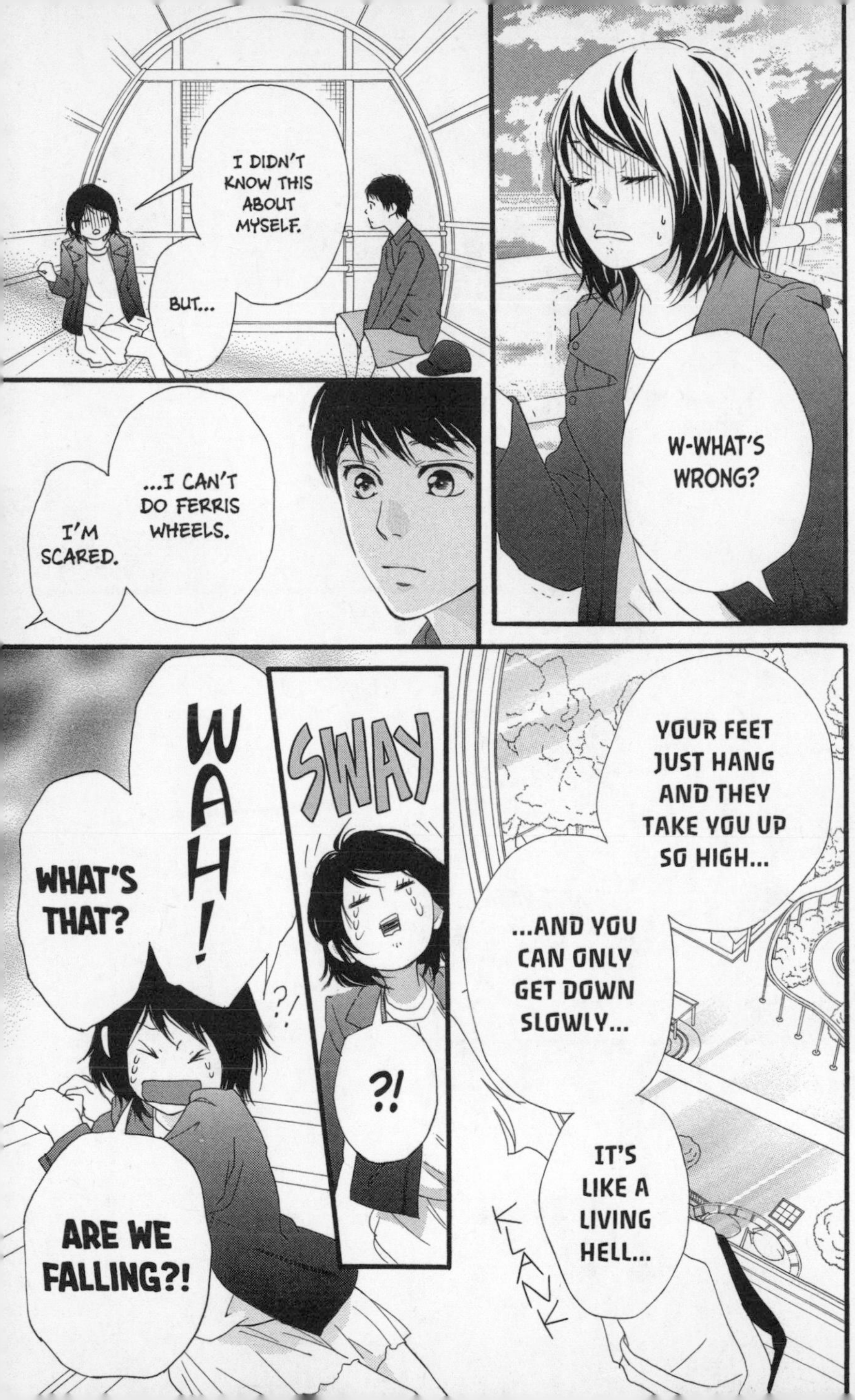
W-WHAT'S WRONG?
I DIDN'T KNOW THIS ABOUT MYSELF.
BUT...
...I CAN'T DO FERRIS WHEELS.
I'M SCARED.
YOUR FEET JUST HANG AND THEY TAKE YOU UP SO HIGH...
...AND YOU CAN ONLY GET DOWN SLOWLY...
IT'S LIKE A LIVING HELL...
KLANK
SWAY
?!
?!
WAH!
WHAT'S THAT?
ARE WE FALLING?!

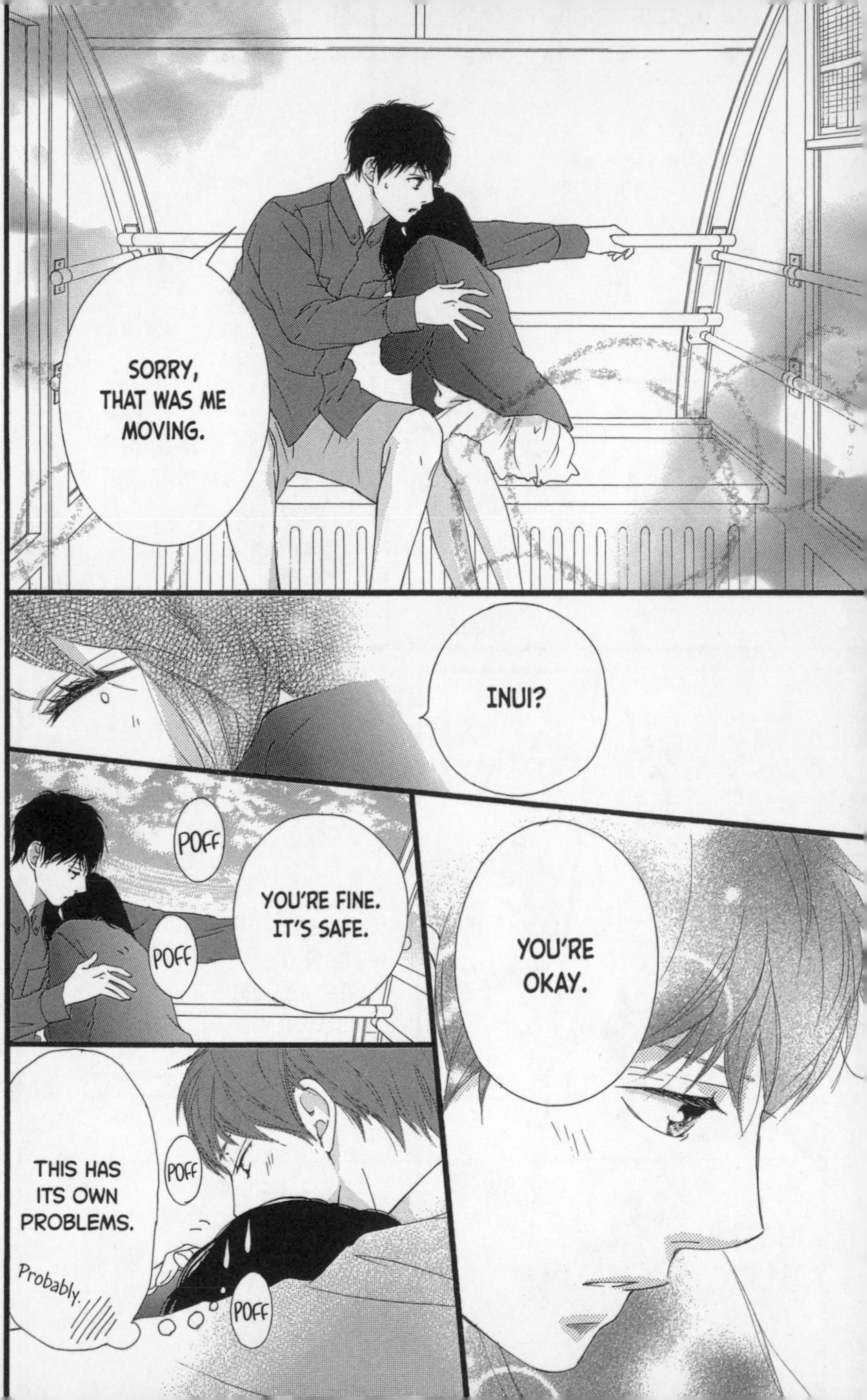
SORRY, THAT WAS ME MOVING.
INUI?
YOU'RE OKAY.
POFF
YOU'RE FINE. IT'S SAFE.
POFF
POFF
THIS HAS ITS OWN PROBLEMS.
POFF
Probably.

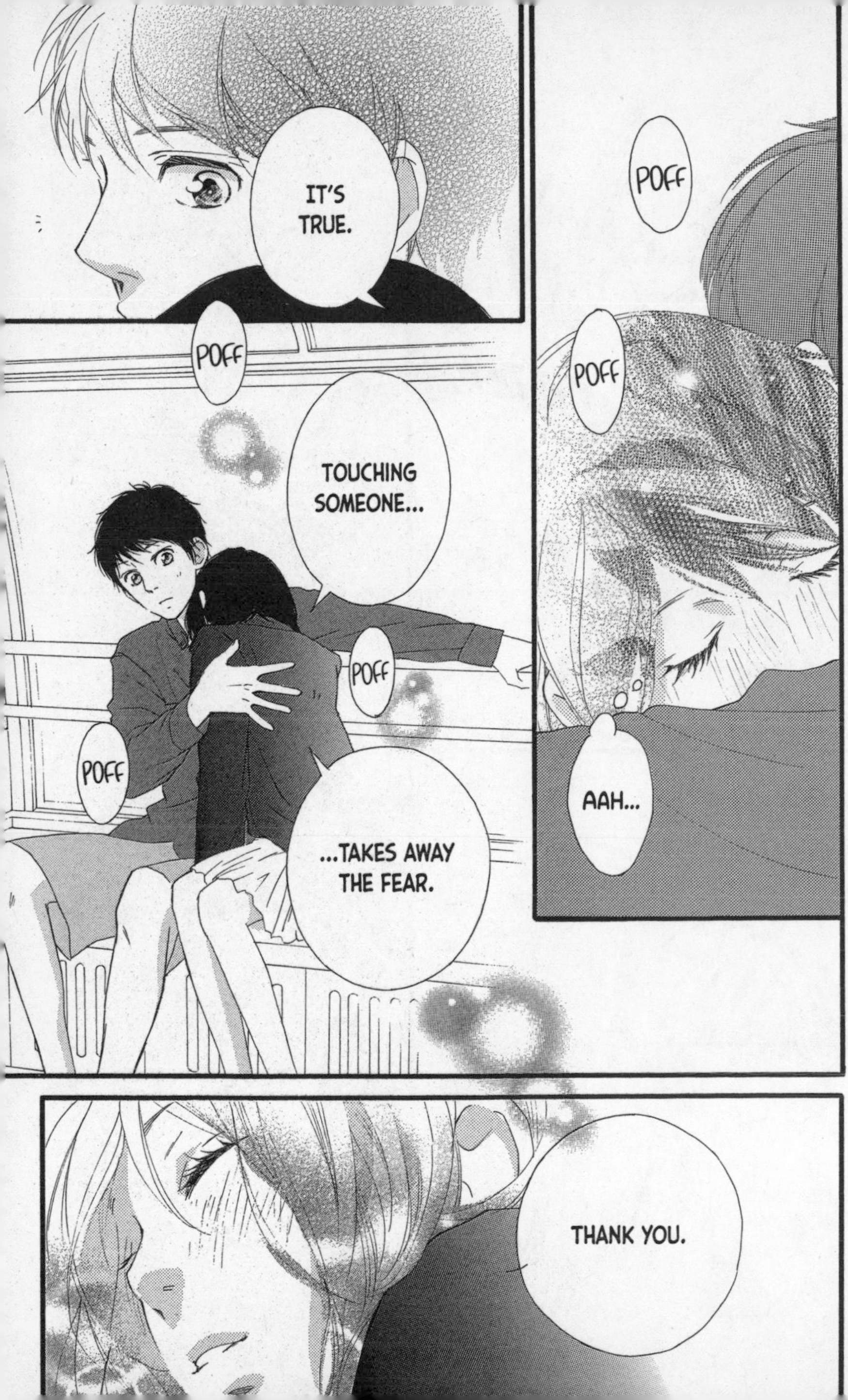
POFF
POFF
AAH...
IT'S TRUE.
POFF
TOUCHING SOMEONE...
POFF
POFF
...TAKES AWAY THE FEAR.
THANK YOU.

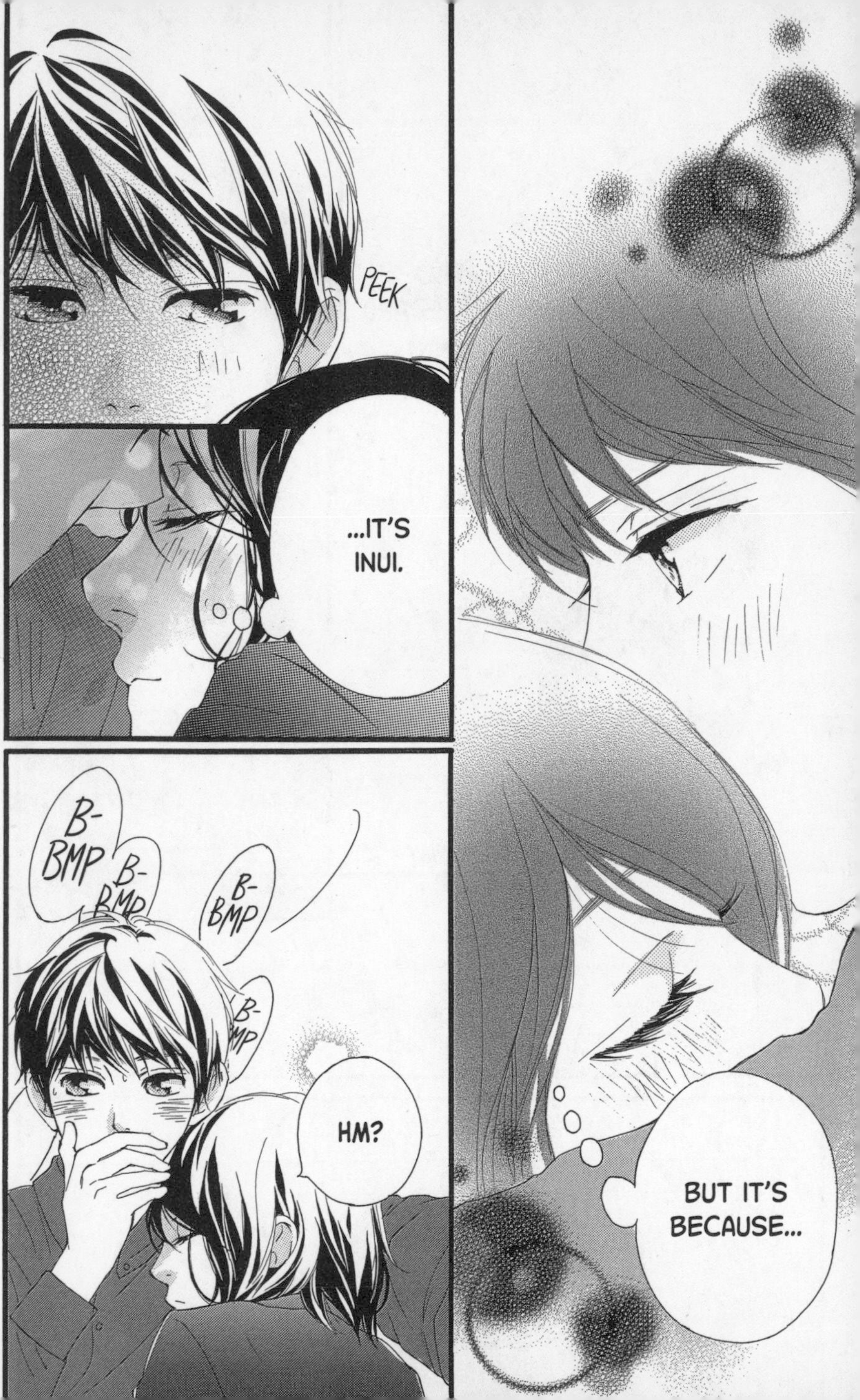
BUT IT'S BECAUSE...
PEEK
...IT'S INUI.
B-BMP
B-BMP
B-BMP
B-BMP
HM?

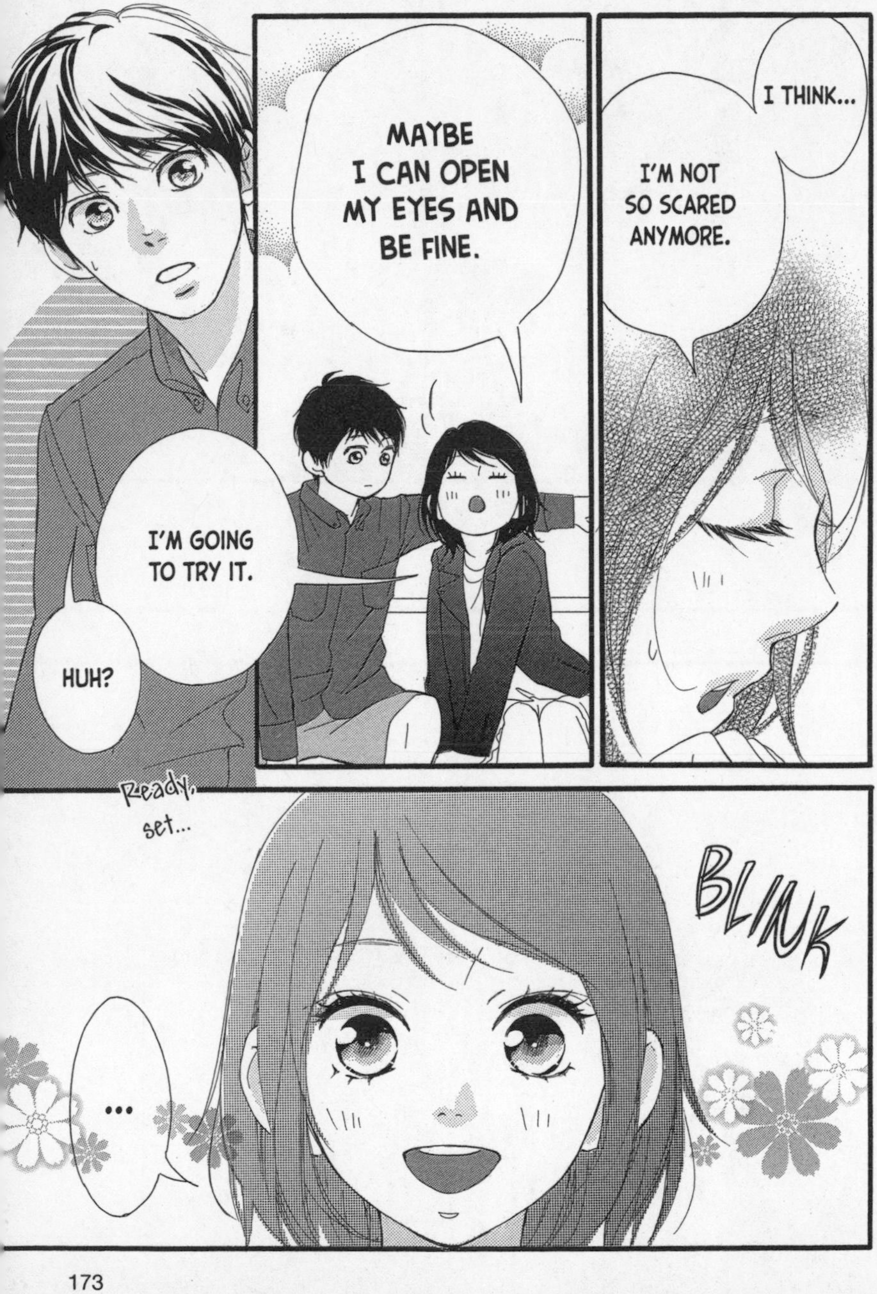
I THINK...
I'M NOT SO SCARED ANYMORE.
MAYBE I CAN OPEN MY EYES AND BE FINE.
I'M GOING TO TRY IT.
HUH?
Ready, set...
BLINK
...

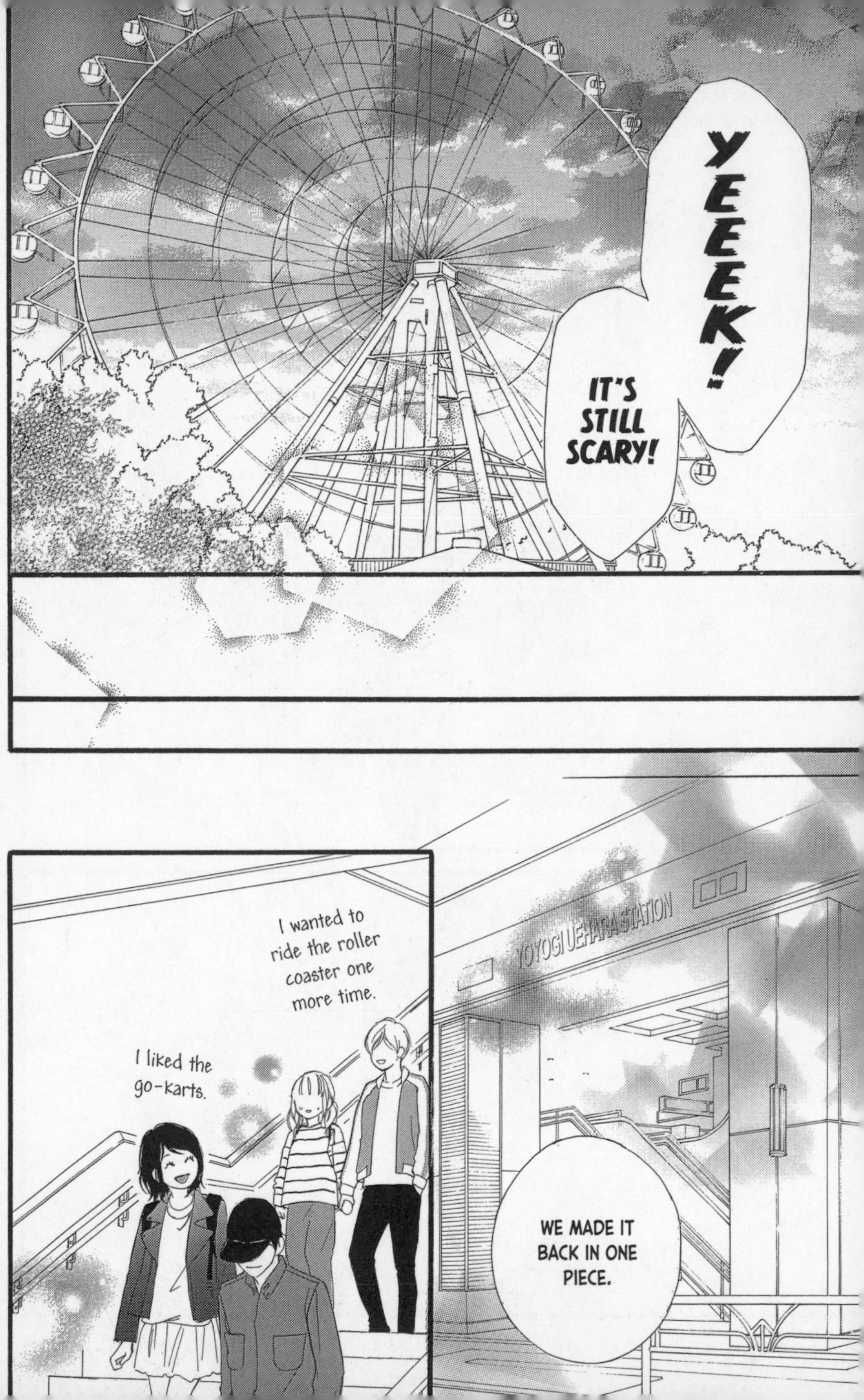
YEEEK!
IT'S STILL SCARY!
YOYOGI UEHARA STATION
WE MADE IT BACK IN ONE PIECE.
I wanted to ride the roller coaster one more time.
I liked the go-karts.

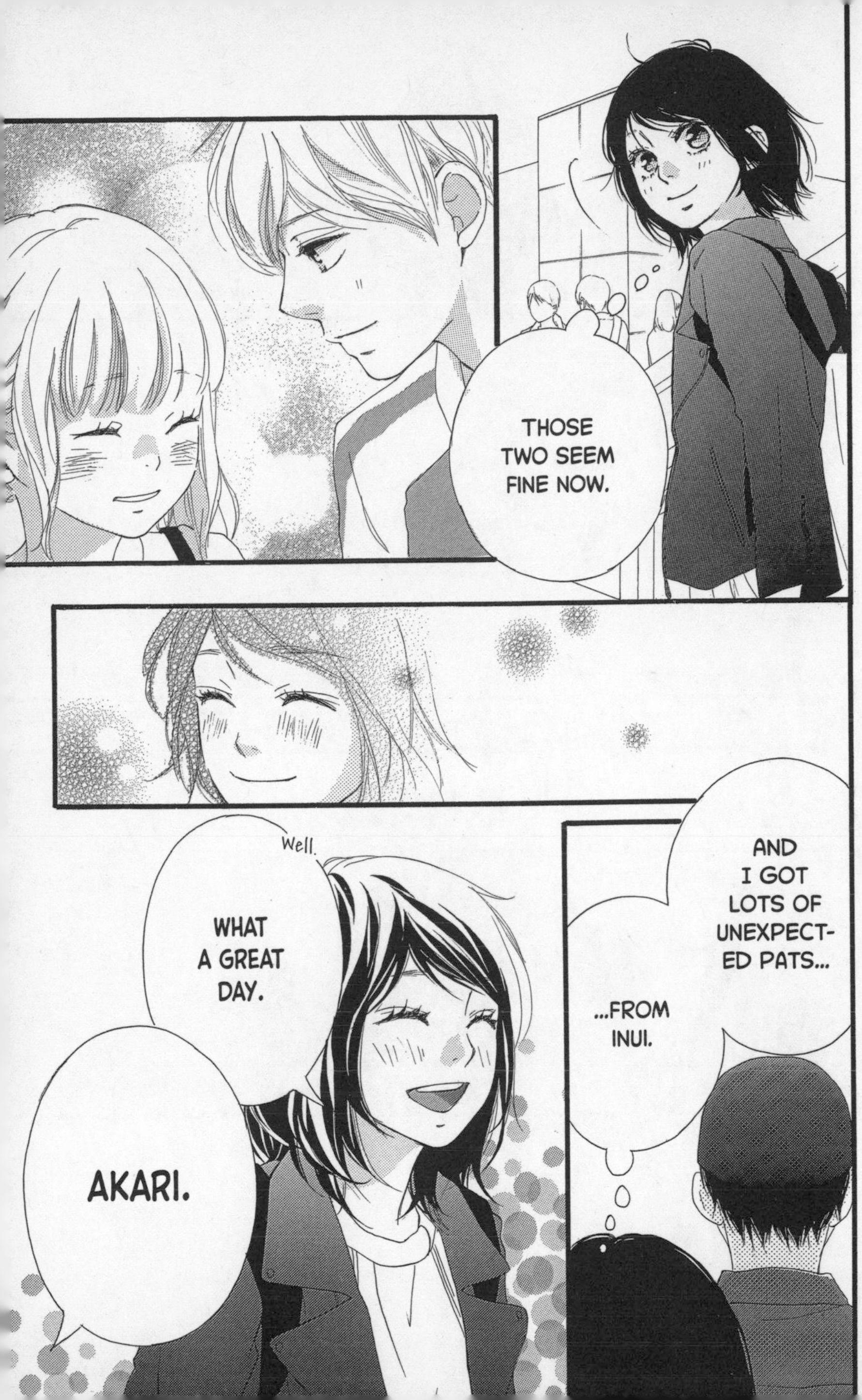
THOSE TWO SEEM FINE NOW.
AND I GOT LOTS OF UNEXPECTED PATS...
...FROM INUI.
Well.
WHAT A GREAT DAY.
AKARI.

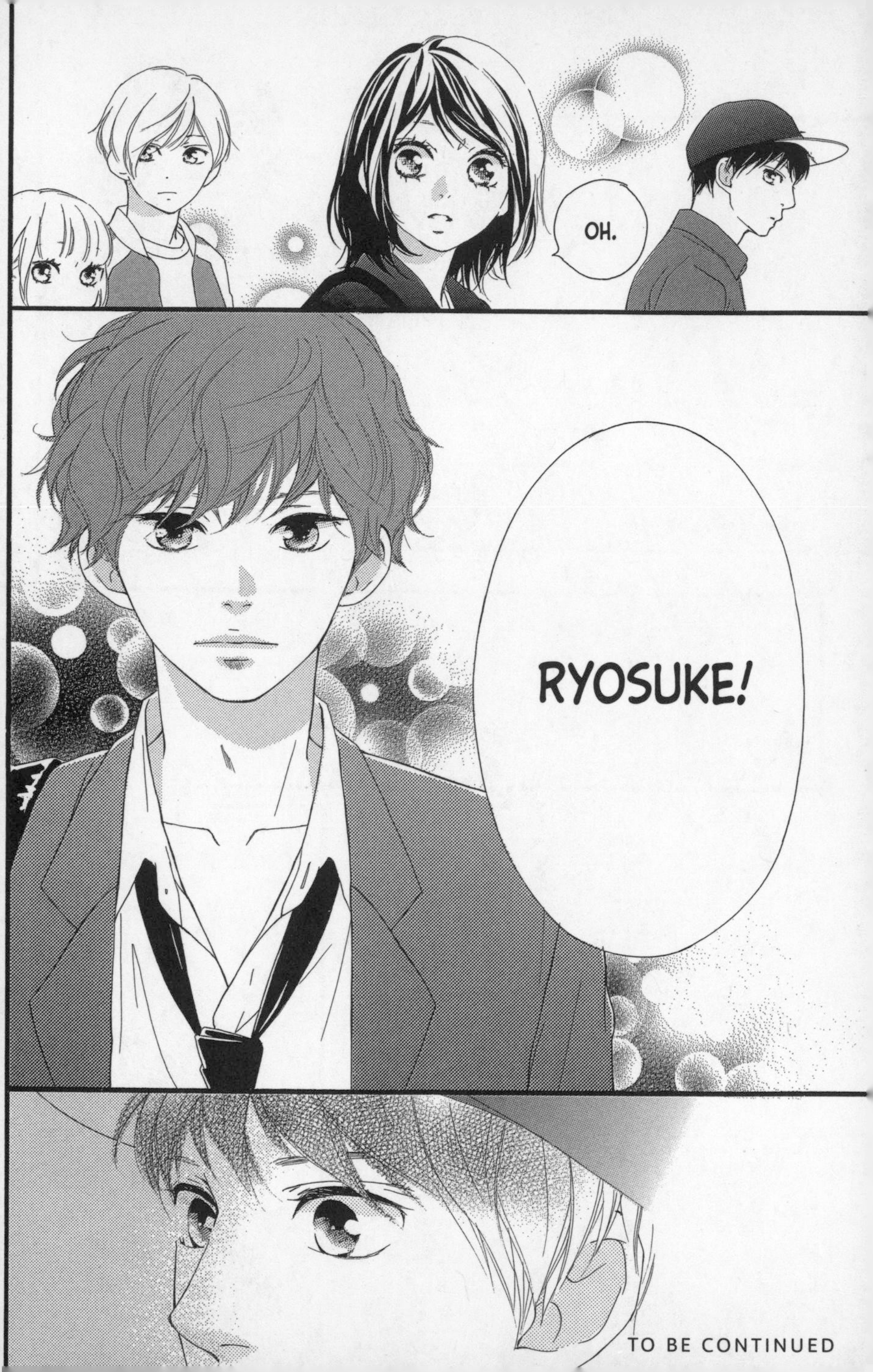
OH.
RYOSUKE!
TO BE CONTINUED

AFTERWORD

Andrew & Cinnamon

Thank you so much for reading this through to the end!

The air in winter is so dry that my skin feels like paper. It's not just my skin—my manuscript paper feels drier too. Sometimes I'll get a paper cut from it, and that's not great. I have a humidifier to help, but the new one I bought last year is already having problems. It was fine yesterday, so what's wrong now? This can't be happening. I tried to tinker with it, and apparently that wasn't good because it's stopped working completely. I learned you can't casually take things apart and to never throw away the warranty in case something like this should happen. Oh, the guilty me who thought, "No way am I going to break it," and threw out that piece of paper. In this very dry season, I hope this volume will fill your heart. My heart will fill in response. But I'm going to get a new humidifier.

See you in the next volume! ✿ ✿

Io Sakisaka

Some time ago, I started to feel an urge to cut off my hair. But my hairstylist advised, "If you feel even a little hesitation, it's better that you don't." So here I am, unable to take that step, while the desire is still inside me, growing hotter.

Io Sakisaka

Born on June 8, Io Sakisaka made her debut as a manga creator with *Sakura, Chiru*. Her series *Strobe Edge* and *Ao Haru Ride* are published by VIZ Media's Shojo Beat imprint. *Ao Haru Ride* was adapted into an anime series in 2014, and *Love Me, Love Me Not* will be an animated feature film. In her spare time, Sakisaka likes to paint things and sleep.

Love Me, Love Me Not

Vol. 7
Shojo Beat Edition

STORY AND ART BY
Io Sakisaka

Adaptation/Nancy Thistlethwaite
Translation/JN Productions
Touch-Up Art & Lettering/Sara Linsley
Design/Yukiko Whitley
Editor/Nancy Thistlethwaite

OMOI, OMOWARE, FURI, FURARE © 2015 by Io Sakisaka
All rights reserved.
First published in Japan in 2015 by SHUEISHA Inc., Tokyo.
English translation rights arranged by SHUEISHA Inc.

Printed in the U.S.A.

Published by VIZ Media, LLC
P.O. Box 77010
San Francisco, CA 94107

10 9 8 7 6 5 4 3 2 1
First printing, March 2021

PARENTAL ADVISORY
LOVE ME, LOVE ME NOT is rated T for Teen and
is recommended for ages 13 and up. This story
centers around teenage relationships.

viz.com   shojobeat.com

Ao Haru Ride

STORY AND ART BY
IO SAKISAKA

Futaba Yoshioka thought all boys were loud and obnoxious until she met Kou Tanaka in junior high. But as soon as she realized she really liked him, he had already moved away because of family issues. Now, in high school, Kou has reappeared, but is he still the same boy she fell in love with?

Honey
So Sweet

Story and Art by *Amu Meguro*

Little did Nao Kogure realize back in middle school that when she left an umbrella and a box of bandages in the rain for injured delinquent Taiga Onise that she would meet him again in high school. Nao wants nothing to do with the gruff and frightening Taiga, but he suddenly presents her with a huge bouquet of flowers and asks her to date him—with marriage in mind! Is Taiga really so scary, or is he a sweetheart in disguise?

viz.com

SHORTCAKE CAKE

STORY AND ART BY suu Morishita

An unflappable girl and a cast of lovable roommates at a boardinghouse create bonds of friendship and romance!

When Ten moves out of her parents' home in the mountains to live in a boardinghouse, she finds herself becoming fast friends with her male roommates. But can love and romance be far behind?

RATED T TEEN

VIZ

Stop!

You may be reading the wrong way.

In keeping with the original Japanese comic format, this book reads from right to left—so action, sound effects and word balloons are completely reversed to preserve the orientation of the original artwork. Check out the diagram shown here to get the hang of things, and then turn to the other side of the book to get started!

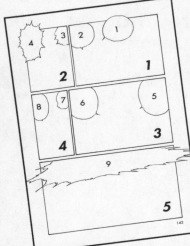